British Internment and the Internment of Britons

British Internment and the Internment of Britons

*Second World War Camps,
History and Heritage*

Edited by
Gilly Carr and Rachel Pistol

BLOOMSBURY ACADEMIC
LONDON • NEW YORK • OXFORD • NEW DELHI • SYDNEY

BLOOMSBURY ACADEMIC
Bloomsbury Publishing Plc
50 Bedford Square, London, WC1B 3DP, UK
1385 Broadway, New York, NY 10018, USA
29 Earlsfort Terrace, Dublin 2, Ireland

BLOOMSBURY, BLOOMSBURY ACADEMIC and the Diana logo are trademarks of
Bloomsbury Publishing Plc

First published in Great Britain 2023
This paperback edition published 2024

Copyright © Gilly Carr and Rachel Pistol, 2023

Gilly Carr and Rachel Pistol have asserted their right under the Copyright, Designs and
Patents Act, 1988, to be identified as Editors of this work.

Photograph © L/Cpl Dennis Phillips. Died on June 3rd 1947, British Military Hospital,
Cologne, Aged 19 yrs. Courtesy of Jersey Heritage

All rights reserved. No part of this publication may be reproduced or transmitted
in any form or by any means, electronic or mechanical, including photocopying,
recording, or any information storage or retrieval system, without prior permission in
writing from the publishers.

Bloomsbury Publishing Plc does not have any control over, or responsibility for, any
third-party websites referred to or in this book. All internet addresses given in this
book were correct at the time of going to press. The author and publisher regret any
inconvenience caused if addresses have changed or sites have ceased to exist, but can
accept no responsibility for any such changes.

Every effort has been made to trace the copyright holders and obtain permission to
reproduce the copyright material. Please do get in touch with any enquiries or any
information relating to such material or the rights holder. We would be pleased to rectify
any omissions in subsequent editions of this publication should they be drawn to our
attention.

A catalogue record for this book is available from the British Library.

A catalog record for this book is available from the Library of Congress.

ISBN: HB: 978-1-3502-6625-4
PB: 978-1-3502-6629-2
ePDF: 978-1-3502-6626-1
eBook: 978-1-3502-6627-8

Typeset by Newgen KnowledgeWorks Pvt. Ltd., Chennai, India

To find out more about our authors and books visit www.bloomsbury.com
and sign up for our newsletters.

To Jon and Alan, now married to academics who only intended to ask them a few questions about what happened to their formerly interned fathers …

In memory of Robin Bartlett, interned in Compiègne and Biberach camps; Kurt Morgenroth, interned in several British and Australian camps including Tatura; and Kate Lack, scholar of Besançon internment camp

Contents

List of Figures ix
List of Tables xiii
List of Contributors xv

British internment and the internment of Britons: An introduction 1
   Rachel Pistol and Gilly Carr

Part 1   British Camps: Continentals Interned in Britain

1   Early internment camps in the United Kingdom: A forgotten history and heritage   13
   Rachel Pistol

2   'Once again to live their bit of private life, free from camping like gipsies': The case of a refugee camp in the Garden of England   31
   Clare Ungerson

3   Legacy and heritage of the Arandora Star tragedy in Britain and Italy: A transnational perspective   47
   Terri Colpi

4   Huyton: A transit camp near Liverpool   67
   Jennifer Taylor

5   Written out of history: The impact of Sefton Camp's post-war invisibility on memory and belonging   83
   Rob David

6   Rushen Camp, Isle of Man – Camp W (women and children), Camp Y (married), 'Treat them with kindness'   101
   Rushen Heritage Action Team in order of authorship: David Wertheim, Pamela Crowe, Alison Graham, Jane Saywell, Sandra Davidson, Hugh Davidson, Doreen Moule

Part 2 Continental Camps: Britons Interned on the Continent

7 An autograph book, a piano and a body hanging on the wire: British memories of the French transit and internment camp of Royallieu, Compiègne — 117
   Gilly Carr

8 P. G. Wodehouse and the men of Tost — 135
   Christine Berberich

9 The Golden Cage: The orphan story of British women and internment in Vittel — 149
   Ayshka Sené

10 The internment of British enemy aliens in Fascist internment camps: The case study of *Anglo-Maltesi* — 167
   Pierluigi Bolioli

Part 3 Camps in the British Dominions: Continentals interned by the British abroad

11 In detention: Memories of Jewish refugees interned in Atlit near Haifa — 189
   Verena Buser

12 The operation, experiences and legacy of the Prem Nagar Central Internment Camp at Dehra Dun in British India, 1939–present — 207
   Joseph Cronin

13 Civilian internment in the Raj: Central and family internment camps c.1939–43 — 221
   Alan Malpass

14 The British sent them to Australia from around the World: The internment of enemy aliens in the Second World War at Tatura Camps 1 to 4 — 239
   Alan Morgenroth

15 Grass growing is like forgetting: A case study of the heritage of the Second World War–internment camp B-70 New Brunswick, Canada — 261
   Todd E. Caissie

Index — 277

Figures

1.1	Map of the early camps mentioned in this chapter *Source:* © Rachel Pistol.	15
1.2	Images of Butlin's Clacton, Dixon's Paignton and Warner's Seaton holiday camps in the 1930s and 1940s *Source:* Postcards from the Pistol-Morgenroth Personal Collection.	16
1.3	Illustrations of Prees Heath by Wilhelm Jondorf *Source:* Images courtesy of Harry Jondorf.	22
1.4	The Warth Mills memorial sculpture and plaque *Source:* Images courtesy of Richard Shaw.	26
3.1	Italian Ambassador, Boris Biancheri, with some of the newly decorated *Cavalieri*, London, 1990 *Source:* © Terri Colpi Archive.	51
3.2	Conference poster, Picinisco, 2019 *Source:* Courtesy Comune di Picinisco.	52
3.3	Arandora Star Memorial, St Peter's Italian Church, London *Source:* © Terri Colpi Archive.	53
4.1	Sketch map of Huyton Camp by Martin Dalheim, 1941 *Source:* Courtesy the Estate of Martin Karl Eberhard Dalheim.	68
5.1	Werner David's journal: Part of the entry for 17 October 1940 describing his departure from Huyton Camp for the Isle of Man *Source:* © the author; journal deposited in Imperial War Museum Archive: Document 25027.	85
5.2	The Sefton Hotel and Church Road in 2014. The facades of these buildings have changed little since 1940–1 *Source:* Courtesy Julian Sale.	86
5.3	Martin Bloch: View from Sefton Camp *Source:* Courtesy Martin Bloch Trust.	93
6.1	HMS *Princess Josephine Charlotte* *Source:* Courtesy of Nigel Thornton.	103
6.2	Port Erin Promenade 1930s–50s	105

6.3	Port St Mary Promenade 2019, much as it was in 1940	110
	Source: © Doreen Moule.	
7.1a-c	Google Earth imagery showing the camp buildings in 2001, 2010 and 2018. The compounds and barracks C4 and C8 which held Islanders are marked in Figure 7.1a	128
	Source: © Google Earth with annotations by Gilly Carr.	
7.2	Survivors from the Channel Islanders present at the 2008 opening ceremony of the *Mémorial*	129
	Source: © Gilly Carr.	
7.3	The Wall of Names at Compiègne Memorial	130
	Source: © Gilly Carr.	
8.1	Tost Memorial	144
	Source: Photo by kind permission of Sybille Krägel, NKWD-Lager Tost/Oberschlesien 1945.	
8.2	Tost camp hospital building	145
	Source: Photo by kind permission of Andrzej Morciniec, www.promafot.pl.	
8.3	Tost NKVD camp memorial plaque	145
	Source: Photo by kind permission of Andrzej Morciniec, www.promafot.pl.	
9.1	Dr J. de Morsier inspects British Red Cross parcels in Vittel on 4 July 1941	153
	Source: © ICRC, 04/07/1941, 'War 1939–45. Vittel. Camp for British civilian internees. Warehouse', V-P-HIST-03022-25.	
9.2	Nuns assembled outside the *Grand Hôtel* in October 1943	155
	Source: © ICRC, 10/1943, 'War 1939–45. Vittel. Camp for American and British civilian internees. Nuns assembled in the park', V-P-HIST-03021-01.	
9.3	The steps outside the Grand Hôtel in September 2015	156
	Source: © Ayshka Sené.	
9.4	Plaque at the Musée de la Résistance et Déportation in Besançon 2015	157
	Source: ©Ayshka Sené.	
10.1	Map of main camps for *Anglo-Maltesi*	176
	Source: Created by the author with ArcGIS.	
10.2	One of the few remains of the Ferramonti di Tarsia Camp	179
	Source: CC BY 3.0 credits: Salvatore Magliari, 2005.	
10.3	The Fraschette di Alatri Camp	179
	Source: Photo courtesy of Maria Novella De Luca, 2021.	

Figures

11.1 Illustrated page from the diary of Egon Weiss showing the layout of Atlit camp, compiled during and immediately after his detention in the camp — 192
Source: © USHMM Photo Collection, image 70188.

11.2 Dr Ella Freund — 197
Source: Courtesy and © Yotam Moked.

11.3 A page of the children's book '*The spotlight of Atlit*' — 198
Source: © Atlit Detention Center Database.

12.1 The 'Enemy Foreigners Order', copy published in *The Gazette of India*, 3 September 1939. British Library, India Office Records: L/PJ/8/41: 'Coll 101/10B; Aliens in India: Indian Foreigners Orders, Ordinances and Acts; British measures under Aliens Order, 1920' — 209
Source: © The British Library Board.

12.2 British Library, India Office Records: L/PJ/8/31: 'Coll 101/10AA; Nominal rolls of internees and parolees in India' — 213
Source: © The British Library Board.

13.1 Civilian Internment Camps in India c.1939–45 — 223
Source: Map adapted by the author from https://d-maps.com/carte.php?num_car=285&lang=en.

13.2 ICRC Archives (ARR), 1942. Purandhar. Civilian Internees Camp. General view of the camp — 229
Source: V-P-HIST-03480-19A.

13.3 ICRC Archives (ARR), 1942. Purandhar. Civilian Internees Camp. Barrack — 230
Source: V-P-HIST-03480-23A.

13.4 ICRC Archives (ARR). 1944. Satara, Parole Center. Civilian internees camp. Barracks of the German wing — 231
Source: V-P-HIST-03478-01A.

14.1 Points of departure of internee deportations to Australia and locations of wartime camps and memorials in the Tatura district — 240
Source: © Alan Morgenroth.

14.2 'Tatura Camp 1' — 248
Source: Annotated compilation of official photographs c.1943 now in the public domain courtesy Australian War Memorial.

14.3 Tatura Irrigation and Wartime Camps Museum; Mural and *Arandora Star* Memorial and HMT *Dunera* Model — 255

Source: Compilation of images by Alan Morgenroth. Leonard Adams Arandora Star memorial watercolour reproduced courtesy of Mary-Clare Adams.

15.1 Photograph of the superstructure base of the water tower next to the sign indicating location of the original camp   262
Source: Image © Todd Caissie.

15.2 Four photographs of University of New Brunswick Biology Hall   268
Source: Image © Todd Caissie.

15.3 Photograph of students building scale model of the internment camp   270
Source: Image © Todd Caissie.

Tables

10.1	Major Deportations of *Anglo-Maltesi* from Libya	170
10.2	Secondary Deportations of *Anglo-Maltesi* from Libya	171
10.3	Foreigners Expelled from Libya as Provided by Prefectures in February 1943 on the Request of the Ministry of Interior	174
14.1	Internees Deported from the United Kingdom on HMT *Dunera*	242
14.2	Internees Deported from Singapore	243
14.3	Internees Deported from Palestine to Australia	243
14.4	Internees Detained by the British in Iran September 1941	245
14.5	Tatura Internment Camps: A Guide to the Use and Occupancy of Each Camp and Compound 1940 to 1947	247

Contributors

Christine Berberich is Reader in Literature at the University of Portsmouth, UK. She has published widely in the field of national identity construction (in particular Englishness) as well as in the area of Holocaust Studies. She is the author of *The Image of the English Gentleman in Twentieth-Century Literature: Englishness and Nostalgia* (2007), editor of *The Bloomsbury Introduction to Popular Fiction* (2014), *Trauma and Memory: The Holocaust in Contemporary Culture* (2021) and *Brexit and the Migrant Voice: EU Nationals in Post-Brexit Literature and Culture* (2022), and co-editor of *Land & Identity: Memory, Theory, Practice* (2011), *These Englands: Conversations on National Identity* (2012) and *Affective Landscapes in Literature, Art and Everyday Life* (2015). She is currently at work on an edited collection on Brexit and the Migrant Voice, a monograph on 'Nazi Noir' and a monograph-length work on P. G. Wodehouse and the Men of Tost.

Pierluigi Bolioli earned his BA in political sciences and his MA in modern history both at the University of Pisa. He is now undertaking PhD research in geopolitics at the same university. His research is mostly based on primary sources and he intends to compare internment of Italian civilians in the British Empire with the internment of British civilians in the Fascist Empire. His research interests are international relations, fascism, imperialism and concentration camps.

Verena Buser earned her PhD from the centre for Research on Antisemitism at Technical University Berlin. Her research focuses on the areas of Hachshara and non-Zionist emigration preparations; Jewish functionaries under Nazi rule childhood and youth during and after the Shoah; the forced Germanization of Polish children; and the history of social work. Her work has been supported by the Blavatnik Archives Foundation, the Szloma-Albam Stiftung in Berlin, the Memorial Foundation for Jewish Culture and the Leo Baeck Institute in New York, the Hadassah Brandeis Institute in Waltham and the Edith Saurer Fonds in Vienna. Together with Boaz Cohen (Western Galilee College) she is founder of the project Children after the Holocaust, War and Genocide (cwg1945.org).

Todd E. Caissie is the Director of New Brunswick Internment Camp Museum and a PhD candidate in Cultural Heritage and Preservation Studies and Art History at Rutgers University. He recently co-authored a chapter on the NB Internment Camp, titled 'The New Brunswick Internment Camp Museum: Preserving the History of Camp B-70', in the edited collection *Civilian Internment in Canada: Histories and Legacies* (2020). Todd is also the curator of the exhibition *Escape: Art from New Brunswick's Internment* Camp at the Beaverbrook Art Gallery (October 2023–December 2023). He has published several public history articles on the museum and camp B-70.

Gilly Carr is Associate Professor and Academic Director in Archaeology at the University of Cambridge's Institute of Continuing Education. She is also Fellow and Director of Studies in Archaeology at St Catharine's College. Gilly publishes in the fields of conflict archaeology, post-conflict heritage studies, Holocaust studies and Second World War history, and is the author of thirteen monographs and edited volumes. Her most recent monograph *Victims of Nazism in the Channel Islands: A Legitimate Heritage?* was published in 2019. She is currently writing *A Materiality of Internment* about the arts and crafts made in civilian internment camps. Gilly is also on the UK delegation of the International Holocaust Remembrance Alliance and is on the academic advisory board of the UK Holocaust Memorial in Westminster. In 2020 she was awarded the European Heritage Prize.

Terri Colpi is an Honorary Research Fellow at the University of St Andrews specializing in the migration, history and geographies of Italian communities in Britain. After her doctorate at Oxford University, in 1991, she published *The Italian Factor: The Italian Community in Great Britain* and *Italians Forward: A Visual History of the Italians in Great Britain*, with a further book in 2015 on Italians in Scotland. Terri frequently presents at conferences and gives public lectures. She collaborates with the Italian Ministry of Foreign Affairs on research initiatives and sat on the Advisory Board of the AHRC (Arts and Humanities Research Council) Transnationalizing Modern Languages project. Her latest television appearances include *CNN*'s 'Searching for Italy', and Sky Arts, 'Treasures of the British Library'. Terri Colpi's contribution to the field of Italian Studies has been recognized by the Italian government through conferment of the title *Cavaliere Ordine al Merito della Repubblica Italiana*.

Joseph Cronin is a Lecturer in Modern German History at Queen Mary University of London. He works on twentieth-century Central and East European history, particularly German Jewish history, migration history and the history of the Holocaust and its legacies. His current research project focuses on Jewish refugees in India during the Second World War.

Rob David's professional career was in history and education, mostly in colleges in the northwest of England. He has a BA from the University of Exeter and an MA and PhD from Lancaster University. More recently, influenced by the silence surrounding his family's history and anniversaries associated with events of the world wars, he has examined the experiences of Germans and Austrians living in Cumbria during the Great War, and the history of refugee communities and organizations in the northwest of England in the 1930s and 1940s. There have been various publications on these subjects, the most recent of which is *A County of Refuge: Refugees in Cumbria 1933–1941* (2020).

Alan Malpass is a Lecturer in Military History at Bishop Grosseteste University. He completed his PhD in 2016 at Sheffield Hallam University. His first monograph *British*

Character and the Treatment of German Prisoners of War, 1939–48 was published in 2020. His current research explores the captivity of civilian internees and prisoners of war in India during and after the Second World War.

Alan Morgenroth is an independent researcher into the experiences of the German and Austrian refugees interned by the British during 1940 and deported to Australia and Canada. Initially inspired by research into his own father's experiences as a '*Dunera* Internee', he has spent fifteen years delving deep into all aspects of the subject. As a retired chartered accountant and entrepreneur, Alan has investigated the daily lives within the Australian camps, with particular attention to the camp economics and their banking systems. In January 2023 he presented a paper to the 'Beyond Camps and Forced Labour' conference comparing the deportations to Canada and Australia and the effect on Jewish refugee trajectories.

Rachel Pistol is a digital historian of immigration and Second World War internment in the United Kingdom and United States. She is currently based in the Digital Humanities Department at King's College London where she is the National Coordinator for EHRI-UK and on the Project Management Board of the European Holocaust Research Infrastructure (EHRI). She is the Honorary Historical Advisor for World Jewish Relief and an Honorary Research Fellow at the University of Exeter. Rachel has published widely on Second World War internment in the United Kingdom and the United States including her monograph *Internment during the Second World War: A Comparative Study of Great Britain and the USA* in 2017. She has discussed Second World War internment in documentaries and debates on TV and radio and has written articles comparing internment with modern day issues that have appeared internationally including in *Newsweek*, *The Independent* and *Huffington Post*.

Rushen Heritage Action Team (the Second World War Women's Internment Heritage Action Team) has, over the past six years, generated new research on internment through research and local interviews. The team created and ran an exhibition in May 2015 called 'Friend or Foe? 1940–1941' to which over 3,000 tourists and local residents visited, including the former CEO of the British Museum, Sir David Wilson, who said the exhibition was of 'outstanding quality'. Courtesy of Betty Kelly, the team also published 'The Illustrated Roll Call' on 19 May 2015. In 2016, the Heritage Action Team extended the 'Friend or Foe?' exhibition, exploring the creation of the world's only married camp in the Second World War. Based on the successful exhibition the team published its second book on Rushen Internment in 2017.

Ayshka Sené is a Research Associate at the University of York where she is currently working on the Leverhulme Trust funded 'Archiving the Inner City Project: Race and the Politics of Urban Memory'. Her research focuses on French history and memory, particularly the history, memory and legacy of British women's internment in Vittel and Besançon during the Second World War. Ayshka achieved her doctorate at Cardiff University in 2018, funded by the AHRC South, West and Wales Doctoral Training Partnership. Prior to taking up her current post, Ayshka worked on an

AHRC funded project at Nottingham Trent University and on the EU-funded H2020 project, 'Unsettling Remembering and Social Cohesion in Transnational Europe' at the University of Bath. Her research interests include French history, oral history, the Second World War, memory, gender and national identity.

Jennifer Taylor studied German at the Universities of Bristol and London, and the Freie Universität Berlin. She is a founder member of the Centre for German and Austrian Exile Studies at the Institute of Languages, Cultures and Societies, University of London. She has published widely on exile topics, including radio propaganda and the exile press. Other relevant publications include the chapter on internment in *Changing Countries* (2002), an oral history project of the Research Centre and *Civilian Internment in Britain during WW2: Huyton Camp* (2012), an edited compilation of eye-witness accounts of the camp.

Clare Ungerson is Professor Emeritus of Social Policy at the University of Southampton. As such, she published many books and articles in the field of social policy, specializing in the areas of gender and of care. Shortly before retirement in 2004 she began archival research on the Kitchener camp at Sandwich in East Kent, which she continued post retirement, using archives in London and Jerusalem. Her book, *Four Thousand Lives: The Rescue of German Jewish Men to Britain, 1939*, was published in 2014, and republished in paperback in 2019. It was named as a 'book of the year' in the TLS (Times Literary Supplement) in December 2019. She was a founder member of the Kitchener Descendants Group and is chair of its organizing committee

British internment and the internment of Britons: An introduction

Rachel Pistol and Gilly Carr

In recent decades there has been a marked growth in scholarship on the internment of continentals in Great Britain during the Second World War, yet more information is still coming to light to build an even more nuanced and full picture of what happened to 'enemy aliens' during this period. From fragmented records, detective work has been required to fully reconstruct exactly what happened during this time period and how it has been remembered and commemorated. This volume has been created to fill a gap in internment scholarship and to offer a comparative approach that considers the internment of continentals in Britain alongside the internment of Britons on the continent. As historian Jürgen Kocka has noted, the 'merits of the comparative approach to history are undeniable … Comparison helps to make the "climate" of historical research less provincial'.[1] By telling the histories of internment in Britain and by the British abroad with the history of Britons interned in Europe, it is possible to compare policy and conditions of internment and how these differed across Europe and beyond. It is a way of combatting exceptionalism in narratives of the camps and of highlighting lesser known aspects of Second World War internment. Furthermore, not only does this collection seek to set internment into a larger global narrative, but it also seeks to address the heritage of the camps and consider what has happened to the sites of internment since 1945. By doing so, we can assess what each country has chosen to remember. It is hoped that by highlighting the status of former sites of incarceration, we can draw attention to the curation and protection – and, conversely, the neglect – of the histories of these physical landscapes. By examining the way in which these heritage sites are presented to the public today – or utterly ignored – we can gain insight into the way in which the memory of the interned has been remembered or forgotten. Previous volumes have largely ignored this important insight.

Internment, when used in this volume, refers to the state of civilian confinement caused by citizenship of a belligerent country, and so this volume does not explicitly cover the treatment of military Prisoners of War captured as combatants during the conflict. Before the 1980s, little was written on the topic of internment in Great Britain, with a few notable exceptions including François Lafitte's seminal text written in 1940,

The Internment of Aliens.² It was not until the 1970s and 1980s that a growth in interest in refugee history and lesser known narratives of the war led to a re-evaluation of internment, particularly in Britain. This was encouraged in part through television and media, including the *World at War* series and the now famous *That's Life* episode that featured the late Sir Nicholas Winton and his role in the *Kindertransport*, an umbrella term that covers the rescue of refugee children from Nazi-controlled Europe by a number of agencies.³ This resurgent interest in what happened to continentals resident in Great Britain during the Second World War coincided with the release of a significant number of government documents in the 1970s under the thirty-year rule, leading to two of the first modern seminal works on internment in Peter and Leni Gillman's *Collar the Lot* and Ronald Stent's *A Bespattered Page*, both published in 1980.⁴ Building on this research, David Cesarani and Tony Kushner held a conference at the Wiener Holocaust Library in 1990 to discuss new research on internment in Britain, with papers later published in an edited volume, with a further internment-focused edited volume collated by Richard Dove in 2005.⁵ Both these edited collections contained chapters on both the First and Second World Wars, with the latter covering the deportation of internees from Britain to Australia and Canada, as well as exploring some of the camp newspapers, artistic and literary portrayals of internment using sources that had only recently become available. These works have, notably, mostly come about during anniversary years, starting with the fortieth anniversary of internment in 1980. It is fitting, therefore, that this volume of new research was conceived during the eightieth anniversary of British internment in 2020, during the Covid-19 pandemic.

Scholarship has not, of course, been limited only to anniversary years. Charmian Brinson, for example, has published extensively on the internment of women and children; one of the editors of this volume, Rachel Pistol, published a comparative study of Second World War internment in the United Kingdom and the United States in 2017; and Tony Grenville and Swen Steinberg edited a collection of essays titled *Refugees from Nazi-Occupied Europe in British Overseas Territories* in 2019.⁶ Beyond the history and experiences of internment camps, in recent years, there has been a huge growth in examining art and creativity within internment camps, including Gilly Carr and Harold Mytum's *Cultural Heritage and Prisoners of War: Creativity Behind Barbed Wire*, which, despite its title, includes civilian internment, and Monica Bohm-Duchen's edited collection based on the Insiders/Outsiders Festival that focuses on contributions to British culture by refugees from Nazi Europe.⁷ Yet there is still more that has been, and is being, discovered in this area. Digitization of previously unseen or hard-to-access documents is making research more accessible, and the growth in sharing of micro-archives – records held not by institutions but by families and other interested individuals – is adding to the growth of resources available to modern scholars of wartime internment.

This volume is the first time a comparison has been made between what happened to continentals interned in Britain with what happened to Britons on the continent, offering brand new insights and an opportunity for a much greater understanding of Second World War internment and how experiences varied from country to country. Furthermore, this collection is the first to focus on post-1945 heritage, legacy and memory and its significance on the narrative of internment. To do this in the most effective way, this book is structured in three sections that cover continentals interned in Britain, Britons interned on the continent, and continentals interned by the British abroad. In this way, this collection offers a comparative approach, not only to show how internee experiences varied between camps and countries but also to demonstrate many similarities in how the internees organized their lives and attempted to create order out of chaos in whatever way they could.

Once Britain declared war on Germany, all German and Austrian citizens living in Britain or British territories automatically became enemy aliens. This classification also applied outside of Britain, including, for example, all Britons living in German-occupied territories. During international armed conflict, enemy aliens can be interned based on the potential threat they pose to a country's internal security. Essentially, enemy aliens can be detained as criminals for no other reason than their nationality and held in prison camps for the duration of the armed conflict if deemed necessary by the interning state. The 1929 Geneva Convention only applied to Prisoners of War, and therefore, civilian internees during the Second World War were at the mercy of the social conventions of the country in which they were residing at the outbreak of hostilities.[8] For continentals living in Britain, and Britons living on the continent, conditions were monitored in each country by the Red Cross and voluntary organizations, with reports sent to both Allied and Axis governments. Pressure was exerted not only from the fear of British citizens abroad being mistreated as a result of poor treatment of German nationals living in Britain, and vice versa, but also from government representatives in Britain such as Eleanor Rathbone, Josiah Wedgwood, Victor Cazalet and others, who read the reports on the treatment of civilians in Britain and objected to the treatment of thousands of refugees from Nazi oppression. Overall, this mutual monitoring via the neutral Swiss led to a certain mutually agreed minimum standard for internment conditions, though reprisals certainly did happen at various points during the war, such as in the case of Germans deported to Australia from Persia 1941 that ultimately led to the deportation of Channel Islanders to the continent in 1942.[9]

So-called enemy aliens were not the only threat to national security, however, at this time. Though fears may have been rife regarding the prospect of an enemy Fifth Column of spies and saboteurs who had entered Britain under the pretence of being refugees, there was also the possibility of British citizens themselves supporting the cause of Britain's enemies. Many Britons admired Adolf Hitler and what he was perceived to have achieved in strengthening Germany's faltering economy; Oswald Mosley and his Black Shirts were some of the most recognizable of Hitler's supporters. While international law supported countries interning enemy alien civilians, new laws had to be created to justify the detention of British citizens. Defence Regulation 18B enabled the detention of British citizens if he or she were subject to 'foreign influence or control' or had 'sympathies with the system of government' of a foreign power.[10] This volume does not focus on the cases of 18B detention, though it is a subject deserving of further study, as the comparative nature of this edited collection is of enemy aliens living in foreign nations during the Second World War, i.e. British citizens in Nazi-occupied Europe and Germans, Austrians and Italians in Britain or British territories.

This collection is a particularly exciting development in internment studies for several reasons. Firstly, there is a huge amount of new and under-represented research in the following pages. Rob David's chapter, for example, focuses on Sefton Camp on the Isle of Man, one of the smallest and least remembered of all the Manx camps. The Rushen Heritage Action Team, a group of volunteers who dedicate their time to preserving the memory of the women's, children's and married camps on the south of the island, have written a chapter on their work preserving this heritage, balancing out the tendency to focus only on the male experience of internment. Many descendants of former internees are only aware of their forebears' time on the island and assume they must have travelled directly there. Rachel Pistol's chapter helps to explain the multiplicity of the transit camps on the British mainland, demonstrating how internees were moved, often several times, between overcrowded and poorly equipped temporary camps before the Manx camps were opened from the end of May 1940. In Britain, most is known about the camps established on the Isle of Man, though Jennifer Taylor's chapter provides new information on the heritage of the largest camp on the British mainland, Huyton, in Liverpool. Kitchener Camp near Sandwich in Kent is often thought of as an internment camp but was in fact a rescue camp that was part of the British response to the refugee crisis of the 1930s. Clare Ungerson offers an exploration of the memory and heritage of this camp that was, until recently, relatively unknown and deserving of recognition for the thousands of lives saved. The memory of camps rarely focuses on lives destroyed or lost. By way of contrast with Kitchener, we might consider the internment of members of the Italian community in Britain, and the tragedy of the sinking of the *Arandora Star* in July 1940, in which the Italian community in Britain was disproportionately affected. How this tragedy has been commemorated and the 'pockets of affect' it created is addressed in Terri Colpi's chapter.

There are also chapters that take new approaches to the treatment of internees who were deported to Canada and Australia from Britain. Though much has been written about the '*Dunera* Boys' and their time in Hay Camps 7 and 8 in Australia, very little is understood about what happened after Hay, particularly at Tatura. Although often referred to in the singular, Alan Morgenroth explains the multitude of camps established in Tatura and the complexities of memory and heritage on a site where so many different categories of internees were housed. By comparison, much less is known about the camps in Canada than Australia, which makes Todd Caissie's discussion of camp B-70 in New Brunswick and the creation of the New Brunswick Internment Camp Museum, one of only two internment museums in Canada, highly significant. Beyond the British Isles, internment was also conducted by the British in Palestine and India. Verena Buser's chapter on Atlit uses refugee testimonies to tell the story of the harsh conditions of the detention camp near Haifa, while Joseph Cronin and Alan Malpass offer new insights into internment in India, articulating an exceptionally thorough picture of both the conditions and the camps' post-war legacies.

Of course, one of the unique features of this book is how the internment of continentals in Britain or by the British is placed next to explanations of how Britons were treated on the continent, an area deserving of much greater awareness. Gilly Carr uses her chapter to show what happened to Channel Islanders deported to France, and how the treatment of the Channel Islanders differed from the German internment of the French political prisoners and French Jews in the same camp. Another camp which held British detainees was Vittel, and Ayshka Sené focuses on the little-known experiences of British women interned there, providing another stark reminder of the differences in the ways the British were treated compared with Jewish internees. These women have been hidden from British and French national memories because their experiences are considered insufficiently heroic, stoic or tragic, requiring a re-addressing of the historical record. The editors had also hoped to include a chapter from Katherine Lack on Besançon in France, but, tragically, Kate passed away during the production of this book. To read more about the case of Besançon, we recommend reading her earlier publication, *Frontstalag 142: The Internment Diary of an English Lady*.[11]

In Italy, the British *Anglo-Maltesi* from Libya were interned, as we learn from Pierluigi Bolioli's chapter. Bolioli tells us that this community, a small percentage of whom were Jewish, lost their homes and possessions in the expulsion, many of whom eventually emigrated to Australia after the war. Finally, though many will be familiar with P. G. Wodehouse's disastrous involvement with the German authorities during the war, fewer will be aware of the conditions British internees – including Wodehouse – experienced in Tost, Poland, as demonstrated in Christine Berberich's chapter.

If there is one overriding, common theme that unites almost all of the memory and heritage of the camps and groups of internees discussed in this volume, then it is one of decades-long, post-war state silence, indifference and forgetting, followed by belated acknowledgement fought for by activists, small organizations, family members, local communities and individuals. One might be tempted to characterize this initial reaction by the state as simply one of national shame when dealing with a difficult history. William Logan and Keir Reeves discuss sites such as those in this volume as places of 'pain and shame' which 'bring shame upon us now for the cruelty and ultimate futility of the events that occurred within them and the ideologies they represented'.[12] Yet, while we too may characterize civilian internment camps in such a way, the reasons for the silence and politics of forgetting are much more varied than we might think at first glance.

The chapters in this volume reveal the wealth of quite reasonable explanations as to why state-sponsored heritage and memory of civilian internment was lacking, and in some cases, is still insufficient, even today. We must remember that we are not starting afresh, in the twenty-first century, with these sites wholly intact and coming up with arguments and heritage plans to protect them now. Rather, many of these sites of internment underwent changes – often irrevocable – immediately after use, only partially recoverable now through archaeology. While reference to a 'politics of forgetting' implies a certain intentional blindness to that which still exists, so many sites of internment were destroyed, taken down or replaced with other buildings soon after the war. It is clearly far easier to forget about something that no longer exists. Huyton camp, just outside Liverpool, for example, became swallowed up in a growing housing estate after the war, complete with roads put back into use and cars driving through the middle of what was once the camp. Jennifer Taylor's chapter shows us that even the footprint of the former camp was hard to identify after this. In Italy, two of the more once-prominent camps, Ferramonti di Tarsia and Servigliano, are today a highway and a sports ground, although some features remain.

Brevity of occupation was another factor which militated against remembrance. Rob David writes about Sefton Hotel in Douglas on the Isle of Man, used from October 1940 to March 1941. So easily forgotten was this location of internment that at least one former camp inmate forgot the name of the camp where he was interned, thinking for decades that he was held elsewhere. Rachel Pistol writes about the earliest internment camps in use for the first nine months of the war. Some of these were in use for only weeks or months. It is easy to see how such brief use can be overshadowed by lengthier post-war functions of sites, and just as easy for those who do not support remembrance projects to dismiss such brief histories.

Many internment camps were re-used for purposes which had a far greater longevity, often by the military, who sometimes also occupied the sites before the war. Gilly Carr tells us how Compiègne internment and transit camp in France, for example, was a military barracks from 1913 to 1997; the war years could thus be posited as a brief interlude which was better covered up and ultimately bulldozed, given the story of French antisemitism and collaboration that it threatened to spotlight. Alan Malpass discusses the camps in India during the British Raj, many of which were former military camps and later used as military schools for Indian forces. His chapter reveals that some were re-used as sites of internment for members of the Indian National Congress such as Nehru; this event is better remembered than their role as a place of internment of Europeans. Joseph Cronin also reminds us that memories of the internment camps in the subcontinent raise difficult issues of India's colonial past and Germany's Nazi past, as the inmates were only there due to a combination of Nazism and British colonialism. Military histories of camps and other, more troubling, narratives can often dominate the story told at sites, overshadowing the (seemingly) 'tame' histories of 'comfortable' civilian internment. The struggle between narratives does not have to be a zero-sum game, with some narratives 'winning' at the cost of others. While it is clearly possible to tell many stories at a single site, some clearly capture the public imagination or receive more political support (and funding) than others.

In Eastern Europe, other narratives have come into play. In Poland, for example, any events of the Nazi occupation, which included the internment of civilians in Tost, have been overshadowed not just by the post-war and Soviet-period re-use of this particular camp as an NKVD prison, as Christine Berberich tells us, but also by the presence of nearby Auschwitz-Birkenau. Both the prison and the concentration camp were places of far worse deprivations, malnourishment, disease and ill-treatment of prisoners, and so it is no wonder that the original buildings of the internment camp at Tost are virtually silent on the former use of the site as a place where Britons were interned in far preferable conditions. It can be hard to garner sympathy within local communities, either now or during the war, for internees who were perceived to have had a 'better time' than those who were not interned. This was also the case in Vittel, France, as Ayshka Sené informs us, and in Italy, in the areas near the camps in which *Anglo-Maltesi* were held, as we learn from Pierluigi Bolioli. This is also a view often repeated in the Channel Islands today when talking about those deported to France and Germany. In both cases, the quantity and reliability of food supply is often perceived as the defining factor in deciding such things.

It is not only the military who claim or reclaim sites after use by internees; Clare Ungerson tells us how the Pfizer pharmaceutical company purchased the land of the Kitchener refugee camp in Kent, England, after the war, and the buildings were destroyed that had previously housed Jewish refugees rescued from Nazi camps in Germany. Ayshka Sené writes about the luxury hotels in Vittel which were used to house British internees and then returned to their former use. Memorial plaques to those interned are here physically marginalized at best. One of the reasons for new site owners or national governments keeping certain wartime narratives at arm's length, for so many of the chapters in this volume, is because of the British (and French and Italian) internment of Jews. While in Britain we do not see the antisemitic policies instituted in occupied Europe, the internment of enemy aliens often meant that both Nazi sympathizers and Jews, both groups of which held German citizenship, were often interned together in Britain and its dominions, with predictably turbulent consequences. These groups were eventually separated, and opportunities were provided for release through a series of White Papers drawn up from July to October 1940, but the majority of those interned only wished to help Great Britain, not harm it. As Heinrich Fraenkel titled his book, written from behind barbed wire in Hutchinson Camp on the Isle of Man, *Help Us Germans to Beat the Nazis!*[13] It is important to remember that, as Tony Kushner argues, Britain has had a 'tendency towards self-congratulation that has never really disappeared' when it comes to its war narrative, despite its failures with regard to the Holocaust and refugees from Nazism.[14]

Despite the factors which combine to silence or marginalize narratives of civilian internment, there are those who seek to combat the politics of forgetting. More often than not, these activists are the descendants of the internees. Local communities and academics, too, can work with (or class themselves as) activists, and such groups can be vigorous in promoting the memory of those once interned. The Rushen Heritage Action Team who write about Rushen Camp, the camp that held women and children in the Isle of Man, have worked tirelessly to raise awareness, put on exhibitions, written text information boards and offered tours. In New Brunswick, Canada, camp B-70 housed enemy aliens deported from Britain. A teacher at a local junior high school was responsible for leading an amateur excavation at the site with his students, and the resulting objects discovered were used to found an internment museum. In his chapter, Todd Caissie tells us about how local activism grew from this one teacher, Todd's father, with a bright idea. Organizations comprising former internees can also ensure the longevity of the legacy of their members. The Association of Jewish Refugees (AJR) based in London, among whose numbers are former internees, has also been active in sponsoring Blue Plaques. Such plaques can be found in the town of Sandwich in Kent to commemorate the Kitchener refugee camp and in Douglas in the Isle of Man in remembrance of the internment camps there.

Descendants of internees often have the greatest incentive to fight on behalf of their family member, even if it takes decades. From Alan Morgenroth's chapter on the *Dunera*, a deportation vessel which carried internees to Australia, some of whom later chose to stay in the country after the war, we learn that descendants have been active in keeping memory in the public domain. It helped matters that many of the deportees were widely perceived to have (disproportionately for their number) positively influenced Australian society through their innate talents and qualities. This went a long way in helping Australians to honour those who had become almost forgotten in the United Kingdom. Terri Colpi also writes about those on board a deportation vessel, specifically the Italians on board the ill-fated *Arandora Star*, who are remembered differently in their native land compared to in the United Kingdom. In Italy, memory appears to thrive in the native towns of the emigrants through the positive connotations of 'innocent emigrants' who were 'making a contribution to British society'. In the United Kingdom, the Italians were seen as 'untrustworthy enemy aliens', some of whom had fascist sympathies. Although there are places in the United Kingdom where Italian communities have memorialized the dead of the *Arandora Star*, there is a clear conflict in the way that the interned Italians are remembered by the British and Italian states. Today, like the families who remember the '*Dunera* boys', the communities who remember the *Arandora Star* have become connected through social media such as Facebook, which hosts dedicated memorial pages. The Kitchener descendant group, too, have found each other through social media, and such ways of uniting people as support for heritage activism is today very popular.

In conclusion then, while most internment sites were places of pain for internees, they have long since ceased to be places of shame for most governments. This is through a fortuitous (for them) combination of little remaining to be seen and because, where the state now acknowledges their role in dark histories (often because of the work of activists), the events were too distant for current governments to be touched by the wrongdoing of their predecessors. In some cases, the state that once interned civilians, such as Fascist Italy, no longer exists. For those heritage and memory activists still fighting for acknowledgement of their camp, it is important to remember that even though their internees may have been few, briefly interned, treated well or whose stories have become overshadowed by seemingly more important events that happened at the site of their camp, they are doing important work. Honouring the memory of those submitted to national and transnational injustices is also part of the fight of holding governments to account for their policies and highlighting the long-term and far-reaching impacts of internment. As Tony Kushner puts it, 'At a time of increasing ethnic and racial tensions at a global level, and the worst refugee crisis since the Second World War, critical perspectives are more than ever required in the dialogue between "then" and "now".'[15] Activists should remember that they often also hold a trump card: while the state may refuse to open or permit access to key archival files, or where these records have been lost, activists often have access to unpublished diaries, memoirs, letters, artwork, handicrafts and oral testimony. All of these are sufficient to give a detailed insight into the daily life and experiences of the interned. These alternative sources of knowledge can, in the end, be more powerful in educating the public and understanding the lived experiences of the interned.

Notes

1. Jürgen Kocka, 'Comparison and Beyond', *History and Theory* 42/1 (2003): 39.

2. Francois Lafitte, *The Internment of Aliens* (London: Libris, 1988); Yvonne Kapp and Margaret Mynatt, *British Policy and the Refugees, 1933-1941* (London: Cass, 1997); Judex, *Anderson's Prisoners* (London: Victor Gollancz, 1940).
3. *The World at War* was first broadcast on ITV in 1973/4; the Nicholas Winton *That's Life* episode was first broadcast on the BBC in 1988. See also Andrea Hammel and Bea Lewkowicz, eds, *The Kindertransport to Britain 1938/39: Yearbook of the Research Centre for German and Austrian Exile Studies* (Leiden: Brill, 2012) and Jennifer Craig-Norton, *The Kindertransport: Contesting Memory* (Bloomington: Indiana University Press, 2019).
4. Leni Gillman and Peter Gillman, *'Collar the Lot!', How Britain Interned and Expelled Its Wartime Refugees* (London: Quartet Books, 1980); Ronald Stent, *A Bespattered Page? The Internment of His Majesty's 'Most Loyal Enemy Aliens'* (London: Deutsch, 1980).
5. David Cesarani and Tony Kushner, eds, *The Internment of Aliens in Twentieth Century Britain* (London: Cass, 1993), 1-24; Richard Dove, ed., *'Totally Un-English'? Britain's Internment of 'Enemy Aliens' in Two World Wars* (Amsterdam: The Yearbook of the Research Centre for German and Austrian Exile Studies, vol. 7, 2005).
6. Charmian Brinson, '"Loyal to the Reich": National Socialists and Others in the Rushen Women's Internment Camp', in *'Totally Un-English'? Britain's Internment of 'Enemy Aliens' in Two World Wars*, ed. Richard Dove (Amsterdam: The Yearbook of the Research Centre for German and Austrian Exile Studies, vol. 7, 2005), 101-19; Charmian Brinson, '"In the Exile of Internment" or "Von Versuchen, Aus Einer Not Eine Tugend Zu Machen": German-Speaking Women Interned by the British during the Second World War', in *Politics and Culture in Twentieth-Century Germany*, ed. William Niven and James Jordan (Rochester, NY: Camden House, 2003), 63-87; Charmian Brinson, '"Please Tell the Bishop of Chichester": George Bell and the Internment Crisis of 1940', *Kirchliche Zeitgeschichte* 21/2 (2008): 287-99; Rachel Pistol, *Internment during the Second World War: A Comparative Study of Great Britain and the USA* (London: Bloomsbury, 2017); Swen Steinberg and Anthony Grenville, eds, *Refugees from Nazi-Occupied Europe in British Overseas Territories* (Leiden: Brill, 2019).
7. Gilly Carr and Harold Mytum, eds, *Cultural Heritage and Prisoners of War: Creativity Behind Barbed Wire* (Abingdon: Routledge, 2017); Monica Bohm-Duchen, ed., *Insiders/Outsiders: Refugees from Nazi Europe and Their Contribution to British Visual Culture* (London: Lund Humphries, 2019).
8. It was not until the Fourth, 1949 Geneva Convention that extensive protection for civilian internees was instituted. For more information see International Committee of the Red Cross, 'Civilian Internees | How Does Law Protect in War? – Online Casebook', https://casebook.icrc.org/glossary/civilian-internees (accessed 18 November 2021).
9. See chapters by Gilly Carr and Alan Morgenroth in this book for more information.
10. Aaron L. Goldman, 'Defence Regulation 18B: Emergency Internment of Aliens and Political Dissenters in Great Britain during World War II', *Journal of British Studies* 12/2 (May 1973): 122. See also A. W. B. Simpson, *In the Highest Degree Odious: Detention Without Trial in Wartime Britain* (Oxford: Clarendon Press, 1992).
11. Published by Amberley Publishing in 2012.
12. 'William Logan and Keir Reeves, 'Introduction: Remembering places of pain and shame', in *Places of Pain and Shame: Dealing with Difficult Heritage*, ed. W. Logan and K. Reeves, 1-14 (Abingdon: Routledge, 2009).

13. Heinrich Fraenkel, *Help Us Germans to Beat the Nazis!* (London: Victor Gollancz, 1941).
14. Tony Kushner, 'The Holocaust in the British imagination: The official mind and beyond, 1945 to the present', *Holocaust Studies* 23/3 (2017): 374.
15. Ibid., 376.

Bibliography

Bohm-Duchen, Monica, ed. *Insiders/Outsiders: Refugees from Nazi Europe and Their Contribution to British Visual Culture*. London: Lund Humphries, 2019.

Brinson, Charmian. '"In the Exile of Internment" or "Von Versuchen, Aus Einer Not Eine Tugend Zu Machen": German-Speaking Women Interned by the British during the Second World War'. In *Politics and Culture in Twentieth-Century Germany*, edited by William Niven and James Jordan, 63–87. Rochester, NY: Camden House, 2003.

Brinson, Charmian. '"Loyal to the Reich": National Socialists and Others in the Rushen Women's Internment Camp'. In *'Totally Un-English'? Britain's Internment of 'Enemy Aliens' in Two World Wars*, edited by Richard Dove, 101–19. Amsterdam: The Yearbook of the Research Centre for German and Austrian Exile Studies, vol. 7, 2005.

Brinson, Charmian. '"Please Tell the Bishop of Chichester": George Bell and the Internment Crisis of 1940'. *Kirchliche Zeitgeschichte* 21, no. 2 (2008): 287–99.

Carr, Gilly, and Harold Mytum, eds. *Cultural Heritage and Prisoners of War: Creativity Behind Barbed Wire*. Abingdon: Routledge, 2017.

Cesarani, David, and Tony Kushner. 'Alien Internment in Britain During the Twentieth Century: An Introduction'. In *The Internment of Aliens in Twentieth Century Britain*, edited by David Cesarani and Tony Kushner, 1–24. London: Frank Cass, 1993.

Dove, Richard, ed. *'Totally Un-English'? Britain's Internment of 'Enemy Aliens' in Two World Wars*. Amsterdam: The Yearbook of the Research Centre for German and Austrian Exile Studies, vol. 7, 2005.

Gillman, Leni, and Peter Gillman. *'Collar the Lot!', How Britain Interned and Expelled Its Wartime Refugees*. London: Quartet Books, 1980.

Goldman, Aaron L. 'Defence Regulation 18B: Emergency Internment of Aliens and Political Dissenters in Great Britain during World War II'. *Journal of British Studies* 12, no. 2 (May 1973): 120–36.

Judex. *Anderson's Prisoners*. London: Victor Gollancz, 1940.

Kapp, Yvonne, and Margaret Mynatt. *British Policy and the Refugees, 1933–1941*. London: Cass, 1997.

Kocka, Jürgen. 'Comparison and Beyond'. *History and Theory* 42, no. 1 (2003): 39–44.

Lafitte, Francois. *The Internment of Aliens*. London: Libris, 1988.

Pistol, Rachel. *Internment during the Second World War: A Comparative Study of Great Britain and the USA*. London: Bloomsbury, 2017.

Simpson, A. W. B. *In the Highest Degree Odious: Detention Without Trial in Wartime Britain*. Oxford: Clarendon Press, 1992.

Stent, Ronald. *A Bespattered Page? The Internment of His Majesty's 'Most Loyal Enemy Aliens'*. London: Deutsch, 1980.

Part One

British Camps: Continentals Interned in Britain

1

Early internment camps in the United Kingdom: A forgotten history and heritage

Rachel Pistol

Introduction

With the expectation that Great Britain would soon be at war with Germany in 1939, MI5 prepared lists of potential threats to national security including German and Austrian nationals known or suspected of being members of the National Socialist and Communist Parties. In the days before the Second World War was declared, arrests started of individuals based on these lists and the first internees were already detained before a formal declaration of war was made. The British government was aware that the majority of Germans and Austrians residing in Britain were refugees from Nazi oppression. To avoid mass internment, tribunals were instituted and every 'enemy alien' was given a category of either 'A' – a threat to national security needing immediate internment, 'B' – placed under certain restrictions including not being able to travel more than a few miles from their home or 'C' – considered to be genuine refugees of Nazi oppression and left at liberty. The tribunals were inconsistent in their approach to classification but, for the most part, genuine refugees were able to remain at liberty. As a result of the MI5 arrests, 'A' classifications, and enemy alien merchant seamen arrested on boats in British ports at the outbreak of war or from merchant vessels captured at sea during the war, up to 2,000 men were interned on the British mainland by the end of April 1940. Not until May 1940, with the imminent threat of German invasion, was a policy of mass internment enacted, which led to the numbers of internees swelling, soon exhausting accommodation capacity. Most discussion of internment camps in Britain during the Second World War has focused on the more permanent camps set up on the Isle of Man. However, the earliest of these camps on the Isle of Man did not open until the end of May 1940 and they were not immediately ready to hold the thousands of men, women and some of their children who had been detained. This chapter will discuss the early, temporary, internment camps that enemy aliens were housed in prior to their travel to the Isle of Man, Canada or Australia.

The earliest camps – September 1939 to April 1940

As soon as it was clear that at least some enemy aliens were to be interned, the question arose of the best place to put these individuals. The first detainees, arrested under the Prerogative by the police on the basis of MI5 lists, were held at the Empire Exhibition Halls at Olympia in London and in prisons across the country. The police were expected to classify aliens into two classes – 'A' and 'B': 'A' for internees considered to be of the officer class and deserving of better camp conditions, and 'B' for other internees. The British wanted to ensure that diplomats and other important British civilians held by the Germans were treated well under reciprocity, hence the creation of 'A' class. Olympia formed the main collecting centre and, as early as 11 September 1939, there were a number of camps designed for the different classes of internee. For class 'A': Donington Hall, Leicestershire; and Craigmillar's Hostel, Edinburgh were open; and for class 'B': the Ordnance Store, Gainsborough; Donaldson's School for the Deaf, Edinburgh; Times Mill, Lancashire; Weeting Hall, Suffolk; Lingfield Racecourse; and Hemsby Camp, Norfolk; with Butlin's Holiday Camp at Clacton taking both 'A' and 'B' classes (Figure 1.1).[1]

Out-of-season holiday camps were the obvious accommodation solution for some of these early sites of internment. These camps were self-contained and had plentiful accommodation, catering and exercise facilities. The Butlin's camp at Clacton-on-Sea was new when the internees arrived in 1939, having only opened on 11 June 1938. Eugen Spier, interned the day before war broke out and initially held at Olympia, wrote of the huts at Clacton that 'the beds were extremely comfortable, with plenty of white woollen blankets ... the hut was very comfortably furnished: we had a wardrobe, a mirror, hot and cold running water ... the food was good, but quite insufficient'.[2] The main problem at Clacton was the mix of Nazis with anti-Nazis, and the balance shifted significantly in favour of the Nazis when merchant seamen were moved into the camp.

In October 1939, internees at Clacton were told they were to be moved to holiday camps on the south coast. Internees who could afford to pay 4s 6d a day were moved to the upmarket Dixon's holiday camp in Paignton and those who could not were sent to the downmarket Warner's holiday camp in Seaton (the contrast in hut quality can clearly be seen in the postcards in Figure 1.2). Spier noted the contrast of the two camps by describing Seaton as being 'far from a luxury camp' where the huts were 'of poor make, and in appearance resembled enlarged dogs' kennels. The thin timber boards, which represented the walls of these huts, were perforated with holes which provided a free passage for wind and rain'.[3] Rainer Radok, another internee, described the Warner's camp as

> an extended rectangular compound which in the past has served as a low class seaside holiday camp: Two double rows of tiny plywood huts, a swimming pool, tennis courts and a football field occupying the space in between. Two barbed wire fences, added to the holiday scheme, surround this arrangement with a gangway in between for the guards. The industrial-type building facing the main road into town contains mess facilities, kitchen, camp office, a theatre with stage and a canteen. The sea, on the other side of the road, can be heard occasionally. When

Figure 1.1 Map of the early camps mentioned in this chapter

Source: © Rachel Pistol.

Figure 1.2 Images of Butlin's Clacton, Dixon's Paignton and Warner's Seaton holiday camps in the 1930s and 1940s

Source: Postcards from the Pistol-Morgenroth Personal Collection.

there is a real storm, the sea crosses the road and inundates the camp. This is to happen several times during the Winter, when cold conditions lead to formation of ice on all footpaths.[4]

A key feature of the camp was the way the internees separated themselves between the Nazi and anti-Nazi elements, with Nazis and Nazi-sympathisers occupying the two western rows of huts, the eastern rows of huts occupied by anti-Nazis and refugees, and tents in between the two rows of huts for those reluctant to join either side.[5] The Nazis were separated in March 1940 into their own camp in Swanwick, near Derby.

The internees at Seaton started their own 'Popular University' with classes in languages, mathematics and sciences. There was a library with a range of English books and English newspapers, workshops for tailoring, bootmaking, carpentry and other trades, with a small plot of land next to the camp given over to cultivation.[6] The fiercely cold winter conditions of 1939/40, for which the camp huts were woefully inadequate, caused the greatest problems. Initially there was no heating in the huts, each accommodating three internees who were issued with four blankets per person, which was not enough to keep them warm at night. Eventually heating coils were installed in the huts which made the camp's electrical bill soar.[7] At Paignton the conditions were much more comfortable. Considered a 'privilege camp' for class 'A' internees, the men were given greater privacy and lived 'in pairs in the separate huts, which are heated by oil stoves, and have a dining room and lounge, with easy chairs, and the use of an entertainment hall, with stage'.[8] In the early days the internees were provided with a wireless, and they were permitted to go on supervised 'nature rambles'.[9] At Paignton's height there were up to 100 internees in the camp, so it was never particularly crowded. However, as soon as an internee lost the ability to pay for their upkeep they were transferred to Seaton, as happened to several men.

For the women, Holloway Prison was their temporary home if arrested in the first nine months of the war. Women were taken through a humiliating admission procedure and were initially denied contact with other internees. However, as their numbers grew they were able to find mutual support and were able to organize activities like classes in languages and other subjects.[10] Aware that prison was not a good long-term solution, the Prison Commission did consider alternative accommodation, but these alternatives were never used either because they were considered too expensive, as in the case of the Royal Victoria Patriotic Naval School at Wandsworth Common, or unsuitable, such as the Bishop's Palace at Southwark, which had inadequate heating.[11] It was not until Rushen Camp opened on 28 May 1940 on the Isle of Man that women were accommodated outside of prison.

Racecourses around the country were also commandeered to use as internment camps with their grandstands and other buildings turned into dormitories, kitchens and recreational spaces. Again, during the early days of internment there was no separation between Nazis and anti-Nazis, leading to confrontation and some violence, although uneasy truces were usually mutually agreed upon by both sides before the two groups were separated by the authorities. As in Seaton, the camps self-divided into opposing factions. At Lingfield racecourse, different buildings were used to separate civilian internees from merchant seamen, and, later, Germans from Italians. There was also a financial divide between these two groups as the civilians tended to be wealthier than those who worked on ships. In December 1939, it was noted that Lingfield camp was not big enough for the men to be comfortable as the 'ground for exercise consist[ed] only of the space enclosed by the buildings, and for a permanent camp of this size is much too small'.[12] A very small number of class 'A' internees paid 4s 6d a day for more luxurious accommodation. In general, the food was considered good if inadequate. By May 1940, part of Lingfield was designated as a school camp for boys up to the age of eighteen, of whom about 180 had been removed from merchant ships. Some Jewish boys had also been sent to the camp by this point but they were soon transferred onwards.[13] York was another racecourse in use early in the war and housed only merchant seamen in January 1940. It was much less crowded than Lingfield and had more exercise space with additional land available for cultivation.[14] Another early camp, also for merchant seamen, was the winter headquarters of the Bertram Mills Circus in Ascot. Ascot was described as 'a good deal less satisfactory' than the other camps due to overcrowded conditions and lack of sufficient washrooms.[15]

Mass internment – May and June 1940

The situation in the early camps remained relatively unchanged until 12 May 1940 when arrests were made of all enemy aliens on the East Coast, then followed by all Category 'B' men four days later, and all Category 'B' women on 28 May 1940. At this point, not only were many new camps opened but the existing camps hosted a number of internees for just a few nights at a time as they were moved around the country. The sudden arrests of around 4,000 individuals living on the East Coast in what had become 'protected areas', followed in quick succession by 6,000 Category 'B's, placed a huge strain on the camp system as insufficient beds were available. The authorities scrambled to requisition suitable accommodation including fields that could be surrounded with barbed wire and filled with bell tents. The overcrowding was further compounded by the order to arrest all male Category 'C' aliens in round ups that started 25 June 1940.

There were many different sites where enemy aliens were held after their arrest for up to a week, including the cells at their local police station. Others were taken to temporary sites such as barracks, bus garages and drill halls. These temporary facilities were often army properties, such as Fenham Barracks, used to house internees arrested in Newcastle, while elsewhere Beverley, Chichester, Chelsea, Wellington, and Albany Street barracks amongst others were used.[16] Gainsborough had a new bus depot which the army requisitioned to house newly arrested internees. Rainer Radok, held temporarily in the bus depot, noted that 'obviously, England is not prepared for the war, at least not for the imprisonment of large numbers of persons'.[17] In the more established camps such as Seaton, approximately 650 men were housed in the camp in May 1940. There was not room for more, although tents had been delivered to the camp in case extra accommodation was needed.[18] Once the Category 'C' arrests began, enemy aliens who were sent to Seaton only stayed for a matter of days. Paul Jacobsthal, professor of archaeology at Oxford, was taken to Seaton for two days after an initial night at Cowley Barracks. At Cowley Barracks the internees had slept twelve to a room on the floor, whereas Seaton was 'spacious and pleasant' with each hut having 'bunks for two and a mattress on the floor for a third'.[19]

Kempton Park racecourse was opened in May 1940 as an internment camp to take many of the enemy aliens arrested in the greater London area. H. Enoch was arrested 6 June 1940, spending one night at Bow Street police station and the next night at Albany Street Barracks. He arrived on 8 June at Kempton Park where

> apart from the quantitatively and qualitatively very poor food Kempton Park was quite good for my health in view of the good quarter and the lovely warm summer-weather. Psychologically, however, was the separation from my mother and the withholding of any news of her and of the war very tormenting.[20]

In a handful of the camps, including Kempton Park, there were issues with regards to the treatment of the internees by the guards. Kurt Frankenschwerth, arrested 25 June 1940, recalled of his arrival at Kempton Park that he was

> shouted at, forced to queue up, searched; we had to give up our papers, money, lighters, knives, razor blades. Then we had to queue up once more for blankets and a mattress, tin bowl and plate. We were to spend the night with 500 others on the concrete floor of a big hall. In the evening someone poured tea into our bowls and put two slices of bread on the plate. I found myself in the middle of a mass of unhappy people.[21]

Ludwig Spiro recalled of his time at Kempton Park that the camp was 'totally unprepared' and he was thankful the weather was warm, as it took a day or so to get a blanket.[22] Another internee wrote a report of his month-long stay in July and early August: 'What struck us at once was the unfriendly and rough tone and the very unpleasant way the body search and searching of luggage was carried out.'[23] Furthermore,

> accommodation at Kempton Park was not too good: one had to sleep on mattresses on the concrete floors, no beds at all in the camp. Each internee received two blankets. Food at this camp was simply 'a disgrace': At 8 o'clock in the morning one slice of bread with jam (no margarine) and a cup of some stuff called tea without sugar. At noon there was cabbage soup and a small slice of dry bread. The internees were actually half starved. Our group was lucky to leave so soon.[24]

Not all those arrested in London were sent to Kempton Park; many were sent to Lingfield, which had already been in operation for several months. Lingfield was further segregated into more accommodation groups as more arrests were made; the Italians were kept separate from the Germans and Austrians and housed in recently refurbished stables.[25] George Leiser, arrested 26 June 1940, recalled that

> I must have spent most of my Lingfield days peeling potatoes, which was better than nothing because there were no facilities for anything other than sleeping and eating, and the latter activity was very severely rationed. Fortunately, the weather

was warm and dry, and one could at least walk round certain parts of the course or even lie on the grass, interrupted only by roll calls morning noon and night.[26]

Steven Vajda remembered of his time at Lingfield that the 'food was army style, basic but adequate, dealt out from mobile food trailers'.[27] The improvised nature of the early camps meant that food was often bland, inadequate in supply, and cooked by those with little or no experience of mass catering. Some racecourses were used for stays of less than two weeks and very little surviving record is available. Enemy aliens arrested on the south coast of England in May, for example, were held temporarily at Brighton racecourse. The setup of this camp was similar to that of Lingfield and Kempton, with the grandstand and tote betting halls used for accommodation with parts of the racetrack for exercise. Arnold Rosenstrauch, a dentist in Brighton, was arrested and taken to Brighton racecourse where internees were expected, as at most other camps, to fill palliasses with straw so that they might sleep on the floor of the grandstand. There were no Nazis at the camp, and religious services were held to lift the men's morale.[28] K. H. Farnham, also sent to Brighton, recalled the guards as being 'extremely friendly' and rejoiced that the internees 'received plenty of newspapers, books and games and there was little military discipline except for the nightly roll-call'.[29]

Ascot camp had room to hold some of the Category 'C' internees after their arrests at the end of June. Fred Uhlman, arrested 25 June 1940, described the camp as

> several long narrow huts which were connected by a long corridor, a large hut and a lofty hall with a corrugated iron roof. This last had reportedly once been used to house elephants. One could still see the rings to which the wild animals had been tied. Now university professors were supposed to live there. Behind the huts there was a kind of wasteland that was surrounded by barbed wire.[30]

On entering the sleeping quarters,

> the first thing we saw was a urinal and a lavatory, separated from the dormitory only by a fairly low wall. Then came the dormitory, a long hall containing 90 wooden bunks. In each, three men slept above and three below one another. At the end of the hall was the washroom which, in contrast to the lavatories, could be closed off by a door. Apart from the wooden bunks, there were two long tables down the middle and a few chairs. We were given straw with which to fill our mattresses and two woollen blankets.[31]

Later, Ascot was used to house internees held under Defence Regulation 18B, which allowed the detention without trial of British citizens believed to be actively opposed to the war who could be a potential threat to the war effort. These internees included members of the British Union of Fascists. Relatively few male 18B detainees arrested at the beginning of the war were held in prisons; however, when their numbers grew in May 1940, men were taken to Ascot, and the women to Holloway Prison before being moved to Rushen Camp on the Isle of Man.

The camps discussed so far all had some form of permanent structures in which to house the internees. Not all camps had such luxury – Prees Heath, near Crewe, and Sutton Coldfield, just outside Birmingham, were both tented camps (see Figure 1.3). Prees Heath had been used during the First World War to house multiple regiments in wooden huts while they trained for trench warfare.[32] It was, therefore, on the radar for future use, and in May 1940 until the autumn of 1940 it was turned into a temporary internment camp consisting of four compounds surrounded by barbed wire, three for friendly enemy aliens and one for pro-Nazis. A contemporary report described the fact that the tents provide only a very cramped accommodation:

> 5–8 are sleeping together in one tent. There is very little space for placing their few possessions. The large tents for communal purposes are only accommodating about half of the number of internees at a time. During meals or spells of bad weather, as well as during the blackout hours, great numbers are therefore forced to remain lying in their tents. The rubber ground-sheets in the tents are certainly of excellent quality. But the palliasses and blankets inevitably tend to get exceedingly damp on account of the ground mists.[33]

The conditions were not ideal for older internees, who were transferred out of the camp in July 1940.[34]

Sutton Coldfield opened in early August and conditions were also rudimentary. The camp consisted of bell tents with marquees for dining and hospital purposes. During the first two weeks of the camp's existence there was a real shortage of essential items including palliasses and straw to fill them, meaning the men had nothing to sleep on but groundsheets.[35] Many of the internees sent to Sutton Coldfield had come from Kempton Park and Lingfield. At one of these two camps the men had been divided into two groups of under fifty and over fifty years of age. The younger men had been sent to Prees Heath with the expectation that the older men would go to a camp with built accommodation; they were, however, sent to Sutton Coldfield. The basic nature of this camp caused problems for the older men but they soon organized religious services and public lectures to occupy their time.[36] The basic nature of the camp was further compounded by a mass influx of internees at Sutton Coldfield after Kempton Park was abruptly emptied for an unspecified urgent purpose.[37] The unsuitability of the tented camp was brought up in parliamentary debate when Eleanor Rathbone berated the government for making 'sick and elderly internees … sleep on the bare ground' and asking 'why was the place reported ready when it was not ready in any sense?'[38] However, by far the most notorious of the transit camps was Warth Mills in Bury, a disused cotton mill, which was often mistakenly referred to as 'Wharf Mills', or perhaps more accurately as 'Wrath Mills' by former occupants.[39] In July 1940, the camp was described as consisting of 'an old mill building, said to have been empty for ten years. Part is on ground level, part three storeys. The building is naturally in a bad state and there is great difficulty in getting it reasonably clean'.[40] The Society of Friends visited all the internment camps and agreed that Warth Mills was the worst of all they had seen, and the men in camp complained that 'internment under these conditions is cruel and punitive'.[41] The most basic of facilities were not available. Regarding the toilet

Figure 1.3 Illustrations of Prees Heath by Wilhelm Jondorf
Source: Images courtesy of Harry Jondorf.[42]

provision, 'there were very few indeed, and with such large numbers of adults, everyone had to queue literally for hours to be able to use one of them, so the authorities placed a number of provisional W.C.'s, a fairly large pail and some canvas round them for a minimum of privacy'.[43] Some effort to lift morale at the camp was given with the annexation of a small patch of grass adjacent to the factory to be used for exercise and football games.[44] Such were the ghastly conditions at Warth Mills that German artist Hermann Fechenbach organized a hunger strike with demands for improvements in camp.[45]

The largest of all the UK transit camps, which also became the largest male internment camp, was Huyton, just outside of Liverpool. The camp consisted of an unfinished housing estate surrounded by barbed wire. Some of the first internees arriving at the newly opened camp recalled that the barbed wire fences were still being erected when they moved in on 18 May 1940.[46] An early description of the camp was that

> all houses were unfurnished and we took our three meals in special huts. The food was entirely insufficient and did not improve for weeks. Breakfast consisted of 1–2 thin slices of bread, 1/4 oz. of margarine, awful tasting porridge and bitter tea with a tin of milk per 100 cups. Lunch consisted of indescribable rotten stuff, 1/2 a potato, 6 bitter beans and mostly no meat at all. Supper one slice of bread, tea, a little margarine and less cheese … In all other respects things were very bad, postal service did not function for some time, beds were taken away again, no soap or toilet paper was available, the camp was overcrowded and at last the young people under 25 were put in tents and had to put up with very filthy conditions … Soon we were 3000 people and the officers were unable to cope with all the work … Yet there was a pleasant side, if I may be allowed to call it thus. We had lectures, concerts and variety shows and a number of visitors were allowed.[47]

The internees in tents struggled to keep their belongings dry, especially during early July.[48] Arnold Rosenstrauch remembered that internees were left mostly to themselves, and 'roll calls must have annoyed the guards as we were not the most disciplined lot as people would get bored and move around and either get counted twice or not at all!'[49] Both Warth Mills and Huyton held Italians, who were kept separately to the Germans and Austrians. Being close to the docks at Liverpool, Huyton was well situated for transfers to the Isle of Man, or deportation to Canada or Australia. The size of the camp and its key location meant a significant proportion of internees passed through Huyton.

Heritage

The early camps were designed as transit camps and were, by their very nature, temporary. Consequently, no permanent structures were created for the internees and the sites were quickly returned to their original use after the internees moved on. Some of these early camps were only in existence for a matter of days, others for weeks, with a small number existing for a few months. It is much easier to gather information about the more established camps on the Isle of Man or in Canada and Australia than these early camps, influencing how much physical heritage exists.

The holiday camps at Clacton, Seaton and Paignton no longer survive. In October 1983, Butlin's closed its Clacton camp, and after a failed venture by an amusement park on the site it was eventually sold for housing.[50] The story is much the same for both Seaton and Paignton. The Warner's camp site at Seaton was closed in 2009 and is now a combination of a housing development and a Tesco Extra. Dixon's camp in Paignton was bought by Pontins after the war and closed in 1988, when the site was developed into the King's Ash housing estate. No physical evidence remain of the camps, although there are photographs and reminiscences of the camps' glory days online. Many websites make mention of the fact that the camps were briefly used for internment; however, the information provided is often wrong or contradictory. For example, Seaton Town Council's history of the area during the Second World War states:

> When World War II erupted in 1939, Warner's Seaton camp was commandeered and used as an internment camp, where people deemed as 'enemy aliens' – a mixture of Germans, Italians, Japanese and others who were resident in Britain at the outbreak of the war, along with those considered to be politically dangerous – were imprisoned.[51]

At first glance, this is a well-informed paragraph; however, it also perpetuates the myth that is commonly held in Devon that Seaton was used to hold Italian and Japanese internees. Paignton held some Italians who were willing to pay for the privilege of better conditions, but Seaton only held German and Austrian nationals.

Most of the racecourses used to house internees are still in existence, but only in two instances do the public histories offered on the racecourses' websites mention what happened in the Second World War. The Kempton Park website says the site 'played a major role in accommodating Prisoners of War throughout World War II' and makes no reference to the fact Kempton was home to civilian internees.[52] Lingfield Park says of the war that the 'War Office requisitioned the estate for use as a prisoner of war internment camp for Italians', again with no reference to civilian internees or the Germans and Austrians who were interned there.[53] The confusion over the differentiation of prisoners of war and civilian internees is common because merchant seamen started as internees and were re-designated as prisoners of war, but normally this confusion is due to a lack of understanding. It is still clear that little is understood in these locations about the true nature of these camps. Kempton Park also refers to German and Italian soldiers but does not refer to civilians at all. With regards to Huyton, which was the site of an internment camp and then later a prisoner-of-war camp, there seems to be much more of an understanding of its combined heritage, with the local council and news sources recognizing the difference.[54] It is important that this differentiation is made, as the legal status and treatment of prisoners of war and civilian internees is not the same.

Furthermore, few camp buildings survive, so the only guide to the appearance of the camps is provided by artworks created by the internees themselves. No photographs of the early camps exist, as photography was prohibited until August 1940. However, photographs taken pre-internment provide an idea of the facilities at the holiday camps and the grandstands and other buildings at the racecourses, but nothing survives of the tented camps. An amateur film held at the British Film Institute shows some of the buildings used by the internees in 1939 at the Ascot camp.[55]

In contrast, Warth Mills and Huyton have some tangible heritage. At Huyton, Knowsley Council has created a number of videos relating to internment at Huyton including walking tours and interviews with surviving former internees.[56] In 2017, funding was provided by the Heritage Lottery Fund to create the Warth Mills Digital Archive to research and inform the public about what happened in Bury, and a website was created to showcase internee stories and highlight art and artefacts from the camp.[57] In the summer of 2018, a historical exhibition was held, accompanied by a number of talks, concerts and an art showcase, which significantly elevated the public awareness of this camp.[58] Furthermore, the Warth Mills project commissioned a memorial, making it the only early camp with a permanent commemorative feature. In December 2018, a plaque and sculpture featuring a pile of suitcases was unveiled (Figure 1.4), which is hugely symbolic as many items were confiscated from internees during their time at the camp. The sculpture gives particular reference to those men transported from Warth Mills to be boarded onto the ill-fated *Arandora Star*.[59]

Conclusion

At the start of the war, the government was keen to ensure internment camps were well organized and that internees considered 'officer class' were treated well. The holiday camps initially used the existing kitchen staff, which meant that, unlike later camps, the internees were catered for by professionals; subsequently, internees were responsible for the cooking themselves. Food is commonly used as a marker of conditions within the camp and frequently mentioned in diaries and interviews related to internment. As the internees had lost control over almost all aspects of their existence, it is no surprise that food formed a key element of all camp descriptions, confirmed by the quotes in this chapter. Once the internees reached the Isle of Man, they had more control over the cooking of the food they consumed, and this usually greatly improved camp conditions and morale.

In terms of the physical sites of internment, the camps varied hugely in terms of accommodation. As more civilian enemy aliens were arrested, the quality of the transit camps deteriorated. Internees were moved after their initial arrest to larger collection centres that included racecourses and tented camps. Existing buildings were modified for use for the internees, but no lasting construction was made. Consequently, as soon as the barbed wire was removed, almost all traces of the internees could easily be forgotten. The internees themselves offered vivid descriptions of these camps through diaries, memoirs, interviews and artwork, and it is only by using these sources that a

Figure 1.4 The Warth Mills memorial sculpture and plaque
Source: Images courtesy of Richard Shaw.[60]

full narrative of early internment can be created, especially since official records are incomplete or lost.

In terms of the physical aspects of the former internment camps, only at Warth Mills has there been any attempt to establish tangible monuments with the erection of both a plaque and a specially commissioned sculpture. The disappearance of many of the former sites of internment makes physical reminders more problematic but not impossible. Much more could be done to better inform the general public, particularly in the local areas where these camps once stood. The fact that there are now comments about internment on websites related to local history groups is very positive, but this information needs to be factually correct since inaccurate myth and folklore are often included, reinforcing these errors to the extent they are assumed to be factual. As more resources become available on the history of internment, let us hope that more accuracy will be woven into the heritage and commemoration of these early internment camps on the British mainland during the Second World War.

Notes

1. Memorandum 8 September 1939 in Prison Commission and Home Office, 'Reception and Internment of Aliens: List of Internees', n.d., PCOM 9/661, National Archives, Kew.
2. Eugen Spier, *The Protecting Power* (London: Skeffington, 1951), 31.
3. Ibid., 51.
4. Rainer Radok, *Before and After the Reichskristallnacht: The History of a Königsberg Family*, n.d., http://mpec.sc.mahidol.ac.th/radok/life/ECONTENTS.HTM?fbc lid=IwAR2Bahap53RYHsbI2Dq80ffQlsKKikh-vf-R__iF1Y4NOEbnZGXfeTXER_A (accessed 5 May 2021).
5. Ibid.
6. Reports on Seaton Camp 21 December 1939, 8 March 1940 and 21 May 1940 in 'FCRA/25/40 Internment Camps Reports: Alphabetical 1939–1941', n.d., Society of Friends.
7. Radok, *Before and After the Reichskristallnacht*.
8. Report on Paignton Camp 9 March 1940 in FCRA/25/40.
9. Ibid. and F. Sittner, 'Personal Correspondence of F Sittner', n.d., Imperial War Museum.
10. Charmian Brinson, '"In the Exile of Internment" or "Von Versuchen, Aus Einer Not Eine Tugend Zu Machen": German-Speaking Women Interned by the British during the Second World War', in *Politics and Culture in Twentieth-Century Germany*, ed. William Niven and James Jordan (Rochester, NY: Camden House, 2003), 64–6.
11. See Prison Commission and Home Office, 'Reception and Internment of Aliens: List of Internees', n.d., PCOM 9/662, National Archives, Kew.
12. Report on Lingfield Camp 18 December 1939 in FCRA/25/40.
13. Ibid.
14. Report on York Camp 26–27 January 1940 in FCRA/25/40.
15. Report on Ascot Camp 16 January 1940 in FCRA/25/40.
16. Craig Armstrong, 'Aliens in Wartime: A Case Study of Tyneside 1939–45', *Immigrants and Minorities* 25/2 (2007): 127; Rachel Mendel, '*Behind Barbed Wire*' (Held at the

Manx National Archives, Douglas, Isle of Man, 2009); H. Enoch, 'Private Papers of Dr H Enoch' (n.d.), Documents.10961, Imperial War Museum.
17. Radok, *Before and After the Reichskristallnacht*.
18. Report on Seaton Camp 21 May 1940 in FCRA/25/40.
19. Paul Jacobsthal, *Memoirs of Professor Paul Jacobsthal, Onetime Internee of Hutchinson Camp* (Held at the Manx National Archives, Douglas, Isle of Man, n.d.).
20. Enoch, 'Private Papers of Dr H Enoch'.
21. Kurt Frankenschwerth, 'Released', *AJR* September (1960): 9.
22. IWM, Ludwig Spiro Interview (Held at the Imperial War Museum, 1979), http://www.iwm.org.uk/collections/item/object/80004313 (accessed 15 May 2021).
23. Report of an internee on his experiences in Camp 10.7.-8.8. in FCRA/25/40.
24. Ibid.
25. Spier, *Protecting Power*, 118–19.
26. George Leiser, *History of George Leiser*, n.d., 74.
27. John A. Bather, Steven Vajda Interview (Held at the Manx National Archives, Douglas, Isle of Man, 1994).
28. Arnold Adlbert Rosenstrauch Interview (IWM, 1996).
29. K. H. Farnham, 'Private Papers of K. H. Farnham', n.d., Documents.1921, IWM.
30. Charmian Brinson, Anna Mueller-Haerlin and Julia Winckler, *His Majesty's Loyal Internee: Fred Uhlman in Captivity* (Portland, OR: Vallentine Mitchell, 2009), 52.
31. Ibid.
32. 'Prees Heath History', https://www.preesheathcommonreserve.co.uk/page-4487369.html (accessed 15 May 2021).
33. Report on Prees Heath 5–6 September 1940 in FCRA/25/40.
34. Report on Prees Heath 31 July 1940 in FCRA/25/40.
35. Report on Sutton Coldfield 13 August 1940 in FCRA/25/40.
36. Ibid.
37. HC Deb 20 August 1940, n.d.
38. Ibid.
39. Jacobsthal, *Memoirs*.
40. Report on Wharf [sic] Mill 10 July 1940 in FCRA/25/40.
41. Ibid.
42. The author would like to thank the Jondorf and van der Zyl families for their very helpful correspondence and for allowing the publication of these images. Thanks particularly to Darrell van der Zyl for his assistance.
43. Gaetano Rossi, *Memories of 1940 Impressions of Life in an Internment Camp* (Held at the Manx National Archives, Douglas, Isle of Man, 1991).
44. Ibid. and Report on Wharf [sic] Mills in FCRA/25/40.
45. 'Conditions at Warth Mills • Warth Mills Project', Warth Mills Project, https://www.warthmillsproject.com/stories/conditions-at-warth-mills/ (accessed 28 May 2021).
46. Farnham, 'Private Papers of K. H. Farnham'.
47. Ibid.
48. Judex, *Anderson's Prisoners* (London: Victor Gollancz, 1940), 69.
49. Arnold Adlbert Rosenstrauch Interview.
50. Norman Jacobs, 'Clacton History', Butlins Memories, http://www.butlins-memories.com/clacton/history.htm (accessed 5 May 2021).
51. 'The Great Wars', *Seaton Town Council* (blog), https://seaton.gov.uk/history/the-great-wars/ (accessed 5 May 2021).

52. 'The History of Kempton Park Racecourse', The Jockey Club - Kempton Park, https://www.thejockeyclub.co.uk/kempton/about/history/ (accessed 5 May 2021).
53. 'History | Lingfield Park', Lingfield Park, https://www.lingfieldpark.co.uk/lingfield-park/history/ (accessed 5 May 2021).
54. For an example of how Huyton's camps are remembered by people living in the area see Jess Molyneux, 'The Merseyside Housing Estate with a Dark Wartime Past', Liverpool Echo, 7 July 2019, https://www.liverpoolecho.co.uk/news/liverpool-news/merseyside-housing-estate-dark-wartime-16525964 (accessed 15 May 2021).
55. 'Watch Horses at Ascot, Winter Quarters, Ascot', BFI Player, https://player.bfi.org.uk/free/film/watch-horses-at-ascot-winter-quarters-ascot-1939-online (accessed 15 May 2021).
56. Terry Hughes Remembers Huyton's WW2 Internment Camp, 2016, https://www.youtube.com/watch?v=8wX6R_YUtOQ; Interview with Dr John Goldsmith, Former Internee at Huyton in WW2, 2018, https://www.youtube.com/watch?v=mi7TXxzDdJQ (accessed 15 May 2021); *Monologues from Huyton's WW2 Internment Camps*, 2018, https://www.youtube.com/watch?v=NsZOM4O_-Hk (accessed 15 May 2021). Molyneux, 'The Merseyside Housing Estate'.
57. 'Home • Warth Mills Project', Warth Mills Project, https://www.warthmillsproject.com/ (accessed 17 May 2021).
58. 'Events • Warth Mills Project', Warth Mills Project, https://www.warthmillsproject.com/events/ (accessed 17 May 2021); Rachel Pistol, 'From World War II "enemy" Internment to Windrush: Britain Quickly Forgets Its Gratitude to Economic Migrants', The Conversation, http://theconversation.com/from-world-war-ii-enemy-internment-to-windrush-britain-quickly-forgets-its-gratitude-to-economic-migrants-98331 (accessed 17 May 2021).
59. Warth Mills Project, 'Warth Mills Memorial Post', Tweet, *@WarthMills* (blog), 17 December 2018, https://twitter.com/WarthMills/status/1074689009404796934 (accessed 17 May 2021).
60. The author would like to thank Richard Shaw for the use of his photographs and for the wonderful work he has done commemorating the Warth Mills internment camp.

Bibliography

Armstrong, Craig. 'Aliens in Wartime: A Case Study of Tyneside 1939–45'. *Immigrants and Minorities* 25, no. 2 (2007): 119–40.

Brinson, Charmian. ' "In the Exile of Internment" or "Von Versuchen, Aus Einer Not Eine Tugend Zu Machen": German-Speaking Women Interned by the British during the Second World War'. In *Politics and Culture in Twentieth-Century Germany*, edited by William Niven and James Jordan, 63–87. Rochester, NY: Camden House, 2003.

Brinson, Charmian, Anna Mueller-Haerlin and Julia Winckler. *His Majesty's Loyal Internee: Fred Uhlman in Captivity*. Portland, OR: Vallentine Mitchell, 2009.

Judex. *Anderson's Prisoners*. London: Victor Gollancz, 1940.

Spier, Eugen. *The Protecting Power*. London: Skeffington, 1951.

2

'Once again to live their bit of private life, free from camping like gipsies': The case of a refugee camp in the Garden of England

Clare Ungerson

This chapter tells the story of a very large refugee camp for German-speaking Jewish men which was in operation between February 1939 and May 1940. For some of the men who were accommodated there, the refugee camp was a prelude to actual internment; for others the refugee camp may have felt, at times, like internment but there were, as we shall see, important differences between the two experiences. The camp was located in one of seven First World War military camps on the east Kent coast in south-eastern England. From each of these camps many thousands of men had been sent, via the nearby port of Richborough, to the trenches of the Western Front. When one of these old military camps became a refugee camp just before, and at the start of, the Second World War, it was known by the men who lived there as the 'Kitchener camp' (named after Lord Kitchener, Secretary of State for War in 1914), while the officials of the Central British Fund for German Jewry (CBF) who oversaw their rescue always called it 'Richborough camp'.[1]

Just beside the small market town of Sandwich, Kitchener was a rather unusual place to house nearly 4,000 German speaking Jewish men. Most of these men would have been accustomed to city life in Berlin or Vienna, while Sandwich, with a population at the time of only 3,800, probably had only a few inhabitants who had ever visited London (eighty miles away), and very few indeed who had ever travelled overseas – except to fight Germans in the First World War two decades earlier.

The refugee camp was initiated, funded and managed by the CBF. The CBF had, in response to the atrocities of Kristallnacht in November 1938, set up two rescues of Jews from Greater Germany. The first, the Kindertransports, which brought nearly 10,000 unaccompanied children to Britain, has generated a large literature and is continually referred to in current British debates on refugee policy.[2] The second, the rescue of nearly 4,000 men from Greater Germany, many of whom had very recently been released from concentration camps to the Kitchener camp, has had far less attention. Both rescues constituted a mass exodus, under very similar conditions and organized in exactly the same way, of refugees to the United Kingdom, but only for temporary residence in Britain. It was thought that the children and the men would move, on a more permanent basis, to other countries. For the children this objective was rapidly forgotten.

However, as far as the men were concerned, one of the criteria for their selection by the Jewish agencies in Berlin and Vienna was that they could demonstrate that they had the means to leave the United Kingdom within about a year of their arrival in Sandwich. This had been a condition laid down by the Home Office and the CBF strictly implemented that condition.[3] The men could demonstrate the temporary nature of their stay through documents: visas for the United States, permission to emigrate to Palestine, shipping-line tickets for ships leaving Britain for anywhere else in the world. Thus, the camp was construed by the CBF as a transit camp. Norman Bentwich, the distinguished Secretary to the CBF who was largely responsible for making certain that the Kitchener camp rescue was implemented, stated that the CBF:

> sponsored the movement for a transit city of refuge, designed particularly to rescue those who had not friends or relatives in this country to guarantee their maintenance. It was to have a floating population, for the intention was to arrange as rapidly as possible the overseas emigration of those brought to England.[4]

The idea that these men were in transit was at the core of this rescue. Thirty thousand Jewish men had been taken to concentration camps immediately after Kristallnacht and many thousands more were threatened with incarceration by the Nazis. The CBF had in mind that the population of the camp at any one time would never rise above 5,000 (later reduced to 3,500), but they hoped, nevertheless, that they would rescue many thousands more by ensuring that each man's stay at the Kitchener camp was brief.

In order to ensure that rapid movement outwards took place, the CBF also construed it as a training camp. The intention, drawn from a long-standing policy for funding Jewish training camps in Greater Germany, was that men would be equipped at Kitchener with skills that would render them attractive to many countries of the world, particularly Palestine and other developing countries such as those of Latin America, colonial Africa and Australia. Training in agriculture, mechanical engineering, car mechanics and carpentry was to be given high priority. Amongst the selection criteria for men to participate in this rescue was whether or not they already had such skills and could train others, or whether they had already demonstrated an aptitude for craft and artisan work.

Internment and rescue – similarities and differences

In certain respects this refugee camp was a forerunner of the British government-run internment camps. In memoirs and accounts of the period there is often confusion on precisely this point – it is easy to find, even from such respectable bodies as the Washington, DC, based United States Holocaust Memorial Museum, that a slippage in the catalogue between describing the Kitchener camp as an 'internment camp' and a 'refugee camp' often occurs.[5] The Kitchener camp certainly looked and in certain respects felt like a British government-controlled prison. The Union Jack flew at its entrance, there were crowded huts, fences and a single exit gate. As with the internment camps, there were considerable challenges in managing order amongst a large concentration of damaged and sometimes angry men. A system of devolved camp management developed at both Kitchener and in the larger internment camps, whereby the men policed themselves in their huts and houses. In Kitchener there was even a large camp police force, drawn from the refugees themselves, which guarded the fences and the single exit gate and reported misdemeanours to the salaried senior camp management.

There were similarities but there were also profound differences. Unlike the internment camps, which were run by personnel drawn from state organizations such as the British army and the British police,[6] Kitchener was a camp funded by Jews and managed by Jews for Jews. While the British state had given permission for its existence, and the Home Office and the local constabulary kept a close eye on its progress, the Kitchener camp was, in essence, the outcome of Jewish voluntary activity and philanthropy and it constituted a rescue. While there are reasons to query as to why this rescue involved a camp at all, it certainly, in essential and foundational ways, did not have the feature of incarceration that characterized the British internment camps.

Moreover, unlike the people who were later interned, the men in Kitchener had fought hard to be rescued. Despite the camp's privations, the alternative had been the brutal and deadly regimes of Dachau, Sachsenhausen and Buchenwald concentration camps. For these Kitchener men, residence in a democracy, even if it was in a camp, had been their goal for some considerable time, and the hope was that the camp facilities – a post office, a telephone exchange, an advice bureau and an allowance of two international stamps a week – would facilitate the process of bringing their families out of Greater Germany and into the safety of England.

In their daily lives, the Kitchener men, unlike internees, had a relative amount of freedom of movement beyond the camp. So long as they had completed their work tasks for the day they could develop relationships with people living beyond the camp and join in neighbourhood activities. They were, however, as part of the agreement between the CBF and the Home Office, forbidden to take up paid employment beyond the camp. In addition there was a nightly curfew – 10 pm – and the camp hut leaders and camp police (all of them refugees themselves) were responsible for ensuring that everyone was accounted for by that time. That said, it was also possible for the men to apply to the camp Director (himself a British Jew) for permission to leave the camp overnight, which was almost always granted.

A further important distinguishing feature between the internment camps and the Kitchener camp was the question of time-management of the inmates. For those in the internment camps, their time was their own. In response to their unstructured day, the internees quickly and effectively, in many camps, put in place a form of structured time. One internee was astonished to observe that, on his very first day after his arrest in June 1940 and arrival at a makeshift internment camp, 'on the field I saw everywhere groups of eight, ten or more people listening to a man who talked. The system of self-preservation by learning had begun … largest group round chap teaching English … someone is teaching French, someone – I could hardly believe it – probably an actor, recited large parts of Goethe's *Faust*.[7] Indeed, the development of very broad educational activities was such that one commander of the Hutchinson camp on the Isle of Man called these activities the 'Camp University' and strongly supported them with his own 'Cultural Department'.[8] Daily life morphed into higher education. Culture, critique, intellectual curiosity, all for their own sake, became the major occupation of many internees. Out of these camps emerged important art from, for instance, Kurt Schwitters, Fred Uhlman and Hugo Dachinger, and world class music from the Amadeus String Quartet.

No such important contributions to the visual arts and music emerged from the Kitchener camp, and this may well be because the men's time was not their own. Rather than higher education and culture of the mind, the emphasis was on productive work and purposeful training. When the camp first started as a refugee camp in February 1939, the working day was very long indeed. After an early breakfast, work began at 7.30 am and ended at 6 pm (or dusk, whichever was the earlier), with half an hour off for lunch. Moreover, there was very little opportunity for days off; particularly in the early days of the camp, the men worked on both Saturdays and Sundays, despite protests.[9] The reason for this intensive work schedule was the state of the huts in the Kitchener camp. Most of them had stood completely empty since the end of the First World War, and were consequently in a state of serious disrepair. Moreover, the camp senior staff (two Jewish brothers, Jonas and Phineas May) were, at the start of the life of the camp, in daily expectation that hundreds if not thousands of refugees might arrive on their threshold at any moment.[10] The work pressure was at its hardest in the first few months when there were small numbers in the camp facing the apparently monumental task of making over forty derelict huts fit for human habitation. It took until August 1939 for the full complement of a little over 3,500 men to become resident. Once the numbers began to increase significantly, in the months of July and August 1939, the intensity of the work began to fall away and the men were allowed to take one day off in three.

The May brothers approached the huge task of repairing the huts, refurbishing the communal washing and cooking facilities, building the camp roads and digging the drains with military discipline and energy. They were not short of skilled and experienced labour: many of the men who were rescued to the Kitchener camp were selected precisely because they already had the skills needed to put the camp to rights. The selection process, organized by the Jewish agencies in Berlin and Vienna but orchestrated by the CBF, was supposed to reflect the urgency of need of the men who had applied to be sent to Kitchener, in particular whether they were already in concentration camps or whether they were in imminent danger of arrest. But useful skills could trump threat to life and liberty. For example, two Jewish training schools in Berlin were encouraged to send their appropriately trained students and, in the case of the school at Niederschönhausen near Berlin, their director of training, as well as – very unusually – his wife, to take charge of the training programme at Kitchener.

This gentleman, Poldi Kuh, became a salaried member of staff. In July 1939 he produced an elaborate report entitled 'Work and Training in Kitchener Camp', which outlined a six-month training programme, at the end of which each man who had a satisfactory work and attendance record and had completed his training tasks would be rewarded with an elaborate 'Certificate'.[11] Round the borders of the draft certificate appear vignettes of men tailoring, bricklaying, roofing, working on telegraph poles, building walls, blacksmithing, watch repairing and tilling the soil. Its bottom border consists of tools for manual work: spanners, lathes, mallets, compasses, paint brushes and an old fashioned plate camera.

The entire document on 'Work and Training' is a demonstration and outcome of the way in which the CBF understood there to be a logical link between training and transit. If they could train the men to be competent and *credentialized* artisans in a range of skills, they would be more attractive to countries other than the United Kingdom and would, as expected and hoped, move on rapidly, making way for further refugees. Whether this scheme was ever put into place in its entirety is doubtful, but some of it was. The report itself states that, of the 1,901 men resident in Kitchener in mid-July 1939, no less than 552 men were occupied in 'Workshops and Campshops'. A further 782 were employed in 'Organization', which included the camp police, the accountancy section and the medical department; 177 were in 'agricultural training'; and 390 were employed in the kitchens. A 'camp university' it was not; daily life in the Kitchener camp was modelled on a German technical high school.

The camp in the community

The arrival of many thousands of Jewish German-speaking men on the edge of Sandwich must have been something of a surprise to the people of the town. As one of the many refugees put it, writing in the *Association of Jewish Refugees Journal* twenty years later,

> Not only did the erstwhile military barracks change into a veritable camp city with all amenities, but also the old, picturesque town of Sandwich awoke from their centuries-long sleep. Suddenly, thousands of men thronged her narrow lanes, talking in loud voices, dressed outlandishly, who did not understand English or, worse, mutilated it by their pronunciation.[12]

This self-conscious comment, which exaggerates the numbers that 'thronged' Sandwich (the camp guards would never have allowed 'thousands' to leave at once) and over-emphasizes the strangeness, to Sandwich residents, of the men involved, nevertheless captures an essential grain of truth. Sandwich was a small market town, and very suddenly there seemed to be another larger town, full of German-speaking Jews, located at its edge – this in a year, 1939, when war with Germany was drawing ever closer. Moreover, English nationalism, antisemitism and general xenophobia had found a promising foothold in Sandwich – the President of the Sandwich Chamber of Commerce, an aristocrat, Lady Grace Pearson, who owned businesses and was a landlord to many tenants in Sandwich, was a prominent member of the British Union of Fascists (BUF) and had insisted that all her workers join the BUF. Another even more prominent fascist, Captain Robert Gordon-Canning, who owned one of the BUF's journals and was a close friend of Oswald Mosley, the leader of the BUF, lived two miles away in a gated community known as the Sandwich Bay Estate.[13] The CBF and the camp management were well aware that there were grounds to be anxious. In an early effort to estimate organized trouble to come, the Board of Deputies of British Jews, in February 1939, took a close look at the Sandwich fascists, sending a spy to sit in one of the twenty-seven pubs in Sandwich and converse with the locals about politics. The spy, in a fascinating anonymized report, decided there was nothing to worry about – the local fascists were mainly those compelled to belong to the BUF by their fascist employer, Lady Pearson.[14]

Somewhat reassured by this information, the camp management and the CBF recognized that, given freedom of movement, there would inevitably be social interactions between the Kitchener men and the people of Sandwich and its surrounding villages. Rather than try to prevent these interactions or be over-anxious about them, the CBF and the camp management decided to foster them but with a careful eye on the surrounding press and publicity. Press releases about the Kitchener camp, picked up in both the national and the local press, were commonplace from the start. The first, published in the *Times*, the *Sunday Times* and the *East Kent Mercury* in late January/early February 1939, stressed the training that the refugees would receive and the temporary nature of their stay: 'All the men would emigrate in due course and would be no liability on the country'.[15] The articles in the national press continued to appear, but only occasionally. In contrast, the local press began to pay considerable attention as – at least every fortnight, and later every week – an article about the events at the Kitchener camp appeared in the *East Kent Mercury* between February 1939 and August 1939. Short pieces, detailing camp concerts, joint activities with local chess clubs, football teams, table tennis clubs, joint sports activities with the local boys' grammar school and bicycle rides into the Kentish countryside with the local cycling clubs appeared regularly on the page where activities in the villages were reported. It was as though the Kitchener camp had become just another Kentish village, and part of the familiar landscape. A typical entry appeared in the *East Kent Mercury* on 15 April 1939:

> On Saturday evening there was an enjoyable concert, and on Sunday the camp was visited by the Sandwich Sea Cadets with their band, and the playing of 'The Retreat' was watched with considerable interest by the crowd of refugees gathered round. In the evening the band gave a musical performance which was greatly appreciated, and in return the refugees had arranged a variety entertainment which disclosed considerable talent, many of the 'turns' being equal to any seen in an English music-hall. There was dancing and singing with violin, cello and accordion selections. Later in the evening a party of some 120 refugees arrived from Vienna and received a warm welcome from those already in the camp, being greeted like long-lost relations. There are now at the camp a total of 650 refugees. On Monday a football match with the Ramsgate Technical Institute was the chief attraction.[16]

The mention of a camp concert is significant. At first, camp concerts were restricted to performance for fellow refugees but, during the summer of 1939, public concerts became very popular events to which Sandwich people flocked. The first public concert, attended by about 700 'English friends' (as the newspaper headline put it) in the first week of May, began with 'God Save the King' immediately followed by Elgar's 'Pomp and Circumstance'. The professional pianist wife of the camp's Liberal Rabbi (both themselves refugees from Berlin) then played some Chopin etudes, and other refugees put on comic turns satirizing camp life. The entire event concluded with 'The Blue Danube'.[17] It was a masterful programme, clearly designed to demonstrate both new loyalties to England and old nostalgias for previous and very different lives. Such concerts continued, drawing ever greater numbers from Sandwich and its hinterland. Word got out and just before war broke out the BBC was in correspondence with the camp management about broadcasting one of them, although war prevented this from happening.[18]

There was intrinsic pleasure and amusement for all those who participated and were the audience to these activities. But it is also clear that there was a certain deliberateness about these organized interactions such that (writing in 2021) many years later it could be called a 'public relations strategy'. The strategy was effective. By the end of the summer of 1939, many of the men at Kitchener had received invitations to the homes of local residents, at least three men were engaged to be married to local girls and some of the wives of Kitchener men who had managed to reach safety were lodging with Sandwich landladies. When war broke out on 3 September 1939, good relations were further cemented when the Kitchener men began to help with building sea defences, planting 'dragons' teeth' along the beaches of Sandwich and Ramsgate (which are still visible) and digging for sand bags on Dover beach.[19] It is noticeable that the Sandwich fascists had run their own campaign in the local newspaper, writing vicious letters about the dangers of miscegenation, particularly with Jewry, and spreading rumours about sexual misbehaviour amongst the Kitchener men.[20] No doubt to their disappointment, nothing unpleasant between fascists and refugees had occurred that summer. In November 1939, the Board of Deputies of British Jews asked for a further report on antisemitism and fascism in Sandwich. The reply was short and to the point: 'East Kent: no evidence of any increase in antisemitism. Neutral area'.[21]

War and a new regime

The outbreak of war brought considerable change to the Kitchener camp. Perhaps the most surprising aspect was the arrival of some 200 of the men's wives and even their children at Kitchener. Having managed to reach England, possibly on domestic service visas, these women had found their way to Sandwich and taken lodgings there. But as soon as war was declared, Sandwich was designated as an evacuation destination for London children and the wives were compelled by their landladies, with the force of the state behind them, to leave their accommodation to make way for the evacuees. The camp authorities took responsibility to house them at Kitchener. A fence was erected to keep them apart from their husbands for most of the day and certainly at night.[22] This odd arrangement probably lasted a month at the most, and eventually most of these couples were allowed to leave the camp and move elsewhere.

At the same time, in October 1939, the Home Office became concerned that, now that Britain was at war with Germany, there was the possibility that these one-time Germans and German speakers constituted a dangerous fifth column. Six tribunals, headed by lawyers, were established in order to assess how many of the Kitchener men were 'enemy aliens' under the Aliens Act, 1919. They interviewed every one of the approximately 3,800 men, and every one of them bar two (one of whom was later reclassified), was found to be 'a victim of Nazi oppression', a phrase which was stamped on their documents. But that was not the end of the matter: the stories that the men told these senior British lawyers of what had happened to them in Greater Germany were so compelling that, when the work of the tribunals was over, the six lawyers composed a letter recounting what they had heard from the Kitchener men and sent it to the *Times*. That newspaper, very unusually, used an entire page to publish their letter on 1 November 1939 under the banner headline, 'The Dark Age. German witnesses in England. A letter from the Tribunals'.[23] The Kitchener men had been given, fleetingly, a collective voice and were able to tell the nation, and, most particularly, the *Times* reading British establishment what was happening to the Jews of Greater Germany.

Amongst those who noticed must have been senior personnel in the War Office. Here was a group of German-speaking men, all of them with very good reason to hate the Third Reich, and all of them classified as 'friendly'. Within weeks, Lord Reading, himself a Jew, arrived at Kitchener to recruit men for the Pioneer Corps, the unarmed section of the British Army. About 2,000 of the refugees enlisted immediately.[24] The Kitchener camp rapidly changed into a hybrid camp; by January 1940 it was both a military camp, known as Pioneer Corps Training Centre no. 3, and a refugee camp. For those men who had enlisted, camp life became very different: instead of training in workshops they were now training to be soldiers – albeit unarmed ones – but nevertheless, soldiers in British army uniform, working to British army daily routines and earning British army wages of fourteen shillings a week.

Those who did not enlist were under considerable pressure from the CBF to do so. The CBF had, by December 1939, exhausted its funds and was desperate to move the financial responsibility for the men's upkeep to the British army.[25] However, for many Kitchener men, enlistment did not seem to be an option: aged between 17 and 45, they were (variously) too young, too sick, too close to getting a visa for Palestine or the USA, too war-weary from the First World War to contemplate going to war again and, most of all, too anxious about the repercussions on their families left behind in Germany should they be captured by the German army. As the Kitchener camp became increasingly like an army camp in discipline and culture, it must have seemed obvious to the refugees who were still civilians that they should be able to leave, but the CBF had other plans. They wanted the civilian refugees to stay at Kitchener in order to service the army personnel by cooking their meals, altering their uniforms and maintaining the huts.

The civilians became increasingly restive, making frequent trips to London to beseech the CBF to help them get their wives and children out of Germany,[26] or to pay their fares so they could take up the offer of a visa to the United States.[27] The atmosphere between them and CBF staff became hostile, such that the staff began to write letters to each other that were, quite frankly, rude about the refugees. For example, the London-based Chaim Raphael who worked at CBF headquarters wrote in December 1939 to Julian Layton, by then the acting Director of Kitchener,

> I was very nearly stabbed in the back by one of your spiritual children who refused to take no for an answer when I refused to give him any money for fares in London or the return journey. He was one of those who wished he were back in the Concentration Camp, and I agreed with him.[28]

It is clear that by December 1939, morale at the camp among the civilian refugees had broken down. On 5 December, a group of refugees who said they were acting on behalf of all those who had been granted visas to the United States and were desperate to leave the United Kingdom wrote a letter to Norman Bentwich pleading with him to arrange that their 'ship tickets' be paid for by the CBF and explaining why it was impossible for them to enlist:

> These are men who suffered very very much in Germany, who passed the hell of Germany, they are broken men who endured years of physical and psychical (sic) terror and persecutions, who were tortured in German concentration camps for months and years, whose homes are torn up, whose families are dispersed all over the world, they have nothing in their heart but one ardent desire. Once again to live like a normal man, to have a home, to be united with their families, once again to live their bit of private life, free from camping like gipsies (sic) and all these things … It would be the best thing to help them as soon as possible, to send them away if they have proceeded so far, to enable them to build up a new life before it is too late, before the passing time make them unable for that they become useless members of the human Community and a public charge forever …[29]

Letters between the CBF staff indicate that at one point the civilians threatened to go on strike[30] and that there was a tendency for some of the men to go up to London and then simply disappear.[31] Nevertheless, large numbers stayed. In March 1940, Norman Bentwich wrote to the Home Office official in charge of the camp's oversight that 'the number of men on the Camp roll is 1572 … that is of course exclusive of the men who are enlisted'[32] By March 1940, most of the enlisted men had joined the British Expeditionary Force in France, so at that stage the camp accommodated about half the number it had housed at its peak in September 1939. Archival sources are not forthcoming as to how the civilians occupied their days at this stage of the camp's life but we do know that a group of the younger men who had been too young to enlist were used as listeners and interpreters in a camp radio station designed to intercept the messages of German shipping in the English channel.[33]

In late Spring 1940 this way of life came to an abrupt end. The momentous events of May 1940 overtook Kitchener: France fell to the invading German forces, Winston Churchill became Prime Minister and the idea that 'aliens' were a potential fifth column took hold of the nation's discourse. An exclusion zone embracing most of Britain's eastern seaboard, and a much stricter policy of internment of enemy aliens, were put into action. The continuing presence of Pioneer Corps Training Camp no. 3, with its complement of non-British soldiers, on the very edge of the English Channel and within twenty five miles of the French coast, became out of the question. At the end of May 1940, with twenty-four hours' notice, the Kitchener camp, both as an army camp and as a refugee camp, was closed. To the shock of Sandwich residents, the enlisted men along with the civilian refugees were marched to Sandwich railway station under armed guard and put on trains to London.

The soldiers were immediately sent on to alternative Pioneer Corps camps in Devon,[34] but for the civilian refugees their fate was internment on the Isle of Man. Julian Layton, who had been the director of the civilian side of the camp since December 1939, followed them there in order to be their advocate and protector. He installed himself in a hotel in Ramsey and in early June received a letter from Lord Reading. It reflected the breakdown in relations that had occurred between the CBF and the civilian refugees:

> The move of that rabble from Sandwich must have taxed all your powers of organisation. I expect they are pretty difficult to handle in present conditions. It cannot be amusing to go from a concentration camp to an internment camp, especially after an interval of liberty. But, sorry though I am for them in many ways, I can't altogether forget that they had their chance and rejected it. I told them quite plainly that, if they did not join the Army, they had only themselves to thank if later on spy-fever raged and they found themselves interned, but they would not believe me.[35]

Thus, on a somewhat sour note, the Kitchener camp, both as a refugee camp and as an army camp, had come to an end. The paths of two sets of refugees had diverged: those who had enlisted were regarded by the British state as a useful resource, while those who were still civilians were regarded by the same state as untrustworthy and possibly extremely dangerous, so much so that they had to be placed behind barbed wire on an island in the Irish Sea.

Forgetting and remembrance

As the Second World War progressed, the site of the Kitchener camp became wholly militarized, at first used to house other units of the British army and later to house men of the Canadian air force based at RAF Manston, an important airfield very close by. Immediately post-war, the camp was purchased by a local manufacturing firm which used it to house both their factory and their workers. In the 1950s, the international pharmaceutical company, Pfizer, bought most of the Kitchener land and almost all the residential huts were demolished or modernized and rendered unrecognizable. Only the large sheds, located on the other side of the main road running north from Sandwich, which had been used for the workshops and the concert hall during the refugees' days, are retained. Some of these sheds are still in use and have become part of the so-called Sandwich Industrial Estate. There is nothing else of the camp that still exists.

The Jews had left little trace apart from in the hearts of a few long-standing Sandwich residents, who, many decades later, wrote short memoirs.³⁶ Very occasionally, in the pages of the journal of the Association of Jewish Refugees (AJR), an article appeared about the Kitchener rescue.³⁷

Only Norman Bentwich, and later his wife Helen Bentwich, made efforts to keep the memory of the Kitchener camp alive, writing histories of pre-war refugee policy and their part in it or, in the case of Helen Bentwich, a privately published *History of Sandwich in Kent*.³⁸ Neither Bentwich, though very distinguished in other fields, were academic historians and they wrote without mentioning sources or bibliographies, which was hardly likely to endear them to academic discourse. One book, by the post-war archivist of the CBF (now 'World Jewish Relief'), did include a chapter on the Kitchener rescue and used conventional historical methods, but not being located within a university department may have hindered the use of this study by other historians.³⁹ The historiography of British refugee policy which developed in the 1980s and 1990s (see, e.g. Kushner, London, Shatzkes) had remarkably little to say about the Kitchener camp, and in public knowledge the other rescue – the Kindertransports – became the popular way of understanding and promoting the British response to the refugee crisis of the 1930s.⁴⁰

Material memorials did not exist at all in Sandwich until 1973. In that year the AJR, almost certainly prompted by Helen Bentwich whose husband Norman had died two years earlier, funded a plaque which memorializes the Kitchener camp. Placed on the medieval gate to Sandwich which stands between the centre of Sandwich and site of the Kitchener camp half a mile away, the plaque is rather more misleading than it is informative. It refers to the 'Richborough Transit Camp' rather than Kitchener, and suggests that '5000 men found refuge from Nazi persecution on the Continent'. The number of 5,000 was, at one time, for the camp's founders, aspirational but was never achieved. Moreover the plaque fails to mention that these refugees from Nazi persecution were Jews. The wording was almost certainly devised by Helen Bentwich, who in her *History of Sandwich in Kent* refers to 5,000 refugees and claims that no less than one quarter of them were Christians.⁴¹ The archives indicate that there were 100 so-called non aryans at Kitchener who were separately funded by the Quakers. Quite why the AJR chose, at the time, to fund a plaque which failed to mention Jews is not known.

In the past ten years, the Kitchener rescue has become more generally known and more accurately described. The shift in the historiography has been largely the result of the efforts of the present author; the development of a website by the daughter of one of the rescued men which brings together memoirs, images, and contemporary primary sources; and the formation of an organization, the Kitchener Descendants' Group, whose membership consists of descendants of the men who lived at Kitchener sometime between early 1939 and spring 1940.⁴² Moreover, a grant from the Heritage Lottery Fund has meant that the Sandwich Museum, which until recently had not memorialized the Kitchener camp at all, does, since its refurbishment in 2017, have a small display of Kitchener-related items which descendants have donated. There have been two Kitchener exhibitions, at the Wiener Library and at the Jewish Museum, both in London, the first prompted by the publication of the present author's book which used archive material sourced, amongst other places, at the Wiener Library. The second was put together by Clare Weissenberg, herself a Kitchener descendant, using materials from the website she had founded and curated. This latter exhibition is designed to be mobile and the intention is for it to travel to other parts of the United Kingdom and internationally. Finally and most recently, the AJR has funded another and more accurate plaque. It has been placed by the front door of the Bell Hotel Sandwich, very close to the gate on which the original AJR plaque is affixed. The words on the plaque were written by the Kitchener Descendants Group and reads, 'The Bell Hotel – a meeting place for Jewish refugees from The Kitchener Camp Richborough Sandwich 1939–40'. The unveiling of this plaque, in September 2019, was something of an occasion, with descendants coming from as far away as Australia and the United States. There were strong emotions present – of sadness driven by loss and of joy at new lives built across the world.

Notes

1. Norman Bentwich, *I Understand the Risks* (London: Victor Gollancz, 1950), 25–34; Norman Bentwich, *They Found Refuge* (London: The Cresset Press, 1956), 102–14.
2. Jennifer Craig-Norton, *The Kindertransport: Contesting Memory* (Bloomington: Indiana University Press, 2019).
3. Minutes of the Executive of the Council for German Jewry (January 1939), Central British Fund for World Jewish Relief: Archives 1933–1960, MF Doc 27, Wiener Holocaust Library, London.
4. Bentwich, *I Understand the Risks*, 26.
5. There has recently been a striking improvement in the way in which Kitchener-related documents are described by the US Holocaust Memorial Museum Library and the camp is now rarely referred to as an 'internment camp'. It is, however, noticeable that catalogued family papers still often refer to the camp as an internment camp, presumably reflecting the perception of the men who were resident there which has passed, by word of mouth, down the generations.
6. Rachel Pistol, *Internment during the Second World War: A Comparative Study of Great Britain and the USA* (London: Bloomsbury Academic, 2017), 37–40.
7. Charmian, Brinson, Anna, Muller-Harlin, and Julia Winckler, *His Majesty's Loyal Internee: Fred Uhlman in Captivity* (London: Vallentine Mitchell, 2009), 18.
8. Charmian Brinson, 'Exile, Internment – and a Camp "full of once and future Very Important Persons"', in Brinson et al., *His Majesty's Loyal Internee*.
9. Phineas May, 'Kitchener Camp Diary 1939', entry for 24 March 1939, MS 644/1, Wiener Holocaust Library, London. Typescript of the diary available online at http://www.kitchenercamp.co.uk/research/phineas-may-kitchener-camp-diary-1939/ (accessed 8 February 2019).
10. May, 'Diary', entries throughout February 1939.
11. Poldi Kuh, 'Work and Training in Kitchener Camp', uncatalogued, Sandwich Guildhall Archives.
12. Herbert Freeden, 'Sandwich Revisited', *AJR Information* 14/3 (1959).
13. Clare Ungerson, 'Two Sandwich Fascists in the 1930s', *The Sandwich Society Journal* 2/15 (2016): 35–9.

14. Board of Deputies of British Jews Archives, minutes of Jewish Defence Committee special meeting, 13 February 1939, Wiener Holocaust Library, London.
15. 'Kitchener Camp to take 3,500 Refugees: To be trained for emigrants', *East Kent Mercury*, 4 February 1939.
16. 'Kitchener Camp', *East Kent Mercury*, 15 April 1939.
17. 'Kitchener Refugee Camp: Refugees entertain English friends', *East Kent Mercury*, 13 May 1939.
18. Phineas May, 'Kitchener Camp diary 1939', entries for 18 August, 21 August, 23 August, 30 August, 1939.
19. Bentwich, *I Understand the Risks*, 30; Bentwich, *They Found Refuge*, 107.
20. Clare Ungerson, *Four Thousand Lives: The Rescue of German Jewish Men to Britain, 1939* (Stroud: The History Press, 2014), 118–26.
21. Board of Deputies of British Jews Archives, Defence Committee minutes, 8 November 1939, Wiener Holocaust Library, London.
22. Bentwich Papers, Norman Bentwich to Mr H.L.Oates 18 September 1939, File P174/13b, The Central Archives for the History of the Jewish People, Hebrew University, Jerusalem.
23. 'The Dark Age: German Witnesses in England: A Letter from The Tribunals', *The Times*, 1 November 1939.
24. Bentwich Papers, Norman Bentwich to E. N.Cooper at the Home Office 13 March 1940, File P174/20a, The Central Archives for the History of the Jewish People, Hebrew University, Jerusalem. This may well have been an exaggeration rather typical of Norman Bentwich: a contemporary document on the Kitchener camp website indicates that in January 1940, 805 men were actually fully fledged soldiers in the Pioneer Corps at Richborough. Documents of Wolfgang Priester, 26 January 1940, http://www.kitchenercamp.co.uk/documents/wolfgang-priester-documents/ (10 November 2020).
25. Minutes of the Executive of the Central Council for Jewish Refugees, 14 December 1939, Central British Fund for World Jewish Relief: Archives 1933–1960, MF Doc 27, Wiener Holocaust Library, London.
26. Bentwich Papers, Norman Bentwich to Jonas May 13 November 1939, File P174/15c, The Central Archives for the History of the Jewish People, Hebrew University, Jerusalem.
27. Bentwich Papers, Letter from six Kitchener Camp men, possibly addressed to Robert Waley Cohen with a copy to Norman Bentwich 5 December 1939, File P174/12d, The Central Archives for the History of the Jewish People, Hebrew University, Jerusalem.
28. Bentwich Papers, Chaim Raphael to Julian Layton 18 December 1939, File P174/15c, The Central Archive for the History of the Jewish People, Hebrew University, Jerusalem.
29. Bentwich Papers, Letter from six Kitchener Camp men.
30. Julian Layton Papers, Robert Waley Cohen to Lord Reading 1 April 1940, document 1205/2/14, Wiener Holocaust Library, London.
31. Bentwich Papers, Robert Waley Cohen to Jonas May 26 October 1939, File P174/15c, The Central Archives for the History of the Jewish People, Hebrew University, Jerusalem.
32. Bentwich Papers, Norman Bentwich to E. N.Cooper at the Home Office, 13 March 1940, File P174/20a.
33. Hans Jackson (n.d.), *The Art of Hans Hermann Josephy*, http://www.kitchenercamp.co.uk/the-art-of-hans-hermann-josephy/ (20 July 2020).

34. Helen Fry, *Jews in North Devon during the Second World War: The escape from Nazi Germany and the Establishment of the Pioneer Corps* (Tiverton: Halsgrove, 2005).
35. Julian Layton Papers, Lord Reading to Julian Layton, 1 June 1940, document 1205/2/21, Wiener Holocaust Library, London.
36. Hilda Keen, 'A Sandwich resident remembers the Kitchener Camp', Association of Jewish Refugees Journal, January 2010, 4–5; Patrick Miles (n.d), personal communication to Clare Ungerson concerning his mother's memories.
37. Herbert Freeden, 'Sandwich Revisited', *AJR Information*, March 1959, page unknown; Anthony Grenville, 'Saved by a transit visa', Association of Jewish Refugees Journal, May 2009, 1–2.
38. Bentwich, *I Understand the Risks*; Bentwich, *They Found Refuge*; Norman Bentwich, *My 77 Years: An Account of My Life and Times 1883–1960* (Philadelphia: The Jewish Publication Society of America, 1961), 142–66; Helen C. Bentwich, *History of Sandwich in Kent* (Deal: T. F. Pain, 1971), 151–7.
39. Amy Zahl Gottlieb, *Men of Vision* (London: Wiedenfeld and Nicolson, 1998), 135–45.
40. Tony Kushner, *The Persistence of Prejudice: Antisemitism in British Society during the Second World War* (Manchester: Manchester University Press, 1989); Tony Kushner, *The Holocaust and the Liberal imagination* (Oxford: Blackwell, 1994); Louise London, *Whitehall and the Jews, 1933–48* (Cambridge: Cambridge University Press, 2000); Pamela Shatzkes, *Holocaust and Rescue* (London: Vallentine Mitchell, 2004).
41. Bentwich, *History of Sandwich*, 152.
42. Clare Ungerson, *Four Thousand Lives;* 'Kitchener Camp -Refugees to Britain in 1939'. http://www.kitchenercamp.co.uk (28 October 2019).

Bibliography

Bentwich, Helen C. *His tory of Sandwich in Kent*. Deal: T. F. Pain, 1971.
Bentwich, Norman. *I Understand the Risks*. London: Victor Gollancz, 1950.
Bentwich, Norman. *My 77 Years: An Account of My Life and Times 1883–1960*. Philadelphia: The Jewish Publication Society of America, 1961.
Bentwich, Norman. *They Found Refuge*. London: The Cresset Press, 1956.
Brinson, Charmian. 'Exile, Internment – and a Camp "Full of Once and Future Very Important Persons"'. In *His Majesty's Loyal Internee: Fred Uhlman in Captivity*, edited by Brinson, Charmian, Anna Muller-Harlin and Julia Winckler, 13–33. London: Vallentine Mitchell, 2009.
Brinson, Charmian, Anna Muller-Harlin and Julia Winckler. *His Majesty's Loyal Internee: Fred Uhlman in Captivity*. London: Vallentine Mitchell, 2009.
Craig-Norton, Jennifer. *The Kindertransport: Contesting Memory*. Bloomington: Indiana University Press, 2019.
Fry, Helen. *Jews in North Devon during the Second World War: The Escape from Nazi Germany and the Establishment of the Pioneer Corps*. Tiverton: Halsgrove, 2005.
Kushner, Tony. *The Holocaust and the Liberal imagination*. Oxford: Blackwell, 1994.
Kushner, Tony. *The Persistence of Prejudice: Antisemitism in British Society during the Second World War*. Manchester: Manchester University Press, 1989.
London, Louise. *Whitehall and the Jews, 1933–48*. Cambridge: Cambridge University Press, 2000.

Pistol, Rachel. *Internment during the Second World War: A Comparative Study of Great Britain and the USA*. London: Bloomsbury Academic, 2017.
Shatzkes, Pamela. *Holocaust and Rescue*. London: Vallentine Mitchell, 2004.
Ungerson, Clare. *Four Thousand Lives: The Rescue of German Jewish Men to Britain, 1939*. Stroud: The History Press, 2014.
Ungerson, Clare. 'Two Sandwich Fascists in the 1930s'. *The Sandwich Society Journal* 2, no. 15 (2016): 35–9.
Zahl Gottlieb, Amy. *Men of Vision*. London: Wiedenfeld and Nicolson, 1998.

3

Legacy and heritage of the Arandora Star tragedy in Britain and Italy: A transnational perspective

Terri Colpi

Introduction

The wartime sinking of the SS *Arandora Star* on 2 July 1940 by a German U-boat forms a unique episode within the internment narrative and is the focus of this chapter. Now over eighty years on and slipping beyond the realm of living memory, the legacy of this incident has nonetheless never been stronger when considering the Italian victims. Over half of all those on board,[1] a mixture of German and Austrian Jewish refugees, German POWs, British servicemen and crew and Italian internees, drowned, Italians suffering the greatest proportionate and total loss – 446 of 712 men.[2] Representing an historically complex outcome of internment policy, the sinking sent powerful ripples not only down through the history of Italian presence in Britain, but also into the emigration narrative from Italy, creating a resilient memory and heritage in both countries. To understand the potency of the legacy and its evolution, the chapter begins by contextualizing the sinking event, moves through discussions of attitudes and representations, and evaluates the progression of remembrance cultures and heritage activism. An innovative transnational approach explores varying emphases between a current of unresolvedness predominantly in Britain where memory of being 'enemy aliens' lingers, and a determination not to forget its emigrants in Italy. Drawing on circumstances and interpretations from British and Italian sources, a more nuanced and balanced appraisal emerges, contributing new dimensions, particularly assessment of Italian perspective, to *Arandora Star* (*AS*) scholarship.

Historical context and troubled legacy

By the 1930s, the Italian community in Britain, numbering 24,000 Italian-born plus an estimated 10,000 British-born Italians, was well-established and nationally dispersed. An infrastructure of small family businesses primarily in the foods sector, some specialist trades such as mosaic and terrazzo and, in London, employment in hotels, restaurants and gentlemen's clubs supported the community. Broadly, integration was characterized by varying degrees of marginalization and prejudice. Family ties with origins remained durable, the community's growth achieved through 'chains of migration' and relationships with specific areas in Italy. This non-random pattern of migrant selection, and to some extent the consequential distribution of Italians in Britain, can be understood as partly responsible for creating what I have defined as 'pockets of affect' in terms of *AS* losses[3] – essentially places and provinces in Italy and towns and cities in Britain that were impacted by the tragedy. These transnational pockets of affect provide conceptual basis for the chapter, characterising sources of emotion and remembrance activism.

As Mussolini sought to envelop the worldwide Italian diaspora during the 1930s,[4] growth of fascism amongst British Italians became increasingly worrying to the Security Services, especially after 1935 with the invasion of Abyssinia and politically oriented anti-British messages.[5] The rank and file of the community became progressively associated, especially in the cities where *fasci* (fascist clubs) were located, with appointed and committed leaders. Yet, in the build up to war no legislation was passed making the *fasci* organizations illegal and, more saliently, no assessment of the Italians' loyalties was undertaken. Other than the now infamous MI5 list of 1,500 'dangerous characters' based on *fascio* membership, no interviewing or categorization of Italians occurred.[6] Italy's declaration of war on 10 June 1940 resulted in immediate arrest of Italian-born males between the ages of sixteen and seventy with less than twenty years residence in Britain. Those on MI5's list were to be deported to the Dominions; *fascio* membership was believed to equate with real threat to national security. However, lack of clarity and preparedness ensured inconsistent national implementation of the round-up.[7] Local constabularies, tasked with the arrests, interpreted and executed instructions differently with varying degrees of error, leniency and zealousness.[8] While all Italian communities were affected by the sinking, the uneven pattern of seizure worked as a second variable influencing pockets of affect by creating unexpectedly high or low impacts. Losses were higher in Ayr and Edinburgh, for example, than relative numbers of Italians might have predicted. By contrast, there were almost no *AS* fatalities in Liverpool or Sheffield, despite not only large Italian communities but also the presence of *fasci*. From amongst the internees, only around half of those on MI5's list could be identified, and selections for deportation to make up the numbers were randomly and hurriedly made, picking Italians regardless of *fascio* membership, age or kinship configurations.[9] Although the *fasci* were in the cities, a third of the drowned men were from small towns.[10]

The selection and status of Italians on board has given rise to debate over 'innocence', an ethical question woven into *AS* legacy in both countries. Originating in Italian literature,[11] the conception of 'innocent victims' has been criticized by some British scholars as presenting an all-inclusive guilt-free impression.[12] Discourse nevertheless continues, centring on the majority aboard.[13] Any militant fascistic intent amongst a minority remains largely unresolvable, with some files at the National Archives remaining closed until 2041, while others are 'missing' or 'destroyed'. An unprecedented statement by Italy's president, Sergio Mattarella, in 2020, marking the eightieth anniversary of the sinking in which he referred to '*vittime innocenti*', innocent victims,[14] foregrounds the issue's continued relevance. In Italian media and academia, those who perished tend to be depoliticized and cast primarily as '*emigranti*'. Indeed, the 'tragedy', exemplifying heartbreak and catastrophe, is routinely referred to as a 'massacre' or 'slaughter of emigrants', thus acquiring the particular emphasis of that perspective.[15] Both in Italy and the Italian community, the actuality of a potentially damaging fascist element in Britain is downplayed, falling into the myth of Italians as '*brava gente*',[16] good people, deployed post-war to minimize guilt in fascist atrocity. This finds reverberation in Britain where a self-absolving memory is often associated with AS victimhood that does not fully register pre-war fascistic acquiescence. A further aspect underpinning the troubled legacy in post-generations focuses on the ship itself and the contributory negligence that led to the sinking. Around the year 2000, the disquiet in AS memory coalesced into 'calls for apology', emanating both from British and Italian pockets of affect.[17]

From silence to representation and beyond

During the war and its aftermath, a silence engulfed the memory of the AS in Britain and Italy, but for different reasons. Silence in Britain was endemic, attributable to several interrelated factors. Within the family, effects of trauma and repression of pain, a void of communication – many never receiving the 'missing presumed drowned' notifications – and lack of materiality in mourning with very few identified bodies recovered,[18] all contributed to memory internalization. As enemy aliens, unable to find pathways for expression of individual or collective grief, and faced with official indifference in their quest for information, an inflexible muteness was inescapable. Ongoing anti-Italian discrimination after the war juxtaposed with an overriding desire to 're-integrate' orchestrated further memory suppression; 'neutralising difference by silence' became a survival technique.[19]

This silence or seeming amnesia took four to five decades to dissipate, the fiftieth anniversary in 1990 forming a watershed. Survivors and victims' families began to 'speak out' and 'tell', the anniversary acting as both catalyst and conduit through which memory was recovered and articulated. Representing a grassroots phenomenon, the emergent narrative was then nourished by diverse media broadening the mnemonic community. For example, in 1991 in Edinburgh, a ground-breaking national exhibition, *The Italian Scots* drew attention to the war experience and an influential play, *Tally's Blood* by Ann Marie Di Mambro, first performed in 1990, was of great potency in remediation.[20] Alfio Bernabei's complex documentary, *Dangerous Characters* (1987), included interviews with AS survivors, again helping reach a wider public consciousness.[21] In London, survivors were invited to record their memories at the Imperial War Museum, indicating changing British establishment attitudes.[22]

In Italy, the story took longer to surface and circulate. According to John Foot, AS 'memories and silences varied in time and space, were patterned by politics, local factors and myths, as well as by the activities of individuals'.[23] Outside pockets of affect, wherein the memory remained 'contained', dispersal of victims' relatives amongst the general population meant little interconnection or even knowledge of each other's existence. The case of Edoardo Ceresa, born 1890 in Bollengo (Torino) and resident in Britain for thirty-two years by 1940, illustrates the total lack of information in Italy, breakdown in wartime communication and the frequent isolation of victims' families. News of Edoardo's drowning took six months to reach his widow who had returned to Bollengo from Manchester with the children in 1939. The family then remained unaware of the scale of the tragedy, even at a local level, until Edoardo's grandson began research from his home in Stepps in 2013. Despite signifying a first large-scale loss of life after Italy's war entry, only small 'notices' of the torpedoing appeared contemporaneously in the press, making no mention of the human cargo. With mainly Italian and German victims, no detail followed due to suppression by the fascist regime embarrassed by their German ally's blunder. When hostilities ended, any questioning of the sinking was again submerged, due to the hegemony of the new Allies and their liberation of Italy from German occupation. Thus, as Umberto Sereni argues, the tragedy was consequently 'twice forgotten' in Italy.[24]

After the war, whereas in Britain a 'victors' paradigm was overarching and exclusionary, Italy's complicated war as simultaneously occupied, resister, loser and victor generated a range of conflicting experiences and identities with no natural unifying memory or master narrative.[25] Reconstruction of the Italian political landscape, transforming monarchy into republic and fascism into democracy, was marked by intense political and social struggle, achieved only by suppressing or 'forgetting' certain narratives, most notably fascism, while promoting others. Further political transformation in the early 1990s after the collapse of the communist bloc allowed repressed and overlooked war chapters to surface, such as the Foibe massacres in Italy's borderlands with former Yugoslavia.[26] The memory of emigrant relatives deported from Britain and lost at sea as enemy aliens thus represented an un-divisive episode in the fragmented and contested national narrative; it was much less problematic to incorporate than internment, especially the *AS* affair, in Britain.[27] Significantly, first Italian official recognition came in 1990 when twenty-one surviving *AS* survivors, resident in both countries, were decorated *Cavaliere della Repubblica Italiana* by President Francesco Cossiga (see Figure 3.1). During a state visit to Britain the same year, Cossiga met with Italian communities at mass gatherings giving further weight and prominence to the anniversary.

Yet, it was not until 2002 in Italy, with the publication of an eponymous book and first major newspaper feature, that the *AS* narrative emerged from obscurity.[28] Dissemination was then rapid, supported by immaterial contexts of memory and promoted by intentional choreography drawing individuals together and forming a mnemonic community. For example, centred on the Lucca provincial pocket of affect with around thirty *AS* losses,[29] the *Fondazione Paolo Cresci per la Storia dell' Emigrazione Italiana* – Foundation for the History of Italian Emigration – became pivotal in memory retrieval and transmission. A documentary film, *Arandora Star, La Tragedia Dimenticata*, The Forgotten Tragedy, was produced in 2004 in association with Noi TV, touring other pockets of affect, generating conferences, screenings and press attention.[30] Despite publication in Britain in 1991 of the Home Office Missing List revealing the extent and composition of the tragedy,[31] this was not picked up in Italy until 2008. However, its reproduction in a second book,[32] meaningfully with parallel

Figure 3.1 Italian Ambassador, Boris Biancheri (second from left), with some of the newly decorated *Cavalieri*, London, 1990

Source: © Terri Colpi Archive.

Italian and English text, generated intense interest. Memory-narrative remediation began to flourish, becoming transnationally fluid and dialogic, particularly through the performing arts[33] and conferences[34] (see Figure 3.2). Exhibitions highlighted the *AS*,[35] literature in memoire, autobiography and fiction grew,[36] and although texts were again slower to appear in Italy,[37] once launched they have had considerable influence, the authors becoming spokespersons for the tragedy. For example, Caterina Soffici has described the incident as not so much a war story, but one of immigration and prejudice,[38] a recurrent theme in the Italian press. National and regional newspapers in pocket of affect areas give anniversary coverage, often with full-page articles. Reporting tends to be partisan, highlighting 'injustices', abusive treatment of internees and laying 'blame' with Churchill.[39] In Britain, the *AS* seldom receives national attention,[40] although newspapers such as the *Scotsman* consistently allocate space, albeit steering a more politically neutral course than Italian counterparts. The word 'forgotten' is ubiquitous in Italian writing, the emigrant victims thus demonstrably perceived as 'belonging', part of both war and emigration history. In Britain, 'forgotten' very rarely appears, suggesting the Italian experience remains outside the mainstream war narrative, something 'other' and apart.

The gathering of mnemonic communities in digital spaces provides further and dynamic forums for heritage encounter. There are currently four *AS* Facebook groups, the most fertile with 1,200 members,[41] where news, information and photographs circulate multi-directionally. Posts appear in English and Italian, and individuals living

Figure 3.2 Conference poster, Picinisco, 2019

Source: Courtesy Comune di Picinisco.

internationally also connect and 'remember'. Repetition of limited documentation, photographs, models of the ship and pictures of *AS* memorabilia from pre-war cruising days highlight the material void. The most dynamic development due to the Covid-19 pandemic was a proliferation of online conferences at the eightieth anniversary in 2020. By bringing together a range of people who may not otherwise have assembled, such as members of the Italian parliament, Italian diplomats in London, mayors from Italian pockets of affect, historians, journalists, authors and *AS* activists, these meetings signified important transnational dialogue and themselves contributed to memory-making.[42]

Commemoration and heritage

The attitudes, behaviours and active performances of remembering described above are related to tangible heritage since there they find embodiment that becomes 'a reservoir of memory allowing for the survival of collective identity'.[43] Memorialization has thus been important in *AS* narrative assertion, cultural preservation and heritage development. With over half of all Italian victims from London, the first memorial, a bronze bas-relief of a lifeboat with outstretched arms, manifested in 1960 at St Peter's Italian Church (see Figure 3.3). Representing all Scottish victims, a colourful mosaic depicting explosion was mounted in 1975 at the *Casa d'Italia* in Glasgow. The semiotics of these early markers evoked the drama of the sinking, visual messages not

Figure 3.3 Arandora Star Memorial, St Peter's Italian Church, London

Source: © Terri Colpi Archive.

encapsulated in later memorials. However, at a time when not all victims were known, such monuments inevitably lacked names, an important aspect of commemoration in acknowledging the unique worth of the individual.[44] Situated in community-bound locations, their discreet, non-mainstream sites were preordained in a post-war environment that obliged inconspicuousness of Italianness. Nevertheless, without graves to visit and tend, these memorials signified the first physical sites of individual and community mourning and remembrance.

In Italy, the most impacted and largest provincial pockets of affect were Parma and Frosinone, each with around seventy victims. An epicentre of *AS* impact was the small town of Bardi (Parma), which lost forty-eight of its migrants.[45] The victims had mostly been resident in Wales, the sinking thus creating two interlinked pockets of affect. In contrast to the early British memorials, at Bardi, in 1968, names were inscribed on marble panels alongside individual enamelled photographs in a purpose-built chapel. Predating release of the Missing List, this testifies to the community's closeness in terms of victim knowledge, connectedness with its emigrants and also municipal support. Indeed, it is conceivable that the chapel provided unifying and non-factious remembrance focus in an area at the heart of the Resistance and considerably 'war-torn'; for example, the Battle of Osacca was fought in the commune of Bardi between local fascists and partisans on Christmas day 1943.[46] *AS* remembrance was thus a conflict-free memory with which Bardigiani on both sides of the fraught political divide could identify. Elsewhere in Parma and contiguous Massa Carrara province, memorial stones were similarly placed at village pockets of affect in the 1960s and 1970s. At Picinisco the largest village pocket of affect in Frosinone, with twenty-two victims, in 1969 several were named on a general tablet to 'civilian victims who had innocently lost their lives'. Yet, it was not until the late 1990s that both Picinisco, near Monte Cassino and on the German Gustav line, and the Fubine (Piemonte region) pocket of affect where 'civil war' murders were particularly acrimonious, joined the *AS* memorial landscape, again indicating the 'forgotten' and entangled layers of Italian war narrative. Within the overall Italian war memorial topography, *AS* victims were rarely recognized amongst the war 'fallen', the monument to two world wars at Vernasca (Piacenza), naming *AS* victims, an unusual inclusion.

Arguably framed within European commemorative obsession, between 2005 and 2010, a further four memorials were unveiled at Italian pockets of affect. In 2005, a symbolic funnel-shaped monument was installed at Lucca outside the *Fondazione Paolo Cresci*, and at Borgotaro (Parma) names were added to a restored existing stone in the town's square. In 2008 at Barga (Lucca), and 2010 at Pontremoli (Massa Carrara), memorials were sited. Although commemorating '*vittimi innocenti*', the Barga plaque does not name victims. Alternatively, commissioned not only by the civic administration but also by the *Istituto Storico della Resistenza Apuana* – Historical Institute of Apennine Resistance – the Pontremoli plaque names seventeen victims in a distinctively political and narrative-constructing marker:

> In memory of the hard-working Pontremoli emigrants in Great Britain on whom Italy's entry into the war cast an unjust shadow of suspicion and who, destined for

imprisonment by the English government, perished in the tragic sinking of the Arandora Star on 2 July 1940.[47]

In 2020, demonstrating the latency of memory at pockets of affect, the transnational quality of remembrance, and the role often played by individuals as 'memory choreographers',[48] the latest commemorative marker manifested at Bollengo (Torino). In the form of a funnel-shaped monument, conceptually similar to Lucca, it names nine victims. Commissioned and designed by Edoardo Ceresa, grandson of the previously mentioned victim, its positioning on the Via Francigena pilgrims' route to Rome ensures considerable passing foot-traffic. New tribute to the *Arandora* as a war memory manifested during the 4 November celebrations for National Unity and Armed Forces Day at Bedonia (Parma) in 2021, where three victims' names were added to the town's monument of war fallen.

In Britain, after the initial memorials, from 1975 to the millennium no further commemorative responses occurred, reflecting continued dominance of the victors' master narrative and residual prejudice and, at the same time, reticence amongst the marginalized war generations to challenge the status quo. However, with the passing of memory custodianship to post-generations, mounting drive for public recognition ultimately created a nationwide infrastructure encompassing seven new memorials. Unlike their predecessors, these new materializations were almost all located in public and civic spaces, indicating not only changed attitudes allowing articulation of this facet of Italian identity but also a performative resilience some seventy years after the sinking. Yet, only the memorials on Colonsay and at Liverpool arose from British initiative,[49] the others stemming from Italian community pressure. The Hebridean island of Colonsay, where *AS* bodies washed ashore and were buried, led the way siting a memorial stone in 2005, coinciding with the second phase of memorialization in Italy. Moreover, the islanders embraced the shared transnational commemorative heritage by organizing civic receptions and exchanges with Borgotaro.[50] As part of Liverpool's European City of Culture in 2008, the city projected its European credentials by harnessing the transnationality of the Italian victims. In a unique historic arena, local and Italian authorities, emissaries from Lazio, Toscana and Emilia-Romagna, the regions containing pockets of affect, victims' families from both countries, the last Italian survivor and members of the Italian community were assembled.[51] As the *AS*'s port of departure, the Liverpool event not only accomplished emotional catharsis, but also symbolized a 'moment of reception' engendering a sense of belonging, a key aspect of commemoration.[52] Liverpool's success encouraged and motivated participants to formulate their own memorial plans. However, due to the historic community's assimilation into different socio-political backdrops, post event, the protagonists went their separatist 'national' ways with no predisposition to collaborate towards a 'British' memorial to the 446 Italian victims. Since 'diaspora politics are about assertions of identity, community, needs, interests and belonging, in the context of a host society's political system',[53] consequent commemorative enterprise has varied. While outcomes were positive in Wales and Scotland, this has been less so the case in England.

The first subsequent memorial was realized at Middlesbrough in 2009, a pocket of affect where ten of the thirteen victims had ties to Frosinone province. Italians enjoyed support from local MP, the late Sir Stuart Bell, who had intended to launch a campaign for government apology and the town's mayor who 'apologized' at the ceremony.[54] In 2010, at Cardiff's St David's Cathedral, the first 'national' memorial emerged. It followed a highly efficacious touring exhibition, *Italian Memories in Wales*. The exhibition was the first of its kind in Wales dedicated to immigration and a specific migrant community, taking place almost two decades after *The Italian Scots*. Marco Giudici explains changing attitudes towards diversity in Wales with its new inclusive discourse as integral to 1997 devolution and observed how museums and exhibitions played a pivotal role in nation-building.[55] Inspired then, not only by Liverpool, but fortified by the strong sense of worth and belonging bestowed by *Italian Memories*, a committee of Welsh Italians secured Heritage Lottery funding for an *AS* memorial. Although listing fifty-three Welsh Italian victims by name, the memorial remembers *all* who perished, being created 'in furtherance of the spirit of reconciliation and peace among nations'.[56] Welsh slate and Italian terracotta visually embody the aim 'to reinforce the Welsh-Italian bond by celebrating [the] Italians' successful integration within and contribution to Welsh society'.[57] The underlying conception therefore aligned with the Welsh political ideal of tolerance and inclusion, the initiative receiving institutional support from government officials and the Catholic Church's hierarchy. However, reflecting a time-delay when compared with narrative emergence elsewhere, it was also only in 2010 that an *AS*-specific exhibition, *Wales Breaks Its Silence: From Memories to Memorial*, acted to release repressed memory.[58] Overlapping with the physical commemoration, the narrative thus forcibly entered the public sphere, notably through television coverage.[59]

The 2011 'Italian Cloister Garden' dedicated to ninety-four Scottish victims at St Andrew's Cathedral in Glasgow embodied similar concepts as the Welsh initiative, but differed substantially in scale and spatiality. The largest and most architecturally ambitious of the British commemorations, it delivers the most public and dynamic legacy, again acting as a 'national' memorial. In a large outdoor setting incorporating monumental sculpture and suggestive water features, the underlying aim of remembrance was once again overlain with ideals of reconciliation and peace. Instigated and choreographed by the late Archbishop Mario Conti, an Italian Scot, but paid for by the Italian community, the monument marked 'the contribution which Italian Scots have made to Scottish society',[60] thus defending a sense of belonging and place in Scottish history. As in Wales, these inclusionary ideas resonated with the recently devolved Scottish government, First Minister Alex Salmond describing the Italian community as 'one of the brightest threads in the tartan that makes up our country', continuing, 'I believe it is entirely fitting that we should remember those Italians that were taken from their homes, their families and their lives in Scotland when Italy entered the war'.[61] Yet, 'support by both devolved governments reflects their disconnection and nuanced disassociation from the wartime decisions of Whitehall, in which they played no part'.[62]

Such support has not been mirrored in England by the more remote Westminster administrations. The London pocket of affect, accounting for over three-quarters of English Italian victims, has achieved little extra-community recognition for the *AS* due to impenetrability of the political elite and the competitive 'super diversity' of the capital.

The subaltern situation is compounded by the presence of St Peter's Italian church around which activity has traditionally been focused, leading to a conceptual if no longer spatial separation of the historic community. Unlike Mario Conti's Archdiocese, which utilized a strategic and unifying mode within the Italian community and with the Scottish authorities, St Peter's, as a 'parish' church, connects to London Italians solely in a spiritual and social capacity, assuming no wider representational or more political mission. Champions for civic and public memorialization within the erstwhile territory of 'Little Italy' did not emerge from the Mazzini-Garibaldi Club through which the *AS* London Memorial Trust is run. Opposition from English Heritage, the Diocese of Westminster historic churches committee and the Pallottini fathers hierarchy to site a new memorial adjacent to the 1960 bronze in the church's loggia, visible to passers-by, reveals much about the complexity in the power relationships. Reflecting weaker political agency, in 2012 a new memorial panel naming 241 victims was mounted inside, at the rear of the church. Remembrance strategy has been more inward looking resembling the 'antagonistic memory mode' adopting a more exclusionary and divisive 'us' and 'them' approach.[63] Although attended by local officials including constituency MP, Labour Party leader Sir Keir Starmer, the commemoration event placed little emphasis on the contribution of Italians to London or sense of belonging within English-British society. A book published in 2015 to mark the seventy-fifth anniversary, emphasized the troubled legacy and privileged suffering over reconciliation thus distancing the Italian community from a more inclusionary identity and fortifying isolation of *AS* memory.[64] Further challenge to memory transmission occurred when a 'permanent' display from the seventy-fifth anniversary exhibition, *The Arandora Star Tragedy: 75 Years On*, was removed from the Italian Consulate General. Not only did a small piece of commemorative heritage vanish but also a key opportunity for communicating the narrative to the '*expatriati*', the new generation of Italian migrants. No *AS* memorial or plaque has ever been accommodated at any of the numerous Italian Ministry of Foreign Affairs buildings in Britain indicating diplomacy in transnational memory.

Yet, Italian governments are once again keen to re-envelop not only the *emigranti* and *expatriati* but also '*italo-discendenti*', Italian descendants. Overall policies of encouraging diasporic consciousness and enhancing Italian identity are evidenced through cultural projects,[65] promoting 'roots tourism' and facilitating political participation to maintain bonds with *comuni* of origin and a wider imagined 'Italy'. 'Return' is conceptually encouraged. Envoys regularly visit the main *AS* memorial sites and the Ministry tweets supportive messages annually at the July anniversary. In 2009, the new *Museo Nazionale Emigrazione Italiana* in Rome, which acknowledges the role of the emigrants in Italy's history and in nation-building, featured the *AS* tragedy. The circumstances and scale of *AS* losses have fostered a legacy of uniqueness giving it special place not only in the history of emigration but also in that of the worldwide diaspora. The spectre of the coal mine disaster at Marcinelle in Belgium in 1956 with 136 Italian fatalities or the New Orleans lynching of eleven Sicilians in 1891 are invoked as similar diasporic catastrophes with emigrant 'sacrifice' and 'injustice' embodied in all three narratives.[66]

During the past decade, transnational interaction between pockets of affect has intensified and become symbiotic. For example, in 2014 the *Amici Val Ceno Galles*,

Friends of Val Ceno (incorporating Bardi) in Wales, donated a sculpture to Bardi by Susanna Ciccotti, the artist who crafted the Cardiff memorial, deepening common bonds. In 2016, London's *AS* Memorial Trust exhibition, *The Arandora Star Tragedy*, travelled to Bardi and was displayed during August. Notwithstanding the role of the *Fondazione Paolo Cresci* in its outreach and organizational capacity, 'over time, Bardi has developed into the centre of ceremonies for all Italian victims of the tragedy'.[67] The road named '*Via Vittime Arandora Star*' in the town's centre bears a plaque listing all affected provinces, thereby conceiving Bardi's nodality and memory guardianship. Moreover, isolated victims' families seek inclusion in the *AS* chapel and gather in Bardi at the anniversary. The tireless efforts of Bardi 'memory choreographer', Giuseppe Conti, great-nephew of a victim, have further influenced remembrance vitality. In 2002, President Carlo Azeglio Ciampi attended the anniversary occasion, and in 2016, designation as an 'event of national interest' by the government's Council of Ministers was achieved for the 2 July commemoration. A recent national television war documentary series included an episode with Conti discussing the *AS* at Bardi.[68] Echoing both Welsh and Scottish ideals of tolerance and inclusivity, Conti stresses that part of Bardi's *AS* committee's aim in curating the memory is to understand problems that 'arise from the new immigration to Italy'.[69]

Although some activists envision a 'national' memorial in Britain, or Italy, the phase of physical memorialization appears largely complete with virtually all pockets of affect represented,[70] an exception being Manchester with some fifteen victims. Some contestation of place has recently arisen in Scotland with calls from the Edinburgh pocket of affect for a separate memorial,[71] where two further tangible sites of memory also exist. The gargantuan three-part public sculpture, *The Manuscript of Monte Cassino*, by Edinburgh-born Sir Eduardo Paolozzi, who lost his father, maternal grandfather and uncle on the *AS*, was partly conceived in remembrance of the sinking,[72] and references war-ravaged Frosinone from where the family originated. Symbolic preservation of protective wartime shutters at Valvona & Crolla delicatessen represents family memorialization by the owners, both of whom lost grandfathers on the *AS*, as well as enacting an *aide-mémoire* to the anti-Italian riots of June 1940. While in Italy, the unrepresented seek inclusion in Bardi's mnemonic community, in England it is less clear where memory of the thirty or so still un-commemorated victims can be remembered publically. The transnational context has led to numerous victims being remembered twice, and in the case of Giuseppe Del Grosso, thrice.[73] Others, like Edoardo Ceresa, recently remembered at Bollengo are unacknowledged in Britain; originally from Manchester, he was ineligible for the Scottish monument where the family now live.

Today, activists are concerned mainly with custodial and informative themes, their work providing a lifeline of historic community identity and also meaningful dialogue with both local communities and Italy. In Glasgow, heritage trail to The Italian Cloister Garden as part of the city's 'Doors Open Festival' attracted almost 650 visitors over just two days in September 2021, around 80 per cent of whom had not visited the garden and monument before, and later, in October, international visitors from the Cop26 summit on climate change, the *AS* touching an ever-wider consciousness. In London, the *AS* Memorial Trust has created a new website and plans to upload biographic details of victims and survivors and hopes that Wales and Scotland will contribute their data. Most significant, however, and representing a new departure and more outward-facing approach, was the leadership role assumed by London in organizing a landmark conference in November 2021, entitled 'Arandora Star Remembered'. The event retrospectively marked the eightieth anniversary but was ground-breaking in bringing together, for the first time, the various strands of the Arandora 'community of interest'. Descendants of victims, academics, community leaders, diplomats, British Italian celebrities, institutional representatives and politicians from both Italian and British parliaments participated. One outcome of this meeting has been impetus for a new public and civic memorial in London, possibly with national connotations memorializing all 446 Italian victims. Additionally, it is anticipated that the scholarly contributions, which presented new research material and perspectives, will be published.[74] If achieved, this will help move the historiography of the Arandora Star forward.

Other ambitious ideas circulate privately in emails, member only newsletters and Facebook groups, such as raising the sand-sunken *AS* lifeboat on a Mull beach, sailing from Ireland to the sea point of the sinking for commemorative service and 'raising' the ship's wreck by remote nautical filming.[75] As noted previously, the realms of intangible memory and cultural heritage demonstrate how, through such performances, memory is both 'living' and 'alive'; it will be a question of whether the depth of heritage now embodied within the *AS* can be sustained into subsequent generations.

Conclusion

The sinking of the *Arandora Star* in 1940 was an historical event that impacted communities in both Britain and Italy. By employing a transnational lens to understand the legacy and heritage that have developed in the ship's wake, two differing perspectives on the wartime incident as well as differential contextualization of the victims have emerged. In Britain, the *AS* remains firmly situated within the wartime milieux of internment, deportation and 'enemies within', the 'alien' and discriminatory roots of the policy being less well articulated. For descendants of victims, a troubled legacy and resilient memory persists, although this is now expressed through a national commemorative infrastructure with some more positive overtones, including reclamation of Italianness, belonging and contribution to British society. In Italy, while wartime content is implicit and a degree of blame is attributed to Britain, contextualization has developed more within the narrative of emigration. The 'tragedy', having been largely depoliticized, epitomizes the suffering and discrimination that emigrants experience. With the eightieth anniversary just past, awareness of the *Arandora Star* continues to grow in both countries. In Italy, there appears to be increasing political willingness to support the post-memory generations in Britain,[76] and indeed high-level perception of the *Arandora* as a vector encouraging reconnection with present-day Italy. Meanwhile, heritage activism is vibrant, especially in Britain, where a flow of new ideas continues to emerge. Looking ahead, only time will tell if performative remembering will endure until the centenary in 2040 and perhaps beyond.

Notes

1. A total of 1,673 men.
2. HO 215/429 'Sinking of the SS Arandora Star: List of Missing Persons' (1942); FO 371/25210/8942 'Internment of Foreign Subjects' (1940), The National Archives, Kew.
3. Terri Colpi, 'Chaff in the Winds of War? The Arandora Star, Not Forgetting and Commemoration at the 80th Anniversary', *Italian Studies* 75/4 (2020): 394–5.
4. Matteo Petrelli, 'Mussolini's Mobilities. Transnational Movements between Fascist Italy and Italian Communities Abroad', *Journal of Migration History* 1/1 (2015): 100–20.
5. Claudia Baldoli, *Exporting Fascism: Italian Fascists and Britain's Italians in the 1930s* (Oxford: Berg, 2003), 67–90.
6. Lucio Sponza, *Divided Loyalties: Italians in Britain during the Second World War* (Bern: Peter Lang, 2000), 95–8.
7. Terri Colpi, 'The Impact of the Second World War on the British Italian Community', in *The Internment of Aliens in Twentieth Century Britain*, ed. David Cesarani and Tony Kushner (London: Frank Cass, 1993), 173–4 and Sponza, *Divided Loyalties*, 103–4.
8. Variation was evident in timing of arrest and modality of detention in addition to inconsistency of decisions on length of residence, citizenship and state of health. Home Office Commissioner, Alexander Patterson, reviewing Italian deportees in Canada reported many had Scottish accents, concluding the Scottish police had interpreted instructions more vigorously than in England. HO 200/117/163 'Civilian Internees sent from UK to Canada: Report by Alexander Patterson to Home Secretary' (1941–1942), The National Archives, Kew.
9. Lucio Sponza, 'The British Government and the Internment of Italians', in *The Internment of Aliens*, ed. David Cesarani and Tony Kushner (London: Frank Cass, 1993), 129.
10. Terri Colpi, *The Italian Factor: The Italian Community in Great Britain* (Edinburgh: Mainstream, 1991), 119.
11. Pietro Zorza, Arandora Star: Il Dovere di Ricordarli (Glasgow: [suppl.] *Italiani in Scozia*, 1985).
12. Wendy Ugolini, *Experiencing War as the 'Enemy Other': The Italian Scottish Experience in World War II* (Manchester: Manchester University Press, 2011), 224, 232–7.
13. Colpi, 'Chaff in the Winds', 398–9.
14. Sergio Mattarella, 'Dichiarazione Del Presidente Mattarella Nell'Anniversario Dell'Affondamento Della "Arandora Star"', *Presidenza Della Repubblica*, 2 July 2020, https://www.quirinale.it/elementi/49634 (accessed 15 March 2021).
15. Pierangelo Campodonico, 'Il Caso "Arandora Star": Tragedia Bellica o Massacro degli Emigranti?', *No-Where-Next|War-Diaspora-Origin*, Cassino, 6 May 2013, https://www.altreitalie.it/la_finestra_di_altreitalie/news/no-where-next__war-diaspora-origin_convergenze_ed_esplorazioni_di_metodo_intorno_allemigrazione_italiana.kl. (accessed 9 August 2021). See also notes 38 and 39.
16. Filippo Focardi, 'Italy's Amnesia Over War Guilt: "The Evil Germans" Alibi', *Mediterranean Quarterly* 25/4 (2014): 9–10.
17. Andrea Tagliasacchi, President of Lucca Province, wrote to Prime Minister Tony Blair. See Richard Owen, 'Britain Urged to Pay for Lives Lost in U-Boat Attack', *The Times*, 11 September 2004, https://www.thetimes.co.uk/article/britain-urged-to-pay-for-lives-lost-in-u-boat-attack-z9k7svjc3wg (accessed 21 April 2021) and The Newsroom, 'Play Sparks Debate Over Whether Italians Deserve Apology for Wartime Internment',

The Scotsman, 11 March 2010, https://www.scotsman.com/arts-and-culture/play-sparks-debate-over-whether-italians-deserve-apology-wartime-internment-1730439 (accessed 5 May 2021).
18. From a total of around 200 bodies recovered on the Irish and Scottish coastlines, 21 Italians were identifiable.
19. Manuela D'Amore, 'Neutralising "Difference by Silence", "Choosing to Remain Peripheral": Xenophobia, Marginalization and Death in Italian Scottish Migrant Narratives of World War II', in *The Migration Conference 2020, Proceedings: Migration and Integration*, ed. Ibrahim Sirkeci and Merita Zulfiu Alili (London: Transnational Press, 2020), 131–4. See also Anne Pia, *Language of My Choosing* (Edinburgh: Luath Press, 2017), 60.
20. Ann Marie Di Mambro, *Tally's Blood* (Glasgow: Hodder Gibson, 2014). The play became a school curriculum text in Scotland for National Level 5 English Study.
21. *Dangerous Characters, The Sinking of the Arandora Star* (1987), [TV film] Dir. Alfio Bernabei. Channel 4, https://www.youtube.com/channel/UCwB2zeKlR4LWEJPXNzoAprg (accessed 22 April 2021).
22. Sound recordings of three Italian *AS* survivors and two other internees followed a commemorative event to mark the fiftieth anniversary of internment in 1990. Imperial War Museum, 'Sound Archive: Italians Interned', https://www.iwm.org.uk/collections/search?query=italians%20interned&filters%5BwebCategory%5D%5BSound%5D=on&pageSize=&media-records=records-with-media&style=list&page=0 (accessed 11 August 2021).
23. John Foot, *Italy's Divided Memory* (London: Palgrave Macmillan, 2009), 80–1.
24. Jenner Merletti, 'Quei 500 Italiani Dimenticati in fondo al Mare', *La Repubblica*, 2 July 2008, https://ricerca.repubblica.it/repubblica/archivio/repubblica/2008/07/02/quei-500-italiani-dimenticati-in-fondo-al.html (accessed 29 April 2021).
25. Rosario Forlenza, 'Sacrificial Memory and Political Legitimacy in Postwar Italy: Reliving and Remembering World War II', *History and Memory* 24/2 (2012): 73–5.
26. Pamela Ballinger, *History in Exile: Memory and Identity at the Borders of the Balkans* (Princeton: Princeton University Press, 2003), 129–67.
27. Panikos Panayi, 'A Marginalized Subject? The Historiography of Enemy Alien Internment in Britain' in *'Totally Un-English'? Britain's Internment of 'Enemy Aliens' in Two World Wars*, ed. Richard Dove (Amsterdam: Rodopi, 2005), 17–26.
28. Maria Serena Balestracci, *Arandora Star: Una Tragedia Dimenticata* (Pontremoli: I Quaderni del Corrieri Apuano, 2002) and Gian Antonio Stella, 'Arandora, Urla dal Silenzio dell' Oceano', *Corriere della Sera*, 30 November 2002, 33.
29. Pocket of affect numbers in Italy vary due to inclusions other than by birth.
30. Fondazione Paolo Cresci, 'Arandora Star', https://www.fondazionepaolocresci.it/search/node/arandora%20star (accessed 8 August 2021); Beatrice Manetti, 'Un Titanic dei Prigionieri Dimenticato per Sessant'Anni', *La Repubblica*, 12 October 2004, https://ricerca.repubblica.it/repubblica/archivio/repubblica/2004/10/12/un-titanic-dei-prigionieri-dimenticato-per-sessant.html (accessed 13 August 2021); and Premio Borgo Val di Taro, *Scritture dell'Emigrazione, Eventi Collaterali*, 21 September 2006, https://www.puntodincontro.com.mx/pdf/premioborgovaltaro.pdf (accessed 13 August 2012). See also Figure 3.2.
31. Colpi, *Italian Factor*, 271–8.
32. Maria Serena Balestracci, *Arandora Star: Dall'Oblio alla Memoria* (Parma: Monte Università Parma, 2008), 236, 367–73.

33. For example, *A Bench on the Road* by Laura Pasetti performed around Scotland and in Milano 2016; *Non Ditelo alle Stelle* by Federica Vicino performed in Pescara and London 2018.
34. AS conferences at Barga 2017, 2020 and Picinisco 2018, 2019 presented speakers from both countries.
35. *Italian Memories*, 2009, *Wales Breaks Its Silence: From Memories to Memorial*, 2010, in Wales; *Arandora Star*, 2010, *Migration Stories*, 2013, *The Scots Italians: A Family Portrait*, 2015–16, in Edinburgh; *Dangerous Characters*, 2015, *The Arandora Star Tragedy: 75 Years On*, 2015, in London and at Bardi, 2016; *Barga Ricorda Le Vittime Dell'Arandora Star*, 2017, at Barga.
36. For example, Joe Pieri, *River of Memory, Memoirs of a Scots Italian* (Edinburgh: Mercat Press, 2006); Mary Contini, *Dear Olivia, An Italian Journey of Love and Courage* (Edinburgh: Canongate, 2006); Natalie Dye, *Arandora Star* (London: Peach Publishing, 2014); and Melanie Hughes, *War Changes Everything* (London: Patrician Press, 2017).
37. For example, Caterina Soffici, *Nessuno Può Fermarmi* (Milano: Feltrinelli, 2017) and Maura Maffei, *Quel che Abisso Tace* (Piacenza: Parallelo45 Edizioni, 2019).
38. Caterina Soffici, 'La Strage degli Italiani Deportati da Churchill, *La Stampa*, 2 July 2020, https://www.lastampa.it/topnews/tempi-moderni/2020/07/02/news/la-str age-degli-italiani-deportati-da-churchill-446-vittime-nel-naufragio-al-largo-della-sco zia-1.39032596 (accessed 26 April 2021).
39. Gianluca Veneziani, 'La Strage Dimenticata. Gli Ottocento Italiani Deportati da Churchill', *Libero Quotidiano Milano*, 9 June 2020, https://www.uniecampus.it/filead min/public/rassegna_stampa/eventi/20200610/Libero_9_giugno_2020.pdf (accessed 22 April 2021).
40. An exception: Charlene Sweeney, 'Last Survivor Tells of Arandora Star U-Boat Tragedy', *The Times*, 28 May 2008, https://www.thetimes.co.uk/article/last-survi vor-tells-of-arandora-star-u-boat-tragedy-gtn2vz9tktf (accessed 5 May 2021).
41. An 'Arandora Star Campaign for Apology' with 150 members is effectively dormant.
42. Partito Democartico Londra, *80°Anniversario Arandora Star*, 2 July 2020, https://www.youtube.com/watch?v=fDnosKFOdLQ (accessed 22 April 2021) and News, '80 Anni Dopo, Il Consolato di Londra Ricorda La Tragedia Dell'Arandora Star', *La Repubblica*, 3 July 2020, https://www.repubblica.it/londra/2020/07/03/news/80_anni_dopo_il_consolato_di_londra_ricorda_la_tragedia_dell_arandora_star-260858179/ (accessed 22 April 2021).
43. Veysel Apaydin, 'The Interlinkage of Cultural Memory, Heritage and Discourses of Construction, Transformation and Destruction' in *Critical Perspectives on Cultural Memory and Heritage: Construction, Transformation and Destruction*, ed. Veysel Apaydin (London: UCL Press, 2020), 17.
44. Zofia Stemplowska, 'Remembering War: Fabre on Remembrance', *Journal of Applied Philosophy* 36/3 (2019): 382.
45. Colpi, 'The Impact', 179.
46. Margherita Becchetti and Ilaria La Fata, 'La Lotta Armata (1943–1945)' in *Storia di Parma VII, Tomo 1, Il Novecento. La Vita Politica*, ed. Giorgio Vecchio (Parma: Monte Università Parma Editore, 2017), 234–40 and Fiorenzo Sicuri, 'La Battaglia di Natale del '43 a Osacca Inizia L'Ora della Resistenza', *Gazzetta Di Parma*, 26 December 2020, https://www.gazzettadiparma.it/spettacoli/cultura/2020/12/26/news/la_battaglia_di_natale_del_43_a_osacca_inizia_l_ora_della_resistenza-4874770/ (accessed 8 August 2021).

47. My translation of Italian original.
48. Brian Conway, *Commemoration and Bloody Sunday, Pathways of Memory* (Basingstoke: Palgrave Macmillan, 2010), 6.
49. Memorials at Colonsay and Liverpool are to *all AS* victims.
50. Giuseppe Del Grosso from Borgotaro washed ashore on Colonsay.
51. Austrian and German officials and surviving British crewmembers were also present.
52. Erin Linn-Tynen, 'Reclaiming the Past as a Matter of Social Justice: African American Heritage, Representation and Identity in the United States' in *Critical Perspectives on Cultural Memory and Heritage: Construction, Transformation and Destruction* ed. Veysel Apaydin (London: UCL Press, 2020), 260–3.
53. Mary M. McCarthy, 'Political and Social Contestation in the Memorialization of "Comfort Women"', in *Public Memory in the Context of Transnational Migration and Displacement. Migrants and Monuments*, ed. Sabine Marschall (Cham: Palgrave Macmillan, 2020), 135.
54. Graeme Hetherington, 'Sad Tale of the Unlucky 13', *Northern Echo*, 3 July 2009, https://www.thenorthernecho.co.uk/opinion/leader/4473099.sad-tale-unlucky-13/ (accessed 19 April 2021).
55. Marco Giudici, 'Migration History and Nation-Building: The Role of Museums and Memorials in Post-Devolution Wales', in *Museums and Migration: History, Memory and Politics*, ed. Laurence Gourievidis (London: Routledge, 2014), 217–21.
56. Paulette Pelosi and David Evans, eds., *Arandora Star Memorial Fund in Wales* (Llanelli: Mike Clarke Printing, 2010), 3.
57. Giudici, 'Migration History', 221.
58. Bruna Chezzi, 'Wales Breaks its Silence: From Memory to Memorial and Beyond. The Italians in Wales during the Second World War', *Italian Studies* 69/3 (2014): 380–1, 392.
59. Television coverage: Cardiff Cathedral, 'Remembering the Arandora Star', https://www.cardiffcathedral.org.uk/remembering-the-arandora-star/ (accessed 14 May 2021).
60. Mario Conti, 'Opening Address', *Italian Cloister Garden Inauguration*, 16 May 2011, http://www.italiancloister.org.uk/message.htm (accessed 12 April 2021).
61. Sweeney, 'Last Survivor'. See note 40.
62. Colpi, 'Chaff in the Winds', 409.
63. Anna Cento Bull and Hans Lauge Hansen, 'On Agonistic Memory', *Memory Studies* 9/4 (2016): 398.
64. Peter Capella, ed., *The Arandora Star Tragedy: 75 Years On – London's Italian Community Remembers* (London: [no pub.], 2015), 10–14.
65. Loretta Baldassar, 'Migration Monuments in Italy and Australia: Contesting Histories and Transforming Identities', *Modern Italy* 11/1 (2006): 60.
66. See: Toni Ricciardi, *Marcinelle, 1956. Quando La Vita Valeva Meno del Carbone* (Roma: Donzelli Editore, 2016); Laura Garavini 'Marcinelle Ferita Indelebile', *Agenzia Internazionale Stampa Estero*, 9 August 2021, https://aise.it/politica/garavini-iv-marcinelle-ferita-indelebile-e-lezione-senza-tempo-su-diritto-al-lavoro-e-alla-sicurezza/164346/115 (accessed 19 August 2021) and Richard Gambino, *Vendetta: A True Story of the Worst Lynching in America, The Mass Murder of Italian-Americans in New Orleans in 1891* (Toronto: Guernica Editions, 2000); Gian Antonio Stella, 'Gli Italiani Linciati a New Orleans', *Corriere della Sera*, 9 April 2019, https://www.corriere.it/opinioni/19_aprile_09/gli-italiani-linciati-new-orleans-2aedd3ac-5ad6-11e9-a26f-7e2e79e4f044.shtml (accessed 7 August 2021).

67. Foot, *Divided Memory*, 81.
68. *Lili Marlene, Le Mille Guerre degli Italiani*, [TV programme] Dir. Pietro Suber. Mediaset Focus: Canale35, 10 June, 2020.
69. Giuseppe Conti, 'Arandora Star. Una Storia da Ricordare', *Valcenoweb*, 15 March 2019, http://www.valcenoweb.it/2019/03/15/23410/ (accessed 23 April 2021).
70. An *AS* memorial plaque was unveiled in Birmingham to four victims in 2015 and in July 2021, a memorial to all Italian victims was placed at Termoncarragh cemetery in County Mayo on the west coast of Ireland where, alongside one identified Italian, unidentified bodies were buried. Michael Higgins, President of Ireland, sent a letter of support, which he read aloud for a YouTube video of the occasion. See 'Arandora Star Lettera Presidente D'Irlanda Michael D Higgins Ottantunesimo Anniversario', https://www.youtube.com/watch?v=2JyeqBBf4ZU&t=4s (accessed 15 July 2021).
71. See David McLean, 'Richard Demarco Calls for Edinburgh Memorial to Arandora Star Victims', *Edinburgh Evening News*, 2 July 2020, https://www.edinburghnews.scotsman.com/heritage-and-retro/retro/richard-demarco-calls-edinburgh-memorial-arandora-star-victims-2902230 (accessed 24 April 2021).
72. Edoardo Paolozzi, 'Texts for Monte Cassino', *Edinburgh Review*, 104 (2000): 19.
73. Remembered at Colonsay, Borgotaro and Italian Cloister Garden, Glasgow. Additionally, there is a gravestone at St Kentigern's Cemetery, Glasgow, where Del Grosso's body was finally buried.
74. A special issue on the Arandora Star has been commissioned by the journal *Modern Italy* for publication in 2024.
75. Edoardo Ceresa, 'The Ceresa Family from Piemonte, 1890–1940 and Beyond', *Anglo Italian Family History Society: Italian Roots Newsletter*, February 2021 (members only access).
76. President Sergio Mattarella of Italy, conferred the prestigious *Medaglia del Presidente della Repubblica* – President's Medal – upon the 'Arandora Star Remembered' conference. According to Italian member of parliament, Onorevole Massimo Ungaro, who participated at the symposium, this can be understood as 'acknowledging the great sacrifice suffered by the Italian community in the UK'.

Bibliography

Apaydin, Veysel. 'The Interlinkage of Cultural Memory, Heritage and Discourses of Construction, Transformation and Destruction'. In *Critical Perspectives on Cultural Memory and Heritage: Construction, Transformation and Destruction*, edited by Veysel Apaydin, 13–19. London: UCL Press, 2020.

Baldassar, Loretta. 'Migration Monuments in Italy and Australia: Contesting Histories and Transforming Identities'. *Modern Italy* 11, no. 1 (2006): 43–62.

Baldoli, Claudia. *Exporting Fascism: Italian Fascists and Britain's Italians in the 1930s*. Oxford: Berg, 2003.

Balestracci, Maria Serena. *Arandora Star: Dall'Oblio alla Memoria*. Parma: Monte Università Parma, 2008.

Balestracci, Maria Serena. *Arandora Star: Una Tragedia Dimenticata*. Pontremoli: I Quaderni del Corrieri Apuano, 2002.

Ballinger, Pamela. *History in Exile: Memory and Identity at the Borders of the Balkans*. Princeton: Princeton University Press, 2003.

Becchetti, Margherita, and Ilaria La Fata. 'La Lotta Armata (1943–1945)'. In *Storia di Parma VII, Tomo 1, Il Novecento. La Vita Politica*, edited by Giorgio Vecchio, 231–65. Parma: Monte Università Parma Editore, 2017.
Capella, Peter, ed. *The Arandora Star Tragedy: 75 Years On – London's Italian Community Remembers*. London: [no pub.], 2015.
Cento Bull, Anna, and Hans Lauge Hansen. 'On Agonistic Memory'. *Memory Studies* 9, no. 4 (2016): 390–404.
Chezzi, Bruna. 'Wales Breaks its Silence: From Memory to Memorial and Beyond. The Italians in Wales during the Second World War'. *Italian Studies* 69, no. 3 (2014): 376–93.
Colpi, Terri. 'Chaff in the Winds of War? The Arandora Star, Not Forgetting and Commemoration at the 80th Anniversary'. *Italian Studies* 75, no. 4 (2020): 389–410.
Colpi, Terri. 'The Impact of the Second World War on the British Italian Community'. In *The Internment of Aliens in Twentieth Century Britain*, edited by David Cesarani and Tony Kushner, 167–87. London: Frank Cass, 1993.
Colpi, Terri. *The Italian Factor: The Italian Community in Great Britain*. Edinburgh: Mainstream, 1991.
Contini, Mary. *Dear Olivia, An Italian Journey of Love and Courage*. Edinburgh: Canongate, 2006.
Conway, Brian. *Commemoration and Bloody Sunday, Pathways of Memory*. Basingstoke: Palgrave Macmillan, 2010.
D'Amore, Manuela. 'Neutralising "Difference by Silence", "Choosing to Remain Peripheral": Xenophobia, Marginalization and Death in Italian Scottish Migrant Narratives of World War II'. In *The Migration Conference 2020, Proceedings: Migration and Integration*, edited by Ibrahim Sirkeci and Merita Zulfiu Alili, 131–4. London: Transnational Press, 2020.
Di Mambro, Ann Marie. *Tally's Blood*. Glasgow: Hodder Gibson, 2014.
Dove, Richard, ed. *'Totally Un-English'? Britain's Internment of 'Enemy Aliens' in Two World Wars*. Amsterdam: Rodopi, 2005.
Dye, Natalie. *Arandora Star*. London: Peach Publishing, 2014.
Focardi, Filippo. 'Italy's Amnesia Over War Guilt: "The Evil Germans" Alibi'. *Mediterranean Quarterly* 25, no. 4 (2014): 5–26.
Foot, John. *Italy's Divided Memory*. London: Palgrave Macmillan, 2009.
Forlenza, Rosario. 'Sacrificial Memory and Political Legitimacy in Postwar Italy. Reliving and Remembering World War II'. *History and Memory* 24, no. 2 (2012): 73–116.
Gambino, Richard. *Vendetta: A True Story of the Worst Lynching in America, the Mass Murder of Italian-Americans in New Orleans in 1891*. Toronto: Guernica Editions, 2000.
Giudici, Marco. 'Migration History and Nation-Building: The Role of Museums and Memorials in Post-Devolution Wales'. In *Museums and Migration: History, Memory and Politics*, edited by Laurence Gourievidis, 216–27. London: Routledge, 2014.
Hughes, Melanie. *War Changes Everything*. London: Patrician Press, 2017.
Linn-Tynen, Erin. 'Reclaiming the Past as a Matter of Social Justice: African American Heritage, Representation and Identity in the United States'. In *Critical Perspectives on Cultural Memory and Heritage: Construction, Transformation and Destruction*, edited by Veysel Apaydin, 255–68. London: UCL Press, 2020.
Maffei, Maura. *Quel che Abisso Tace*. Piacenza: Parallelo45 Edizioni, 2019.
Marschall, Sabine, ed. *Public Memory in the Context of Transnational Migration and Displacement: Migrants and Monuments*. Cham: Palgrave McMillan, 2020.

McCarthy, Mary M. 'Political and Social Contestation in the Memorialization of "Comfort Women"'. In *Public Memory in the Context of Transnational Migration and Displacement: Migrants and Monuments*, edited by Sabine Marschall, 127–56. Cham: Palgrave Macmillan, 2020.

Panayi, Panikos. 'A Marginalized Subject? The Historiography of Enemy Alien Internment in Britain'. In *'Totally Un-English'? Britain's Internment of 'Enemy Aliens' in Two World Wars*, edited by Richard Dove, 17–26. Amsterdam: Rodopi, 2005.

Paolozzi, Eduardo. 'Texts for Monte Cassino'. *Edinburgh Review* 104 (2000): 7–19.

Pelosi, Paulette, and David Evans, eds. *Arandora Star Memorial Fund in Wales*. Llanelli: Mike Clarke Printing, 2010.

Petrelli, Matteo. 'Mussolini's Mobilities. Transnational Movements between Fascist Italy and Italian Communities Abroad'. *Journal of Migration History* 1, no. 1 (2015): 100–20.

Pia, Anne. *Language of My Choosing*. Edinburgh: Luath Press, 2017.

Pieri, Joe. *River of Memory, Memoirs of a Scots Italian*. Edinburgh: Mercat Press, 2006.

Pistol, Rachel. 'Remembering the Internment of "Enemy Aliens" during the Second World War on the Isle of Man, and in Australia and Canada'. In *The Jews, The Holocaust and the Public: The Legacies of David Cesarani*, edited by Larissa Allwork and Rachel Pistol, 93–114. Cham: Palgrave Macmillan, 2019.

Ricciardi, Toni. *Marcinelle, 1956. Quando La Vita Valeva Meno del Carbone*. Roma: Donzelli Editore, 2016.

Soffici, Caterina. *Nessuno Può Fermarmi*. Milano: Feltrinelli, 2017.

Sponza, Lucio, 'The British Government and the Internment of Italians'. In *The Internment of Aliens in Twentieth Century Britain*, edited by David Cesarani and Tony Kushner, 125–44. London: Frank Cass, 1993.

Sponza, Luico. *Divided Loyalties: Italians in Britain During the Second World War*. Bern: Peter Lang, 2000.

Stemplowska, Zofia. 'Remembering War: Fabre on Remembrance'. *Journal of Applied Philosophy* 36, no. 3 (2019): 382–90.

Ugolini, Wendy. *Experiencing War as the 'Enemy Other': The Italian Scottish Experience in World War II*. Manchester: Manchester University Press, 2011.

Zorza, Pietro. Arandora Star: Il Dovere di Ricordarli. Glasgow: [suppl.] *Italiani in Scozia*, 1985.

4

Huyton: A transit camp near Liverpool

Jennifer Taylor

Introduction

The first part of this chapter presents an overview of the location and facilities of Huyton Internment Camp in its early months, before going on to claim that a change of leadership led to reforms resulting in improved morale among the detainees. The chapter later describes the post-war eradication of the camp boundaries, but concludes by arguing that, as some memory of the past is retained by local people, appropriate heritage responses may yet be developed.

The war years

In the 1960s and 1970s, the village of Huyton near Liverpool was well-known as the constituency of Prime Minister Harold Wilson. Decades earlier, however, from 17 May 1940 until October 1941, it had housed up to 5,000 'enemy aliens', German and Austrian civilians, detained in accordance with Churchill's policy of mass internment. In June, when Italy entered the war, these unfortunates (predominantly, although not exclusively, racially persecuted refugees from Hitler) were joined by Italian civilians, and accommodated at the newly built corporation housing estate at Woolfall Heath (Figure 4.1).

Originally, the camp covered a fairly modest area, estimated to be approximately twenty acres, bounded by part of Hillside Avenue, Pennard Avenue as far as the junction with Heath Avenue and part of Altmoor Road. To accommodate the influx of internees experienced in the first few months, tents were erected in the spaces between the houses. Additionally, wooden huts positioned between Parbrook Close and the perimeter fence served as mess huts, as barrack rooms for additional accommodation and, eventually, entertainment venues. As the original area of the camp provided insufficient accommodation, the tented camp area was extended to the west and the north to include Bruton Road and beyond.[1]

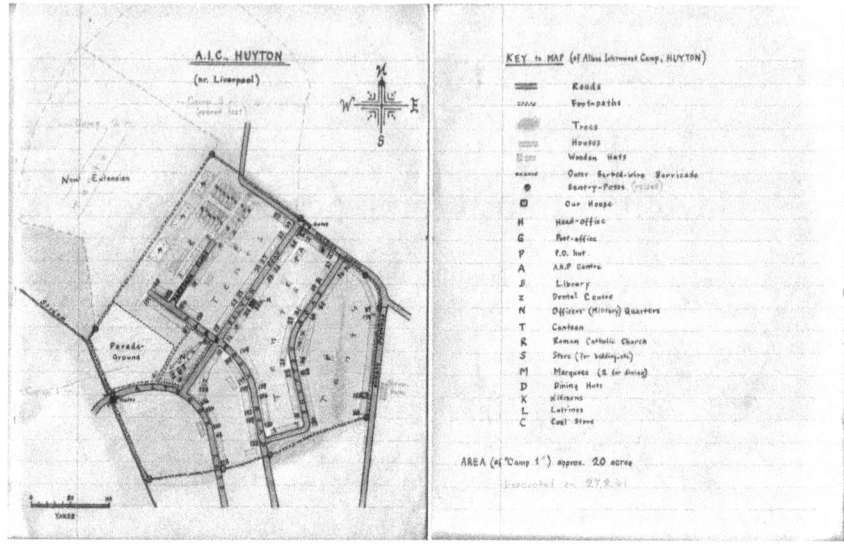

Figure 4.1 Sketch map of Huyton Camp by Martin Dalheim, 1941
Source: Courtesy the Estate of Martin Karl Eberhard Dalheim.

The camp was designated a transit camp, the internees destined to be transferred to the Isle of Man (the principal location of civilian internment camps) or to be deported to the Dominions – its relative proximity to the Liverpool docks presumably one of the factors for the choice of location. Being a transit camp meant numbers were fluid and there was a considerable amount of movement, a circumstance which, as we shall see, adversely impacted conditions in the camp.

In May a government-sponsored film, presumably for broadcasting as a newsreel or similar, recorded the arrival of some of the first internees, documenting aspects of everyday life such as socializing in the street, hanging out the washing and stuffing sacks with straw to make palliasses.[2] However, the high barbed wire perimeter fence, complete with a single guard defending it with a fixed bayonet, also featured.[3] These images were accompanied by the commentary chilling in its callousness: 'To be interned in Britain is like paradise when compared to the Nazi concentration camps.'[4] The description of Huyton, which appeared in the *Liverpool Daily Post* on 22 May, was somewhat more measured in tone although equally misleading in its description of the camp and its facilities:

> The extent of the camp permits the internees plenty of freedom ... each [house] will accommodate some nine persons, and ... has its own bathroom ... the younger members will be able to continue their studies at an educational centre staffed by priests, parsons and professors from the community ... A canteen has been opened.

The optimistic assessments of the situation evinced here did not correspond to the experience of the internees themselves. The relative freedom of the camp outlined in the local press was not apparent to the Austrian novelist Robert Neumann. He was so horrified at the militaristic atmosphere in the camp that he volunteered for the first transport to the Isle of Man on 7 June; Huyton was, he averred, just like hell.[5] Moreover, by July, four suicides had been recorded, and there had been a further two unsuccessful attempts.[6] It must also be remembered that many of those 'younger members' mentioned here had, on reaching the age of sixteen, been summarily arrested and removed from their schools. Such was the experience of John Goldsmith who had been detained shortly before sitting for his O level examinations.[7]

Unlike many camps in the Isle of Man, Huyton could not boast a camp newspaper, but visual evidence of daily life is provided by artwork completed at the camp, and the extent of contemporary records in the form of reports and diaries is such that the available evidence is substantial enough to provide a comprehensive picture of camp conditions.

At first sight the accommodation would seem to be more than adequate, yet the houses were overcrowded, with at least twelve men assigned to each. Moreover, not all could be accommodated in the houses. Some had to sleep in tents while others, like the elderly Viennese engineer Wilhelm Hollitscher, shared a barrack hut designed for twenty with forty-three others.[8] The tents lacked washing facilities and the houses lacked hot water and, most distressingly, furniture. In the circumstances, it was not surprising that the internees resorted to self-help – the doors of many of the houses were ripped off and made into furniture for sale, while the skilled craftsmen among them had obtained additional wood by cutting out portions of the rafters. Since the British soldiers themselves profited from the deals, a blind eye was turned to this abuse of government property. On 31 May, one of the first official visitors to the camp, the Chief Rabbi of Liverpool, found three elderly rabbis sleeping on the floor. The situation improved gradually. In late May, a modest number of beds arrived for the sick and elderly, and once a new commandant was appointed in mid-July, each house was provided with a table, a chair and a bench.

As in all internment camps, the detainees were subject to army discipline. Very soon a system of self-government was set up on hierarchical principles: the internees themselves elected house fathers, street fathers, a camp speaker and deputy speaker.[9] Unfortunately, in the early months of the camp, these representatives exerted little influence on the camp authorities. For example, in May the Austrian composer Hans Gál commented that every suggestion put forward by the detainees met with official opposition on the grounds that implementation would be too difficult.[10]

The men were supplied with army rations which initially proved to be woefully inadequate for the rapidly increasing number of detainees. By the end of May, these rations could be supplemented by food and luxury items such as cigarettes, chocolates and alcoholic beverages purchased from the canteen situated in Hut 14 between Parbrook Close and Belton Road. On 4 August, a Viennese café was opened at 50 Bruton Road, decorated with atmospheric frescoes of the wine harvest and steamers on the Danube. Unfortunately, however, the whole internee population was affected by the mud which, even in July, had to be negotiated on the way to the mess huts. This was due to the unfinished nature of the site since the twelve mess huts were placed in a field between Belton Road and Hillside Avenue.[11] Apart from the food, all other items, such as toiletries, shoe and house cleaning materials, and even medicines, had to be purchased. A small emolument (typically two shillings per week) was paid to those internees involved in the internal administration of the camp; others received grants from charitable sources, such as trades unions or the Quakers. Otherwise, detainees were dependent on funds from their families, which could be sent in the form of postal orders, or grants from the internal welfare fund, which was set up and financed by the internees. Theoretically, each detainee had an account into which his money was paid, but initially internees found it difficult to access their funds.[12]

The camp post office provided an essential service in keeping the men in contact with the outside world. Letter-writing was permitted but censored and restricted in frequency and length, communications had to be on a *pro-forma* of twenty-two lines. While outgoing letters were limited to two per week, there was no restriction on the number of letters and parcels that could be received, although the regulations did not permit letters in parcels. Additionally, no visual material (such as children's drawings) was permitted in letters for security reasons. Telegrams were allowed and, despite their relatively high cost, proved so popular that, in August, the commandant had to order that their use should be for emergencies only. Postal delays had been occasioned by wartime damage to the transport network and by censorship; outgoing mail was censored in the camp and incoming mail in an office in Liverpool. In the first weeks the camp was opened no attempt was made to censor the mail, and so the messages the anxious refugees sent to their families had simply piled up in the camp office. Additionally, the mail for the internment camp had to compete with that of Knowsley Park, the prisoner-of-war camp in nearby Longview Lane, often overwhelming the Liverpool office. Communications were improved when the ban on newspapers was lifted on 15 July and detainees were permitted to listen to radio news broadcasts in the radio shack. This had to be done in a group as private radios were banned.

The easing of restrictions on communications meant a reduction in rumour and speculation and an improvement in morale. Later, however, once the blitz had started, reports of the bombing caused anxiety for the safety of families. One omission from the camp arrangements which caused particular concern was the lack of air raid shelters. Merseyside had its first air raid warning on 25 June and the air raids intensified in early August, continuing for many months. Permission to dig air raid shelters using internee labour was declined, and the men were expected to congregate on the ground floor of their houses during air raids. Although a bomb fell just five yards from the camp on 25 August, and on 30 August an incendiary bomb landed in the camp itself, which was successfully extinguished, no direct hit was received and no casualties suffered. That was just as well as the medical provision was wholly inadequate. There was only one army doctor available for the whole camp, but the medically qualified internees offered their services so a camp hospital could be opened, albeit ill-equipped. The seriously ill were sent to military or prison hospitals.[13]

The impression which emerges from the written records is that conditions were extremely poor in the first three months of its existence. A letter from a newly released internee, which appeared in the press in early August, stated that 'for months the camp was in a state of chaos'.[14] The writer claims the men had no access to their money, which had been confiscated on arrival, but nevertheless a lively black market in smuggled goods had been established. Moreover, the arrangements for the deportations to the Dominions, which took place at the beginning of July, were execrable.

The first holder of the post of camp commandant, a Major, has perhaps mercifully remained anonymous since his incompetence is clear – his efforts to sustain morale were inadequate and he was unequal to the task of administering the camp efficiently. The journalist and political activist Eugen Brehm describes him as a drunken Scotsman, while François Lafitte, whose account of internment was published in the autumn of 1940, edited his name out, presumably for security reasons, stating only that he was a Major, the rank normally held by those exercising such responsibilities.[15] Hans Gál indicates a further reason for this anonymity: the commandant was rarely seen round the camp, delegating the day-to-day running to a certain Captain Tanner. From Gál's account it can be seen that in May, the internees had little more than a roof over their heads although those in tents, which were not waterproof, arguably did not even have that. In sum, there were insufficient rations, inadequate medical provisions for the many sick and elderly, no newspapers or radio, no canteen, no access to money and, finally, no mail was leaving the camp.

On 21 June an anonymous Austrian, whose diary gives a vivid impression of conditions in the early months, wrote, 'I have never been so hungry in all my life.'[16] To be fair to the commandant, some of these deficiencies were beyond his control: newspapers and radio were banned by the War Office, a ban which ended once the Home Office had taken over responsibility for the running of the internment camps. The inadequate rations, too, were in part attributable to the nature of the camp as a transit camp. Gál records on 22 May that the camp was on half rations because too many newcomers had arrived; a similar situation pertained just over a month later, when the Austrian diarist wrote, 'We are completely overcrowded, but in spite of that new people arrive all the time. We have no idea how to feed them.'[17] When approached about the inadequacy of the food, the commandant had replied 'that he was only liable not to let us starve, but he could not give us enough that we would not be hungry'.[18] In a lightly fictionalized account, the painter Alfred Lomnitz is even more scathing, having him say, 'My orders are to keep the men here. I have no instructions about feeding them.'[19] This seems typical of the original commandant's mentality. He had no interest in intervening with the authorities in order to improve conditions. In fact, according to a report by the elderly pacifist Otto Lehmann-Russbueldt,[20] he constantly feared mutiny and revolt, to which end he had all the metal fittings removed: the foot scrapers by the back doors and the gates too, since they had latches on them, so that soon the almost pleasant suburban street scene photographed on 21 May became a thing of the past.[21]

It was hardly surprising that this manner of running the camp led to an atmosphere of suspicion and fear resulting in suicides and attempted suicides. Moreover, when the deportations began, panic at the prospect of being sent overseas to an unknown destination ensued. Lehmann-Russbueldt reports that before the *Dunera* left for Australia, many internees had been forced onto the transport at bayonet point in order to make up the numbers since not enough volunteers had been forthcoming. The approximately forty-eight men who had prudently concealed themselves did not even receive a warning on emerging from hiding the following day.[22] One of these was Siegfried Nissel, later to become a member of the Amadeus Quartet.[23]

Huyton's function as a transit camp can be illustrated by the large-scale movement of men in June and early July. In June, men had been regularly transferred to the Isle of Man: 400 on 7 June, over 2,000 between 13 and 17 June, and 600 on 3 July. On 21 June, the deportations to the Dominions began when the *Duchess of York* left for Canada, carrying a quota of internees from Huyton. Two further ships, the *Arandora Star* and the *Ettrick*, left Liverpool shortly afterwards for the same destination, and the *Dunera*, bound for Australia, left on 10 July, among its passengers some survivors of the ill-fated *Arandora Star* which had been torpedoed and sunk in the Atlantic on 2 July.[24] These departures were matched by a steady flow of arrivals: 780 on 2 July, a transport from Kempton Park on 4 July, 100 on 12 July and 500 on 2 August, so that it was estimated that the camp, which had originally held 2,500, by the end of July accommodated 5,000 men.[25]

Eugen Brehm wondered whether the commandant was relieved of his post because of the way the deportations were mismanaged for, in early July, after barely two months in the job, the original commandant was replaced by a more senior officer, Lieutenant-Colonel S. W. Slatter, who had previously overseen all the recently opened internment camps on the Isle of Man.[26] It is tempting to suppose that the employment of this experienced officer was a measure expressly designed to compensate for the incompetence of his predecessor. In any event he must have been made aware of the camp's shortcomings for it is clear that the new commandant came to the job with a reforming agenda. Rabbi Dr Solomon Schonfeld who, with Bishop Bell, visited the camp on 18 July very soon after Slatter's appointment, commented that the new commandant was determined to improve the spirit of the camp and its facilities.[27] Lomnitz described how the obstructionist mentality of the original commandant and his staff was replaced by a can-do mentality. For example, in the matter of hot water, a compromise was reached; coal could be obtained, but the internees would have to pay for it themselves.[28] A market soon developed, and Hollitscher was able to buy a bucket of hot water for 3d.[29] The introduction of army cooks led to an improvement in the meals; previously the internees themselves prepared the food in a field kitchen in the open air. The diary entry of the factory manager Paul Bondy for 9 November, 'Haven't been to lunch but Neumann brings back Messing Officer's new sticky cake', graphically illustrates the improvement in the catering.[30] Lehmann-Russbueldt observed that, in contrast to his predecessor who rarely showed his face to the internees, the new commandant spent several hours one sweltering Sunday afternoon speaking to the internees and listening to their complaints.[31] Slatter also had the wit to realize that as well as ameliorating the material conditions in the camp, the key to raising morale was to improve communication with the outside world. On 2 August, Bondy noted that '[The] commandant says he is in touch with [the] Chief Censor at Liverpool every second day – personally or by phone'.[32] Lomnitz reported that the commandant returned from one such visit with 2,500 letters which were immediately distributed.[33]

Among the arrivals at Huyton occasioned by the policy of mass internment were men of diverse backgrounds who did not form part of the estimated 70 per cent of the camp's the refugee contingent. There were people who had been resident in Britain for some time but failed to keep their paperwork up to date, for example, a group of young Welsh miners, born in Germany when their fathers were stationed in the Rhineland as part of the occupying forces and a group of elderly Jews from Manchester who had neglected to apply for naturalization.[34] More worrying were the expatriates (estimated by Otto Lehmann-Russbueldt to comprise about 10 per cent of the camp), many of whom were considered to have decidedly Nazi sympathies.[35] Unfortunate billeting decisions caused friction between Nazis and the Jewish refugees. Moreover, as these expatriates were likely to have been employed, they were eligible for the first wave of releases in the summer, leading to the irony that the official procedures initially favoured those who potentially posed the greatest danger to Britain, while the refugees, who were by definition opposed to Hitler, remained interned.

A minority of the internees occupied their time with political activities. At the other end of the political spectrum to the Nazis were the communists. Bruno Retzlaff-Kresse, who shared a house at 57 Bruton Road with the poet Kurt Barthel (known as KuBa) and other young communists, stated that they actively sought employment in the mess huts so that they could use mealtimes for recruitment purposes.[36] Since Gál described mealtimes as chaotic and very noisy, this would seem to be an onerous task. In contrast to the communist attempt at proselytizing, Brehm's associates (mostly members of the socialist splinter groups) operated on the exact opposite basis, employing an almost paranoid exclusion from their meetings of those they suspected. At this time of the German–Soviet pact when German communists were masquerading as Social Democrats, such distrust most probably resulted from the fear of communist subversion.[37]

It is in the matter of artistic and cultural activities that the absence of a newspaper is particularly to be regretted, for it was customary to advertise the diverse activities of the camp and, on occasion, to print reviews of exhibitions and theatrical and musical performances. Although Gál mentions that cultural activity was discouraged by Captain Tanner on the grounds that it was too much trouble, the early period of the camp witnessed one outstanding cultural achievement. Writing for the only musical instruments in the camp that had somehow escaped confiscation, Gál composed the 'Huyton Suite' for flute and two violins. The process of composition and rehearsal of this chamber piece is described in some detail in his diary. As Gál was transported to the Isle of Man in mid June, performance in Huyton was out of the question; the suite was first performed in Douglas on 28 July.[38]

One of Slatter's areas of reform had been to devote more attention and resources to recreational facilities, a sure way of helping to alleviate the psychological pressure on internees worried about their families and facing the fear of deportation. Religious worship, it might be thought, would also contribute to an amelioration of morale. There are records of at least two religious groups: orthodox Jews and pastors of the German Confessional Church whose emigration Bishop Bell had facilitated; but apart from a reference to a Roman Catholic church on Martin Dalheim's map, no details of formal arrangements for worship seem to have survived.[39]

By the summer, frequent musical performances were possible. Maryan Rawicz (later known as half of the popular pianist duo Rawicz and Landauer) performed musical arrangements and songs from operettas.[40] Hollitscher gives detailed descriptions of the musical performances which he attended regularly in July and August.[41] Bondy records a concert performance in Hut 19 on 4 October, while among his papers in an undated flyer advertising a piano recital in Tent 3 by Peter Stadlen.[42] Additionally, both Hollitscher and Bondy make it clear that something approaching a university eventually developed. This was presumably encouraged by the provision of a library which, to a certain extent, compensated for the books and papers which had been confiscated on arrival. The library, organized by Lieutenant Brewer and staffed by six internees, eventually comprised approximately 800 volumes donated by various organizations including Jewish charities, the Red Cross and the Quakers.[43] Hollitscher mentions that his housefather supplied him with a list of lectures, and he frequently noted the title of the lectures he attended.[44] Between 26 July and his release in early December, Bondy records the titles of approximately fifty lectures, covering religion, the arts, economics, geography, history and politics.[45] In contrast, there are few references to the school; at the end of May Gál mentions that the school has an insufficient number of teachers to prepare the boys for their school-leaving examinations, and as we shall see, it receives a reference in Bondy's diary in September.[46]

The pursuit of cultural activities on any meaningful scale was dependent on the good will of the authorities; painters, in particular, needed materials. Alfred Lomnitz received drawing materials and was assigned a room he could use as a studio, and Walter Nessler and Hugo Dachinger were able to produce a substantial body of work portraying life in the camp. Some paintings were shown in Huyton at the end of August in an exhibition entitled *Art behind the Wire*, an event mentioned briefly by Bondy and more extensively by Hollitscher.[47] Dachinger's Huyton paintings were included in a later exhibition of his work, *Art Behind Barbed Wire*, held in Mooragh Camp on the Isle of Man in November 1940.[48]

Although Stadlen's piano recital took place in a tent, there was a designated hut, Hut 19, where dramatic performances could take place, such as 'Mr Dietz goes to Liverpool', presumably a satirical sketch of internee life.[49] Of this piece, only the title survives, but KuBa's dramatic activities are better documented.[50] With his youth group he organized performances of two pieces dealing with the recent history of Czechoslovakia: Louis Fürnberg's *Böhmische Passion (Bohemian Passion)*, and his own *Septembertage (Days in September)*, the latter written at Huyton in collaboration with the seventeen-year-old talented composer Gerhard Hadda. *Böhmische Passion*, an ambitious portrayal of Czechoslovak history with twelve leading roles, is arguably the largest dramatic enterprise of the internment period. *Septembertage*, a much shorter agitprop piece, deals with the events immediately prior to the German invasion of the Sudetenland from the perspective of a group of young anti-fascists. These activists brand the French and British politicians who had ceded Czech territory to Hitler as traitors.[51] On 28 September, Bondy noted that the school had been closed 'owing to communist propaganda', arguably as a consequence of this impertinence. True to his conviction, KuBa was later to become a prominent figure in the cultural scene of the German Democratic Republic.[52]

In 1941, internee numbers were reduced as release procedures took effect, and in October the camp was finally closed to internees and reverted to army use as the Western Command Depot.[53] Although the camp had been in existence for less than eighteen months, it had housed many men who would later play a prominent part in intellectual and political life in Germany, Austria and Britain. Among the former were the art historian Otto Pächt, the trade unionist Hans Gottfurcht and the social democratic politician Gerhard Lütkens, one of the first members of the West German Parliament. Among the latter were the art historian Ernst Gombrich, director of the Warburg Institute in London from 1959–72; the statistician Baron Claus Moser, director of the Central Statistical Office from 1967 to 1978; and the art historian Sir Nikolaus Pevsner, Professor of the History of Art at Birkbeck College, London, author and editor of the *Buildings of England* series.

Post-war developments

Once the army had no further use for the site, the temporary installations were removed and it reverted to the control of Liverpool Corporation for its original purpose of residential accommodation, initially housing families who had been bombed out. This meant that the streets which had formed part of the camp were re-integrated into the Woolfall Heath Estate, a process made all the easier since the roads which formed the perimeter of the camp, Hillside Avenue and Pennard Avenue, had never been completely in the camp area because they had been bisected by the boundary fence, as had Altmoor Road and Parbrook Road. Once the barbed wire had been removed, traffic could flow freely in and out of the area of the former camp. As the camp site was not retained as a discrete entity, the history of the post-war development of the site is synonymous with the development of the area as a whole.

A crucial aspect of this development was the improvement in the transport infrastructure which facilitated communications with Liverpool and the surrounding urban areas. In 1972, the M 57 (the Liverpool ring road) opened to the north; to the west the A 526 provided a convenient connection between this motorway and the A 57 to the south. Within this triangle, the camp area remained a residential enclave. In the course of the progressive urbanization of the area, the land formerly occupied by the camp extension was developed. Residential streets were built in the area between Parbrook Close and Stockbridge Lane, while an extra row of houses was added to Pennard Avenue. Apart from this increase in housing density, the most striking aspect of post-war development was the impact of the Conservative Government's Right to Buy policy in the 1980s, and a recent statistical summary of the post-code area shows a high proportion of owner occupiers.[54] In other respects, there is a high degree of stability and uniformity in the area. Few house sales have been recorded, and there is very little ethnic diversity; Belton Road and Shepton Road are listed as all white, while the majority of the residents fall into social classes C2, D and E, that is, skilled manual, semi-skilled or unskilled.[55] These factors would indicate that the present-day residents of the area are not very different from the first council tenants of the 1940s.

Preserving the memory

In the years which have passed since the war, the memory of the camp has been kept alive not just by the publication of the written narratives of the internees referred to above (publication of which in most cases occurred several years after the events were recorded in these journals) but also by oral history initiatives.[56] The Imperial War Museum holds thirty-eight records of former Huyton internees interviewed between 1978 and 2008, and the academic studies by Kochan and Harkins, which have been quoted above, contain recollections of former internees.[57] Additionally the works of Dachauer and Nessler appeared in public for the first time since the war, in an exhibition entitled *Art Behind Barbed Wire* held at the Walker Gallery in 2004.[58] Unfortunately these artworks, produced as they were under emergency conditions, are too fragile to be on permanent display, but the Gallery is in the process of digitization so that they may be enjoyed by a wider audience.

Memorialization of the site of the camp itself poses several difficulties. Firstly, civilian internment does not figure prominently in the consciousness of the nation. While the detention of military combatants in prisoner-of-war camps is an aspect of war made familiar not least by sensationalist escape narratives, the detention of civilians is a more arcane topic. This is particularly so in the context of the Second World War, for the mass incarceration of refugees from Hitler (including some survivors of concentration camps) runs counter to the myth of British decency. The second difficulty is the nature of the site itself. The re-integration into the housing estate means there are no clear-cut boundaries to distinguish the former camp from the surrounding area. A further difficulty is posed by the location of other former military installations nearby, namely, the U.S. Army transit camp on Blue Bell Lane and the prisoner-of-war camp on Longview Lane. The close proximity of these three historical sites has led to confusion among some researchers. Fortunately, there have recently been local initiatives which have gone some way to addressing these issues. In 2011, a video entitled *Bridge over the Bluebell* was produced as part of a community-led, inter-generational project of the same name funded by the Heritage Lottery Fund.[59] In this video, the civilian internment camp and the prisoner-of-war camp were presented in the context of the history of the Second World War as a whole. Local people who had been children at the time reported on their wartime memories of the camps, emphasizing the friendship and support afforded the prisoners by the local people. A further initiative was the Archive Resource for Knowsley (ARK) project, funded by the Heritage Lottery Fund. This wide-ranging endeavour included the 'World War II Huyton Camps' project, where the experiences of individuals living near the three wartime camps were explored. The culmination was an exhibition entitled 'Huyton Camps' held in Huyton Library in the summer of 2016.

Happily there is also an audio-visual legacy. Sixteen oral history interviews were undertaken, two of which (that of former internee Dr John Goldsmith and local resident Terry Hughes) can be seen on YouTube, while extracts from the interviews of other local residents can be accessed as an audio-file.[60] Dr Goldsmith commented on the internment process from the point of view of the internees, stressing the illogicality of detaining the opponents of Hitler, while Terry Hughes and other interviewees described their childhood experiences of living just beyond the camp boundaries and their daily consciousness of its presence in their area. This testimony could also serve as a source of topographical information to inform an audio-guide to the camp if a trail were to be established. Any proposal to erect a plaque or information board would face the difficulty of the eradication of the camp boundaries, meaning that there is no obvious focal point where these might be placed, although the site of the main gate on Woolfall Heath Avenue might be considered an appropriate location.

Situating the history of the internment camp within the wider context of the history of the city of Liverpool remains problematic. The irony is that the town of Huyton itself was developed in the nineteenth century as a refuge from the polluted city, and in the twentieth century, the corporation estate at Woolfall Heath was designed to serve a similar purpose. The camp must compete for public attention with a museum landscape which ranges from popular music (the Beatles Museum) to post-colonialism (the Museum of Slavery). It can only be hoped that the initiatives which have so far attracted funding from national sources will provide a secure basis for securing the history of Huyton Camp within the wider narrative of the history of Merseyside during the Second World War.

Conclusion

The poor conditions experienced in the first months of the camp were ameliorated by a change of leadership as attested in contemporary journals. Despite this extensive evidence, the preservation of the memory of this camp poses specific challenges. Nevertheless, the pioneering work of local historians provides a firm basis for future development.

Acknowledgements

Grateful thanks to Lin Rice (Archivist) and staff of Archive Resource for Knowsley' before (ARK) for providing me with information and material when the pandemic made a site visit impossible.

Notes

1. See two sketch maps by internees: Harry Seidler (1940) in Jessica Feather, *Art behind Barbed Wire* (Exhibition catalogue: National Museums Liverpool, 2004), 7; Martin Dalheim (1941) in Jennifer Taylor, ed., *Civilian Internment in Britain during WW2: Huyton Camp* (Southend-on-Sea: Anglo-German Family History Society, 2012), 12–13, also reproduced here as Figure 4.1.
2. See Peter and Leni Gillman, *'Collar the Lot!'* (London: Quartet Books, 1980), between 144–5.
3. See Feather, *Art*, 5.
4. Cited in Feather, *Art*, 6–7.
5. See R. Dove, '"KZ auf Englisch": Robert Neumann's Internment Diary', in *'England? Aber wo liegt es?'*, ed. Charmian Brinson, Richard Dove, Marian Malet and Jennifer Taylor (Munich: iudicium, 1996), 160.
6. François Lafitte, *The Internment of Aliens* (Harmondsworth: Penguin, 1940), 108.

7. 'Interview with Dr John Goldsmith, former internee at Huyton in WW2' (2016), https://www.youtube.com/watch?v=mi7TXxzDdJQ&list=PLthp8BKjJtZdonsEq18cErJeo0eRq9oOW&index=2 (28 August 2020); cf. also arrests of schoolchildren in Marian Malet and Anthony Grenville, eds, *Changing Countries* (London: Libris, 2002), 131–2.
8. Hollitscher's diary is published in Ines Newman, *Internment in Britain in 1940* (London: Vallentine Mitchel 2021), 69–137, here 81.
9. See Taylor, *Huyton Camp*, 49–50.
10. Eva Fox-Gál, ed., *Musik hinter Stacheldraht: Tagebuchblätter aus dem Sommer 1940 von Hans Gál* (Bern: Peter Lang, 2003); an English translation of the Huyton section is published in Taylor, *Huyton Camp*, 58–74, here 65.
11. See Seidler and Dalheim's sketch maps.
12. See Taylor, *Huyton Camp*, 65.
13. See Lafitte, *Internment*, 107–8; Margaret Harkins, 'Alien Internment at Huyton during World War II', in *A Prominent Place: Studies in Merseyside History*, ed. J. A. Davies and J. E. Hollinshead (Liverpool: Hope Press, 1999), 113–24.
14. 'I was Anderson's Prisoner', *Reynold's News*, 4 August 1940.
15. E. Brehm, 'Meine Internierung', *Exil* 6 (Frankfurt-am-Main, 1986/2), 41–62 here 44; an English version, 'My Internment', is deposited in Knowsley Archives; Lafitte, *Internment*, 108.
16. This diary was submitted to the Council of Austrians; a redacted version was published in Lafitte, *Internment*, 109–13; the full version in Taylor, *Huyton Camp*, 39–47; here 41.
17. 29 June, Taylor, *Huyton Camp*, 44.
18. 22 June, Lafitte, *Internment*, 110; Taylor, *Huyton Camp*, 41.
19. Alfred Lomnitz, *Never Mind, Mr. Lom* (London: Macmillan, 1941), 54.
20. Otto Lehmann-Russbueldt's report, dated 3 September, was submitted to Lord Lytton's Advisory Council on Aliens; for an English translation see Taylor, *Huyton Camp*, 48–57, here 51.
21. See Feather, *Art*, 9.
22. See Taylor, *Huyton Camp*, 49.
23. See ibid.; Ronald Stent, *A Bespattered Page: The Internment of His Majesty's Most Loyal Enemy Aliens* (London: Deutsch 1980), 150.
24. Additionally, the *Sobieski* left from Glasgow for Canada on 4 July.
25. Estimates are from eye-witness accounts; the army kept no formal record of numbers; see also Stent, *Bespattered*, 150.
26. See Brehm, 'Meine Internierung', 48.
27. Rabbi Dr Solomon Schonfeld, 'A Report on Visits to Internment Camps for Aliens' (1940), https://www.jewishvirtuallibrary.org/a-report-on-visits-to-internment-camps-for-aliens (3 September 2020).
28. See Lomnitz, *Never Mind*, 105.
29. See Newman, *Internment*, 89
30. The diary is held in 'Paul and Charlotte Bondy Papers', Institute of Modern Languages Research/Senate House Library, University of London, GB 0367 PCB; extracts from the diary are published in Taylor, *Huyton Camp*, 80–114; here 86.
31. See Taylor, *Huyton Camp*, 52.
32. Taylor, *Huyton Camp*, 96.
33. See Lomnitz, *Never Mind*, 98.
34. See Harkins, 'Huyton', 119–20; Miriam. Kochan, *Britain's Internees in the Second World War* (London: Macmillan, 1983), 72.

35. See Taylor, *Huyton Camp*, 52.
36. See Bruno Retzlaff-Kresse, *Kerker, Illegalität, Exil* (Berlin: Dietz, 1980), 275.
37. See Jennifer Taylor, '"Die geschworenen Feinde des nationalsozialistischen Deutschland": The Aspirations and Activities of Socialist Politicians Interned in Huyton in 1940', in *Political Exile and Exile Politics in Britain after 1933*, ed. Anthony Grenville and Andrea Reiter (Amsterdam/New York: Rodopi, 2011), 169–86.
38. Further performances followed on 31 July, 5 and 13 August.
39. See Charmian Brinson, 'Please Tell the Bishop of Chichester', *Contemporary Church History* 21/2 (2008): 288; Bishop Bell's reputation has suffered in recent years, but he was indefatigable in his support of the German-speaking refugees as this article shows.
40. See Ulrich Skaller's account in Kochan, *Internees*, 73.
41. See Newman, *Internment*, 95, 96, 99, 103, 104, 106, 112.
42. See note 30.
43. See Taylor, *Huyton Camp*, 54; Kochan, *Internees*, 72.
44. See Newman, *Internment*, 92, 103.
45. See Bondy Diary, entries 26 July–2 December.
46. See Taylor, *Huyton Camp*, 69.
47. An inadequately documented event until corroborated by the publication of the Hollitscher's diary; see Newman, *Internment*, 122.
48. See Feather, *Art*, 16.
49. An undated advertisement is among Bondy's papers.
50. See 'Theater in Huyton', *Freie Deutsche Kultur* (December 1940), 3–4; Brehm, 'Internierung', 51; Alan Clarke, 'Theatre Behind Barbed Wire', in *Theatre and Film in Exile: German Artists in Britain 1933*–1945, ed. Günter Berghaus (Oxford: Wolff, 1989), 189–222.
51. See Michael Seyfert, *In Niemandsland. Deutsche Exilliteratur in britischer Internierung* (Berlin: Das Arsenal, 1984), 98.
52. See Erhard Scherna, 'Kuba', in *Literatur der DDR*, ed. Jürgen Geerdts (Berlin: Volk und Wissen, 1976), 144–60.
53. See Stent, *Bespattered*, 237, cited after Feather, *Art*, 18.
54. 'Postcodes in the L36 region', *Street Check*, https://www.streetcheck.co.uk/postcode/startingwith/l36 (28 August 2020).
55. Ibid.
56. Harry Seidler's diary appeared in 1986; Janis Wilton, ed., *Internment: The Diaries of Harry Seidler May 1940-October 1941* (Sydney: Allen and Unwin, 1986); see also Jo Bondy and Jennifer Taylor, eds, *Escaping the Crooked Cross: Internment Correspondence between Paul and Charlotte Bondy during the Second World War* (Peterborough: FastPrint, 2014).
57. 'Civilian Internment in Britain 1939–1945'. Catalogue and 30 interviews available online: *IWM Collections: Imperial War Museums*, https://www.iwm.org.uk/collections/search?query=huyton+camp&pageSize=&media-records=records-with-media (28 August 2020); Harkins, see note 13, Kochan, see note 34.
58. A selection is reproduced in Feather, *Art*, 21–35; see also Rachel Pistol, *Internment during the Second World War* (London: Bloomsbury, 2017), 106–7.
59. *Bridge over the Bluebell (2011)*, managed and delivered by the Blue Bell Estate Residents' Association and funded by the Heritage Lottery Fund, supported by Knowsley Archives, https://www.youtube.com/watch?v=-TsOa0N7QJA (27 December 2020).

60. Goldsmith, see note 7; 'Terry Hughes, Remembers Huyton WW2 Internment Camp'(2016), https://www.youtube.com/watch?v=8wX6R_YUtOQ&feature=emb_l ogo (4 December 2020); 'Memories of Huyton Internment Camp'(2016). Excerpts available online, https://soundcloud.com/knowsleyarchives (4 December 2020); the full recordings are held in the ARK archive.

Bibliography

Anon. 'Theater in Huyton'. *Freie Deutsche Kultur* (December 1940): 3–4.

Bondy, Jo, and Jennifer Taylor, eds. *Escaping the Crooked Cross: Internment Correspondence between Paul and Charlotte Bondy during the Second World War.* Peterborough: FastPrint, 2014.

Brinson, Charmian. '"Please Tell the Bishop of Chichester": George Bell and the Internment Crisis of 1940', *Contemporary Church History* 21, no. 2 (2008): 287–99.

Clarke, Alan. 'Theatre Behind Barbed Wire'. In *Theatre and Film in Exile: German Artists in Britain 1933–1945*, edited by Günter Berghaus, 189–222. Oxford: Wolff, 1989.

Dove, Richard. '"KZ auf Englisch": Robert Neumann's Internment Diary'. In *'England? Aber wo liegt es?'*, edited by Charmian Brinson, Richard Dove, Marian Malet and Jennifer Taylor, 157–67. Munich: iudicium, 1996.

Feather, Jessica. *Art behind Barbed Wire.* Exhibition catalogue: National Museums Liverpool, 2004.

Fox-Gál, Eva, ed.. *Musik hinter Stacheldraht: Tagebuchblätter aus dem Sommer 1940 von Hans Gál.* Bern: Peter Lang, 2003.

Gillman, Leni, and Peter Gillman. *'Collar the Lot!' How Britain Interned and Expelled Its Wartime Refugees.* London: Quartet Books, 1980.

Harkins, Margaret. 'Alien Internment at Huyton during World War II'. In *A Prominent Place: Studies in Merseyside History*, edited by J. A. Davies and J. E. Hollinshead, 113–24. Liverpool: Hope Press, 1999.

Kochan, Miriam. *Britain's Internees in the Second World War.* London: Macmillan, 1983.

Lafitte, François. *The Internment of Aliens.* Harmondsworth: Penguin, 1940.

Lehmann-Russbueldt, Otto. 'Alien Internment Camp, Huyton Liverpool: Experiences and Observations over Two Months (July – August 1940)'. In *Civilian Internment in Britain during WW2: Huyton Camp*, edited by Jennifer Taylor, 48–57. Southend-on-Sea: Anglo-German Family History Society, 2012.

Lomnitz, Alfred. *Never Mind, Mr. Lom.* London: Macmillan, 1941.

Malet, Marian, and Antony Grenville, eds. *Changing Countries The Experience and Achievement of German-Speaking Exiles from Hitler in Britain from 1933 to Today.* London: Libris, 2002.

Newman, Ines. *Internment in Britain in 1940: Life and Art Behind the Wire.* London: Vallentine Mitchell. 2021.

Retzlaff-Kresse, Bruno. *Kerker, Illegalität, Exil.* Berlin: Dietz, 1980.

Scherna, Erhard. 'Kuba'. In *Literatur der DDR*, edited by Jürgen Geerdts, 144–60. Berlin: Volk und Wissen, 1976.

Seyfert, Michael. *In Niemandsland. Deutsche Exilliteratur in britischer Internierung. Ein unbekanntes Kapitel des zweiten Weltkriegs.* Berlin: Das Arsenal, 1984.

Stent, Ronald. *A Bespattered Page: The Internment of His Majesty's Most Loyal Enemy Aliens.* London: Deutsch, 1980.

Taylor, Jennifer, ed. *Civilian Internment in Britain during WW2: Huyton Camp*. Southend-on-Sea: Anglo-German Family History Society, 2012.

Taylor, Jennifer. '"Die geschworenen Feinde des nationalsozialistischen Deutschland": The Aspirations and Activities of Socialist Politicians Interned in Huyton in 1940'. In *Political Exile and Exile Politics in Britain after 1933*, edited by Anthony Grenville and Andrea Reiter, 169–86. Amsterdam: *The Yearbook of the Research Centre for German and Austrian Exile Studies*, vol. 12, 2011.

Wilton, Janis, ed., *Internment: The Diaries of Harry Seidler May 1940-October 1941*. Sydney: Allen and Unwin, 1986.

5

Written out of history: The impact of Sefton Camp's post-war invisibility on memory and belonging

Rob David

On 18 October 1940 the *Ramsey Courier* reported that '550 German aliens, who have been interned at Huyton, arrived on the island [the Isle of Man] on Wednesday [16 October]. The men were of all ages, and were accommodated at the Sefton Hotel, Douglas, and adjoining houses, which have been commandeered as a detention camp. This is the first batch of aliens to be interned at the Sefton'.[1] Amongst this group of men was a nineteen-year-old Manchester University student by the name of Werner David.[2] After the war, David misremembered the location of his internment as Hutchinson Camp which, as a result of rare conversations, his children came to believe was where he had been interned. He continued to describe being interned at Hutchinson in interviews he gave at the beginning of this century.[3] It was not until after his death in 2010 that a letter came to light which gave his island address as Sefton Camp. David was not alone in wrongly believing he had been interned at Hutchinson. Around 2008 another former internee, Michael Maynard, stated that he had been interned in Hutchinson, although he later corrected this to Sefton.[4]

Even though the story of internment has become better known on the island, the internees of Sefton Camp and their descendants have not been well served by its low profile both on the island and in the historiography of Manx internment, which until recently had focused on an 'élite minority' of middle-aged 'enemy aliens' in camps such as Hutchinson at the expense of those camps which housed the 'ordinary refugee'.[5] Recent interest in the women's and married camps at Rushen has given a voice to the ordinary woman, a voice that is still denied to the ordinary man.[6] This chapter will examine the internment experience of the under-represented Sefton internees, through David's unpublished journal, testimonies from other, mostly young, German Jewish internees, and the few remaining official records. It will also explore the reasons for the camp's relative post-war invisibility and the effect that this had on its internees and their descendants.[7]

Werner David and his internment journal

Werner David was born in Dusseldorf in 1920 to middle-class Jewish parents. During 1933 he was bullied at his secondary school by a Nazi-supporting teacher and some fellow pupils, and aged thirteen his mother brought him to England to continue his education at Buxton College in Derbyshire. In October 1938, he became an undergraduate at Manchester University. He completed his first year without incident, but at the beginning of the second, on 6 October 1939, he was required to attend an Enemy Alien Tribunal in Manchester, where he was assigned Category C. Being designated a 'Refugee from Nazi Oppression' enabled him to continue his studies.[8] Initially only those in Category A were interned, but in May 1940, the government extended internment to include men and women in Category B and men in Category C. Fortunately for him, his arrest came later than for many others; he remained free until mid-July and was thus able to complete his second year at the university.

David began to write his journal on 17 August while interned at Huyton, and he intended it to be a gift for his girlfriend Joan Storey's twenty-first birthday in January 1941.[9] He entitled it *You and I* as it was to be the story of what had become an interrupted relationship. However, in the journal the past and present are constantly intertwined as he also wrote about life as an internee, and the impact of internment on him. It has survived as a fair copy in two handwritten volumes written between 17 August and 16 December 1940. Journal entries for events prior to 17 August represent his memory of what happened. Those from 17 August until his release on 10 December 1940 were written at the time.

David's first experience of internment at the tented camp at Prees Heath in Shropshire coloured his attitude to what happened to him throughout his five months behind barbed wire. At the end of a long day on 17 July 1940, David walked through the barbed wire perimeter fence and into captivity. On arrival his attention was focused on the armed guards, the barbed wire and in particular his loss of freedom:

> One of the doors at the entrance opened and we went in. So I was now definitely leaving freedom. The 2nd door – part of the inner fence didn't open until the outer door was completely shut again. No escape possible. Searchlights were there too. Even inside the camp I saw plenty of barbed wire. The camp was divided into several isolated units and the road on which I had just come in passed right through the middle of the camp. It was just like a zoo – the 'animals' had assembled to see who was arriving today.[10]

In early August, David was transferred to Huyton Camp, and on 16 October he was taken to Liverpool Docks to board a steamer for the Isle of Man (Figure 5.1).

Werner David's journal is of particular value because so much of it was written while at Sefton Camp where relatively little contemporary documentation and testimony has survived. His journal is also significant because it recorded events and thoughts from the perspective of a young man who turned twenty during his internment. Most

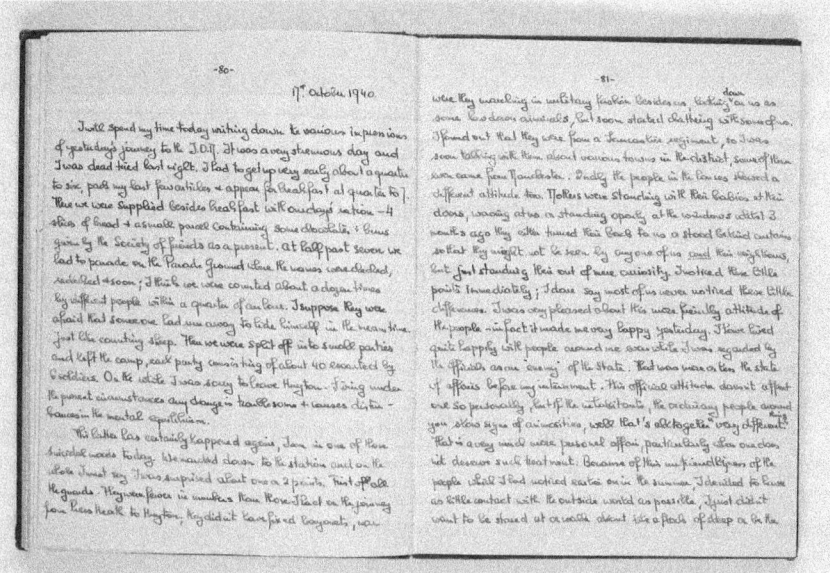

Figure 5.1 Werner David's journal: Part of the entry for 17 October 1940 describing his departure from Huyton Camp for the Isle of Man

Source: © the author; journal deposited in Imperial War Museum Archive: Document 25027.

journals were written by middle-aged internees who, in Ronald Stent's words, were 'once or future very important persons'.[11] Some of these have been published, such as those of the musician Hans Gál (aged fifty in 1940), the artist Fred Uhlman (aged thirty-nine) and the author Robert Neumann (aged forty-three).[12] David's journal is unusual in other ways too. It is written in English because, by 1940, this had become his language of communication, and unusually it was written with an audience in mind, his English girlfriend. In contrast, Gál, Neumann and Uhlman wrote their journals in German, having spent the years since their arrival in Britain lodging with fellow exiles and continuing to speak and write in German. With the exception of Neumann, who wrote his journal for a German-speaking girlfriend, the others appear to have had no audience in mind. For them, journal writing was a discipline which helped overcome long hours of relative idleness and enabled them to record their unusual internment life.

Two preoccupations dominated the lives of many internees. The first involved the anxious wait for letters and parcels from loved ones. David complained about the erratic arrival of parcels of science textbooks which enabled him to keep studying. The second was the yearning for release and the uncertainty surrounding its timing. Both contributed to a pervading sense of frustration and depression, what Livia Laurent has labelled 'the exile of internment', a further exile within an exile, and Michael Seyfert has called 'barbed wire sickness'.[13] David's journal reflects this but amongst the angst is a rare record of life in Sefton camp during the autumn of 1940.

'What a life!': Internment at Sefton

On 1 November 1940, a fortnight after his arrival on the Isle of Man, David wrote: 'Another month has gone and I am still here. What a Life!'.[14] This referenced the famous revue *What a Life!* performed by internees in September at the Palace Theatre in Douglas. Although this was prior to his arrival, and indeed before Sefton Camp had opened, it is clear that the revue had become part of the shared memory of the internee community and clearly David felt the phrase applied to his situation. Sefton was one of the last camps to be opened. The Sefton Hotel and twelve properties in the adjoining Church Road were commandeered in early September 1940 when it became obvious that more accommodation was required (Figure 5.2). Work on erecting the barbed wire fence began immediately, and later in September the surrounding roads were closed to traffic in readiness for the internees' arrival in mid-October.

David described the camp in his journal entry for 17 October. He noted the 'excellent view' which stretched around the bay to Onchan where his younger brother was interned, but what struck him most forcibly was the limited exercise space with islanders walking past. This was also noted by Lord Lytton, the chairman of the Council of Aliens, when he visited the seafront camps at the end of the month. He described them as 'little better than large cages [creating] a most depressing psychological effect'.[15] David wrote:

> The hotel is on the promenade about 400 yards from the harbour and faces the sea. The barbed wire fence runs along this side's curb (sic) and then along the curb (sic) in the side street. That's all we have regarding walking space. Isn't that horrible? Here we not only face the sea, not only the coast of Cumberland but the whole life of Douglas. People young and old walking up and down the promenade, the normal traffic, shopping etc. Young couples just like us two [referring to

Figure 5.2 The Sefton Hotel and Church Road in 2014. The facades of these buildings have changed little since 1940–1

Source: Courtesy Julian Sale.

himself and his girlfriend Joan] walking down the road arm in arm. The real life is constantly presented to me and yet I am banned from taking part in it by a few inches of barbed wire. It is tantalising to an extreme degree. Psychological barbarity I call this. I have no chance to do any walking exercises on this small pavement crowded with some 500 internees. It's just like a monkey's den here, everybody outside looks this way, you are being stared at just like monkeys in the zoo.[16]

He went on to acknowledge that despite some limitations, the accommodation was an improvement on Huyton:

They have of course taken out everything that might contribute to anything like comfort, but the rooms are more habitable and have running hot and cold water. I still sleep on the floor of course, but at last I got a pillow, an improvement! Except a wardrobe there is no furniture in the room. I sleep with 4 others in one that would normally house 2, but it's fairly biggish, I must admit. The window unfortunately does not face the sea [his room was in one of the properties in Church Road].[17]

It took the internees a few days to settle in. Initial disorganization generated 'a large number of angry outbursts by some people, since their nerves are already under great strain'. Jobs were soon allocated, and for many work provided a purpose to their restricted lives. David 'joined the kitchen staff as a waiter [which involved] 6 hours a day of pretty hard work', Manfred Gornitzky worked in an office translating documents, Fritz Adler administered the camp welfare café and Walter Sondhelm, whose internment journey from Manchester University to Sefton mirrored that of David, worked outside the camp perimeter in 'intelligence' where amongst other responsibilities he organized internees' release procedures. Michael Maynard enrolled for a correspondence course. David observed that 'food here is very much less than at Huyton', and he was not pleased to learn that the *Isle of Man Daily Times* was suggesting that conditions in the camps were better than those for the Manx population.[18] Some internees such as Gornitzky received so many food parcels from home that he was often able to avoid eating in the communal dining room.

Work lessened the monotony of camp life as did the supervised walks organized by the Walking Club. David participated but on his first walk he found it disconcerting that 'people kept gazing as we walked like a flock of sheep'.[19] He wrote that on 1 November:

The kitchen staff went out this afternoon as a special privilege; we had 2 soldiers with us but for the first time they carried no rifles with them. I talked with the guard all the time, it was jolly. He was a decent chap. We passed through some lovely country; he took us wherever we wanted to go. It's beautiful up here and so summery still. I went without a coat – inside the house it is colder than outside. It's so marvellous just being fairly free if only for a short time; I feel that I am still a human being for under this dreadful prison life one is apt to forget one's individuality.[20]

As well as the supervised walks there were sporting opportunities, especially football. On 19 November a visit was made to the cinema:

> The first time since four months. Interned 18 weeks today. It was quite exciting to see a movie again. The films were quite good but I have already forgotten their titles. I never imagined I would sit in a cinema without a single woman being there. Of course the female film stars caused some excitement. Most of us haven't seen or heard the voice of a woman for many months.[21]

A few days later on 23 November he enjoyed a modern dress production of Julius Caesar at the adjacent Gaiety Theatre, where 'our dramatic society performed "Julius Caesar" this afternoon. It was a splendid performance. They performed it on a proper stage'.[22]

Despite a library of some 1,200 books, educational opportunities within the camp were limited as the Cultural Department at Sefton existed only on a small scale compared with some other camps and there was only a limited camp university.[23] This was probably due to the small size of the camp, its elderly demographic and its social composition where over a third of the internees categorized themselves as skilled industrial and agricultural workers.[24] The camp newspaper, the *Sefton Review*, reported on lessons in mathematics and English language, as well as technical subjects such as metalworking and welding. The proportion of university-educated personnel was smaller than at Hutchinson and Onchan where lectures on philosophy, science and literature were common. However Rabbi Schonfeld, who visited the camps on behalf of the Chief Rabbi's Religious Emergency Council in November, noted that Sefton Camp had a radio and possessed ten pianos and that music was being encouraged.[25] Few professional musicians were interned at Sefton, but those who were, such as Leo Wurmser, gave concerts as did talented amateurs like Arnold Lorand. Internees such as Gornitzky played the piano for their own interest.[26]

Psychologically, internment began to take its toll. David's fluency in English and declining competence in German may have exacerbated his loneliness. This may have been a particular problem at Sefton where the elderly population most likely spoke German amongst themselves leaving the English speakers feeling isolated.[27] David sought refuge in his studies and does not name any internees in his journal, which possibly reflects his lack of friends. His journal is introspective and he rarely engaged with the experiences of others or in much of the social life of the camp. The camp café is not mentioned and he made little use of the camp bar being put off by the 'music, loud voices, just like a pub, but a terrible sight considering that most of the people in it had once led a respectful life but must now enjoy themselves in that way in order to have a few hours of pleasure – to forget prison life'.[28] His isolation contrasts with the internment life of the artist Fred Uhlman at Hutchinson, and the much older engineer and entrepreneur Wilhelm Hollitscher at Huyton, who name fellow internees and instances of camp camaraderie on almost every page of their journals.[29]

There is a view that younger internees coped better with internment than those who were more elderly. Ronald Stent observed that 'the psychological impact of imprisonment was by no means uniform … some, particularly amongst the younger ones, treated the situation with a sense of adventure', and benefitted from living with people of talent who in some cases 'had a formative, even decisive, influence on their future lives'.[30] Recently, Richard Dove has suggested on the basis of the letters of the twenty-one-year-old Hans Keller that 'it was easier for younger internees to adapt to their constrained circumstances than for older men'.[31] However, this was not the case for every young internee, such as David, and not every young internee had the advantages of someone like Keller who was interned with an older relative and was part of a musical tradition which could thrive even behind barbed wire. The correspondence of another younger internee, Manfred Gornitzky, with his wife Thea, who was pregnant, reflected his low morale as his wife's pregnancy continued without him.[32] In contrast, the younger Michael Maynard took advantage of new opportunities and chose not to return to his pre-war employment, but to join the Auxiliary Military Pioneer Corps (AMPC) as a consequence of 'the fall of France and the great danger to the country'.[33]

David became increasingly indecisive, for example, wondering whether he should join the AMPC and thus gain his freedom or wait until his release came through and he could continue his university studies. The question of release was constantly on his mind. His girlfriend, like the wives and girlfriends of other internees, was charged with doing all she could to expedite his release. After the government added students to their release categories on 17 October 1940, David received a letter on 21 November in which she wrote, 'I am trying to do everything possible at this end, but no one quite knows what we can do'.[34]

Eventually on 8 December 1940 David was notified of his imminent release: 'RELEASED!!! RELEASED!!! Can you believe it? This magic word! I simply don't know what to say. On Tuesday I shall be going back to Manchester.'[35]

The post-war legacy: Memory and belonging

Despite having enjoyed his fellow internees' production of Julius Caesar on 23 November, David was feeling 'rather gloomy' as he wrote his journal later that day. He referred to his internment as 'this disgraceful injustice' and commented:

> There are so many of us here who would rather sleep in London night after night in tube stations than spend one day in an internment camp. I most certainly would. I must admit I miss the air raids. I like to share the same anxieties and hardships of an air raid with the other people of Great Britain, after all we are all fighting against the same foe.[36]

Like many internees, David felt guilty that he was spending wartime in war on a holiday island when so many were suffering the consequences of the blitz.[37] His sense of guilt was probably compounded by unspoken concern for his mother, who since the German occupation of Belgium had been hiding in Brussels without any means of communicating with her three children in England. The contrast between his 'safe' internment and uncertainty over her fate could not have been more marked.

After his release and completion of his university course, his scientific work in London and participation in the Home Guard Anti-Aircraft Command gave him the opportunity to participate in Britain's war effort. Yet, despite this, his continuing reaction to his internment was, as Rachel Pistol suggested, 'to attempt to suppress the memories and simply not mention it'.[38] Pistol identified internees' enforced separation from other family members as especially important in relation to their subsequent silence, and she cited a number of cases including an Italian internee who commented on 'the initial shock of being suddenly and without warning removed from family and daily life'.[39] As David had had little contact with his family since he left Germany in 1933 this was probably not the main reason for his silence. David's silence was probably caused by the way internment had interrupted and challenged 'the difficult processes of assimilation and acculturation'.[40] By 1940, he had lived in England for seven years, could speak and write English almost fluently, had won a place at university and enjoyed the company of an English girlfriend, but in 1939 he had been classed an enemy alien and in 1940 interned by a country he regarded as his home. Other Sefton internees faced a similar feeling of rejection. The fifty-six-year-old artist, Martin Bloch, who had been in Britain since 1934 and had been a founder of the School of Contemporary Painting and Drawing in London, felt, in the words of his daughter recorded many years later, that internment had shaken 'his faith in the United Kingdom' and he felt 'crushed, betrayed and misunderstood'.[41] The younger Manfred Gornitzky, who had been in England since 1937, had sought to merge his Jewish culture with the adoption of a new British identity. In the words of his daughter, he found 'becoming an enemy alien, a painful echo of the dehumanising effect of the Nuremburg laws. His new identity was slipping away from him. He was now simply a Jew behind barbed wire'.[42] Although all three men undoubtedly felt that they had made considerable progress towards cultural citizenship, internment reminded them that they had not progressed towards legal citizenship and that the state still regarded them as 'the other' despite their attempts to assimilate. For all of them this was a painful echo of how National Socialist racial policy in Germany had challenged their 'imagined Germanness' during the 1930s.[43]

Revisiting internment

In 2009, sixty-nine years after his release, David stepped off the ferry in Douglas accompanied by his children to revisit the places associated with his internment, in particular, as he thought, Hutchinson Square, and to see the island beyond the barbed wire which so dominated his memory. By making this journey he was, as Pistol observed, one of a minority of internees who have chosen to revisit where they were interned, usually accompanied by younger family members.[44] His post-war silence on the subject had ended in 1998 when he wrote *The Story of the First Twenty-Five Years of my Life* for his children and grandchildren. In it he explained that he had

> nothing to hide [about his past], but it is probably true that I have spoken too little about my early life because it was so different from the years of my life in England. I have never felt an overwhelming desire to recapture this past. This

perhaps explains why, subconsciously, I have kept my early years in a separate, rather watertight compartment.[45]

Because he talked so little about his early life, his family asked few questions, and as he grew older he realized that there was a possibility that much of his story would die with him.

In fact the memoir added little to what the family already knew about his internment. He referred to 'two weeks at a hastily erected tent campsite behind barbed wire', 'two months on an unfinished housing estate in Huyton', and 'a further two months in a requisitioned hotel in the centre of Douglas'. Beyond saying camp life 'was Spartan but bearable' with the 'monotony [being] relieved by a camp university [and] listening to the BBC News', he revealed little else, but by the time of his visit to the island in 2009 he had become willing to talk more freely in interviews that he enjoyed giving. As the Manx Heritage Foundation interview began though, a problem emerged. Where exactly had he been interned?

Sefton – a forgotten camp

It was obvious on visiting Hutchinson Square that it was not the location of the seafront hotel of David's memory, and which the letter discovered after his death revealed as being the Sefton Hotel. At some point soon after the war David began to identify himself as a member of the 'university' community who inhabited Hutchinson Square. Why had Hutchinson replaced Sefton in his mind? It may have been a consequence of Sefton's post-war invisibility, probably resulting from its small size, its short period of use from October 1940 to March 1941, its relatively few high-profile internees and the small surviving archive.[46] Sefton Camp was little known on the island, and had been rarely mentioned beyond the Isle of Man. It seemed to David and his family that the camp had been forgotten.[47] In 2009, there was no plaque on the exterior, nor information leaflet inside, that explained the hotel's very different function during the Second World War, a situation that has largely continued to the present day. Over the years other camps, in particular Hutchinson, have dominated the public imagination.

In the immediate post-war period, there was little interest in the subject of internment. Two highly critical books about internment policy had been written in 1940, but the policy of post-war governments to keep the documentary record under wraps resulted in little new material for historians to work with.[48] Some documents began to be released in the late 1970s, and this led to a number of publications which addressed various issues relating to refugee policy and internment. Where camps were named, coverage was uneven and Hutchinson and Onchan were most frequently cited. Sefton was so little known that Ronald Stent, despite having been interned on the island, wrongly located it 'outside Douglas'.[49]

By the 1990s, Manx National Heritage sensed that even amongst the island population 'civilian internment was slowly fading from the public consciousness', and this led in 1994 to an ambitious exhibition at The Manx Museum which covered internment in both wars, as well as the publication of a book *Living with the Wire*.[50]

Information about the camps reflected the research that had taken place by that time and once again Hutchinson and Onchan were covered in the most detail, with Sefton in the least. When Panikos Panayi wrote a short historiography of enemy alien internment in Britain in 2005 he aptly entitled it 'A Marginalized Subject', which in many ways it still was.[51] The exhibition and book led to a renewed interest and increased knowledge and the publication of a revised edition of *Living with the Wire* in 2010. However this growth in knowledge was related to the other camps. The section about Sefton remained unchanged.[52]

Interest in internment on the island has continued due to the enthusiasms of Yvonne Cresswell, until recently Curator of Social History at Manx National Heritage, and Alan Franklin, who for many years was librarian at the same institution. In recent years they have written books, devised self-guided walks, created blogs and advised on information boards such as those about the seafront camps, including Sefton, on Douglas promenade, and panels at the sites of Hutchinson and Onchan camps.[53] Most recently the Manx owner of one of the apartments in the Sefton Hotel, unaware that she was living on the site of an internment camp, became interested in its hidden history and has written an account of the hotel as a camp, which she has made available to those interested.[54] Community interest in internment has also recently increased. For example, the Rushen Heritage Group investigated the women's and married persons' camps in its area, which led to an exhibition, a book and a significant online presence. As the exhibition was about both the internees and the community who had hosted them, interest was considerable, with over 3,000 local people and visitors attending, including some surviving internees and their descendants.[55] However in 2022 Hutchinson Camp once again received national publicity when it acquired its own online website accompanied by a substantial volume authored from off the island, focusing as always on the university élite imprisoned there, but many of the other camps, including Sefton, continue to fare poorly in historical literature and on the web.[56]

Historians' interest has widened to examine aspects of other camps, but has lagged behind local enthusiasm. An edited volume in 2005 included chapters on less well-known camps such as Rushen, Central Promenade, Metropole and Granville, but Sefton only received a passing reference in a chapter on camp newspapers.[57] The most recent overview of internment policy again focused on Hutchinson but taking advantage of the new interest in Rushen, also included the women's and married camps.[58] Given the dominance of Hutchinson in the popular imagination, it is unsurprising that when Ali Smith included internment in her novel *Summer*, she chose to locate her imagined internees in Hutchinson Camp, and linked them to the artistic community held captive there.[59] For art historians, Hutchinson has always been the centre of attention given the significant numbers of artists interned there, and who, with the support of the Camp Commandant, Captain H. O. Daniel, were able to improvise art materials, create what has been called 'internment art' and mount selling exhibitions of their work. Artists were also interned at Mooragh, Onchan and Central Promenade, but they have featured less frequently in discussions about internment art. Those who found themselves isolated in other camps, such as the prominent pre-war expressionist artist Martin Bloch at Sefton, have had even less exposure.[60] The first exhibition to include one of Bloch's drawings of Sefton Camp was held in London in 2009 (Figure 5.3), but the accompanying book focused on artists at other camps.[61]

The *Insiders Outsiders* nationwide arts festival which began in 2019 is continuing to give Bloch greater prominence. Some of his Sefton Camp drawings have been

Figure 5.3 Martin Bloch: View from Sefton Camp
Source: Courtesy Martin Bloch Trust.

included in exhibitions, and his grandchildren have given associated talks about him.[62] Unfortunately, an essay on art in the internment camps written for the festival missed the opportunity to widen the discussion on internment art much beyond Hutchinson and Onchan, and Liverpool's Huyton Camp. Both Sefton Camp and Bloch were omitted. The Ben Uri Gallery's biography of Bloch refers to his internment at Huyton Camp, but follows it by saying that he as then interned 'briefly on the Isle of Man'. Again Sefton Camp has not been named.[63]

Given that the politics of internment and the role of the Isle of Man in Second World War internment has been studied by historians and art historians for the best part of forty years, and that Manx National Heritage and community groups on the island have made significant contributions to our understanding of life in the camps, it is not the case that internment *per se* has been out of the limelight. What has occurred is that some camps have been constantly cited and others largely ignored. Sefton is one of those that have fared badly to the extent that even some of those interned there, such as Werner David and Michael Maynard, misremembered the location of their internment and identified with the more high-profile Hutchinson. Was their identification with Hutchinson a consequence of Sefton's invisibility in the internment story, and their longing to have been associated with the intellectual activity that so characterized it? For the visitor to the island or even for the islanders themselves, the fact that some camps are little known and not memorialized may not especially matter. But the relative invisibility of some of the camps did matter for those surviving internees, now mostly deceased, who returned to the island in later life. In the future this will be important for the descendants of internees, guards and staff who will have an interest in the locations where their ancestors' stories played out. Rushen Heritage Group has shown what is possible and in doing so has forged new links to the families of both internees and islanders who were part of the story of the camps at Port St. Mary and Port Erin. More than most of the other sites, Sefton needs its champions so the stories of those interned there and those who looked after them are not forgotten, and relatives left disappointed.

Notes

1. *Ramsey Courier*, 18 October 1940. The first internees may have arrived on 13 October when Manfred Gornitzky wrote a letter describing the boat journey from Liverpool (personal communication, Carry Gorney, Manfred Gortnitzky's daughter).
2. Werner changed his name to Vernon by deed poll in 1948.
3. Ambleside Oral History Group archive: interview MI (2008); Manx Heritage Foundation World War II Oral History Project: Charles Guard talks to Vernon David (2009).
4. MS 11497 (completed questionnaire c2008); and MS 11799/1, Manx National Archives: manuscript memoir, 'Fragments from My Life', by Michael Maynard, 2005. The copy in the archive includes a handwritten note: 'Please note: The author subsequently corrected himself, Hutchinson should read Sefton Camp'.
5. Tony Kushner, 'An Alien Occupation: Jewish Refugees and Domestic Service in Britain, 1933–1948', in *Second Chance: Two Centuries of German-speaking Jews in the United Kingdom*, ed. Werner E. Mosse (Tübingen: J.C.B. Mohr, 1993), 554–5.

6. Rushen Heritage Trust Library, https//www.rushenheritage.org/library (accessed 14 January 2023).
7. I am grateful to Yvonne Cresswell, Wendy Thirkettle and Petra Dudek who accessed material held by Manx National Heritage while the Covid-19 pandemic restricted visits to the island. My sister Maggie Sale and nephew Jayce Sale provided further insights into how Werner David's journal can be read. My wife Sue David has read the text.
8. HO396/15, HO396/250, The Home Office: Aliens Department: Internees Index, The National Archives (TNA).
9. Document 25027 Werner David's journal, Imperial War Museum [IWM] Archive.
10. Document 25027, IWM Archive, 35–9.
11. Ronald Stent, *A Bespattered Page? The Internment of 'His Majesty's Most Loyal Enemy Aliens'* (London: Andre Deutsch, 1980), 172.
12. Hans Gal, *Music Behind Barbed Wire: A Diary of Summer 1940* (London: Toccata Press, 2014); Fred Uhlman, *The Making of an Englishman: an autobiography* (London: Gollancz, 1960); Charmian Brinson, A. Müller-Härlin, and J. Winckler, *His Majesty's Loyal Internee: Fred Uhlman in Captivity* (London: Vallentine Mitchell, 2009); Richard Dove, *Journey of No Return: Five German-speaking Literary Exiles in Britain* (London: Libris, 2000).
13. For a discussion of internees' responses to internment see Uhlman, *The Making of an Englishman*; Brinson et al., *His Majesty's Loyal Internee*, 128–30.
14. Document 25027, IWM Archive, 105.
15. HO215/53, The Home Office: Internment: General Files, TNA.
16. Document 25027, IWM Archive, 88.
17. Document 25027, IWM Archive, 88–9.
18. Ibid, 96; Fritz Adler archive, MS 13381, Manx National Archives; Association of Jewish Refugees: Refugee Voices Testimony interview (RV125). Walter Sondhelm was interviewed by Rosalyn Livshin on 29 April 2003; Carry Gorney, *Send Me a Parcel with a Hundred Lovely Things* (London: Ragged Clown Publishing, 2014) and personal communication with C. Gorney.
19. Document 25027, IWM Archive, 95.
20. Ibid., 106.
21. Ibid., 136.
22. Ibid., 146.
23. *Sefton Review*, 25 November 1940.
24. Connery Chappell observed that Sefton had a significant number of disabled internees as the building had a lift to the upper floors: see Connery Chappell, *Island of Barbed Wire: Internment on the Isle of Man in World War Two* (London: Corgi, 1984), 147. A census was taken on 8 December 1940: see *Sefton Review*, 9 December 1940.
25. HO215/53 The Home Office; Internment; General Files, TNA.
26. C. Gorney; *Sefton Review* 9 December 1940. A list of interned musicians in Suzanne Snizek, 'German and Austrian Émigré Musical Culture in the British Internment Camps of World War II: Composer Hans Gál, *Huyton Suite* and the Camp Review *What a Life!*' (Unpublished Doctor of Musical Arts thesis, University of British Colombia, Vancouver, 2011), does not list any at Sefton; for a study of musical activity based largely on reviews in camp newspapers see Alice Allan, 'Entertainment and Expression: Musical Activity in World War II Internment Camps in the Isle of Man' (Unpublished undergraduate thesis, University of Southampton, 2013) MS 13459, Manx Archives; C. Gorney.
27. Chappell, *Island*, 147. Onchan had a significant population of younger internees.

28. Document 25027, IWM Archive, 110–11.
29. Brinson et al., *His Majesty's Loyal Internee*; Ines Newman, Charmian Brinson, and Rachel Dickson, *Internment in Britain in 1940: Life and Art behind the Wire* (London: Vallentine Mitchell, 2021).
30. Stent, *A Bespattered Page?*, 134, 150, 152.
31. Richard Dove, ' "Most Regrettable and Deplorable Things Have Happened": Britain's Internment of Enemy Aliens in 1940', in *Music Behind Barbed Wire: A Diary of Summer 1940*, ed. Hans Gal (London: Toccata Press, 2014), 29.
32. Gorney, *Send Me a Parcel*.
33. MS 11799/1, Manx National Archives: Michael Maynard memoir, 27.
34. Document 25027, IWM Archive, 143.
35. Document 25027, IWM Archive, 164.
36. Ibid., 146–7. David experienced the Liverpool blitz while at Huyton.
37. There is also a hint of embarrassment in a letter sent by Gornitzky to his wife: 'It is actually as lovely as a picture postcard here. One could live here', Gorney, *Send Me a Parcel*, 107.
38. Rachel Pistol, *Internment during the Second World War: A Comparative Study of Great Britain and the USA* (London: Bloomsbury Academic, 2017), 101.
39. Ibid., 100–1.
40. Brinson et al., *His Majesty's Loyal Internee*, 128.
41. Barbara Grant in conversation with Ann Rau Dawes, 2013: personal communication with Charlotte Grant (16 March 2021). See also 'Identity and Belonging in the Works of Martin Bloch', https://insidersoutsidersfestival.org/event/martinbloch/ (accessed 8 March 2021).
42. Gorney, *Send Me a Parcel*, 91; and C. Gorney.
43. For a discussion of 'otherness' in the context of European Jewry in the mid-twentieth century see Ufuk Topkora, 'Us versus Them: The Steady Narrative of "Othering" in Historical and Contemporary Debates in Germany and the U.S.', *American Institute of Contemporary German Studies*, 21 December 2018, https://www.aicgs.org/publication/us-versus-them-the-steady-narrative-of-othering-in-historical-and-contemporary-debates-in-germany-and-the-u-s/ (accessed 10 February 2021).
44. Pistol, *Internment*, 101.
45. Vernon David, *The Story of the First Twenty Five Years of My Life* (privately published, 1998).
46. Manx National Heritage holds material relating to the camp. See also Alan Franklin, *Involuntary Guests: Enemy Aliens and Political Detainees on the Isle of Man in World War Two* (Ramsey: Lily Publications, 2017), 50.
47. This continuing invisibility was also noticed by Snizek in 2011: 'Sefton is today a beautifully restored luxury hotel, yet there is no visible evidence that the hotel ever housed internees during World War II': see Snizek, 'German and Austrian Émigré Musical Culture', 14.
48. François, Lafitte, *The Internment of Aliens* (Harmondsworth: Penguin, 1940, new edition London: Libris, 1988). Lafitte only referred to the camps at Onchan and Mooragh on the Isle of Man. Yvonne Kapp and Margaret Mynatt, *British Policy and the Refugees 1933–1941* (London: Frank Cass, 1997). This book, also written in 1940 but not published until 1997, did not refer to any camp by name.
49. Stent, *A Bespattered Page?*; Peter and Leni Gillman, *Collar the Lot: How Britain Interned and Expelled Its Wartime Refugees* (London: Quartet Books, 1980). Chappell, Island.

50. Yvonne Cresswell, ed., *Living with the Wire* (Douglas, 1994).
51. P. Panayi, 'A Marginalized Subject? The Historiography of Enemy Alien Internment in Britain', in *'Totally Un-English'?: Britain's Internment of Enemy Aliens in Two World Wars*, ed. Richard Dove (Amsterdam: The Yearbook of the Research Centre for German and Austrian Exile Studies, vol. 7, 2005), 17–26. For example, Mosse, *Second Chance* (1991), explored the history of the Jews in Britain but completely marginalized Second World War internment.
52. Cresswell, ed., *Living with the Wire* (Douglas, 1994; revised edition 2010).
53. Franklin, *Involuntary Guests*. See also 'Douglas Promenade: Second World War Internment on the Isle of Man', https://www.imuseum.im/douglas-promenade-second-world-war-internment-on-the-isle-of-man/ and 'WWI and WWII Information Panels: Queens Promenade, Douglas, Isle of Man', https://www.waymarking.com/waymarks/wm11WPK_WWI_WWII_Information_Panels_Queens_Promenade_Douglas_Isle_of_Man (both accessed 5 March 2021).
54. Elaine Moore, *Sefton Hotel to Internment Camp* (privately published, n.d.), MS14863, Manx National Achives.
55. Rushen Heritage Trust Library, https//www.rushenheritage.org/library (accessed 14 January 2023).
56. S. Parkin, *The Island of Extraordinary Captives* (London: Sceptre, 2022). 'Hutchinson Camp: The Island of Extraordinary Captives', https://www.hutchinsoncamp.com (accessed 14 January 2023).
57. Dove, *'Totally Un-English'?* See chapters by C. Brinson, ' "Loyal to the Reich": National Socialists and Others in the Rushen Women's Internment Camp', 101–20; R. Dove, 'Wer sie Nicht erict hat, der begreift sie nie'. The Internment Camp Review *What a Life!*, 121–38; L. Sponza, 'The Internment of Italians 1940–1945', 153–64; J. Taylor, ' "Something to make people laugh"? Political Content in Isle of Man Internment Journals July-October 1940', 139–52. Taylor provided extensive commentaries on the *Mooragh Times*, the *Onchan Pioneer*, *The Camp* (the Hutchinson paper) and the *Central Promenade Paper*.
58. Pistol, *Internment*. The map of the Isle of Man internment camps on p. 39 does not include Sefton.
59. Ali Smith, *Summer* (London: Hamish Hamilton, 2020).
60. See Nichola Johnson, Amanda Geitner, and Sarah Bacon, *Martin Bloch: A Painter's Painter* (Norwich: Sainsbury Centre for Visual Arts, 2007).
61. Ben Uri Gallery, *Forced Journeys: Artists in Exile in Britain c1933–1945* (London: Ben Uri Gallery, 2009), 15. In 2004 Bloch had been excluded from an exhibition of Huyton artists at the Walker Art Gallery in Liverpool as the gallery did not hold any of Bloch's paintings.
62. For example, 'Refuge: The Art of Belonging', at Abbot Hall Art Gallery, Kendal in 2019, which was accompanied by a talk about the artist by his grandson, Peter Rossiter, and a web talk 'Identity and Belonging in the Works of Martin Bloch', by his granddaughter, Charlotte Grant, in March 2021: 'Refuge: the Art of Belonging: Exhibition of the artists Who Fled Nazi occupation', https://lakelandarts.org.uk/refuge-the-art-of-belonging-exhibition-of-the-artists-who-fled-nazi-occupation/ (accessed 12 March 2021); 'Identity and Belonging in the Works of Martin Bloch', https://insidersoutsidersfestival.org/event/martinbloch/ (accessed 26 March 2021). Martin Bloch is central to an online exhibition 'Painting with an Accent: German-Jewish Émigré Stories' hosted by the Ben Uri Gallery in 2023. https://benuri.org/72/overview (accessed 16 January 2023).

63. Rachel Dickson, '"Our horizon is the barbed wire": Artistic Life in the British Internment Camps', in *Insiders Outsiders: Refugees from Nazi Europe and their Contribution to British Visual Culture*, ed. Monica Bohm-Duchen (London: Lund Humphries, 2019), 147–56. https://benuri.org/artists/229-martin-bloch/overview (accessed 16 January 2023).

Bibliography

Ben Uri Gallery. *Forced Journeys: Artists in Exile in Britain c1933–1945*. London: Ben Uri Gallery, 2009.

Bohm-Duchen, Monica, ed. *Insiders Outsiders: Refugees from Nazi Europe and their Contribution to British Visual Culture*. London: Lund Humphries, 2019.

Brinson, Charmian. '"Loyal to the Reich": National Socialists and Others in the Rushen Women's Internment Camp'. In *The Yearbook of the Research Centre for German and Austrian Exile Studies*, edited by Richard Dove, 101–20. Amsterdam: Institute of Germanic and Romance Studies. University of London, vol. 7, 2005.

Brinson, Charmian, Anna Müller-Härlin and Julia Winckler. *His Majesty's Loyal Internee: Fred Uhlman in Captivity* . London: Vallentine Mitchell, 2009.

Chappell, Connery. *Island of Barbed Wire: Internment on the Isle of Man in World War Two*. London: Corgi, 1984.

Cresswell, Yvonne, ed. *Living with the Wire*. Douglas: 1994; revised edition 2010.

David, Vernon. *The Story of the First Twenty Five Years of my Life*. Privately published, 1998.

Dickson, Rachel. '"Our horizon is the barbed wire": Artistic Life in the British Internment Camps'. In *Insiders Outsiders: Refugees from Nazi Europe and Their Contribution to British Visual Culture*, edited by Monica Bohm-Duchen, 147–56. London: Lund Humphries, 2019.

Dove, Richard. *Journey of No Return: Five German-Speaking Literary Exiles in Britain*. London: Libris, 2000.

Dove, Richard. '"Most Regrettable and Deplorable Things Have Happened": Britain's Internment of Enemy Aliens in 1940'. In *Music Behind Barbed Wire: A Diary of Summer 1940*, edited by Hans Gal, 28–40. London: Toccata Press, 2014.

Dove, Richard, ed. *'Totally Un-English'? Britain's Internment of Enemy Aliens in Two World Wars*. The Yearbook of the Research Centre for German and Austrian Exile Studies. Amsterdam: Institute of Germanic and Romance Studies. University of London, vol. 7, 2005.

Dove, Richard, '"Wer sie Nicht erict hat, der begreift sie nie": The Internment Camp Review *What a Life!*'. In *The Yearbook of the Research Centre for German and Austrian Exile Studies*, edited by Richard Dove, 121–38. Amsterdam: Institute of Germanic and Romance Studies. University of London, vol. 7, 2005.

Franklin, Alan. *Involuntary Guests: Enemy Aliens and Political Detainees on the Isle of Man in World War Two*. Ramsey: Lily Publications, 2017.

Gal, Hans. *Music Behind Barbed Wire: A Diary of Summer 1940*. London: Toccata Press, 2014.

Gillman, Leni. *'Collar the Lot': How Britain Interned and Expelled Its Wartime Refugees*. London: Quartet Books, 1980.

Gorney, Carry. *Send Me a Parcel with a Hundred Lovely Things*. London: Ragged Clown Publishing, 2014.
Johnson, Nichola, Amanda Geitner and Sarah Bacon. *Martin Bloch: A Painter's Painter*. Norwich: Sainsbury Centre for Visual Arts, 2007.
Kapp, Yvonne, and Margaret Mynatt. *British Policy and the Refugees 1933–1941*. London: Frank Cass, 1997.
Kushner, Tony. 'An Alien Occupation – Jewish Refugees and Domestic Service in Britain, 1933–1948'. In *Second Chance: Two Centuries of German-Speaking Jews in the United Kingdom*, edited by Werner E. Mosse, 553–78. Tübingen: J.C.B. Mohr, 1993.
Lafitte, François. *The Internment of Aliens*. Harmondsworth: Penguin, 1940; new edition London: Libris, 1988.
Newman, Ines, Charmian Brinson and Rachel Dickson. *Internment in Britain in 1940: Life and Art behind the Wire*. London: Vallentine Mitchell, 2021.
Panayi, Panayi. 'A Marginalized Subject? The Historiography of Enemy Alien Internment in Britain'. In *The Yearbook of the Research Centre for German and Austrian Exile Studies*, edited by Richard Dove, 17–26. Amsterdam: Institute of Germanic and Romance Studies. University of London, vol. 7, 2005.
Parkin, Simon. *The Island of Extraordinary Captives*.London: Sceptre, 2022.
Pistol, Rachel. *Internment during the Second World War: A Comparative Study of Great Britain and the USA*. London: Bloomsbury Academic, 2017.
Smith, Ali. *Summer*. London: Hamish Hamilton, 2020.
Sponza, Lucio. 'The Internment of Italians 1940–1945'. In *The Yearbook of the Research Centre for German and Austrian Exile Studies*, edited by Richard Dove, 153–64. Amsterdam: Institute of Germanic and Romance Studies. University of London, vol. 7, 2005.
Stent, Ronald. *A Bespattered Page? The Internment of 'His Majesty's Most Loyal Enemy Aliens'*. London: Andre Deutsch, 1980.
Taylor, Jennifer. ' "Something to make people laugh"? Political Content in Isle of Man Internment Journals July-October 1940'. In *The Yearbook of the Research Centre for German and Austrian Exile Studies*, edited by Richard Dove, 139–52. Amsterdam: Institute of Germanic and Romance Studies. University of London, vol. 7, 2005.
Uhlman, Fred. *The Making of an Englishman: An Autobiography*. London: Gollancz, 1960.

6

Rushen Camp, Isle of Man – Camp W (women and children), Camp Y (married), 'Treat them with kindness'[1]

Rushen Heritage Action Team in order of authorship: David Wertheim, Pamela Crowe, Alison Graham, Jane Saywell, Sandra Davidson, Hugh Davidson, Doreen Moule

Introduction

Rushen Camp was unique on several fronts: initially it was only for women and their children; it was controlled by the Home Office and run by landladies rather than the military; it accommodated many women who had lived in England for many years; and it also included British women married to German men and visitors who were just passing through. This chapter tells the story of these women who were arrested with little warning, brought to the Isle of Man, treated fairly and released as soon as possible.

When war with Germany broke out in September 1939, there were some 75,000 people of Germanic origin in Britain, mostly refugees from Nazi persecution,[2] some 65,000 were of Jewish origin.[3] This included the 9,354 children registered by the Movement for the Care of Children from Germany who were rescued on the *Kindertransport*.[4] They became 'enemy aliens' overnight and the next day Sir John Anderson, the Home Secretary, told the Commons that tribunals would be established to 'determine which of [the Germans and Austrians in this country] can properly be left at large and which should be interned or subjected to other restrictions'.[5] Numbering 120 and chaired by barristers, Justices of the Peace and judges with police as secretaries, the alien tribunals commenced in the first week of October 1939 and operated behind closed doors. The chairmen had considerable discretion. Refugees were not permitted lawyers but at the request of the Home Office the refugee organizations provided liaison officers who often acted as interpreters for those refugees possessing little or no knowledge of the English language. They categorized the enemy aliens into 'persons to be interned' (Category A); 'persons to remain at liberty but with certain restrictions' (Category B) and those certified as 'refugees from Nazi oppression' and freed from restrictions other than those applied to friendly aliens (Category C). By the end of February 1940, the tribunals had examined over 73,000 cases, placing 569 and 6,782 into Categories A and B, respectively, with the remaining roughly 66,000 into Category C, of which over 55,000 were classified as 'refugees from Nazi oppression'. Decisions were often arbitrary and inconsistent between tribunals.[6] Of those appearing before tribunals, 27 per cent of the men and 17 per cent of the women were doctors, dentists, pharmacists, opticians, psychologists, teachers, architects or consulting engineers. One quarter of the women had entered Britain as domestic workers, a category that offered them relatively easy entry to Britain to escape from the Nazis.[7]

On 24 October 1939, Viscount Cobham, Under-Secretary of State for War, told the House of Lords that the Government had decided against mass internment based on injustices during the First World War, stating that 'it is not likely to happen', while newly appointed Home Secretary, Sir John Anderson, made a similar statement in the House of Commons.[8] By May 1940, the situation had changed dramatically. On 9 April 1940, the Germans invaded Denmark and began invading Norway. On 10 May, the German Luftwaffe attacked Allied airfields in France. On 12 May, German forces attacked the Netherlands, and on 15 May, the Netherlands surrendered. A failed British and French military response fed the mythical belief in a fifth column of local collaborators. Britain was facing defeat and the prospect of invasion, as the 'superb German Army' prepared to destroy the French army and sweep the less well-trained and equipped British Expeditionary Force (BEF) into the sea.[9] Significantly, also on 10 May, Winston Churchill replaced Neville Chamberlain as prime minister. On 11 May, chairing his first War Cabinet Churchill agreed to the recommendation of the Chiefs of Staff to arrest male enemy aliens aged sixteen to sixty living in a substantial area covering no fewer than thirty-one counties from Hampshire to northeast Scotland.[10]

Events leading up to the mass arrest of Category B women are recounted by Peter and Leni Gillman from the meeting of the Joint Intelligence Committee on 2 May, at which the term 'fifth column' first appeared in government papers.[11] This was compounded by the fertile imagination of Sir John Bland, British Minister to the Dutch Government, who escaped to England on 14 May after witnessing – but misinterpreting – the effective German use of paratroops. In his account to Foreign Minister, Lord Halifax, entitled 'Fifth Column Menace', he included the statement 'The paltriest kitchen maid … generally, is a menace to the safety of the country', ending with the conclusion that 'ALL Germans and Austrians at least ought to be interned at once'.[12] On 23 May, with the BEF facing defeat, the War Office requested the internment of all enemy aliens. At their meeting the following day, in a partial victory for Anderson, the cabinet agreed to limit internment of German and Austrian women to some 3,600 in Category B. The police were instructed to start the arrests on 27 May and to spare only those who were invalid, infirm, heavily pregnant or with dangerously ill children. Mothers were expected to take any children under the age of sixteen with them. Homes were searched and any plans found for assisting the enemy were to be reported to MI5. Policewomen were to accompany police officers and assistance was enlisted from the Women's Voluntary Service.[13]

Lack of preparations for mass internment meant there were insufficient facilities available. During the First World War, the Knockaloe Camp outside Peel had been home to some 23,000 male internees, but it was not decided until early May 1940 to send most of the internees to the Isle of Man. Eventually nine men's camps were established on the Island under military control, and the first in Ramsey received its initial internees on 27 May. In mid-May the clerk to Port Erin Commissioners, Alec Clague, received instructions from the Lieutenant-Governor to establish a women's camp. He visited the hotels and guest houses in the southern villages of Port Erin and Port St Mary in the sheading of Rushen (one of the six administrative divisions of the Isle of Man), enquiring whether the landladies would take internees. This camp differed significantly from the men's camps as it was under Home Office jurisdiction.

Following their arrest, the women, some with children, were taken to temporary accommodation whilst awaiting transportation to the Isle of Man. The accommodation included Holloway Prison in London for Category A internees and some Category B internees.[14] They were then taken by train to Liverpool. On arrival at the ferry port, they discovered the nature of their destination.

The Isle of Man Steam Packet Company's vessels had been mostly commandeered for war service and those that remained had been pressed into use for the Dunkirk evacuation. Three of those vessels would be lost to the enemy over the coming days together with twenty-four Manx crew members. To accommodate this shortage, a Belgian cross-channel ferry, the HMS *Prinses Josephine Charlotte* (Figure 6.1), was taken into service. After carrying the first shipment of male internees to Ramsey on

Figure 6.1 HMS *Princess Josephine Charlotte*
Source: Courtesy of Nigel Thornton.

27 May, she was used to take three further shipments of women and children from Liverpool to Douglas. The first arrived on the morning of 29 May. After disembarking soon after 7.30 am on to the quay in Douglas, the women, some with children, walked, carrying their single suitcases, the half mile to Douglas railway station where three trains and a fleet of buses waited to take them the fifteen miles to their new homes in Port Erin and Port St Mary. On 29 and 30 May, the *Prinses* made two crossings with a total of 2,589 women and 259 children. Its final crossing on 31 May raised the numbers to about 3,000 women and 300 children.[15] On 7 June, the SS *Snaefell* transferred a further 267 women.[16] The Rushen Camp reached its peak occupancy in the second week of August when it housed approximately 4,000 women and children, after which releases started.[17]

Two very different Commandants

Dame Joanna Cruickshank (1875–1958)

Even though Sir John Anderson had advised against mass internment, he was not unprepared when Churchill is alleged to have announced in May 1940, 'Collar the Lot'. Provision for male internment was established on the Isle of Man, a Crown dependency of the United Kingdom, an independent Island with its own Parliament and with experience of internment in the First World War. No female camps existed, but Sir John identified an area in the south of the Island for this purpose. Sir John knew exactly the person to establish a female camp. A volunteer working within his Ministry as the Matron in Charge of all Auxiliary Nursing Services, she was a heroine of the First World War. Dame Joanna Cruickshank who, as founder Matron of the Princess Mary Royal Air Force Nursing Service (PMRAFNS), had established five military hospitals around the world was the ideal choice. Sir John discovered that Dame Joanna had been struck down by another bout of recurring pernicious malaria, so he was reluctant to ask for her help. However, Sir John's private secretary mentioned the dilemma they were in, and although still unwell, Dame Joanna readily agreed to establish a female camp on the Island, referenced in her resignation letter, dated May 10th 1941, 'In those grim days of May last year there was nothing one could refuse to do if it was likely to help, even in the smallest way, the government and the country.'[18]

The sixty-four-year-old Dame Joanna arrived on the Island in late May. The camp was to encompass the two beautiful seaside villages of Port Erin (Figure 6.2) and Port St Mary. Well-used to the role of Commanding Officer and with her experience of establishing hospitals, she set about her task with a military precision. Owners of luxury hotels, guest houses and private homes with spare bedrooms were told they must house internees. The only request from the Commandant to the hosts was that they should treat the internees kindly. The fear of the impending influx of enemy women was in some part allayed by the payment of one guinea a week for accommodation and food for each internee.

The end of May 1940 saw the arrival of around 3,000 women and children. They were escorted from the railway station in Port Erin to the local church hall where they

Figure 6.2 Port Erin Promenade 1930s–50s

were registered. A handful of helpers escorted them to the hotels and guest houses. Dame Joanna saw that many of the arrivals were heavily pregnant and was relieved that, at her direction, a small hospital had been created in one of the hotels. She had established a place of safety for the refugees and others in her charge. As in her nursing career, all were cared for to the best of her ability with no distinction made between religion or nationality. With the recognition that extra staff were required, the camp thrived. Education for all, art for all, music and drama. Although there was still some resentment of the internees, most residents of the villages integrated with the internees.

However, the pressure of the task of establishing the camp took its toll on Dame Joanna's health. A year after establishing the camp she wrote to Sir John stating that as she had never been formally appointed there was no need for a formal resignation. A dedicated nurse to the end, she finished her letter with the good news of an unexpected delivery of a baby that evening.

Cyril Roy Mitchell Cuthbert 1902–1984

An enthusiastic amateur forensic scientist, Cuthbert joined the Metropolitan Police Force in 1924. He had some medical and dental knowledge after dropping out of dentistry and medical courses and taking evening classes in chemistry. He invested in a second-hand microscope and set himself up as 'the scientific policeman'. However, his superiors viewed his activities as highly inappropriate, and he came close to losing his job. In time, a Police Forensic unit was established, and Cuthbert became the clerk to the unit. He remained fascinated by the work of the unit, making notes on procedures and the forensic investigative skills of the scientists. In 1958, he published *Science and the Detection of Crime* 'detailing the cases he had observed'.[19]

At the outbreak of war, Cuthbert, now an Inspector, was transferred as clerk to the Alien Tribunal at Bow Street Magistrates court in London and, in September 1940, he applied to be transferred to the Tribunal administration team in Douglas, Isle of Man. By Spring 1941, the need for tribunals was declining rapidly and Inspector Cuthbert would be due to return to the British mainland, but he saw an opportunity to transfer to Port St Mary where a new internment camp was being established. He contacted the

Home Office and applied to be Commandant of the Married Camp. He was appointed, working alongside Miss Wilson, a former prison governor, who had single-handedly progressed Dame Joanna Cruickshank's vision for the Married Camp.[20]

On 8 May 1941, 162 reunited couples, who had both been on the Island but in different camps without knowing, moved into Port St Mary, and Cuthbert took up residence in the luxurious Ballaqueeney Hydro Hotel as Commandant of the Port St Mary Camp with approximately 500 internees in total, a big difference from the 4,000 Dame Joanna had to manage. When rumours circulated that Dame Joanna was unwell and was retiring, Cuthbert wrote to the Home Office suggesting he was in an ideal position to take on the role of commandant of both camps.[21] Dame Joanna's resignation letter had clearly referred to a new female commandant, 'I think it will be far wiser if the 18Bs and others do not come until the new Commandant is installed as then she can make whatever arrangements she thinks best for them',[22] but Miss Wilson, the woman who had been such a valuable deputy to Dame Joanna, was overlooked. After questions in Parliament about the suitability of a man in charge of the women's camp, 'women's interests' were to be the responsibility of Miss Wilson in her capacity as Deputy Commandant. Cuthbert certainly won over the local landladies. As good looking as the film actors of the day, they described him as a 'ladies' man, but despite his charming manner, the Home Office sent him stern reprimands for altering official orders referring to 'internees' to read 'aliens', and for seeking to appoint an officer with known prejudice to internees.[23]

By August 1942, the internee numbers were so dramatically reduced that the Married Camp was moved to the Spaldrick area of Port Erin. Inspector Cuthbert moved into a house in St Georges Crescent, Port Erin. We know from one of the camp messengers that Cuthbert spent most of his time in his office in Victoria Square, compiling the extensive Cuthbert Report from newspaper cuttings, which appears to be an actual report of the camp. The Home Office acknowledged receipt of the document but stated that it had not been requested.[24] Cuthbert remained in Port Erin until the camp closed in September 1945 when he returned to London and assumed his liaison responsibilities at the Metropolitan Police Forensic laboratory. After receiving the Kings Medal – he had written to suggest that he was a worthy recipient – and his promotion to Detective Superintendent, he retired from the police in 1951. He travelled around Asia and India selling scientific instruments.

Security, including the role of the constabulary

Rushen Camp was initially set up for the detention of women and children and latterly it became a mixed camp enabling married couples to be billeted together. It operated very differently from other camps in the Island, the UK and Europe. There were no military guards, just the 'Rules of the Camp', pinned to the inside of internees' doors in their billets, and a modest barbed wire fence forming the boundary of the entirety of Port Erin and Port St. Mary Camps, necessitating the issue of ID cards and/or permits for internees and residents alike, to be checked at the barriers leading into and out of the camps.

Property owners were responsible for the day-to-day running of the camp, ensuring that the internees' needs were met, as directed by the Home Office. They had to ensure the internees did not gain access to radios, torches, newspapers, candles and similar items, and that they abided by the rules, returning in time for curfew. As time went on, many of the reluctant hosts and their internees became firm friends, corresponding for many years, others returning to the Island on many occasions.

To help keep law and order within the female camps, the Isle of Man Government requested assistance from the Home Office and the Metropolitan Police, in the form of a team of Women Police Constables (WPC), there being no women in the Isle of Man Police Force at that time. By July 1941, there were around seven WPCs. Their duties consisted mainly of custody and escort of the internees within the Port Erin and Port St. Mary Camps, where internees could meet up with friends and visit shops on an allocated two days each week, make trips to the cinema, take walking trips and, in some cases, work alongside those internees who worked on farms. The WPCs would be called upon to accompany an internee who required medical treatment not available on the Island and where the internee's detention case was being heard in Douglas or the United Kingdom.[25]

Commandant Dame Joanna Cruickshank was responsible for dealing with minor indiscretions such as petty theft, unruly behaviour and ruling on disputes reported from the elected Internee District Supervisors. Port Erin Police Station was utilized on occasions for overnight detentions. Incidents of a more serious nature would be dealt with by the local judiciary and would be heard before the Civil Courts. Many internees were effectively destitute and had no means of supporting themselves once back in the United Kingdom and resorted to theft from other internees of items such as jewellery, clothing, anything of value that could be sold later. All internees preparing for departure had their belongings searched by the WPCs. If any such items were found, the internee would temporarily lose their right to freedom. Many of those responsible for the security of Rushen Camp understood and empathized with the internees' situation and remained until the closure of Rushen Camp, their final assignment being to escort the remaining internees back to the United Kingdom.[26]

The welfare of women in Camp

Many of the internees had been arrested in the United Kingdom and had spent time in Holloway prison, a Victorian gaol in London. After the nightly bombing raids, frugal food rations and no idea of their fate when transported, the internees must have been relieved to arrive in the beautiful seaside villages at the southern tip of the Isle of Man. Now they were safe from the bombing, reasonably well-treated and housed in grand hotels, guest houses and private homes. Waking to the sight of the beautiful sunlit bay of Port Erin or the harbour in Port St Mary must have provided some reassurance, but it could not alter the fact that most, despite being committed to British victory, were unjustly imprisoned and had lost their freedom.

Dame Joanna Cruickshank, a qualified nurse and midwife, established a small hospital in the hotel close to her office and required all qualified doctors and nurses amongst the internees to assist in medical care in the camp. Three hundred women had arrived in various stages of pregnancy and others also needed immediate medical advice or care, but she made it clear to all that no distinction was to be made in terms of religious or political persuasion when treating patients. Sister Anna, the Matron of Dalston Hospital, London, and thirty-nine of the Lutheran Deaconess nursing sisters, assisted in maternity care, and worked with the local doctors at the internee clinics in both villages. For the mothers, who understandably found difficulty in coping with a baby without the support of a husband, a mother-and-baby home was established. Local doctors and dentists provided medical and dental care for internees.

The internees were encouraged to work in the fishing/farming communities of the twin ports, helping at the farms replacing men away at war. Land was provided for the internees to grow vegetables, keep chickens and there was even a small pig farm. The food was used by the internees. Each house had a Captain who allocated the cooking and cleaning duties. Local residents were introduced to continental delicacies: dandelion leaf salad, rollmop herring, Viennese coffee and cakes. A Kosher house was established in Port St Mary to cater for the dietary needs of the Orthodox Jewish women, and the arrival of the German Red Cross Food parcels for refugees meant extra rations.[27] The internees grew some of their own vegetables on allotments[28] and could barter these with the locals for items that were hard to come by.[29] All the churches in the camp helped provide comfort. A small Jewish community living in Port Erin helped organize Jewish services, and for those who did not understand the English mass, the Commandant authorized a mass in German. At Christmas, prayer meetings took place in many of the hotels. The Quaker Religion was also represented by a permanent camp official.[30]

The glorious summer of 1940, which saw the internees sunbathing and swimming, could not compensate for loneliness and the separation from loved ones. There was also a financial divide in the Camp. Some of the refugees who had fled Germany had only the support of refugee agencies and the Lutherans seemed to have no financial support, but many others had money to purchase whatever they wished. Shops, hairdressers and cafes were all open, and internees could purchase most things, causing some resentment among local residents whose purchases were controlled by clothing coupons and Food Ration books,[31] while internee rations were provided by the Home Office. Recognising the difficulties, a group of enterprising internees under the direction of Ruth Borchard, who held a doctorate in economics and social psychology from the University of Hamburg, with a twenty-five-pound grant from Dame Joanna, established a barter system known as the Service Exchange. Soon a haircut could be had for a bunch of carrots (for example). The system proved highly beneficial with thousands of hours being bartered and people able to utilize their talents to provide for themselves.[32]

From the first weeks of the camp, entertainment was popular, and choirs and orchestras were formed. There were many talented musicians, and internees and residents joined together to perform. Concerts and plays were much appreciated as was the cinema, which was open all day. However, as the balmy days of summer departed, the Commandant realized that boredom would be a challenge. Qualified teachers, led by the distinguished Minna Specht, were appointed, and after weeks of playing on the beach, children now had to attend school and education was available from kindergarten to high school. An educational programme for adults proved very popular, with both academic courses and practical skills courses offered. In January 1941, health, welfare and education were all well established. Dame Joanna resisted many calls to segregate the internees by political persuasion but the camp was organized and orderly. When Bertha Bracey, chairman of the Central Department for Interned Refugees and general secretary of the Germany Emergency Committee of the Society of Friends, made her second visit to the camp in January 1941, she wrote in her report in *The Manchester Guardian* on 21st February 1941 about the differences between her first and second visits:

> [First visit] The double bed seems to be a system throughout the Isle of Man, so it was no fault of the commandant if sick and healthy, Nazi and anti-Nazi women and children were found sharing rooms and even beds. The commandant's office, by the way, was hopelessly inadequate.
>
> [Second visit six months later] The staff has been increased to about thirty. The commandant now has a good office with the necessary equipment. There is a resident woman medical officer, two clinics and a nursing home and in these, internees with nursing and medical qualifications assist the British staff. Surgical, mental and complicated medical cases are sent to island hospitals outside the camp. Women who require kosher food are in one house and one or two houses have been set aside for Nazis. There are two schools, one in Port St Mary and one in Port Erin, staffed by internee teachers.[33]

We know from the Camp Messenger, Mrs Corrin, that she never saw any trouble as she cycled on her rounds of the camp. There were no swastikas daubed on the village walls or crimes of violence. It was a remarkable achievement recognized by the International Committee for Refugees in Europe.[34]

Post-war

Many of the buildings used for internment in the Isle of Man have reverted to their original use as hotels and boarding houses or become private homes, while others have been demolished and replaced with modern apartments. The continued presence of so many of the buildings means that the visitor experience for those interested in internment is enhanced by the knowledge that they are seeing what would have been familiar to the internees. The buildings mentioned here are only a small proportion of what is still in situ.

On arrival at Port Erin Railway Station, the internees were escorted to St Catherine's Church Hall, where they were registered before being billeted in one of the hotels, boarding houses and the occasional private home. These two buildings were of significance, and if the internees were to return to Port Erin, they would instantly recognise both the station and the church hall which are in constant use, with the same railway locomotives and carriages still being used. The railway was the only means of travel by the internees, under escort, when they went to Douglas, the capital, for tribunal hearings or medical appointments. St Catherine's Church, and its hall, built in 1880, is the Anglican church in Port Erin and, along with the other Anglican and Catholic churches and Methodist chapels in both Port Erin and Port St Mary, opened its doors to welcome the internees in their time of need. The internees took regular part in the services of the churches and chapels, and this is recorded in the local newspapers.[35] Baptisms also took place, one such being of Professor Eva Rieger,[36] at the Victoria Square Methodist Church, which is now the Erin Arts Centre, but retains its ecclesiastical façade. Also, at St Catherine's Church there were confirmation services which included a number of internees.[37]

Collinson's Café, the hub of the internee community with its educational activities and social and entertainment facilities, would also still be recognizable to internees. It is now a private home but continues to be one of the most outstanding buildings in Port Erin. Unfortunately, time has not been so kind to the Marine Biological Station (MBS) where forty internees were registered to do research work and to give lectures to other suitably qualified internees. In return, the internees catalogued thousands of papers on marine biological and hydrographical topics. The MBS is currently awaiting redevelopment.

Many of the then luxury hotels on the Promenade in Port Erin,[38] where the internees were billeted, have now been replaced with apartments except for The Falcon's Nest (the first and last hotel in Port Erin). However, the Promenade in Port St Mary (Figure 6.3) looks very much the same as it did in 1940 when the internees arrived and in 1941 when the Married Camp was based there.[39] This includes the Town Hall, where there was a synagogue in the basement, and Cowley's Café and Cornaa Boarding House

Figure 6.3 Port St Mary Promenade 2019, much as it was in 1940

Source: © Doreen Moule.

(now a private residence) where Minna Specht set up a kindergarten and a school for older children, respectively.⁴⁰ The other building of importance in Port St Mary was the Ballaqueeney Hotel at the far end of the Promenade. It was a luxury hotel and became a kosher house where the Jewish internees were billeted and a room was provided for their religious prayers and ceremonies.⁴¹

The buildings mentioned above, plus the other buildings used as part of the camp, did, for the most part, return to their former uses after the war. By the end of the twentieth century, some of them had become unfit for purpose and they have been demolished and replaced, in the case of the Port Erin hotels, with apartments. The grandeur of the buildings has mostly been forgotten, but some of the names have been retained – Windsor House, Bay Cliffe, Bradda Glen to name but a few, while the Port St Mary buildings have mostly survived. There was no bomb damage to the area, so the return of the tourist industry meant that the camps were forgotten until more recent years when interest in the period has revived.

Conclusion

Our research has shown us that the internees, in most cases, were wrongly arrested, but this was a time of fear amongst the British population and when the British government were under extreme pressure to be seen to address the situation. The Isle of Man, which had internment experience from the First World War, when 23,000 men were interned at Knockaloe, was once again chosen as a secure place to intern enemy aliens.⁴² We have reached the conclusion that, for the most part, the internees were treated well, they were safer than they would have been in the rest of Britain, many made lifelong friends with local people and some returned regularly for holidays.⁴³

Since 2014, one of the goals of Rushen Heritage Action Team (RHT) has been to celebrate Rushen Internment Camp in as many ways as possible. There have been two exhibitions which attracted international interest, both officially opened by people with internee ancestry – Katherine Hallgarten (daughter of Ruth Borchard) and Baroness Henig (daughter of Elfrieda and Kurt Munzer), and a book about life in the camp, its places and its personalities, was published in 2018.⁴⁴ As part of preserving memories for the future, interviews have been recorded with people who were children during the war, both internees such as Dr Hans Christoph Rieger⁴⁵ and local people such as Keith McArd.⁴⁶ A series of presentations and character outlines are part of a schools' programme which is being developed. A digitized record of events is on the Rushen Heritage Trust website where we also do our best to assist descendants who periodically ask for help, not forgetting the Manx Museum, which holds approximately 70 per cent of the original registration cards. In future, self-guided walks are being planned with information boards to be appropriately placed around the two villages, and a new heritage/exhibition/visitor centre is now open as an active preservation of history.

These are all part of the ways in which the heritage of Rushen Camp is being preserved through the work of RHT. It is essential that the commemoration process continues for future generations to access, so that they understand the events that happened during that period in our history, what caused them, how ordinary people dealt with the difficult situations they found themselves in and the overall effects both at the time and since. It is impossible to move forward unless we understand what went before.

Notes

1. Parts of this chapter are republished from *Surviving Together Beside the Sea*, ISBN 978-0-9932914-1-8.
2. Connery Chappell, *Island of Barbed Wire: World War Two Internment on the Isle of Man* (London: Robert Hale, [1984] 2005), 20.
3. Amy Zahl Gottlieb, *Men of Vision: Anglo-Jewry's Aid to Victims of the Nazi Regime 1933–1945* (London: Weidenfeld and Nicolson, 1998), 150.
4. Ibid., 125.
5. Hansard, 4 September 1939, vol. 35, Col. 36.
6. Peter Gilman and Leni Gilman, *Collar the Lot: How Britain Interned and Expelled its Wartime Refugees* (London: Quartet Books, 1980), 43–5; Chappell, *Island of Barbed Wire*, 21.
7. Gottlieb, *Men of Vision*, 168.
8. Gillman, *Collar the Lot*, 7–8.
9. Julian Thompson, *Dunkirk: Retreat to Victory* (London: Pan Macmillan, 2017), xiv.
10. Gillman, *Collar the Lot*, 94–5.
11. Ibid., 84–6.
12. Ibid., 102–4.
13. Ibid., 132–3.
14. Charmian Brinson, '"In the Exile of Internment" or "Von Versuchen, Aus Einer Not Eine Tugend Zu Machen": German-Speaking Women Interned by the British during the Second World War', in *Politics and Culture in Twentieth-Century Germany*, ed. William Niven and James Jordan (Rochester, NY: Camden House, 2003), 65–6.
15. *Isle of Man Times*, 'German Women Internees Arrive', 1 June 1940, 5.
16. *Isle of Man Times*, 'The Female Internment Camp', 8 June 1940, 3; Chappell, *Island of Barbed Wire*, 121.
17. Chappell, *Island of Barbed Wire*, 35; Gilman, *Collar the Lot*, 121.
18. Dame Joanna Cruickshank, 'Resignation letter, 10 May 1941', HO 215/405, National Archives, Kew.
19. Cyril Roy Mitchell Cuthbert, *Science and the Detection of Crime* (London: Hutchinson, 1958).
20. Doreen Moule et al., *Friend or Foe?* (Isle of Man: Rushen Heritage Trust, 2018), 39, 43.
21. Cyril Cuthbert, 'Papers of Cyril R Cuthbert, One Time Commandant of Married Internees Camp', MS 11196, Manx National Archives.
22. Cruickshank, 'Resignation letter'.
23. Cuthbert, 'Papers'.
24. Ibid.
25. Unpublished memoirs of Miss Dorothy Olivia Georgiana Peto, OBE: *Detention of Enemy Aliens*, Metropolitan Women Police Service.
26. *Isle of Man Examiner*, 'Internees Leave', Friday, 7 September 1945, Front page, Col. 5.
27. Alan Franklin, *Involuntary Guests* (Isle of Man: Lily Publications, 2017), 152.

28. Moule et al., *Friend or Foe?* 60.
29. Ibid., 90.
30. Ibid., 150.
31. Ibid., 90–1.
32. Ruth Borchard, 'Experiment in Planned Economy: The Service Exchange', The Manchester Guardian, 29 August 1942.
33. Bertha Bracey, 'Isle of Man Internment Camps: The Great Improvement made in Six Months, The Manchester Guardian, 21 February 1941.
34. Moule et al., *Friend or Foe?* 42.
35. *Isle of Man Examiner*, Friday 1 November 1940, 6, Col. 2.
36. Moule et al., *Friend or Foe?* 139.
37. *Isle of Man Examiner*, Friday 8 November 1940, 6, Col. 3.
38. Moule et al., 228 (illustration).
39. Ibid., 48 (illustration).
40. Angela W. Little et al., *Living with the Sea* (Isle of Man: Rushen Heritage Trust, 2019), 193.
41. Ibid., 196.
42. Ibid., 17.
43. Ibid., 214–15.
44. Moule et al., *Friend or Foe?*
45. Ibid., 140–7.
46. Ibid., 155–7.

Bibliography

Chappell, Connery. *Island Lifeline 1830–1980*. Prescot: Stephenson, 1980.
Chappell, Connery. *Island of Barbed Wire: World War Two Internment on the Isle of Man*. London: Robert Hale, [1984] 2005.
Cuthbert, Cyril Roy Mitchell. *Science and the Detection of Crime*. London: Hutchinson, 1958.
Dalheim, Rosemarie. *The Sunny Hours*. Brighton: Indepenpress, 2011.
Davidson, Hugh, ed. *The Illustrated Roll Call*. Isle of Man: Rushen Heritage Trust, 2015.
Franklin, Alan. *Involuntary Guests*. Isle of Man: Lily Publications, 2017.
Gillman, Peter, and Leni Gillman. *Collar the Lot: How Britain Interned and Expelled its Wartime Refugees*. London: Quartet Books, 1980.
Gottlieb, Amy Zahl. *Men of Vision: Anglo-Jewry's Aid to Victims of the Nazi Regime 1933–1945*. London: Weidenfeld and Nicolson, 1998.
Kelly, Peter. 'Hut Dwellers'. *Isle of Man Victorian Society*. Newsletters 99 and 100. Interview with Malcolm Kinley, March and July 2015.
Lafitte, François. *The Internment of Aliens*. London: Penguin, [1940] 1988.
Mackie, Mary. *Wards in the Sky: The RAFs Remarkable Nursing Service*. Cheltenham: The History Press, 2014.
Moule, Doreen. 'Enemy Aliens in Port St Mary'. In *Living with the Sea*, edited by Angela Little et al. Isle of Man: Rushen Heritage Trust, 2019.
Moule, Doreen, Pamela Crowe, Alison Graham, David Wertheim, Sandra Davidson, Jane Saywell and Hugh Davidson. *Friend or Foe?* Isle of Man: Rushen Heritage Trust, 2018.
Thompson Julian. *Dunkirk: Retreat to Victory*. London: Sidgewick and Jackson, 2008).

Part Two

Continental Camps: Britons Interned on the Continent

7

An autograph book, a piano and a body hanging on the wire: British memories of the French transit and internment camp of Royallieu, Compiègne

Gilly Carr

Introduction

Royallieu, a transit camp in Compiègne, near Paris, is best known as a place of internment for French Jews and political prisoners before their deportation to concentration camps. Yet, for more than three months in 1943, it held a group of approximately 130 British citizens. Rounded up from the German-occupied Channel Islands, these civilians, comprising large families from Sark, British Jews, convicted political prisoners and their families and former army officers and their wives, were deported to the camp en route to their more permanent places of internment in Germany. During their deportation by train after reaching France, families were separated and the train carriages decoupled. The younger men were sent to Laufen internment camp in Germany and the others, to the camp in Compiègne.

The presence of Channel Islanders in Compiègne was undocumented and unacknowledged at the site's memorial museum when it opened in 2008. Yet a small number of survivors who were children and teenagers when in the camp still live in the Channel Islands. Evidence for their experiences lie in their and their parents' diaries, memoirs and letters and in their oral testimony. A small number of archival records also reside in the Islands' archives and in London. This chapter is the first work to unite all known surviving records and interviews to present an account of the British experiences in this French camp.

After providing the historical background to the deportation and internment, this chapter examines who was targeted for deportation and why before examining the evidence for one of the most controversial parts of this episode: the extent to which there was foreknowledge among the Islands' local authorities of the splitting up of families on the journey. The chapter then tells the story of the three months of internment through the eyes of the islanders, a narrative which focuses predominantly on their fellow prisoners – the American internees and French Jews – but also on the hardships of the camp. It concludes with an appraisal of the post-war biography of the camp and its museum, an account from which Channel Islanders have been almost entirely omitted.

Historical background

The Channel Islands were occupied by German forces from the end of June 1940 until 9 May 1945. During this period, a variety of deportations to different categories of camps took place at different times. Those affected were Jews without British nationality, people who committed offences against the occupiers and large numbers of Islanders in both September 1942 and February 1943. In the first wave of these mass deportations, over 2,000 Islanders were deported to the neighbouring civilian internment camps in Germany of Wurzach (for those from Jersey) and Biberach (for Guernsey families). Those targeted were men aged between sixteen and seventy years old born outside the Channel Islands, along with their dependants. This was in retaliation for the British internment and deportation to Australia of German civilians working in Iran who were deemed to be 'furthering the war aims of Germany'.[1]

The subsequent deportations of February 1943, which primarily targeted British Jews, large families from Sark, political prisoners and former army officers, should not have been a complete shock to the Islands' authorities. In his post-war affidavit to war crimes investigators, John Leale, President of the Controlling Committee (the Island's wartime cabinet) in Guernsey, reported that eighteen months beforehand, 'the German authorities had ordered and been supplied with' a list of former officers.[2] The Germans had also asked for – and been given – lists of those who had served prison sentences for offences against the Germans. On 8 January 1943, Inspector Lamy of the Island Police in Guernsey had handed over to the Germans a list of all people 'convicted by a German court' up until 9 December 1942.[3] In Jersey, Clifford Orange, Jersey's aliens officer, stated that lists were supplied to the Germans of retired officers in the island in November 1941.[4] Earlier, and within a month of their arrival in the Channel Islands, the Germans asked for lists of aliens of all nationalities; this marked the start of hunting down Jews in the Islands, a period marked by numerous requests for list of various nationalities of aliens. By 25 November 1940, the Germans were in possession of their desired list of Jews.[5] Those without British nationality were deported to France in April 1942, from where they were taken to Auschwitz a few months later. Those in Guernsey who had acquired British nationality through marriage were on the deportation lists of February 1943. In total, six Jews were deported from the Channel Islands at this time and the husbands of two of the Jewish women were also deported. The youngest to be deported was toddler Janet Duquemin, daughter of Elisabet Duquemin née Fink from Vienna. In summary, all of the information needed by the Germans to deport Islanders was, in one shape or another, supplied to them by the Islanders themselves.

A final group, who comprised over one-third of all of those deported to Compiègne at this time, included forty-eight people from the Channel Island of Sark.[6] This was a result of a British commando raid on Sark the previous October, during which some Germans had been taken prisoner. As the German troops were consequently to be billeted in the more protected centre of the island, those living in that area were deported.[7]

While the first wave of deportations in September 1942 had targeted non-indigenous Islanders for reasons of retaliation, the second wave appeared to have additional objectives. Removing former trained soldiers was clearly a move to get rid of those who could carry out or train people in armed resistance. Those who had been previously convicted by German courts (often for acts of protest, defiance and resistance) were clearly 'trouble makers' who might similarly have got involved in (further) acts of resistance. The other groups were, like those previously convicted, 'undesirables' (in German eyes) of one sort or another.

Foreknowledge of the splitting of families

Members of the Guernsey Deportee Association have long maintained that the separation of families on the deportation journey was something that was not known about or announced in advance, and was a cruel act inflicted without warning. It is the most often cited part of the story of the February 1943 deportations. The truth of this story is slightly harder to establish. That the train deporting Islanders was decoupled some time after its departure from St Malo, with the separation of families to different camps, is not in doubt. What is less clear is the degree to which it was known in advance – and by whom – that families would be split. Dates are also crucial here: while the dates of deportation were 12 and 25 February from Guernsey and 13 and 25 February 1943 from Jersey, how far in advance did anyone know about the planned separations? In Guernsey, the Reverend Douglas Ord, Guernsey's best-known occupation-period diarist (who rarely revealed his sources of privileged information) recorded on 10 February that 'a cruel Order directs the luggage of men and women to be packed separately ... it may simply be to facilitate arrangements in camp, but the fears of separate internment camps are growing. Nothing can eradicate the conviction that at the basis of the movement lies sheer vindictiveness'.[8]

Closer to the centre of power was diarist Louis Guillemette, Liaison Officer and the Bailiff of Guernsey's private secretary. In his unpublished diary entry for 9 and 10 February 1943, he recorded that 'today we have received the ominous order to see that luggage belonging to men is packed separately from that belonging to women and children. Apparently families are to be split up and all men under 64 years of age are to be put in a separate camp. What this means can only be imagined'.[9] In other words, this is clear evidence that the Guernsey authorities knew, just a couple of days before the deportations, that families would be separated.

Violet Cortvriend's memoir, which drew on the files of the Controlling Committee with the assistance of John Leale and Louis Guillemette, was first published in 1947. She is the sole source of an anecdote about Ambrose Sherwill, Attorney General of Guernsey, who was deported because of his status as a former army officer. She states that he was given a letter by the Feldkommandantur stating that he was the head of the Guernsey contingent, and was informed that the families were to be split up, that the women and children were to be sent to a camp in Compiègne in France, and that all men under 63 years of age were to proceed to Germany.[10] He was asked to break this news to them during the journey and this caused, as may be imagined, great additional suffering.[11]

Had it not been for Guillemette, Ord or Cortvriend, our suspicions of German foreknowledge of the separation of families would have been confirmed by the transport lists themselves. These survive in both the Island Archives in Guernsey and in Jersey Archives, and are complicated by crossings-out and ticks in various coloured pencils. The lists for Guernsey are headed *Transportliste fuer Lager Laufen* (62 names) or *Compiègne* (96 names, but with 8 of these crossed out, leaving 88); there is a third *Transportliste* with no camp stated but with 38 names listed; these people were deported on the later date of 25 February.[12] Those who were subsequently sent to Compiègne and Kreuzburg feature on the untitled list; based on age and sex, one can deduce that 25 of them were sent to the former camp. All three lists contain columns for the name, date of birth and reason for deportation clearly stated in German.[13] The transport lists surviving in Jersey are headed by the initial of the name of the camp. From these we learn that 12 of those deported on 13 February were destined for Compiègne, followed by just 3 more on 25 February.[14]

Thanks to these lists, we can work out that 113 people from Guernsey and just 15 from Jersey – 128 people in total – were deported to Compiègne. This figure is confirmed by the Biberach camp register, which recorded 128 arriving from Compiègne on 21 May 1943.[15] This number is further supported by a list issued by the International Red Cross and published in the Channel Islands Refugees' Committee in March 1944. We know that the Islanders were deported and arrived at the camp in two batches: the first appears to have accounted for 98 people; records of the International Committee of the Red Cross note this many 'inhabitants of the Channel Islands, including 68 women and 18 children' in the camp on 17 February 1943.[16]

Deportation and arrival

For those deported from Guernsey, the experience began with medical inspections for former officers held at the Regal Cinema at the end of January 1943. In his diary, Louis Guillemette wrote that he attended in order to

> see that there was nothing to complain about in the arrangements, and one of the first arrivals was an old soldier who had spent quite a long time in the mental hospital as a patient. The fact of having to submit himself for examination by German doctors brought on a bout and his roars and struggles in the empty theatre, with three or four people, including a German soldier, holding him, lent a weird and hellish atmosphere to the whole proceedings.[17]

For the others, the deportation orders arrived on 6 February.[18] Fifteen-year-old Nellie Le Feuvre née Gallienne from Sark was deported with her grandparents, mother and brother; she was allowed to pack only what she could carry: a 'blanket, knife, fork, dessert spoon, teaspoon, cup, saucer, plate and clothing. We also had to leave a trunk to follow with clothing'.[19] Those from Sark were put on the boat to Guernsey, and those to be deported gathered and waited at the Gaumont Cinema (the designated 'collecting station') where they were given a basket of food while more medical examinations took place. Eventually they were put on board a boat. They had hardly left the harbour at 5.30 pm when a strong gale struck and sea started coming in through the portholes. Nellie recorded being 'terribly seasick'. In the middle of the night some others on board came to where they were sitting and told Nellie that there was more sea water on the other side of the boat and the crockery was floating.[20] Things were not much better for the Jersey contingent sailing the following day; Ruby Still noted that she was 'seasick under awful conditions. Luckily we had the pie dish. We shared it and emptied the contents on the floor. As the boat lurched, so did our wooden benches and so did we'.[21]

The Guernsey deportees arrived at St Malo in the middle of the night and first thing in the morning they were put on a train, where they waited for another twenty-four hours for the contingent from Jersey to arrive. During that period, the train was caught in an air raid. It is likely that, while waiting, Ambrose Sherwill broke the bad news to the Islanders about the splitting up of families. Lieutenant Colonel Robert Randall reported that 'during the afternoon there was an air raid after which we were ordered out of the train and divided up, the men 64 and over with the women and children were put in the rear portion of the train and the other men in the front part'.[22] After the train set off, at Le Mans station[23] the train was decoupled and the families were split; they were not to see or hear directly from each other for six months.

On arrival at Compiègne train station, open carts (of the sort used to transport livestock) pulled by horses, hay wagons pulled by oxen[24] and lorries met the train. The women and children were put in the carts, and the men into the lorries; Randall later wrote that his lorry 'had been used for carrying coal and the floor was broken in places'.[25] Nellie Le Feuvre was frightened in the cart because 'we could hear the horse's hooves on the cobblestones and it made me feel as if I was going to the guillotine. The next thing we saw was all these searchlights bearing down on us, then these great big gates, then these awful barracks'.[26]

The Islanders had arrived at the camp of Royallieu at Compiègne, Frontstalag 122, a transit and internment camp comprising three different compounds arranged around three sides of a parade ground and separated internally by barbed wire. In compound or 'Block' A, down one side of the parade ground, were eight barracks for mainly French political prisoners and communists. Block B, down the other side of the camp, comprised another eight barracks for American nationals, trapped in occupied territory after America entered the war and arrested as nationals of an enemy power. Some other foreign nationals from countries at war with Germany were interned with them. Joining these two compounds was Block C, made up of eight barracks arranged in groups of two, used by mostly French Jews and Jews of other nationalities.

The shape of the camp betrayed its earlier origins; it was originally constructed in 1913 as a military barracks for the 54th infantry regiment, serving as a military hospital during the First World War. From 1919 it was returned to its former use until 1939, after which it briefly became a hospital once again. In 1940, it was used as a Prisoner of War camp for French and British soldiers, becoming *Frontstalag* 170, but from June 1941 it became *Frontstalag* 122, designated as a 'concentration camp for active enemy elements'. The management and supervision of the camp was entrusted to the German military administration; the guards were soldiers of the Wehrmacht and not the SS.[27]

Life in Compiègne

Between June 1941 and August 1944, around 50,000 people of various categories passed through the camp. It was primarily a camp for gathering together people deemed 'deportable' and became the principal place of departure for political prisoners towards the Reich, thus holding the status of a transit camp for deportation to concentration camps. During the war, approximately forty convoys left from Compiègne station,[28] taking people to the concentration camps of Buchenwald, Auschwitz, Mauthausen, Sachsenhausen, Dachau, Neuengamme and Ravensbrück.[29] Channel Islanders witnessed the arrival and departure of some of these prisoners.

Prisoners in each of the three compounds were treated differently and were of different status, as witnessed by the Channel Islanders, who were placed in corner barracks C8 (women and children) and C4 (older men)[30] (see Figure 7.1a), bordering the American and Jewish compounds and separated from them by barbed wire. They had more contact with the Americans and – one must assume given the anecdotes recorded by Islanders – were not forcibly prohibited from interacting with them, which was not the case with the Jews. The Americans were given privileges and rights that those in other compounds did not have; for example, they received Red Cross parcels and could purchase additional food in their own canteen.[31] When the Channel Islanders first arrived in the camp, they initially had no access to the American canteen but appeared to have contact with a 'German messenger' who bought 'what he could' in Paris. Using this method, which clearly relied on having cash, Wilhelmina Quin from Guernsey was able to buy a 'shoe and clothes brush and soap powder but no foodstuffs as they are all rationed'.[32] Despite this statement, after just under a month in the camp, Wilhelmina referred to paying for various fresh vegetables, which were 'rather dear, but we must have a change from soup'[33] – a reference to the camp-issued basic rations.

Randall explained in his memoirs that camp rations were drawn each day from 'our own kitchen, which was used to cook the children's food and small things for the grownups. We lined up in the corridor for soup for dinner. This was mostly swede soup ... This and the mint tea for breakfast and tea was prepared by the American kitchen and brought down to us under guard'.[34] In her post-war affidavit to war crimes investigators, Elsie Henry stated that, in addition to the breakfast of mint tea, the Islanders were given 'at 11am a small wedge of bread followed at noon by a small basin of turnip, swede or carrot soup, which was mostly water. We never received any meat or solid foods other than occasionally a little macaroni, jam or honey'.[35]

The Channel Islanders were not issued Red Cross parcels as the Germans had apparently notified the Red Cross that the internees' stay was only temporary;[36] however, the Americans kindly shared theirs with the Islanders at a rate of around one every seven to ten days.[37] The sharing of food in adversity was partly no doubt due to fellow-feeling among allies, but there was more to it than that. Five of the Americans in Block B had been deported from the Channel Islands on 2 January 1942; just one of them, Arthur McGahy, kept a diary of his experiences. Although only a single volume of this survives, unfortunately not covering the period during which the contingent of Islanders was in the camp, McGahy's diary is extremely valuable in shedding light on the experiences of those in the American compound and his own role within it.

Through McGahy we learn that the American compound held about 200 men upon his arrival. He appears to have become a barrack leader or volunteered for some kind of responsibility within the American camp. According to the Channel Islanders, he is named as the man who helped the women and children down from the horse-drawn carts upon their arrival in the camp.[38] In his memoirs, Randall recorded that when the American camp captain heard that Channel Islanders were coming to the camp, he asked the Americans from the Channel Islands to prepare the barracks. They consented and,

> thanks to them the camp quarters were cleaner than they would have been and only clean straw was put into the mattresses and pillow cases; they also lit the stoves before we arrived and [had] hot mint tea ready for us. The first night everyone was housed in the one building but the next day the men moved into another [barrack] hut, [where] a room was also [put] aside for church services and a school.[39]

The new arrivals were given metal discs with their internee number stamped on them; they also had their fingerprints taken.[40] Their barracks comprised both dormitories which slept eighteen people[41] and smaller rooms for families with children. Nellie Le Feuvre was lucky enough to be placed in a room with 'three beds, lockers, a table and three chairs, and a small fire in a round stove in the corner of the room' with her mother and brother.[42]

The Islanders were indeed fortunate to have benefactors in the American camp who provided some Islanders with postcards to contact their relatives in England or back home.[43] Gwen Ashton later credited Arthur McGahy for getting Red Cross parcels to the Islanders via the German guards.[44] Randall recorded in his memoirs that the Americans 'brought down our coal and wood ration in a cart which we men had to unload and put in a coal cellar'.[45] Margaret Godfrey, ten years old in the camp, remembered being deported in her mother's old cut-down fur coat: 'In the evening at dusk, I would stand near the wire that separated us from the Americans and hide packets of biscuits, chocolates and packets of food that the Mr McGahy and his friends had collected for us children. In the end there was no fur left on the sleeves. It had all been pulled off by the barbed wire.'[46]

An event which underscored the kindness of the Americans, mentioned by several Islanders, took place on 5 April 1943, on the occasion of the twelfth birthday of Doris Bougourd from Guernsey. 'They brought up a piano to the barbed wire, and dressed up as Hawaiians and they sang and it was very nice', she later recalled. Doris and her friend Margaret tap-danced for them in return, and she passed her autograph book to the men for them to sign. Arthur McGahy inscribed the first page with the following rhyme and signed it with his internee details:

> Just think of our friendship true
> While in Frontstalag 122.
> Some time we must part
> But we'll meet again
> True friendship always do.
> —Arthur W. McGahy, 2365, Frontstalag 122 (American), Compiègne-Oise, France[47]

The Americans also sent over to the Islanders an old wind-up gramophone for the day. 'We put it in the hallway', recalled Doris, 'and anyone passing had to give it a wind. It played *Springtime in the Rockies*.'[48] Ruby Still from Jersey wrote that 'the whole camp was present. There was a wonderful string band with variety turns in between. It was much appreciated by a very enthusiastic audience'.[49]

The friendliness and generosity between the Americans and Islanders was almost impossible to extend to the Jews in the neighbouring compound. The Islanders were 'under the strictest instructions by the Germans not to give them anything to eat … we were warned not to have anything to do with them. They were supposedly "bad people"'.[50] The Islanders witnessed much ill-treatment of the French Jews. Nellie Le Feuvre wrote that they

> saw some terrible cruelty in the Freh camp. They had roll calls three times a day and they were eating grass, they were so hungry. When they had to collect their heavy containers of food, they were so weak that they dropped them at times and we saw them eating the food off the ground. One of our internees decided to throw some bread over to them. They were nearly killing one another to get at it. We were warned not to ever do that again. Now and then the Germans would send some of these French people away, we didn't know where, and those poor things would sing their French anthem with such gusto.[51]

Una Heaume from Guernsey wrote that 'we were surrounded by starving prisoners who were continually begging for scraps of food through the barbed wire fences'.[52] Ruby Still wrote in a letter home that 'the French … are very harshly treated. They are not allowed to pick up bread which finds itself on their side of the wire. If they should make a small fire, it is kicked over by the guards. They march into camp signing the Marseillaise. There is always the sound of shooting at night'.[53] When interviewed almost seventy years later, Gwen Ashton remembered that children were among the Jewish prisoners: 'The Germans had taken children off the streets and they were starving … and were calling out "*du pain, Madame, du pain,*" but you couldn't give it to them or you'd be shot.'[54]

These distressing images stayed with the Island children in the camp. Doris Bougourd remembered hearing machine guns and being told that the prisoners would be shot if they picked up bread. From a window in a barrack room she could see a body 'caught on the wire and left there for a good few days'.[55] Four of the Hamon brothers from Sark, children and young teenagers in the camp, remembered a small number of Jewish men coming into the camp wearing just blankets. 'You could rest a cigarette in the grooves in their back where they had been whipped ... there was an old chap with a beard and they bashed him. They killed him because he went to try to get some food. There was blood coming out of his mouth.' They, too, remembered the prisoner left on the wire 'as a warning to others'.[56] They also remembered these prisoners picking nettles and trying to boil them in water, and the Germans kicking out their fires. The guards would 'throw soup on the ground and kick the bread out of the hands of the French prisoners'.[57] As the Islanders were near the road at the back of the camp, they also saw friends or family of the other prisoners coming close to the barbed wire, by the outdoor toilets, when the guards weren't looking, and throwing messages tied to stones into the camp, looking for their loved ones.[58] This was dangerous as the German guards would fire on them if they were spotted.[59]

Islanders recalled seeing prisoners taken away from and arriving in the camp; Arthur McGahy also recorded the arrival and departure of convoys of prisoners in his diary entries: on 27 March 1942, he wrote, 'Jews on the move – about 580, dinner 12 [o' clock], Jews went out at 4 o'clock.'[60] Camp records show that this entry was a deportation of Jews to Auschwitz. Arrivals and departures sometimes happened at night, presumably to avoid the gaze of local people. On 28 April 1942, McGahy noted, '620 arrivals with 130 guards, 4 machine [guns], extra guards ... lots of commotion during the night'. From 28 August 1942, the Americans were forbidden from 'having anything to do' with the political prisoners or Jews in camp.[61]

Of the British Jewish women deported from the Islands to Compiègne, we are extraordinarily lucky to have the diary of one, the letters of another and the memories of the daughter (deported as a toddler) of a third. The Germans appointed Elisabet Duquemin as the Channel Islands' camp leader because she was bilingual in German and English. Her daughter Janet described this as the 'worst aspect of Compiègne' because it meant that her mother was 'very much in the spotlight where the Germans were concerned. Her papers identified her as Jewish and in the next-door camp [Jewish] people were being loaded onto transports and taken off to concentration camps. As a result it must have been an enormous relief when we left Compiègne'.[62] Fellow Jew, Esther Pauline Lloyd (née Silver), used her diary to castigate herself for her honesty in declaring her Jewish heritage when the Germans required Jews to register in the island. 'Never shall I be honest again', she wrote while in Compiègne. 'If I hadn't declared myself this wouldn't have happened. It's dreadful.'[63] What she witnessed in the camp almost certainly increased her fear of the consequences of her actions.

Despite the support of the Americans, life in the camp was still extremely difficult for the Islanders. Of particular concern to them were the filthy camp toilets and poor washing facilities. A number of people soon developed hair lice. Elisabet's daughter Janet remembered becoming infested with lice, much to her mother's horror, and had to have all her hair cut off.[64] Nellie Le Feuvre, too, remembered the lice, and how fellow Islanders from Sark would come to visit her mother, who had a fine-tooth comb.[65] Nellie also remembered, as many did, the washing facilities or *lavoir* (for both people and clothes), which comprised a long trough, as if for cattle, with cold taps above. It was in a doorless, open air hut. The Islanders were also allowed to take communal showers in the American camp, in a 'tin hut',[66] but this was not a regular occurrence and not everyone took the opportunity. Doris Bougourd remembered that 'they put up old blankets and curtains to screen us but there was some peeping by the American men'.[67] Marjorie Lawrence, too, remembered that the American showers had glass ceilings through which the men watched.[68] For those unwilling to go into the American compound, it was possible to use 'a sheet and a chair' and have 'a rig-up and a bit of privacy for our bucket of cold water in the corner'.[69] As Marjorie remembered, they had to use the same bowl for both soup and washing.[70]

The nearby outdoor toilets were just holes in the ground with a slab either side for the feet, which was very difficult for the older Islanders. Lieutenant Colonel Randall's representation to the Germans eventually secured toilet seats in the form of chairs with holes,[71] but these quickly became filthy because of camp diet-induced diarrhoea.[72] There were 'bins' underneath the toilets, emptied from time to time. Gwen Ashton recalled that her friend from Jersey 'got caught. They were emptying the bins and my friend heard "pardon, mademoiselle." She didn't know whether to continue or what!'[73] The toilets were up a flight of steps and the doors were insufficient for privacy, meaning that those outside could see the person's feet and face, which was degrading for the women. The women were too scared to use these outdoor toilets at night because of the nearby watchtowers: 'There was always someone on guard, with searchlights going all night', as Nellie Le Feuvre wrote later.[74]

A daily routine established itself during the Islanders' three months in Compiègne. The children attended school in the men's barrack every day, 'for which we were thankful; we had little peace when they could not get outside to play – the barracks were hell', as Randall later recalled.[75] Church services were held twice on a Sunday. The only other activity remaining to the women was a little needlework, where some of the women cut pieces off their bed sheets to make embroidered pinafores for their growing children.[76] Exercise in their tiny compound was possible, as was cleaning.[77] Teenagers Nellie Le Feuvre and her friend Beryl Bouget were asked to scrub the corridors and washroom every night.[78] Randall wrote that the men in his room 'took turns as room orderly', which involved sweeping out the room, washing down the washroom and toilets and emptying the urine bucket. Randall also chopped wood for the kitchen fire and swept the chimneys. There were also eleven graves of French soldiers from an earlier period within the grounds of the Islanders' compound. Randall kept this cemetery weeded: 'My trowel was a piece of corrugated iron or the coal shovel … We also painted the crosses at the head of the graves.'[79]

With time on their hands, the younger women who had been separated from their husbands suffered 'mental anxiety' as to where their husbands were.[80] Some teenage boys had also been separated from their families and sent to Germany; Bert and Ruby Still longed to hear from their sixteen-year-old son, Michael,[81] who had been sent – unbeknown to them – to Laufen civilian internment camp. They were not to be reunited with their loved ones until 6 August 1943 in Biberach civilian internment camp in southern Germany. The Islanders finally themselves left Compiègne for Biberach, after four false starts,[82] on 21 May 1943. They had been in the camp for just over three months.

Camp heritage

After the war, the camp at Compiègne reverted to military use; a function it continued in various guises until 1997, when the 51st Signal Regiment left. This was the last use of the site until the *Mémorial de l'internment et de la deportation du Camp de Royallieu* opened in February 2008.

Google Earth allows us to see historical satellite imagery; this function shows us that still, in 2001, the camp remained intact in its original U-shape form, but by 2008, when the *Mémorial* was inaugurated, all but three barracks (Block A, barracks one to three) had been demolished (Figure 7.1a-c). At that time, two billboards stood in front of the camp. The first announced the opening of the new *Mémorial*, and the second, in front of a large area of cleared ground, heralded the building of a new *quartier* of the city. This 'integrated development zone' was to comprise houses, local shops and amenities and extension of the local university with accommodation for students.

A field trip made by the author to the *Mémorial* in 2020 revealed the completed *quartier*. No traces of the old camp, apart from the three barrack blocks comprising the *Mémorial*, remained. While the roads around the perimeter of the camp remained intact, some now bearing war-related names such as 'Avenue des Martyrs de la Liberté' and 'Rue du 67E Régiment d'Infanterie', new ones had been built within the area of the old camp. Some of these were named after famous prisoners of the camp, such as 'Rue Geneviève Anthonioz/de Gaulle'; others reflect the former use of the camp, such as 'Avenue du Camp de Royallieu'. While the camp's former footprint has been eradicated, different kinds of traces remain.

As for the *Mémorial* itself, when a group of camp survivors from Guernsey and Sark, accompanied by the Bailiff of Guernsey, attended the opening of the camp in 2008 (Figure 7.2), they found no trace of the Channel Islanders in the museum display. The exhibition was cutting-edge and impactful: film and photographs were beamed onto the walls of the barrack huts such that the people shown within them were the same size as visitors. Drawings by American internees were similarly enlarged to help the visitor better visualize the space as it had been during the war. Interactive digital tables, activated not just by touch, but by a hand interrupting a light beam, allowed visitors to read and hear letters written by prisoners. Such features were placed with minimal intervention into the original camp barracks, allowing the tiled floors and walls with original layers of flaking paint to retain their atmosphere.

The Islanders, accompanied by the author, were impressed at the display, but their experience was one of dissatisfaction and anticlimax. The first disappointment was, of course, that the three remaining barracks did not include those which once held Islanders. The outline of a map of Europe traced on the floor of one of the barracks showing Nazi-occupied territory excluded the Channel Islands altogether. On the floor of another barrack room, a diagram showed the connections, marked by lines, of prisons across France with Compiègne in the centre, the last stop before deportation to concentration camps. The Channel Islands were not mentioned here, and no black line connected them to the camp. The display relating to the American internees, who had played such a large part in the experience of the Islanders, did not mention them either.

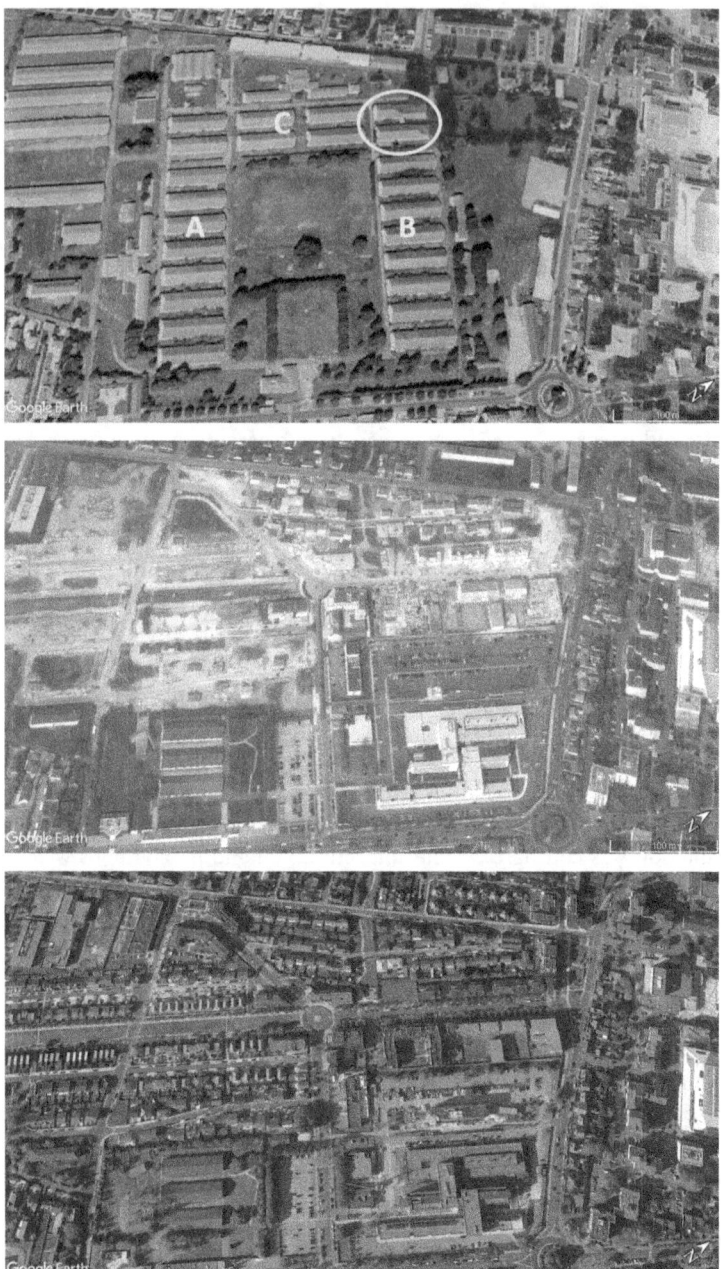

Figure 7.1a-c Google Earth imagery showing the camp buildings in 2001, 2010 and 2018. The compounds and barracks C4 and C8 which held Islanders are marked in Figure 7.1a

Source: © Google Earth with annotations by Gilly Carr.

Figure 7.2 Survivors from the Channel Islanders present at the 2008 opening ceremony of the *Mémorial*

Source: © Gilly Carr.

Even the Wall of Names at the entrance of the camp omitted the names of the Channel Islanders, and the camp chapel did not contain any Channel Islands flags.

Before the opening ceremony began, the Islanders located the director of the *Mémorial* to announce their presence, both then and during the war. Taken aback, he had been unaware of their chapter in the camp's history. He was even more surprised to see a metal dog tag carried by a son of one of the deported Islanders. As most of the camp inhabitants had ended their lives in the concentration camps, he had never before seen a dog tag from the camp.

Although the director visited Guernsey with his team to meet the camp survivors in 2010, no changes to the exhibition had been made by 2020. While the Islanders' names have now been added to the Wall of Names (Figure 7.3), no other changes are visible. Even the multiple stations throughout the exhibition where audioguides elucidate content – surely the easiest part of the exhibition to update – are silent on this matter.

Today, many of the more impressive interactive displays have now stopped working and the exhibition needs refreshing. Although the current *Mémorial* staff want to include information about the Channel Islanders when the exhibition is renovated,[83] one of the hindrances in telling their story has been a lack of a coherent narrative – until now. Staff are also inevitably faced with financial constraints, with annual budget decreases.[84]. Looking beyond the omission of Channel Islanders from the current

Figure 7.3 The Wall of Names at Compiègne Memorial
Source: © Gilly Carr.

display, one of the more shocking aspects of the camp of Compiègne is not just the fact that it took until 2008 to recognize the role that the camp played in the Holocaust, but that so very recently the majority of the camp (including the Jewish compound) was allowed to be bulldozed. It was perhaps no mistake that three barracks that once housed political prisoners were preserved, echoing the French war narrative which has long championed the Résistance.[85]

We might usefully compare the situation of late recognition at the site of Compiègne with that of the better-known Jewish transit camp at Drancy, also just outside Paris. Although the camp today is now used for social housing for immigrants, the process of preserving and classifying the camp was completed only in 2001. Nearby, its associated Centre for History and Education was opened in 2012. The sites of both Compiègne and Drancy are implicated in France's history of collaboration and antisemitism during the war and, as such, their role today as places of national 'pain and shame'[86] – and embarrassment – are surely behind not just their late recognition but also Compiègne's destruction.

About the narratives in the exhibition at the *Mémorial* today, there is perhaps little justification, we must acknowledge, for the recognition of 128 British internees, especially given that 50,000 French people passed through the camp en route to concentration camps. Their story is neither one of victimhood nor involvement in the Holocaust (although a small number of the deported Islanders were Jews). Neither can these Islanders claim a share of the heroic narrative of the French resisters represented in the permanent exhibition. And, unlike those in the American compound, the Islanders were in the camp for just three months, which gives curatorial staff even less reason to include them in the permanent exhibition.

In the Channel Islands, their story has become subsumed with that of other internees. Compiègne is rarely mentioned in local museums; the focus – where mentioned at all – is always on Biberach and Wurzach civilian internment camps, the final destination of most deportees. Once again, the 128 Islanders are a minority within their own Islands' story of deportation, making up scarcely 6 per cent of all of those deported. Marginalized in both France and in the Channel Islands, the memory of this small group has had to vie for attention with that of the whole population who were either evacuated, occupied, imprisoned or deported to German internment camps. It is not surprising that they have failed to find a platform.

Acknowledgements

The author would like to thank many Islanders for their interviews, including Margaret Godfrey, Marjorie Lawrence, Gwen Ashton, Doris Bougourd and the Hamon brothers. She would like to thank Nellie Le Feuvre for permission to quote from her memoirs; Peter Boon, for the copy of his grandfather's memoirs; Jose Day, for sight of relevant pages of the diary of her father, Louis Guillemette; and Mark Boléat, for allowing her to quote from his grandmother's letters and mother's memoirs.

Notes

1. Channel Islands – general correspondence and various papers. The National Archives, TS 26/89.
2. Affidavit of John Leale, 15 June 1945. The National Archives, TS 26/89 and WO 311/105.
3. List of those convicted by a German court up until December 1942. Island Archives, Guernsey, FK 12-12.
4. Affidavit signed by Clifford Orange, 12 June 1945. The National Archives, WO 311/105.
5. Letter from Inspector Sculphur to the Bailliff, 25 November 1940. Island Archives, Guernsey, CC/3-20; letter from the Bailiff to John Leale, Acting President of the Controlling Committee, 26 November 1940. Island Archives, Guernsey, CC/3-20.
6. In the matter of German war crimes and in the matter of Sybil Mary Hathaway, affidavit sworn 30 June 1945. The National Archives, WO 311/105.
7. Roger Harris, *Islanders Deported* (Ilford: CISS Publishing, 1979), 34.
8. Douglas Ord, *Guernsey Occupation Diaries 1940–1945* (Guernsey: Blue Ormer, 2020).
9. Entry for 9–10 February 1943, Louis Guillemette's diary, consulted by kind permission of Jose Day.
10. The men older than 63 years of age were sent to Compiègne.
11. Violet Cortvriend, *Isolated Island* (London: Streamline Publications, 1947), 116.

12. Affidavit of John Leale, 15 June 1945. Channel Islands – general correspondence and various papers. The National Archives, TS 26/89.
13. Transport lists. Island Archives, Guernsey, FK 12–14.
14. List of persons transported to Germany, February 1943. Jersey Archives, B/A/W80/1.
15. Biberach camp register. Guernsey Museum, GUELI: GMAG 4090 a and b.
16. Note of Dr de Morsier, 17 February 1943, folder 'lettres reçus, 1/43–6/43, box 315. Archives of the ICRC (International Committee of the Red Cross), G 8/51.
17. Entry for 29–31 January 1943, Louis Guillemette's diary, consulted by kind permission of Jose Day.
18. This date has implications for the degree of German foreknowledge of the separation of families given that the transport lists would likely have been drawn up before those targeted were notified.
19. Nellie Le Feuvre, *A Sark Teenager's Deportation* (Privately printed, 2013), 3.
20. Ibid., 5.
21. Peggy Boléat, *A Quiet Place* (Guernsey: Villette Publishing, 1993), 147.
22. Memoirs of Lt. Colonel R. W. Randall, folio 9, file on Compiegne compiled by Tom Remfrey, Island Archives, Guernsey.
23. The location of the decoupling of the train has been in doubt, but Elsie May Henry and her husband Ernest John Henry both name this as happening in Le Mans; affidavits signed 16 May 1945, The National Archives, WO 311/105.
24. Interview between author and Margaret Godfrey, 19 April 2011.
25. Memoirs of Lt. Colonel R. W. Randall.
26. Le Feuvre, *A Sark Teenager's* Deportation, 6.
27. Beate Husser, Jean-Pierre Besse, and Françoise Leclère-Rosenzweig, *Frontstalag 122 Compiègne-Royallieu: Un camp d'internement allemande dans l'Oise 1941–1944* (Beauvais: Archives Départementales de l'Oise, 2008), 22.
28. Husser et al., *Frontstalag 122 Compiegne-Royallieu*, 21.
29. Ibid., 149–50.
30. As identified in a sketch of the map by Margaret Godfrey, former Guernsey internee, interviewed by author 19 April 2011.
31. Diary of Arthur McGahy. Island Archives, Guernsey, AQ 209/06.
32. Letter of Wilhelmina Quin, 23 February 1943, in private possession.
33. Ibid., 10 March 1943.
34. Memoirs of Lt. Colonel R. W. Randall.
35. In the matter of German war crimes and in the matter of Elsie May Henry, 16 May 1945. The National Archives, WO 311/105.
36. Harris, *Islanders Deported*, 150.
37. Letter of Wilhelmina Quin, 10 March 1943, in private possession; Memoirs of Lt Colonel R. W. Randall.
38. Interview between author and Margaret Godfrey, 19 April 2011.
39. Memoirs of Lt. Colonel R. W. Randall.
40. Le Feuvre, *A Sark Teenager's Deportation*, 7.
41. Letter reported in the diary of Douglas Ord, entry for 6 March 1943.
42. Le Feuvre, *A Sark Teenager's Deportation*, 6.
43. Harris, *Islanders Deported*, 149.
44. Interview between author and Gwen Ashton, 18 December 2009.
45. Memoirs of Lt Colonel R. W. Randall.
46. Interview between author and Margaret Godfrey, 19 April 2011.

47. Autograph book of Doris Bougourd, in private ownership.
48. Interview between author and Doris Bougourd, 6 December 2010.
49. Boléat, *A Quiet Place*, 149.
50. Interview between author and Margaret Godfrey, 19 April 2011.
51. Le Feuvre, *A Sark Teenager's Deportation*, 7.
52. Compensation claim for Nazi persecution, Una Heume,. 10 June 1965. The National Archives, HNP/1342.
53. Boléat, *A Quiet Place*, 148.
54. Interview between author and Gwen Ashton, 18 December 2009.
55. Interview between author and Doris Bougourd, 6 December 2010.
56. Interview between author and Bill, Arthur, Peter and Alan Hamon, 20 April 2011.
57. Ibid.
58. Interview between author and Doris Bougourd, 6 December 2010.
59. Le Feuvre, *A Sark Teenager's Deportation*, 8.
60. McGahy, entry for 27 March 1942.
61. McGahy, entry for 28 August 1942.
62. Janet de Santos, 'Survivor story', in *In Living Memory*, ed. Olympia McEwan (Guernsey: Blue Ormer, 2020), 36.
63. Esther Pauline Lloyd, *Camp Diaries*, entry for 6 May 1943. Wiener Holocaust Library ref. 1607.
64. De Santos, 'Survivor Story', 36.
65. Le Feuvre, *A Sark Teenger's Deportation*, 6.
66. Interview between author and Marjorie Lawrence, 9 December 2010.
67. Interview between author and Doris Bougourd, 6 December 2010.
68. Interview between author and Marjorie Lawrence, 9 December 2010.
69. Interview between author and Gwen Ashton, 18 December 2009.
70. Interview between author and Marjorie Lawrence, 9 December 2010.
71. Memoirs of Lt. Colonel R. W. Randall.
72. Le Feuvre, *A Sark Teenager's Deportation*, 8.
73. Interview between author and Gwen Ashton, 18 December 2009.
74. Le Feuvre, *A Sark Teenager's Deportation*, 10.
75. Memoirs of Lt. Colonel R. W. Randall.
76. Interview between author and Margaret Godfrey, 19 April 2011.
77. Boléat, *A Quiet Place*, 149.
78. Le Feuvre, *A Sark Teenager's Deportation*, 10.
79. Memoirs of Lt. Colonel R. W. Randall.
80. Compensation claim for Nazi persecution, Una Heaume, 10 June 1965. The National Archives, HNP/1342.
81. Boléat, *A Quiet Place*, 149.
82. Memoirs of Lt. Colonel R. W. Randall.
83. Email from *Mémorial* curator Gabrielle Perissi to author, 17 September 2020.
84. Email from *Mémorial* curator Gabrielle Perissi to author, 22 May 2022.
85. For example Henry Rousso, *The Vichy Syndrome: History and Memory in France since 1944* (Cambridge: Harvard University Press, 1991); Pieter Lagrou, *The Legacy of Nazi Occupation: Patriotic Memory and National Recovery in Western Europe, 1945–1965* (Cambridge: Cambridge University Press, 2000).
86. William Logan and Keir Reeves, *Places of Pain and Shame* (London: Routledge, 2009).

Bibliography

Boléat, Peggy. *A Quiet Place*. Guernsey: Villette Publishing, 1993.
Cortvriend, Violet V. *Isolated Island*. London: Streamline Publications, 1947.
Harris, Roger. *Islanders Deported*. Ilford: Channel Islands Specialist Society, 1979.
Husser, Beate, Besse Jean-Pierre and Françoise Leclère-Rosenzweig, Françoise. *Frontstalag 122 Compiègne-Royallieu: Un camp d'internement allemande dans l'Oise 1941–1944*. Beauvais: Archives Départementales de l'Oise, 2008.
Lagrou, Pieter. *The Legacy of Nazi Occupation: Patriotic Memory and National Recovery in Western Europe, 1945–1965*. Cambridge: Cambridge University Press, 2000.
Le Feuvre, Nellie. *A Sark Teenager's Deportation*. Privately printed, 2013.
Ord, Douglas. *Guernsey Occupation Diaries 1940–1945*. Guernsey: Blue Ormer, 2020.
Rousso, Henry. *The Vichy Syndrome: History and Memory in France since 1944*. Cambridge: Harvard University Press, 1991.
de Santos, Janet. 'Survivor story'. In *In Living Memory*, edited by Olympia McEwan, 34–7. Guernsey: Blue Ormer, 2020.

8

P. G. Wodehouse and the men of Tost

Christine Berberich

Introduction

If you are on the fast InterCity between Krakow and Wroclaw, chances are that you will entirely miss the small station of Toszek that your train is steaming through. It is just one of many small-town places in Poland, with a train station in the middle of fields, a few kilometres away from the town centre. You would be excused for missing the relevance of this small town in Second World War history. In the early 1940s, Toszek, then named Tost, was the site of a Nazi internment camp, the Ilag VIII, which housed predominantly British, French, Dutch and Belgian civilian internees, among them, for some months, the celebrated British novelist P. G. Wodehouse.. The scant internet results for searches on 'Tost' inevitably bring up Wodehouse's name as his time at the camp became his downfall: he accepted Nazi proposals that allowed him to exchange captivity at Tost for civilian accommodation in hotels and as the guest of German landed families, in return for broadcasting a series of light-hearted but badly judged radio talks from Berlin that seemed to depict his Nazi captors in a positive light and that led to accusations of treason. This chapter will not go into either Wodehouse's broadcasts, nor the long-term damage to his reputation, but will firmly focus on the camp of Tost and the experiences of the internees. It will start by locating the town of Toszek within the geography of contemporary Poland, move on to the capture of the internees in Northern France, chart their journey across Europe, with stays at holding camps near Lille and Liège, and then focus, in more detail, on day-to-day life in Ilag VIII Tost, before concluding with a look at post-war and contemporary Toszek and the problems of finding research materials on a woefully under-researched aspect of the Nazi past.

A Small Town in Silesia

Toszek is located in Upper Silesia, close to Gliwice and only around 50 km northeast of the better known and much bigger Katowice. Krakow is roughly 130 km to the southeast, Wroclaw (formerly Breslau) 150 km to the northwest, and Warsaw 290 km to the northeast. Its current population stands at about 4,000. In the late eighteenth century, Upper Silesia was annexed by what was then the Kingdom of Prussia and, as such, became part of the German Empire in 1871. After the First World War, the Eastern part of Upper Silesia became Polish; the rest remained part of the Weimar Republic, with the populations divided sharply into Polish and German speakers. With the German invasion of Poland in 1939, Polish Silesia once again became part of the German Reich. In 1945, after the end of the Second World War, Upper Silesia became Polish, and German-speakers were largely expelled. Polish once more, Tost became Toszek.

Today, travellers find a small sleepy place, off the beaten tourist track. The town is home to Toszek Castle which has its origins in the eleventh century, and which now functions as a cultural centre and popular wedding venue. Sir Ludwig Guttmann, the pioneer of spinal cord injury treatment and founder of the Paralympic Games was born nearby and the town celebrates his memory with regular talks and events held in the castle.[1] There are not too many tourist amenities to be found. A quick search on Tripadvisor mainly advertises the castle and a local church; for restaurants and especially hotels, the weary traveller would probably be best advised to try nearby Gliwice.[2] Toszek, in short, is not the kind of place one would normally associate with important wartime events, with internment camps or with 'dark tourism' and throngs of research visitors. Yet, it is only a brisk ten-minute walk from the Cultural Centre at Toszek Castle, via the centre of town, to Gliwicka Road, and it is here, in a building now housing a psychiatric hospital, that we find the site of the former Nazi Ilag VIII.

Ilag is an abbreviation of the German word *Internierungslager*, different from the more infamous *Konzentrationslager*, or KZs. The Ilags were predominantly created to house British and other Allied civilians during the war – and they are generally not covered in much depth or detail in research. In fact, as far as Ilag VIII Tost is concerned, most of the existing work has been done by relatives and descendants of former internees. I have been very fortunate in having been granted access to the private collection of letters, cards and photographs of the internee Tom Sarginson, whose daughter Jeanne Gask, herself the author of a book on her own experiences in domestic internment in Northern France, has offered valuable insights and recollections.[3] In France, Frédéric Turner, the son and nephew of former Tost internees, has, over the course of more than seventeen years, painstakingly compiled a list of internees and their stories, and produced a book that, although a valuable research resource, is not easily obtainable. Tellingly, his book is entitled *Les oubliés 1939-45* – the 'forgotten' of 1939-45.[4] Turner also maintains a blog site where he is trying to piece together further histories of French and British prisoners of Tost with the help of their respective descendants.[5] In addition to that, there is the writing of P. G. Wodehouse who, after the war, had been planning to publish what he referred to as his 'Camp book', to be called *Wodehouse in Wonderland*. He had been planning to use this as an official 'Apologia' to offer his side of events leading up to the ill-fated broadcasts from Berlin. *Wodehouse in Wonderland* was never published, but excerpts of it are available in his generally light-hearted *Performing Flea: A Self-Portrait in Letters*, first published in 1953.[6] There is also Iain Sproat's biographical work, *Wodehouse at War*, that tries to reveal 'the extraordinary truth about P.G. Wodehouse's broadcasts on Nazi radio', but fails to provide much insight into actual internment life at Tost, as well as biographical writing on Wodehouse, such as Robert McCrum's seminal *Wodehouse. A Life* that contains a section on internment and the ensuing scandal surrounding the Berlin broadcasts that led to the writer's disgrace.[7] However, to date, there is nothing matching this work in terms of academic engagement with the various Ilags and their internees. After the war and over the past decades, the focus of academic attention has understandably been on the concentration camps. Looking at civilian internment camps by no means diminishes this focus but, rather, adds another important layer of research on Nazi treatment of prisoners in their power. As civilian internees, the men at Tost could receive Red Cross Parcels, and their status differed drastically from that of ordinary prisoners, prisoners of war (POWs) or inmates in the Nazi concentration camps. Their treatment was generally more humane, in as far as that can be said for the treatment of inmates in a Nazi camp. It is high time that more critical light is shed on the civilian internment camps in Nazi-occupied Europe and the treatment of the men (and, in some cases women) within their confines.

From Northern France to Tost

It was on a beautiful summer morning, on 21 July 1940, that the celebrated British writer P. G. Wodehouse was arrested by the occupying German authorities in his house in Le Touquet in the département of Pas-de-Calais. Together with other British detainees he was transported to Loos prison, located in a suburb of Lille about 110 kilometres to the east. This was only the first stop in the detainees' long journey towards Silesia. After a few days in Loos prison, they were moved to army barracks in the nearby Belgian Liège. Wodehouse's biographer, Robert McCrum, explains how Wodehouse, alongside 800 other English internees, was 'crammed into windowless cattle trucks designed for "Quarante Hommes, Huit Chevaux"' and that the journey of just under 200 kilometres took twenty-four hours.[8] Less than a week later, the men were moved on again, this time to Huy Citadel, just thirty kilometres away, where they were to remain for five weeks, in horrendous conditions marked by hunger, cold and dirt.[9] Huy Citadel, a forbidding fortress overlooking the river, was never equipped to be an internment camp and facilities were basic. On 3 August, Wodehouse chronicled his arrival and his forebodings: 'Arrived four-thirty. … things don't look too good. They have put forty of us in a room large enough for about fifteen. No beds. Not even straw on the floor.'[10] Other internees similarly focused on the poor accommodation arrangements. In a letter to his family of 14 August 1940, Tom Sarginson, who had shared Wodehouse's journey from Calais to Loos to Huy, likewise points out the poor if slightly improving sleeping arrangements: 'Loose straw, but we are having bags today'.[11] Wodehouse's diary entries are in his typically humorous tone of voice but their focus on the lack or poor quality of food ('Rumour proved true. Our buckets contained a sort of sweet hot water with prunes floating in it. I have seldom tasted anything so loathsome'; 'Horrible shock today. The bread ration failed …') showcase the hardships he and his fellow internees had to suffer in Huy.[12] In a more serious tone, his biographer McCrum points out that 'for the civilian internees … their sojourn [in Huy] was an experience they would never forget and in some cases never really recover from'.[13] The fact that Huy was never meant to be an internment camp might account for, but not excuse, the very basic conditions. On 8 September, the internees were given new orders. They were marched down the hill to Huy station, packed on to a train and headed 'off into the unknown'; their destination was Tost.[14]

Camp Life: Barred windows, cricket and dreams about food

The internees' arrival was anti-climactic. The journey from Huy took 'three days and three nights' and, apart from hunger and thirst, the men mostly struggled with the fact that they did not know where they were going.[15] Wodehouse's recollections foreground the fact that Tost was so safely tucked away in the middle of nowhere that even the train driver missed the station:

> And when we did get to Tost he passed it without a glance and took us on to Gleiwitz, where we remained at a siding for six hours before somebody happened along and told him to go back till he came to Farmer Schmidt's barn and then left as far as the old mill and after that he'd better ask somebody.[16]

Tost 'station' is described by Wodehouse as consisting of merely 'some planks dumped down in the middle of the woods', and although this is a typical Wodehousean exaggeration, it does emphasize the isolated location of the small town of Tost and the internment camp that was to be the weary men's destination.[17] Famously, Wodehouse would often joke in later life that 'Tost is no beauty spot. It lies in the heart of sugar-beet country … There is a flat dullness about the countryside which has led many a visitor to say "If this is Upper Silesia, what must Lower Silesia be like?"'[18]

Things were not necessarily more welcoming when they finally arrived at their destination, as the internment camp at Tost was housed in a former mental asylum – a fact that greatly tickled Wodehouse who referred to the building complex as 'this Upper Silesian loony bin'.[19] The five-storey building of the former asylum ended up accommodating up to 1,300 internees at a time, and conditions, though not squalid, were certainly cramped. Although a distinct improvement on the conditions at Huy Citadel, the arrangements inside were utilitarian at best. Wodehouse pointed out that 'the walls are bare and the floors are bare, and when you go in or out you climb or descend echoing stone stairs', while Sarginson informed his family that 'the building and grounds are very much like your old college for size and disposition'.[20] George Gregson, another internee who arrived a few months after Wodehouse and Sarginson, kept a diary at Tost and recorded, in particular, the cold in his top-floor dormitory and the fact that 'WC's and baths are all open – no doors at all – so that the lunatics were always under observation as indeed we can be, if necessary'.[21] On arrival, the new internees had to parade, as well as having '[their] baggage examined, [handing] in all money, [and going] before a doctor'.[22] Both Gregson and Wodehouse remarked on the fact that they were also ordered to take a bath – something noteworthy after the long journey and, in particular, the conditions at Huy, although it was less luxurious than it originally sounded. Wodehouse described the baths as 'a number of enormous wooden tubs' in the 'laundry above the cookhouse', and both he and Gregson highlighted that three men had to use the bath simultaneously in order to save time and, presumably, water.[23]

The dormitories, where the men spent most of their time, were overcrowded and poorly ventilated. It was very much luck of the draw which room an internee was allocated. Gregson was initially in an attic dormitory sleeping seventy-two men with no heating whatsoever, which was so cold that it triggered coughs and severe rheumatism for him. He was eventually transferred to room 309 on the third floor that already housed both Wodehouse and Sarginson.[24] Lower floor dormitories such as this benefited from more heating but brought with them other disadvantages, poorer ventilation that often led to arguments among the men as to whether windows should be open or closed at night. Room 309 had been designed to accommodate thirty asylum inmates but, during Wodehouse's time at Tost, averaged sixty-six men.[25] Beds were either singles or bunk beds, with bedding made up of, as Gregson recorded, 'a thin paillasse, two sheets and two blankets', sheer luxury for those men who had come from Huy where they had had to sleep on the floor.[26] In a letter of 12 December 1940, Sarginson told his family that 'I have a bed, what we call a double-decker, with another fellow on top of me, we are 60 per room'. Storage was non-existent; the men had to keep their belongings in bags and boxes stored underneath the beds, drop their clothes on the floor at night or, alternatively, sleep in them.[27] Wodehouse also recounted that 'the window sills were used as storage depots for tin cans, cardboard boxes, cold potatoes and other properties … The space between the double windows served as a Frigidaire'.[28] These descriptions paint a vivid picture of conditions inside the camp and illustrate the way that the men tried to make the best of an unpleasant situation by arranging what little space was available to them in as comfortable a manner as possible. Later on in his internment, Sarginson commented that 'I have flowers growing in window boxes that I have made up', and Gregson recorded the men's attempt to decorate 'a spare parade room … with fur-trees [sic] and a Xmas tree – all the oddments such as stars being made with much ingenuity from the cardboard of parcels and silver paper from cheese'.[29] All of those whose letters, diaries and recollections have been consulted here repeatedly commented on the alternative usages dormitory fittings were put to: the radiators that were used to heat up left-over potatoes, for instance, or even to bake bread pudding from saved up breadcrumbs and jam.[30] Such things gave much-needed structure to their day, created some sense of normality and helped make their internment somewhat more bearable.

Nevertheless, the men were very conscious of the fact that they were not at liberty to come and go as they pleased. One of the things all the internees commented on were the windows: Wodehouse pointed out that 'all the windows at Tost were heavily barred'; Sarginson struggled with the fact that 'I can see outside, the kiddies with sledges & think then of my dear girls last winter. Can you imagine what it feels like to be locked up & see the people free outside!' and, in a different letter, 'From the barred window of my room I see the people free, walking outside & the kiddies going to school on bikes etc.

They look just like in England. It does not make me feel over cheerful!'³¹ Wodehouse's writing makes it clear that, initially, the internees were prohibited from even standing at and looking out of the windows overlooking the street, but that they found this order impossible to obey as they all yearned for something resembling normality: 'It was not that there was anything much to see when you did look out: just a village street with a deserted beer garden across the way; but that mattered little to us. We did not ask for the Grand Canyon or the Taj Mahal. What we wanted was to stand there and goggle.'³² Entries such as these emphasize the isolated and sequestered nature of life at Ilag VIII, a life that saw them cut off not only from their families but also from everyday life in the surrounding town. The windows provided tantalizing glimpses of 'ordinary' town life, so while camp life in general followed a dull but comparatively 'peaceful' routine, it was the bars on them that reminded the internees on a daily basis that they were, to all intents and purposes, prisoners.

There were, however, some small perks to life at Tost: the camp benefitted from a relatively large outside area that the men could use for all sorts of activities. Sarginson's letters mention the park-like space surrounding the camp, with 'many trees, oak, pin [sic], chesnut [sic] etc [where] we take a brisk walk ... for exercise', where the men are 'sunbathing', and where 'cricket, bowling, miniature golf & other games are in full swing'; Gregson recorded regular exercise in the park, and Wodehouse also writes about using a 'private yard ... formed by the main building and ... fenced in with wire' where he spent some quiet time 'basking in the sunshine' until the place was similarly discovered by other internees which put an end to his sunny solitude there.³³ Occasionally, the men were also escorted to playing fields, Sarginson relating that 'We go to a sport field 120 at the time, with guards, to play football & cricket'.³⁴ Those cricket matches – undoubtedly under the bemused stares of the cricket-uninitiated Nazi guards – proved more successful and invigorating than the impromptu and improvised cricket matches played amongst and around the trees in the camp park. Apart from that, though, the men were seldom allowed outside of the camp confines. Sarginson's letters show that, on one occasion, the men had been permitted to visit a local cinema; some men also volunteered for outside work.³⁵ But these were rare occurrences, and contact with the outside world was strictly limited: letters were eagerly anticipated and brought news from family and friends provided they got past the censor; English newspapers were not allowed and most men could not understand the German newspapers or radio stations to which they had access. Sarginson wrote that 'we are [not] allowed to speak to soldiers or civilians', and so the men were largely left to their own devices and to each other's company.³⁶

For many of the men, this led to boredom and depression. Others tried to keep themselves busy. Wodehouse was particularly concerned about the progress of his writing as he had been in the process of completing another novel – *Joy in the Morning* – when he was first arrested. Once he had settled in at Tost, he thought of a new novel – *Money in the Bank* – and set about writing it, as he explained in a letter to his friend Bill Townend of 11 May 1942, 'in a room with fifty other men playing darts and ping-pong'.³⁷ Once the commandant of Tost, *Oberleutnant* Buchelt, had recognized his famous internee, Wodehouse was given access to a separate writing room, 'formerly a padded cell' and was allowed to hire a typewriter.³⁸ With Wodehouse thus occupied, other internees also looked for ways to while away the time. Sarginson, for instance, constantly reassured his family that 'I keep busy with different things': he taught French and also gave some French talks; he sang at concerts; he undertook daily physical exercises and walked as much as possible to remain fit and healthy and, early on in his internment, he also started learning German.[39] As there was such a wide array of internees from different countries and backgrounds, a lot of entertainment was arranged to keep the men engaged and help them pass the time. Arranging these different entertainments, offering classes and organizing sporting events was entirely left to the management of the internees themselves: apart from the sport that the men engaged in in the Park, there were organized boxing matches, pantomimes and theatre performances, musical recitals, film nights and much more.[40] Nevertheless, many of the men succumbed to melancholia and even depression, giving in to the monotony of life as internees: Sarginson reported to his family that 'to some it must be very trying & long, doing sweet nothing all day, on their beds or lounging about corridors, proping [sic] walls & radiators, have not even the guts to read or do slightest effort. What will they do after?'[41] This letter, written twenty months after Sarginson's arrival at Tost, clearly illustrates the toll internment was taking on some of the men: no amount of entertainment and cricket in the park could cover the fact that they were forcibly separated from their families and homes, and that the future was filled with uncertainty.

When reading recollections or letters by internees, it quickly becomes obvious that they all share certain preoccupations, in general circling around food. Food was something never far from their minds. For Gregson, time at Tost started with 'an excellent breakfast of soup, sausage (cold), bread and coffee', a welcome change from treatment the men had experienced at previous internment camps, especially the ones who had been at Huy where food had been scarce and where they had been reduced to eating potato peel.[42] Wodehouse was bowled over by the fact that each man, on arrival at Tost, was given 'porcelain bowls, tin mugs, spoons, knives and forks', a welcome change from 'Huy [where] we had had no forks or spoons and the tin mug which we used for coffee in the morning had to serve for soup at midday', and 'Liège [where] we had been obliged to get along with what we could dig out of the dustbin'.[43] Once Tom Sarginson had finally established regular contact with his wife and daughters, who were in civilian internment in Northern France, and his father- and sister-in-law in Birmingham, a large part of each of his letters focused on food and what the family could do to enhance his supplies. One thing in particularly high demand among the internees was 'plain cake biscuits or anything bready', as well as 'choc, cigs always acceptable', as they could be used for trading.[44]

As civilians, the men at Tost could register their internment with the Red Cross and request and receive parcels to supplement their food supplies. Once these started arriving, the men's diets were much improved and they generally pooled their resources and shared out delicacies such as chocolate. Gregson's diary entries provide a lot of detail about the content of these parcels – '1 Xmas pudding, 1 cake, 1 sardines, 2 big cakes, Nestlé's chocolate, 1 Pascall's sweets, 1 Irish stew, 1 kippers, 1 tin beans and tomato, 1 St Ivel cheese, 1 tin stewed mandarine [sic], 1 tin Nestlé's milk, 1 tea, 1 sugar' – while Sarginson's letters make it clear that he felt well-supplied in terms of food and that, in fact, he worried far more about shortages suffered by his wife and daughters, a fact emphasized by his many letters to his father- and sister-in-law exhorting them to have Red Cross parcels sent to France as well.[45] Nevertheless, food remained a major preoccupation, mainly because the set meal times for breakfast, lunch and dinner punctuated the day and helped ease the monotony and boredom. Mealtimes also helped the communal spirit in the camp, with the men sitting together, sharing out what provisions they had. The standard camp diet was bland and repetitive and while the men were not starving, they were certainly still often hungry and craved those things they could not have. Wodehouse was planning to dedicate an entire chapter in his 'Camp book' to food, explaining, 'We were thirteen hundred internees with but a single thought. A bevy of tapeworms could not have been more preoccupied with the matter of nourishment than the inmates of Ilag VIII.'[46] This preoccupation with food also led to ingenious inventions and experiments. Gregson noted in his diary that

> Dutnall and I have decided to try baking a bit. We have a supply of old crusts so have set them to soak in water and we then propose to squash up the pulps into a tin, put some bits of butter on the top, add jam jelly, made liquid with hot water and sprinkle with sugar and then bake on the radiators,

reporting a few days later that 'our bread pudding was a huge success and we are going to make another as he [Dutnall] now has more sugar available from his parcel'.[47] Despite the official camp food that, as Gregson said, was 'good and sufficient – anyone can live on it', Wodehouse noted that he lost a lot of weight during his time at Tost, and that his attitude towards food was compromised for years after when he had to '[relearn] the technique of dining' and '[re]accustom [himself] to the peace-time method of securing potatoes'.[48] Accounts from POWs, internees or concentration camp survivors from all over the world show a preoccupation with food during their ordeal that affected their lives for years to come; the men of Tost, clearly, were no exception.[49]

Like internees everywhere, the men were desperate for news from friends and family, and also for news about the progress of the war. Rumours were rife: about the progress of the war, about which other countries might now be involved (there was, in particular, speculation about when and how the Americans might join the war effort) and about Allied successes. And there were, of course, also rumours and uncertainties about the men's own future in the camp. Sarginson's letters often mention rumours that wives and children would be allowed to join their husbands in the camp, or that they would all be reunited in a different family camp; Gregson recorded news that those English men who had lived in France for more than fifteen years were to be sent back, and that those over fifty were to be released.[50] In the event, Wodehouse left Tost on 21 June 1941, to be taken to Berlin for his broadcasts. Eventually joined by his wife Ethel, he stayed in various places in Germany – ranging from luxury hotels to private accommodation with civilian hosts – until September 1943 when he moved to Paris to continue civilian internment in a series of apartments there.[51] George Gregson's Tost diary ends on 31 May 1941 and there is some uncertainty concerning his movements after that. His diaries recommence on 2 November 1943, and it appears that he was moved to a POW camp instead of a civilian internment camp[52]. In autumn 1943, after pressure by the Red Cross who argued that, after four years, internees had to be returned to the country from which they had been taken. Tom Sarginson and the others who had arrived with him from Huy returned to France, to be interned in a camp at Giromagny near the Swiss border. The men arrived there in the middle of winter and found a camp that was not fit for living, and that initially barely offered them protection against the cold. Jeanne Gask records that 'anything, absolutely anything at all, that was not wanted was burned on the stoves in the middle of the huts – doors, chairs, wood lying around outside the huts'.[53] In September 1944, with Allied troops steadily progressing further into France after the D-Day landings in June and the liberation of Paris on 25 August, the British men at Giromagny were repatriated to England via Sweden. Sarginson arrived in Liverpool on 16 September 1944. His wife and children were, at that point, still in France. He had been interned for over four years.[54] His experiences at Tost camp had marked him deeply.

Post-War Toszek and blind spots in contemporary memory culture

During the war years, the Nazi internment camp at Tost saw a number of reincarnations. After briefly serving as an Oflag – a POW camp for officers – between July and October 1940, the camp was solely used as an Ilag until September 1943. From December 1943 until April 1944, it served as an Oflag again.[55] In the immediate post-war years, the history of the camp at Tost and the experiences of its inmates were overshadowed by stories and revelations about a much more notorious camp just under ninety km away: Auschwitz-Birkenau. The site at Tost – now renamed Toszek – was taken over by the Soviets and turned into a prison camp for the NKVD, the People's Commissariat for Internal Affairs. It largely housed German civilians who had been brought from parts of Germany now under Soviet control. While conditions during the Ilag days of the camp had been quite cramped, the NKVD camp was terribly overcrowded. Diseases such as dysentery were rife: between June and December 1945, 3,000 prisoners died from disease, malnourishment and torture. In Germany, the bulk of the memory work concerning the NKVD camp at Toszek has been done by Sybille Krägel, the daughter of a prisoner who died within weeks of arriving at Toszek. Krägel, a member of the German organization UOKG (*Union der Opferverbände kommunistischer Gewaltherrschaft/Society of Unions of Victim of Communist Tyranny*), has, for the last thirty years, researched the terror that reigned at the NKVD camp and has managed to compile a list with thousands of names of prisoners, often painstakingly translated and transcribed from Cyrillic transport lists.[56] She is also the driving force behind the organization of a memorial in Toszek (see Figure 8.1).

This memorial was erected on the site of a mass grave of civilian victims of the camp regime. The commemorative plaque reads – in both Polish and German – 'here rest the victims of the NKVD camp Tost, May till November 1945'. The memorial is well kept, mainly due to the efforts of the 'German Friendship Circle' present in Toszek today. Regular annual visits organized by the UOKG are welcomed in the town and

Figure 8.1 Tost Memorial

Source: Photo by kind permission of Sybille Krägel, NKWD-Lager Tost/Oberschlesien 1945.

chronicled by both Polish and German media. The buildings of the former Ilag VIII and NKVD camp now house a psychiatric hospital that specializes in the treatment of addictions. The hospital's website clearly shows the buildings of the former camp.[57] Parts of the buildings in their contemporary incarnation can be seen in Figure 8.2, which shows the part of the complex used as hospital wing during the building's time as a camp.

There is also a memorial plaque on the hospital buildings (Figure 8.3), commemorating the approximately 3,250 prisoners of the Soviets who died in the camp.

Yet, despite the varied history of the site, and notwithstanding the excellent memorial work undertaken on the site's use as an NKVD camp, there are no signs or memorials commemorating its time as an Ilag and Oflag between 1940 and 1944, and this is a troubling blind spot in contemporary memory culture. A smattering of official documentation seems to exist in a number of different archives in Germany, but it appears that no wider-reaching official work on the histories of the Nazi civilian internment camps has been done either in Germany or Poland. In Poland, commemoration by and large focuses on the Soviet use of the camp; a book on the NKVD history of the camp has been published by the historians Sebastian Rosenbaum, Boguslaw Traczl and Dariusz Wegrzyn but currently only exists in the Polish original although efforts are underway to have it translated into German.[58] There is, clearly,

Figure 8.2 Tost camp hospital building
Source: Photo by kind permission of Andrzej Morciniec, www.promafot.pl.

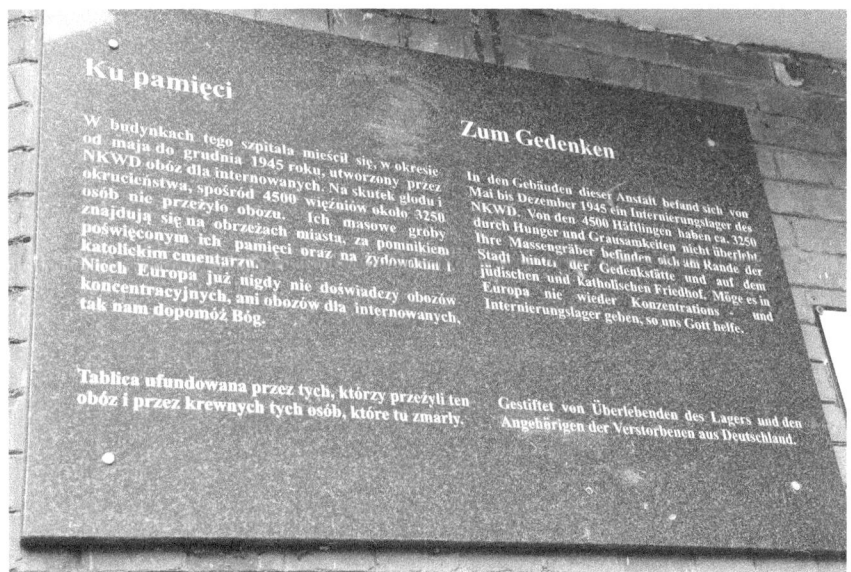

Figure 8.3 Tost NKVD camp memorial plaque
Source: Photo by kind permission of Andrzej Morciniec, www.promafot.pl.

a lot of 'history' around the Ilag VIII at Tost still to be discovered. And while this chapter has offered some insights into what can be termed social history, with a focus on the voices of the internees themselves, it is clear that other, more wider-reaching questions about the camp, its management and the effects on the internees have yet to be asked. These need to include searching questions about not only the complete lack in contemporary Poland of meaningful commemoration of the site's use as a Nazi internment camp but also the absence of the topic as a focus for research in Germany. One thing that this chapter has not been able to touch upon, for example, is the fact that, in April 1942, several hundred Jewish internees were transported from Tost to a new camp opened at Kreuzburg – now Kluczbork – roughly seventy kilometres north of Tost.[59] This chapter is just the starting point for a more in-depth engagement with the Nazi internment camp at Tost and with the various histories and plights of its internees. Fascinating and important stories remain to be uncovered, and this is vital for a more critical and reflective assessment of the past.

Notes

1. See, for instance, https://www.zamektoszek.eu/ (accessed 26 December 2021).
2. See, for instance, https://www.livemint.com/Leisure/3yan1GetM4eXcf0SUofj7L/Toszek-Poland--On-a-Wodehousean-trail.html for a travel report by Aadisht Khanna from 2013 (accessed 26 December 2021).
3. See Jeanne Gask, *Nell and the Girls: The True Story of a British Girl and her Family in Occupied France 1940–1944* (Newcastle-upon-Tyne: Myrmidon, 2015).
4. Frédéric Turner, *Les outlies de 39–45. Les Britanniques internes a Tost, Kreuzburg, Giromagny et Westermke* (Arras: Editions JAFT, 2013).
5. See, for instance, http://anglais62.blogspot.com/search/label/Tost (accessed 26 December 2021).
6. P.G. Wodehouse. *Performing Flea: A Self-Portrait in Letters* (London: Everyman, [1953] 2014).
7. See Iain Sproat, *Wodehouse at War: The Extraordinary Truth about P.G. Wodehouse's Broadcasts on Nazi Radio* (London: Milner, 1981) and Robert McCrum, *Wodehouse: A Life* (London: Penguin Books, 2005).
8. McCrum, *Wodehouse. A Life*, 279–80.
9. See, for instance, Wodehouse, *Performing Flea*, 243–55.
10. Wodehouse, *Performing Flea*, 243.
11. Tom Sarginson, Letter of 14 August 1940. Private collection.
12. Wodehouse, *Performing Flea*, 244, 245.
13. McCrum, *Wodehouse*, 281.
14. Ibid., 255.
15. Ibid., 259.
16. Ibid., 260.
17. Ibid., 263.
18. Ibid., 256.
19. Ibid., 256.
20. Ibid., 257; Sarginson, Letter of 12 December 1940.

21. George Gregson, 'Internment at Tost from November 26 1940 to May 31 1941', entry for 30 November 1940.
22. Ibid., entry for 26 – 29 November 1940.
23. Ibid., entry for 26 – 29 November 1940; Wodehouse, *Performing Flea*, 265.
24. Gregson, 'Internment at Tost', entries for 26 – 29 November; 30 November; 18 December 1940.
25. See Wodehouse, *Performing Flea*, 268.
26. Gregson, 'Interment at Tost', entry for 26 – 29 November 1940.
27. Sarginson, Letter of 12 December 1940; see also Gregson, 'Internment at Tost', entry for 26 – 29 November 1940.
28. Wodehouse, *Performing Flea*, 267.
29. Sarginson, Letter of 26 May 1941; Gregson, 'Internment at Tost', entry for 24 December 1940.
30. See, for instance, Wodehouse, *Performing Flea*, 267 or Gregson, 'Internment at Tost', entry for 21 December 1940.
31. Wodehouse, *Performing Flea*, 257; Sarginson, Letter of 18 December 1940 and Letter of 18 April 1941.
32. Wodehouse, *Performing Flea*, 279.
33. Sarginson, Letter of 12 December 1940; letter of 24 May 1942; Gregson, 'Internment at Tost', for example, entries for 19 December 1940, 3 April 1941, 29 April; Wodehouse, *Performing Flea*, 261.
34. Sarginson, Letter of 26 May 1941.
35. Ibid., Letter of 24 August 1941.
36. Ibid., Letter of 24 May 1942.
37. PG Wodehouse, letter to Bill Townend, 11 May 1942, quoted in McCrum, *Wodehouse*, 287.
38. See ibid., 288, 295. In fact, it was Buchelt who offered to have the completed manuscript of *Money in the Bank* sent to the United States for publication.
39. Sarginson, Letter of 18 December 1940; also Letter of 26 May 1941 and Letter of 30 September 1940. Gregson's diaries similarly reference his attempts to learn German: 'Am considering learning German' and 'had German lesson' (Entries for 2–3 December and 12 December 1940).
40. Incidentally, none of the consulted sources make any reference to the behaviour of the guards. This could be due to concerns about censorship. The impression that most of the letters and diary entries convey is that the camps were largely self-administered by the inmates themselves.
41. Ibid., Letter of 12 April 1942.
42. Gregson, 'Internment at Tost', entry for 26 – 29 November 1940.
43. Wodehouse, *Performing Flea*, 263–4.
44. Sarginson, Letter of 11 October 1940 and Letter of 25 September 1941.
45. Gregson, 'Internment at Tost', entry for 16 January 1940.
46. Wodehouse, *Performing Flea*, 286.
47. Gregson, 'Internment at Tost', entries for 21 and 25 December 1940.
48. Wodehouse, *Performing Flea*, 294.
49. For such accounts see, for instance, Elie Wiesel, *Night* (London: Penguin, [1956] 1986); Art Spiegelman, *The Complete Maus* (London: Penguin, 2003); Takis Würger, *Leon. Von Einem, der Überlebte* (München: Penguin, 2020).

50. For instance, Sarginson, card from 19 December 1941, Letter of 1 February 1942, Letter of 15 February 1942; Gregson, 'Internment at Tost', entries for 23 and 31 May 1941.
51. See McCrum, *Wodedhouse*, for example, 301, 310, 328, 338.
52. See http://www.holywellhousepublishing.co.uk/George_Gregson.html (accessed 26 December 2021).
53. Gask, *Nell and the Girls*, 108.
54. For an account of Sarginson's repatriation see http://www.holywellhousepublishing.co.uk/Tom_Sarginson.html (accessed 26 December 2021).
55. See http://www.moosburg.org/info/stalag/laglist.html for information (accessed 26 December 2021).
56. See https://www.uokg.de/mitglieder/initiativgruppe-nkwd-lager-tostoberschlesien-1945/ (accessed 26 December 2021). In years of painstaking detective work, Sybille Krägel, the daughter of a prisoner at the camp who had died within weeks of arriving there, has compiled a databank of over 4,000 names of former prisoners at the NKVD.
57. See http://www.szpitaltoszek.pl/ (accessed 26 December 2021).
58. See Sebastian Rosenbaum, Boguslaw Traczl and Dariusz Wegrzyn, *Tiurma-lagier Tost. Historia obozu NKWD w Toszku w 1945 roku* (Gmina Toszek, 2017). A brief summary of the work in German and English is available via Academia.edu at https://www.academia.edu/35652789/Tiurma_%C5%82agier_Tost_Historia_obozu_NKWD_w_Toszku_w_1945_roku (accessed 26 December 2021).
59. See https://www.historylearningsite.co.uk/world-war-two/prisoners-of-war-in-ww2/british-internees/ (accessed 26 December 2021).

Bibliography

Gask, Jeanne. *Nell and the Girls: The True Story of a British Girl and Her Family in Occupied France 1940–1944*. Newcastle-upon-Tyne: Myrmidon, 2015.

McCrum, Robert. *Wodehouse: A Life*. London: Penguin Books, 2005.

Rosenbaum, Sebastian, Traczl Boguslaw and Dariusz Wegrzyn, *Tiurma-lagier Tost. Historia obozu NKWD w Toszku w 1945 roku*. Gmina Toszek, 2017.

Sproat, Iain. *Wodehouse at War: The Extraordinary Truth about P.G. Wodehouse's Broadcasts on Nazi radio*. London: Milner, 1981.

Turner, Frédéric. *Les oubliés 1939–45. Les Britanniques internes a Tost, Kreuzburg, Giromagny et Westertimke*. Arras: Editions JAFT, 2013.

Wodehouse, P. G. *Performing Flea: A Self-Portrait in Letters*. London: Everyman, [1953] 2014.

9

The Golden Cage: The orphan story of British women and internment in Vittel

Ayshka Sené

> *This camp benefited from the magnificent installations of the thermal establishment of Vittel, had nothing to compare with the other Nazi camps and, apart from the deprivation of liberty, the internees were not too unhappy and were very well supplied* – Mayor of Vittel, 1948.[1]
> 'Still the best of camps' – Red Cross Report, September 1944.[2]

Between 2007 and 2014, several published biographies emerged about British women interned in a camp in Vittel in eastern France.[3] These biographies were all written by the relatives of former internees, based on wartime diaries, except for *Rosie's War*, which was co-written by a former internee and her daughter.[4] Nicolas Shakespeare's account of his aunt Priscilla's experiences was serialized on Radio 4's *Book of the Week*, and reviews of the book featured widely in the British and American press.[5] These publications indicate a gap in the historiography of British women in wartime France, as well as a popular preoccupation with their lives. In addition to these published accounts, a significant corpus of archival material concerning Frontstalag 142 in Vittel also exists, as well as survivors and their relatives who could be interviewed. Despite these rich sources, the internment of British women in Vittel has received little academic attention, as stories of resistance and female secret agents continue to dominate the field of British women and the Second World War.[6] Combining oral and written testimony with archival material, the first part of this chapter addresses the concept of Vittel as a 'Golden Cage', where inmates were well resourced and protected by the British government, in stark contrast to the Jewish internees with whom they were interned and also French civilians living under occupied rule. The second part of the chapter posits the memory of British women in Vittel as an 'orphan story', by which I mean that their memory has not found a home in French or British national memories. British women have been occluded from national narratives in both countries because their experiences are neither sufficiently heroic nor tragic.

Little has been written about the internment of British civilians in France and neither do British women feature in literature concerning foreign women in France.[7]

Existing research on internment focuses on 'enemy aliens' in British camps, rather than British civilians interned overseas.[8] French historian Dennis Peschanski offers rich insights into the camps run by the French Republic, covering the period before, during and after Vichy, but considers British civilian internees on the edge of his subject specialism and focuses on the internment of others considered enemy aliens by the Vichy regime.[9] Current work on foreign women in wartime France posits them as either vulnerable, persecuted by Vichy (especially if they were Jewish), and perceived as 'outsiders' in local communities, or as combatants, clandestinely engaged in resistance and mobilized against the Vichy and Nazi regimes.[10] British women do not feature in these studies either. Despite these absences, British women in wartime France have been the subject of some research, but this has focused on the experiences of young, female British agents who were part of the F (French) section of the Special Operations Executive (SOE).[11] The memory of SOE has pervaded at a national level and their experiences have been foregrounded in museums, memorials, television series, documentaries, novels and press coverage. There were only thirty-nine women in the F section, all had escaped France before 1942, and this small sample represent an exceptional group of individuals whose 'extraordinary experiences' have been the focus of academic enquiry.[12] Despite this very partial vision, the SOE agent has become the dominant stereotype for British women in France during the Occupation. It is hoped that exploring the lesser known accounts of British women interned in Vittel will nuance perceptions of internment in France and broaden current understandings and memories of British women in France during this period.

Frontstalag 142, Vittel

Situated in a luxury hotel complex in the spa town of Vittel, Frontstalag 142 was the largest camp of British women on French soil. Following the defeat of France and the armistice, from September 1940, British women residing across France were required by the German authorities to report to their local German command office.[13] In December 1940, those who had registered were rounded up and interned by the German authorities at *Caserne Vauban* in Besançon. There were 3,900 British subjects interned in Besançon on 10 December 1940.[14] Only those who were seriously ill could remain in their own homes or in hospital.[15] Upon arrival in Besançon, the most elderly and infirm internees were hospitalized. On 7 December, there were 157 British civilians hospitalized in the Hôpital Saint-Jacques in Besançon, and this number rose quickly to 484 on 20 December 1940 due to the poor conditions in the camp.[16] In January 1941, those in the camp aged over sixty and under sixteen were released by the Germans and were then required to report to their local German command office.[17]

In June 1941, the 1,481 remaining British civilians (of whom 120 were men and 11 were children) who had been held at Besançon were transferred to a new camp in Vittel in eastern France, following complaints from the International Committee of the Red Cross (ICRC) about the conditions in *Caserne Vauban*.[18] Besançon was unsanitary, contaminated with pests, bitterly cold and meagrely provisioned. In contrast, the camp to which they were transferred, Vittel, was very different with good conditions and was hailed as a model internment camp by the Nazis.[19] As well as the series of luxury hotels which accommodated internees, the occupying forces also requisitioned the extensive grounds, tennis courts, ornate gardens and casino, all of which were surrounded with barbed wire fences. In June 1942, under a policy of *regroupement familiale*, husbands of internees who had previously been housed in other camps (most in Saint Denis) were able to join their families in *l'Hôtel des Sources*.[20] From October 1942, American women also arrived in Vittel when the United States entered the conflict, and then at the end of 1942, foreign Jews, notably around two hundred Polish Jews from the Warsaw ghetto, were also sent to the camp. The Jews were kept in a separate hotel to the British and Americans.[21]

Vittel was chosen as the destination for British internees for two reasons: first, the Germans were anxious that British women should be seen to be treated well as this affected the way in which German prisoners were treated by the British. If conditions were not improved at Besançon, Churchill threatened that German civilians interned in Britain would be moved to Canada.[22] Second, Hitler was anxious to dispel the rumours circulating about the concentration camps in Eastern Europe. Vittel was a 'model camp' and served as a very public window into the Nazi party, which propagated the idea that Nazi camps were akin to holiday resorts.[23] Internees recall regular visits from high-ranking Nazi officials who were shown round the camp as well as film crews who gathered footage for propaganda.[24]

The British internees were a diverse group, both culturally and socially, united by their possession of a British passport. They included expatriates, wives or daughters of British businessmen who were resident in France and second-generation British civilians. Other internees had been in France temporarily at the outbreak of hostilities, on holiday or visiting relations. There were nuns from various denominations, some of whom were caring for the elderly, who were interned with their charges. Internees' depth of ties with Britain also varied, since their British status was determined by their spouse or father's nationality if they were not born in Britain, which was the case for several women who were arrested in December 1940. These women considered themselves French, but were interned for four years as British, having never lived in Britain, or even visited, and having no real connection with the country apart from via their husband or father.

Everyday life in Vittel

To date, existing research on civilian internment in France presents this experience as one of lack and deprivation with supplies constantly deficient, particularly vis-à-vis alimentation, fuel (coal and petrol) and medicine.[25] The introduction of the Final Solution in Spring 1942 marked a clear shift in internment policy from the politics of exclusion to the politics of extermination. Vittel reflects this change; it was used as a transit camp for Polish Jews who were transported from there to Auschwitz where they were murdered. However, British women's internment experience does not conform to the concepts of deprivation, lack and incarceration, which we commonly associate with civilian incarceration in France. In fact, sources suggest that British internees in Vittel had a comparatively comfortable and untroubled experience under occupied rule. They experienced a level of protection, resourcing and freedom. This representation of Vittel as a 'Golden Cage' not only nuances perceptions of internment in occupied France, but it also challenges existing narratives concerning British women during wartime. The three themes of resourcing, protection and freedom are briefly explored in this next section, before a final discussion of the memorialization of the camp.

The ICRC regularly inspected the camp at Vittel, describing it in July 1941 as 'the best camp that we have ever visited'.[26] The internees received weekly ICRC parcels, and at the time of the camp's liberation in September 1944, a report stated that 'sufficient parcels are on hand to feed the camp for at least three months'.[27] In terms of activities to keep the internees occupied, there were sports, theatre productions, an orchestra, adult-learning courses and a school for children, art classes, various religious services and séances. According to the American authorities, 'Tennis and golf are particularly popular at the moment, a new putting ground has just been completed.'[28] The ICRC inspectors also noted the tranquil and calm atmosphere in the camp commenting, 'In Vittel, peaceful and practically empty, there is complete calm; we hear some nuns whispering, there is an old gentleman reading whilst smoking his pipe, further on, internees are sunbathing.'[29] These images present a stark contrast to other accounts of internment in France during this period.[30]

British women were better resourced than many civilians living outside the camp, particularly in terms of food supplies. They received Red Cross parcels on a weekly basis and although there were some instances of parcels being taken by German soldiers or French workers in the camp, Vittel had a good supply, as Figure 9.1 illustrates, as well as copious reserves which remained at the camp following the liberation. Supplies were used to barter with local farmers for fresh produce, and each week a table was set up at the workers entrance/exit to the camp, which functioned like a market stall where the internees could exchange cigarettes or chocolate for eggs, fruit and vegetables.[31] Far from being deprived, internees appear to have had more supplies than many of those outside the camp. From 1942, internees were allowed to send home food parcels, to supplement family and friends' ration allowance. They also gave food to local families in need; in August 1941, the mayor of Vittel thanked internees for, 'very generous donations of food, such as: condensed milk, Ovaltine, cocoa, sugar syrup, canned meat, etc … intended to be distributed by us to the poorest and most needy large families … These donations are all the more welcome as many children are currently undernourished.'[32] Vittel had gained a reputation as a camp of abundance. A letter to one internee from an acquaintance in Paris stated, 'I hear that in your camp you have all you want and that most of the internees do [the] black market, sell all that they receive from England at a very high price and also chocolate. Everybody in Paris tells me that you are all getting fat and living a marvellous life.'[33] Vittel challenges the association of the internment experience as one of lack and deprivation, instead suggesting that these internees had more supplies than they needed, to such an extent that they could donate or exchange them, or even that they were overfed.

British women were also afforded a level of protection because of their nationality and, as stated earlier, for fear of repercussions on German civilians interned in Britain. The camp was inspected regularly, and internees were able to request items such as

Figure 9.1 Dr J. de Morsier inspects British Red Cross parcels in Vittel on 4 July 1941

Source: © ICRC, 04/07/1941, 'War 1939–45. Vittel. Camp for British civilian internees. Warehouse', V-P-HIST-03022-25.

musical instruments for the orchestra, books for distance learning courses and material for making clothes. One internee sent a letter to her cousin in Belgium to which she attached pink satin and other material, described as a 'cadeau de la x rouge' [a gift from the Red Cross].[34] In the accompanying letter, she wrote, 'With the packages we receive, we have nothing to complain about, but I am thinking of you, my darlings. If only I could get you what you need.'[35] Internees were evidently aware that they were better supplied within the camps than those on the outside. They looked to the ICRC to supply additional needs, playfully calling supplementary resources 'presents'. The supplies required to maintain this level of resourcing exerted a considerable strain on the town of Vittel. Writing to the camp commandant, the mayor describes an 'excessive consumption' of water, bread and petrol.[36] In a letter to the prefect in Épinal [the capital of the region], the mayor explains that he is obliged to provide around 500 kilograms of bread per day for the internees and is concerned as the flour is running out.[37] He cites an 'extreme urgency' for farmers to accelerate wheat threshing to produce more flour.[38] This indicates that providing sufficient supplies for the camp as well as the local population placed a heavy burden on the town's resources. The well-being of the internees was prioritized, and their needs were brokered by the camp commandant and the ICRC, two parties with significant influence who were difficult for the mayor to refuse.

Concerning the level of freedom given to internees, existing research into enemy aliens under occupied rule indicates that it was their liberty that was first targeted, even before internment was introduced as a policy under Vichy. From September 1939, foreigner's freedom was increasingly encroached upon and they became 'the object of restrictive legislation, discrimination and persecution'.[39] Despite this, British internees were permitted to leave the camp in Vittel with a guard to visit the town or the neighbouring two villages. An interviewee, born in 1936, who was a young boy during the occupation, recalled cycling to Vittel and seeing internees walking in the town with a German escort. Internees would regularly take their German guards to a local bistro, get them drunk and then use the café's telephone to phone their families. He recounted, 'I remember seeing the English women taking the German soldiers by the arm and leading them back to the camp, they [the soldiers] were completely drunk'.[40] This not only suggests that the camp rules were fairly relaxed, but also indicates that internees chose to return to the camp when they could easily have escaped. The benefits of remaining as an internee were so significant that some women who were due to be released because of their age or ill health even elected to remain in the camp as voluntary internees, knowing that they were safer and better resourced inside Vittel.

> The situation of many internees who leave the camp is complex because of supply difficulties in France. Thanks to the support of the British Red Cross and its many food packages, the internees of Vittel are among the privileged. This is why many of them, without great financial resources, prefer to extend their stay in the camp.[41]

This ICRC report from 1941 shows that remaining in Vittel had distinct benefits; one internee deliberately denounced her mother and younger sister who were living outside the camp, so that they could be repatriated to Britain together.[42]

This picture of internment does not resonate with British national memories of stoic and heroic wartime women, it is more akin to French national memories which, more recently, position most of the French population as *attentistes* who waited for the war to end.[43] Although testimony material and archival sources indicate that life in Vittel was privileged in comparison to internees' experiences elsewhere, or indeed Jewish internees in the same camp, there were difficult periods of internment which marked British women's memories even when interviewed seventy years after the war had ended. On the eve of deportation to Auschwitz, several Jewish internees either committed, or attempted to commit, suicide. Memories of this event and the deportation of Jewish internees clearly impacted internees and feature in their written memoirs and interviews.[44] Inhabitants of Vittel also recall these dark periods in the camp's history.[45] It is clear that, despite their comparatively comfortable experience in

Vittel, witnessing these traumatic events first-hand did psychologically impact British internees. The privation of liberty, monotony and strains of communal living also seem to have affected some older women in particular; sources refer to a nervous breakdown and a psychotic episode suffered by two internees.[46]

Memories of Vittel

Having briefly explored some aspects of the quotidian experience for British internees, I would now like to address the legacy of the camp, the importance of the site today and the transmission of memories concerning Vittel.

The hotel complex which once housed civilian internees is now a Club Med holiday destination: Vittel Le Parc promises an 'elegant all-inclusive family resort … [where you can] wander our marble halls and columned walkways … refresh yourself at the thermal water fountain and dream about tomorrow's adventures'.[47] It is unlikely that many of the holidaymakers are familiar with the resort's history, and there is no mention of the internment camp on the company website. Comparing photographs of the camp with the site today, topographically and architecturally, little has changed since 1945.

Figure 9.2 shows a group of nuns positioned on the steps outside the *Grand Hôtel* in Vittel during their interment in October 1943; Figure 9.3 was taken in September

Figure 9.2 Nuns assembled outside the *Grand Hôtel* in October 1943

Source: © ICRC, 10/1943, 'War 1939–45. Vittel. Camp for American and British civilian internees. Nuns assembled in the park', V-P-HIST-03021-01.

2015 and shows that the location remains unchanged. The opulent hotel buildings, landscaped grounds and verdant parklands appear very similar to photographs taken during the war. Interviews with residents confirm that in the park and hotels, many of the features have little altered since the war.⁴⁸

On close inspection, there are subtle references to the site's history; a memorial plaque affixed to the *Villa Sainte Mairie* at the entrance to the *Parc Thermale* (the six-hundred-hectare site in which the hotels are situated) explains, 'Here was the entrance to the camp where American and English civilians were interned between 1 May 1941 and 12 September 1944.'⁴⁹ A second plaque is positioned outside the park boundaries, on the *Hôtel de la Providence* where Jewish internees were held; it reads, 'Here were interned (January 1943 – April 1944) 300 Jews from Poland who,

Figure 9.3 The steps outside the Grand Hôtel in September 2015

Source: © Ayshka Sené.

after agonising peregrinations, perished in Auschwitz on 1 May 1944, victims of Nazi barbarity. Amongst them was renowned poet, Itshak Katsnelson. Plaque affixed by the Federation of Jewish Societies of France, 6 February 1955'.⁵⁰

At Caserne Vauban in Besançon there is no mention that the barracks housed up to 4,000 British internees between December 1940 and May 1941, and the site is being redeveloped into an 'Eco Quarter' with 800 dwellings and 600m² of office and business space.⁵¹ At the *Musée de la Résistance et de la Déportation* de Besançon in the town's Citadel, there is a plaque in one of the buildings at the end of the museum tour which commemorates the British internees held in Caserne Vauban (see Figure 9.4).⁵² Aside from the plaque situated in an adjacent room at the Citadel, there is no mention of the British internees in the museum and no context is given to the plaque about either the internees' identities or the conditions of their internment. Perhaps because British women were interned in Vittel for longer, they feature more at the site of the camp; whereas, in Besançon, the women were interned for only five months and do not form part of local memories of the war. This is further exemplified by the positioning of the memorial plaque, which is situated in a nearby empty building, separate to the museum, propped up on the floor rather than on the wall, and not at the actual site of internment because it is being redeveloped and regenerated. Parallels can be drawn between the plaque and the memory it represents: perhaps British women in Besançon are an awkward and slightly inconvenient part of Besançon's heritage, best

Figure 9.4 Plaque at the Musée de la Résistance et Déportation in Besançon 2015
Source: ©Ayshka Sené.

left 'in another room', set apart from more established memories of the war which are represented in the town's Museum of Deportation and Resistance.

In French national memory, the camp at Vittel has been largely remembered for its role as a transit camp in the deportation of Jews. This has also been the primary focus of existing research into the history of the camp, for example, the documentary *Passports pour Vittel*, and a conference, *Le camp de Vittel et sa relation à Auschwitz* [Vittel camp and its relationship with Auschwitz], held in June 2017 and organized by the town of Vittel in conjunction with the Fondation Auschwitz Bruxelles and other Jewish organizations.[53]

The sites in Besançon and Vittel have played a key role in appraising family members of their relatives' pasts and informing the cluster of biographies which emerged in the late 2000s.[54] In a published account of her great aunt, Fanny Twemlow, who was interned in Besançon and briefly in Vittel, author and historian Katherine Lack describes that she received 'invaluable help' from staff at the *Hôpital St Jacques* and *Musée de la Résistance et Déportation* in Besançon during her fieldwork.[55] Nicolas Shakespeare also retraced his Aunt Priscilla's steps as he returned to *Caserne Vauban*, paying attention to sights and smells, 'recognising' the building in which his aunt had lived thanks to his, and others' research efforts.[56] However, it is Vittel which has been a particularly important *lieu de mémoire*. The *Musée du Patrimoine et du Thermalisme* situated in the *Parc Thermale* in Vittel is a museum and archival holding. It holds a permanent exhibition on the evolution of Vittel during the nineteenth and twentieth centuries, which focuses on different themes including its history as a spa town, tourism and the period during the Occupation when the hotels and park were turned into an internment camp. The museum's website states that the purpose of the archives 'is to research and archive every document concerning all aspects of Vittel (water, business, wars, leading figures, streets, architecture, advertising etc.). Archives are available to everyone: spa clients, Vittel residents, researchers'.[57] The *Musée de Patrimoine* organized a reunion for former internees on the sixtieth anniversary of the camp's liberation in 2004.[58] The invitation to return to Vittel as a site of remembering and to share their memories of internment authenticated the survivors' voices. From an interview with the museum's curator, it was clear that Vittel was an important site of remembering for British women and their families: 'There are four or five people come each year who are interested in the camp. That's for sure, English, or Jewish ... those are the two categories'.[59] The curator of the museum was a key gatekeeper during this research, suggesting survivors to interview, and allowing me to consult the museum's archives. Based on interviews and biographical acknowledgements, it was clear that Vittel functions as a place of pilgrimage for former internees and their relatives. As anthropologist Carol Kidron outlines in her work on family memory and the Holocaust, it is a 'site of remembering ... evoking re-enactment of the past and consensual remembering'.[60] The archival holdings consisted primarily of private collections from former internees which had been donated by them or their relatives. Several of the biographies written between 2008 and 2014 referenced the museum's holdings and quoted from these private collections.

Kidron also argues that the family should 'be understood as an essential co-producer of communal and national memory', which is less evident in the case of

Vittel. In British national memory, the narratives concerning British women in France focus on internees' resilience and their ability to keep calm and carry on.[61] Coverage of Vittel internees in the British press has been minimal. Only one article about Vittel published in *The Mail on Sunday* in January 2000 was identified; the headline read 'Having a wonderful time … we're prisoners of the Nazis'.[62] The central colour photograph features a variety performance in Vittel with the women in costume. Set alongside a swastika, this paradox of fun and laughter taking place in a Nazi camp frames internees as resourceful and resilient. It echoes 'the Blitz spirit', which conveys 'a sense of community spirit, tenacity and stoicism in trying circumstances'. British women are in control; they are protagonists, rather than victims. The women featured are young, carefree and independent. The article mentions 'the relaxed attitude in the camp', and 'that for some women the lack of men was no hardship – they turned to each other for physical comfort'.[63] This last phrase suggests a level of sensationalism in the article around same-sex relations. The piece does not focus on older women who found the camp experience more challenging. The narrative is about rallying together in the face of adversity, the challenging conditions during the internees' five-month stint in Besançon in 'cramped, freezing, and bug-ridden barracks'.[64] A third of the article covers the arrival and later deportation of Polish Jews who were interned in Vittel and mentions Sofka Skipwith and Madeleine White, two internees who worked to save Jewish internees from deportation by smuggling letters to the British Embassy and the Home Office.[65] This memory of Vittel ties in with the SOE narrative concerning British women; they may not have been spies, but they are still resilient survivors who rose to the occasion in the face of adversity and resisted the Nazi threat. Other memories of Vittel which do not correspond to this heroic or stoic narrative are masked in the article by more dominant memories, such as the attempt to delay or prevent the deportation of Jewish internees.

A British comedy war film about Vittel internees, *Two Thousand Women*, was released in 1944 in Britain.[66] The film was made by Gainsborough studios, directed by British director and scriptwriter Frank Launder and starred Phyllis Calvert, Flora Robson and Patricia Roc, three of Britain's leading actresses in the 1940s.[67] An article in the *Picture Post* on 4 December 1943 about the making of the film described it as follows:

> What's it like to be in an enemy internment camp? A film being made by the Gainsborough studios attempts to answer this question on the screen … Three British airmen who bale out and are smuggled away from the Germans by the imprisoned women provide the story. There is a background of romance and intrigue. The internee who is really a Nazi spy, the two tough spinsters who 'keep the flag waving'; the pretty young show girl who had an intrigue with a German then regrets it.[68]

Tensions between internees from different social backgrounds are portrayed as humorous as the women tease each other. There are moments of slapstick comedy when the internees attempt to hide the Royal Air Force (RAF) airmen from the Germans, and apart from 'Mrs King', considered a collaborator, most of the internees are portrayed as resisters who are united against their German captors. There is no mention of the Jewish internees who were held in the *Hôtel de la Providence* in Vittel from 1943 onwards. The film highlights that even before the end of the war, the camp in Vittel was being framed in British propaganda as a hub of action and resistance. The British media wanted to portray internees in Vittel as loyal to the British fighting forces, suggesting that they were so devoted to the war effort that they would even rescue and shelter an Allied airman inside a German internment camp. Former internee, Sofka Skipwith questioned this highly exaggerated representation in her autobiography:

> McTurk had worked in it [the film] as an extra and told us that when she walked onto the set on the first day and saw a lot of huddled figures sitting about knitting or simply waiting, she thought that the producer had really caught the atmosphere. Then suddenly a whistle blew, the figures threw off their coats and galvanized into improbable action.[69]

The reality that British internees in Vittel were often inactive, waiting for the war to end, did not fit with the heroic narrative which needed to be promoted, both during and after the conflict.

Orphaned memories

Having examined importance of local lieux de mémoire in cultivating individual memories of British women's internment in Vittel, this final section addresses the visibility, or rather obscurity, of these memories at a national level. It posits their memories as 'orphaned' since their story sits between France and Britain, an experience claimed by neither national memory context. Three explanations are offered to account for their absence. In his chapter on 'addressing painful memories', Christopher Daase argues that 'collective memories of nations, for the most part, relate to events of either glory or victimhood', and the binary nature of national, collective memory is useful in our analysis of remembering British women in Vittel.[70] One of the problems with these women's experiences is that many do not fit easily in the categories of 'glory' or 'victimhood'; their wartime lives were nuanced and their choices were complicated. It is difficult to compose a narrative which places the women in this study as either victorious or tragically defeated; most simply survived. Daase also asserts that it is important to 'depict the national self as triumphantly victorious or tragically defeated hero respectively – but nevertheless as hero'.[71] The need to focus on either tragic defeat or triumphant victory could also explain the emphasis on poor conditions at the camp in Besançon in biographies and the British press. This narrative fits better with national memory frames than the comparatively palatial surroundings in which women were imprisoned in Vittel. The second explanation for the non-appearance of British women in wartime France is that, as a group, these women sit in between different national narratives: not fully British, not fully French, interned in a German camp, on French soil. Their memory sits between national borders and therefore national collective memories. Aside from the local memory site in Vittel, national memories which correspond to these women's experiences in France between 1939 and 1945 have been largely overlooked in both countries. The third reason, which corresponds to the internment camp in Vittel, is the dominance of the memory of the Holocaust and the deportation of Eastern European Jewish internees from Vittel to Auschwitz. The Shoah is described by memory scholars as both 'a touchstone for the study of twentieth-century memory' and 'a timeless and deterritorialised measuring stick for good and evil'.[72] We can hypothesize that British women's internment experiences have been overlooked because, when compared with the experiences of Jewish internees, they are less harrowing, less 'evil' as Levy and Sznaider suggest in their article on the Holocaust and Cosmopolitan Memory. Speaking about her mother – a former internee – one interviewee referred to this sense of comparison: 'My mother never recovered. And yet it was not a concentration camp … but … but it changed her whole life.'[73] The influence of the Holocaust in how we remember is exemplified in this extract; the interviewee compares her mother's experiences to Jewish internees who were deported to concentration camps. She seeks to acknowledge how much her mother's life was changed by her wartime experiences but cannot do so without referencing the experiences of Jew internees which were far more devastating. Acknowledging the treatment of Holocaust victims interned in Vittel, on both a local and individual level, has led to an omission of British women's wartime experience in the same camps. All memories are not equal, as renowned historian Tony Judt argues, 'Memory is inherently contentious and partisan: one man's acknowledgement is another man's omission.'[74]

In conclusion then, to try and fill these silences and reconcile conflicting accounts, it seems that local sites of memory, such as Vittel, which embrace individual family narratives, are key in validating and informing representations of British women's experiences. The link between the memory site, Vittel and familial memories of British women interned there has been pivotal in cultivating second- and third-generation representations of British women interned in France during the war. The active relationship between the Vittel museum and the families of former internees also reveals the central importance of telling their story as a transnational history. It demonstrates the need to investigate the operation of memory at different levels – local, regional and transnational.[75] This study also echoes recent work on memory studies which contend that 'the national has ceased to be the inevitable or preeminent scale for the study of collective remembrance'.[76] Only in the late 2000s has an increasingly transnational milieu made space for the memories of British women in Vittel to emerge, preserved and promoted by their families in biographical form. The memory work in Vittel demonstrates the interactions between private and public memories and suggests that family stories are helpful in nuancing broader, national narratives. Historian Tomoko Sakai argues that 'trans-generational memory works as an important medium through which a big story of national historical level becomes an essential constituent of the small story of an individual at a personal level'.[77] This study suggests that the small story of an individual is equally necessary in informing and personalizing national memory so that it reflects individual memories at a broader level. It is hoped that the descendants of British women in France during the war will continue to transmit their family stories so that these testimonies can be adopted and integrated into British and French memories of the conflict, rather than orphaned.

Notes

1. 4.5H60.D, 'Letter to Mlle M.C. de Dorlodot from the Mayor, 14 September 1948', Vittel Town Hall Archives, Vittel, France. Translated from French. All translations are mine unless otherwise noted.
2. HO 215/68, Front Stalag 142 and 194, Vittel Vosges, France, 1943–1945, 'Memorandum: Internment camp at Vittel', 11 October 1944, The National Archives, Kew, London.
3. Katherine Lack, *Frontstalag 142: The Internment Diary of an English Lady* (Stroud: Amberley Publishing, 2010); Jane Manley, *Mrs Trewhella's War, 1940–1944* (London: Gatehouse Editions, 2014); Rosemary Say and Neil Holland, *Rosie's War: An Englishwoman's Escape from Occupied France* (London: Michael O'Mara, 2012); Nicolas Shakespeare, *Priscilla: The Hidden Life of an Englishwoman in Wartime France* (London: Vintage, 2014); Sofka Zinovieff, *The Red Princess: A Revolutionary Life* (London: Granta, 2007).
4. Say and Holland, *Rosie's War*.
5. Matthew Bell, 'Paperback Review: Priscilla, By Nicholas Shakespeare', *The Independent*, 24 November 2001, https://www.independent.co.uk/arts-entertainment/books/reviews/paperback-review-priscilla-nicholas-shakespeare-8957948.html; Lucy Lethbridge, 'Priscilla: The Hidden Life of an Englishwoman in Wartime France by Nicholas Shakespeare – review', *The Guardian*, 17 November 2013, https://www.theguardian.com/books/2013/nov/17/priscilla-hidden-life-wartime-nicholas-shakespeare; Anna Shapiro, 'In "Priscilla," Nicholas Shakespeare Looks at Family Mystery', *The New York Times*, 26 December 2013, https://www.nytimes.com/2013/12/27/books/in-priscilla-nicholas-shakespeare-looks-at-family-mystery.html; Matthew Price, '"Priscilla" by Nicholas Shakespeare', *The Boston Globe*, 1 February 2014, https://www.bostonglobe.com/arts/books/2014/02/01/review-priscilla-the-hidden-life-englishwoman-wartime-france-nicholas-shakespeare/mp9r5ZZNHGdRoSiwDLsxzN/story.html; Gaby Wood, 'Nicholas Shakespeare: "My Aunt the Collaborator?"', *The Telegraph*, 28 October 2013, https://www.telegraph.co.uk/culture/books/authorinterviews/10401886/Nicholas-Shakespeare-My-aunt-the-collaborator.html; 'How to Survive: A Tale of Cunning in Wartime France', *The Economist*, 16 November 2013, https://www.economist.com/books-and-arts/2013/11/16/how-to-survive (all accessed 17 August 2021).
6. Juliette Pattinson, *Behind Enemy Lines: Gender, Passing and the Special Operations Executive in the Second World War* (Manchester: Manchester University Press, 2007); Juliette Pattinson, '"The Thing that Made Me Hesitate …": Re-Examining Gendered Intersubjectivities in Interviews with British Secret War Veterans. *Women's History Review* 20 (2011), 245–63; Kate Vigurs, *The Women Agents of the Special Operations Executive F Section: Wartime Realities and Post War Representations* (Leeds, England: University of Leeds, 2011), http://etheses.whiterose.ac.uk/1751/1/Ethesis_FINAL.pdf (accessed 17 August 2021).
7. Shannon Fogg, *The Politics of Everyday Life in Vichy France: Foreigners, Undesirables, and Strangers* (Cambridge: Cambridge University Press, 2009); Maëlle Maugendre, 'Les réfugiées espagnoles en France (1939–1942): Des femmes entre assujettissements et résistances', PhD thesis. Toulouse 2, France (2013); Barbara Vormeier, 'Les Femmes Allemandes dans la Résistance Française' (225–38)and Anne Grynberg, 'Les Femmes Juives dans la Résistance' (203–21). Both in *Les femmes dans la Résistance*

en France, ed. Mechtild Gilzmer, Christine Levisse-Touzé and Stefan Martens (Paris: Tallandier, 2003).
8. Richard Dove, *'Totally Un-English'?: Britain's Internment of 'Enemy Aliens' in Two World Wars* (Rodopi: Amsterdam, 2005); Rachel Pistol, *Internment during the Second World War: A Comparative Study of Great Britain and the USA* (London: Bloomsbury, 2017).
9. Denis, Peschanski, 'Les camps français d'internement: 1938–1946', *Ph.D. Université* Panthéon-Sorbonne: Paris (2000): 352.
10. Maugendre, 'Les réfugiées', 552; Vormeier, 'Les Femmes'; Grynberg, 'Les Femmes'.
11. Pattinson, *Behind Enemy Lines*; Vigurs, *The Woman Agents*.
12. Pattinson, *Behind Enemy Lines* 2.
13. Peschanski, 'Les camps', 101.
14. ACICR CSC, Service des Camps, France (Frontstalags), 'Visite au camp des internés et internées britanniques de Besançon, 28.1.1941', International Committee of the Red Cross (ICRC) Archives, Geneva, Switzerland.
15. FO 916/135, British subjects in France – internment, 1941. 'Visite au camp des internés et internées britanniques de Besançon, 28.1.1941', The National Archives (TNA), Kew, London.
16. 57W 37, Administration des Hospices Civils Réunis de Besançon, Letter from Le Vice-Président de la commission administrative à Monsieur le Préfet du Département du Doubs à Besançon, 20.12.1940, Departmental Archives, Doubs, France.
17. FO 916/135, TNA.
18. ACICR, CSC, Service des Camps, France (Frontstalags), 'Camp d'Internees civiles britanniques de Vittel (Vosges) Frontstalag 142, 4.8.1941', ICRC Archives, Geneva, Switzerland.
19. Claire Soussen, 'Le camp de Vittel, 1941–1944', *Revue d'histoire de la Shoah* 153 (1995): 114.
20. Claude Poinsot, *Le camp des internés civils de Vittel: Britanniques, Américains, Juifs Polonais* (Vittel: Maison du Patrimoine, 2004).
21. Jean Camille Bloch, 'Le Camp de Vittel 1940–1944', *Les Dossiers d'Aschkel* (2007), http://ddata.over-blog.com/1/98/99/81/FICHIERS-PDF/Camp-de-Vittel_Jean-Bloch.pdf (accessed 17 August 2021).
22. FO 916 135, TNA.
23. Soussen, 'Le camp', 118.
24. The internment camp in Theriesenstadt (Terezin), near Prague, was also a Nazi 'show camp', designed to mislead the Jewish and the international communities about the Final Solution. Elderly and prominent Jewish civilians were interned in the camp, propagating the myth that they could 'retire safely' in this spa town. Once the camp had been visited by the ICRC, Jewish internees were deported to Auschwitz up until October 1944.
25. Peschanski, 'Les camps', 233.
26. ACICR, 'Camp d'Internées civiles britanniques de Vittel'.
27. HO 215/68, Front Stalag 142 and 194, Vittel Vosges, France, 1943–1945, 'Memorandum: Internment camp at Vittel', 11 October 1944, TNA, Kew, London.
28. Ibid., U.S. Army Report.
29. ACICR, 'Camp d'Internées civiles britanniques de Vittel'. Translated from French.
30. Peschanski, 'Les camps', 233.
31. Poinsot, 'Le camp', 33.
32. 4.5H60.D, 'Extrait du Registre des Délibérations de la Commission Administrative du Bureau de Bienfaisance, 6 August 1941', Vittel Town Hall Archives, Vittel, France.

33. Letter to Lucie Gumuchian, 26 May 1944, 1. Private papers of Sonia Gumuchian. Paris, France.
34. Letter to Mademoiselle Méliné Covan from Lucie Gumuchian, 15 April 1942, 2. Private papers of Sonia Gumuchian. Paris, France.
35. Ibid.
36. 4.5H60.D, 'Letter from the Mayor to the Camp Commandant, undated'.
37. 4.5H60.D, 'Letter from the Mayor to M. Virtel, 2 September 1943'.
38. Ibid.
39. Fogg, *The Politics of Everyday Life*, 13.
40. Interview with Jean Michel, Vittel, 16 September 2015 (all interviewees have been given pseudonyms).
41. ACICR, 'Camp d'Internees civiles britanniques de Vittel'. Translated from French.
42. Interview, Phillips, 2016.
43. Henry Rousso, *Le Syndrome de Vichy de 1944 à nos jours* (Paris: Seuil, 1990).
44. Interview, Phillips, 2016; Lack, *Frontstalag 142*, 2010; Sofka Skipwith, *The Autobiography of a Princess* (London: Hart David, 1968).
45. Interview, Michel.
46. HO 215/68, YMCA Report to the Home Office, Received in London 23 February 1944, Gabriel Naville, 5, TNA; Lack, *Frontstalag 142*, 2010.
47. Club Med Vittel Le Parc website. https://www.clubmed.co.uk/r/vittel-le-parc/y (accessed 10 May 2021).
48. Interview, Michel.
49. Translated from a photograph taken by the author in September 2016.
50. Ibid.
51. *Ma Commune*, 'Economie, Besançon: Écoquartier Vauban à Besançon: la Maison du projet à disposition des habitants… actualité Besançon Franche-Comté' (2016). http://www.macommune.info/article/ecoquartier-vauban-a-besancon-la-maison-du-projet-a-disposition-des-habitants-177750 (accessed 18 August 2021).
52. Although the plaque states that British women were interned until 30 April 1941, Red Cross archives indicate that some internees remained into May 1941 before being transferred to Vittel.
53. Adam Rutkowski, 'Le Camp d'internement et d'échange pour Juifs de Vittel', *Le Monde Juif* 102 (1981); Soussen, 'Le camp', 1995; Madeleine Steinberg, 'Les camps de Besançon et Vittel (février 1941 à juillet 1944)' Témoignage d'une Internée Civile. *Le Monde Juif* 137 (1990) 6–23; Bloch, 'Le Camp', 2007; *Passeports pour Vittel*. [Film]. Dîr. Joëlle Novic. France: Imjam Production (2007) France 3, Image Plus; The conference organizers were Ville de Vittel, bibliothèque médiathèque de Vittel, Musée du Patrimoine Vittel, Fondation Auschwitz Bruxelles, Les Fils et Filles des Déportes Juifs de France militants de la mémoire, Cercle d'étude de la déportation et de la Shoah – Amicale d'Auschwitz.
54. Lack, *Frontstalag 142*, 2010; Say and Holland, *Rosie's War*; Shakespeare, *Priscilla*.
55. Lack, *Frontstalag 142*, 7.
56. Shakespeare, *Priscilla*, 184.
57. Musée du Patrimoine website. http://www.vittelpatrimoine.sitew.fr/Musee.F.htm (accessed 10 May 2021).
58. Unnamed collection 'Des anciens internés sont venus témoigner de la vie au camp, pendant 3 ans in *Vosges Matin*', 13 September 2004, Musée du Patrimoine archives, Vittel, France.
59. Interview with Madame Clement, Vittel, 14 September 2015.

60. Carol Kidron, 'Survivor Family Memory Work at Sites of Holocaust Remembrance: Institutional Enlistment or Family Agency?' *History and Memory* 27, no. 2 (2015): 51.
61. Ibid.
62. Anna McQueen, 'Having a wonderful time we're prisoners of the Nazis', *The Mail on Sunday*. 16 January 2000. Unnamed collection. Private Papers of Sonia Gumuchian, Paris, France.
63. Lucy Noakes and Juliette Pattinson, eds, *British Cultural Memory and the Second World War* (London: Bloomsbury, 2014), 10.
64. McQueen, 'Having a wonderful time', 64.
65. Skipwith, *The Autobiography*, 226.
66. *Two Thousand Women*. (1944). [Film]. Dir. Frank Launder. London: Gainsborough Studios.
67. Ronald Bergan. *Eyewitness Companions: Film* (London: Dorling Kindersley, 2006).
68. Heal, Jeanne. 'Women from German Camps Act their Story', Picture Post [London]. 4 December 1943. *Picture Post Historical Archive* [digital] 1939–1957, The British Library.
69. Skipwith, *The Autobiography*, 279.
70. Christopher Daase. 'Addressing Painful Memories: Apologies as a New Practice in International Relations', in *Memory in a Global Age: Discourses, Practices, and Trajectories*, ed. A. Assmann (Basingstoke: Palgrave Macmillan, 2010), 19.
71. Ibid.
72. Marianne Hirsch and Leo Spitzer, 'The Witness in the Archive: Holocaust Studies/Memory Studies', *Memory Studies* 2/2 (2009): 151; Daniel Levy and Natan Sznaider, 'The Holocaust and the Formation of Cosmopolitan Memory', *European Journal of Social Theory* 5/1 (2002): 95.
73. Interview with Laura Giraud, Paris, 22 February 2016.
74. Tony Judt, *Postwar: A History of Europe since 1945* (London: Vintage, 2005): 829
75. Patrick Finney, ed. *Remembering the Second World War* (London: Routledge, 2017).
76. Chiara De Cesari and Ann Rigney, *Transnational Memory: Circulation, Articulation, Scales* (Berlin: Wakter De Gruyter, 2014), 2.
77. Tomoko Sakai, 'Trans-Generational Memory: Narratives of World Wars in Post-Conflict Northern Ireland', *Sociological Research Online* 14 (2009): 5.

Bibliography

Daase, Christopher. 'Addressing Painful Memories: Apologies as a New Practice in International Relations'. In *Memory in a Global Age: Discourses, Practices, and Trajectories*, edited by A. Assmann, 19–21. Basingstoke: Palgrave Macmillan, 2010.

De Cesari, Chiara, and Ann Rigney. *Transnational Memory: Circulation, Articulation, Scales*. Berlin: Wakter De Gruyter, 2014.

Dove, Richard. *'Totally Un-English'?: Britain's Internment of 'Enemy Aliens' in Two World Wars*. Rodopi: Amsterdam, 2005.

Finney, Patrick, ed. *Remembering the Second World War*. London: Routledge, 2017.

Fogg, Shannon. *The Politics of Everyday Life in Vichy France: Foreigners, Undesirables, and Strangers*. Cambridge: Cambridge University Press, 2009.

Grynberg, Anne. 'Les Femmes Juives dans la Résistance'. In *Les femmes dans la Résistance en France*, edited by Mechtild Gilzmer, Christine Levisse-Touzé, and Stefan Martens, 203–11. Paris: Tallandier, 2003.

Heal, Jeanne. 'Women from German Camps Act Their Story'. Picture Post [London]. 4 December 1943. *Picture Post Historical Archive* [digital] 1939–1957, The British Library.

Hirsch, Marianne, and Leo Spitzer. 'The Witness in the Archive: Holocaust Studies/Memory Studies'. *Memory Studies* 2, no. 2 (2009): 151–70.

Judt, Tony. *Postwar: A History of Europe since 1945*. London: Vintage, 2005.

Kidron, Carol. 'Survivor Family Memory Work at Sites of Holocaust Remembrance: Institutional Enlistment or Family Agency?' *History and Memory* 27, no. 2 (2015): 45–73.

Lack, Katherine. *Frontstalag 142: The Internment Diary of an English Lady*. Stroud: Amberley Publishing. 2010.

Levy, Daniel, and Natan Sznaider. 'Memory Unbound: The Holocaust and the Formation of Cosmopolitan Memory'. *European Journal of Social Theory* 5, no. 1 (2002): 87–106.

Manley, Jane. *Mrs Trewhella's War, 1940–1944*. London: Gatehouse Editions, 2014.

Noakes, Lucy, and Juliette Pattinson, eds. *British Cultural Memory and the Second World War*. London: Bloomsbury, 2014.

Pattinson, Juliette. *Behind Enemy Lines: Gender, Passing and the Special Operations Executive in the Second World War*. Manchester: Manchester University Press, 2007.

Pattinson, Juliette. '"The Thing that Made Me Hesitate …": Re-Examining Gendered Intersubjectivities in Interviews with British Secret War Veterans'. *Women's History Review* 20 (2011): 245–63.

Pistol, Rachel. *Internment during the Second World War: A Comparative Study of Great Britain and the USA*. London: Bloomsbury, 2017.

Poinsot, Claude. *Le camp des internés civils de Vittel: Britanniques, Américains, Juifs Polonais*. Vittel: Maison du Patrimoine, 2004.

Rousso, Henry. *Le Syndrome de Vichy de 1944 à nos jours*. Paris: Seuil, 1990.

Rutkowski, Adam. 'Le Camp d'internement et d'échange pour Juifs de Vittel'. *Le Monde Juif* 102 (1981): 35–70.

Sakai, Tomoko. 'Trans-Generational Memory: Narratives of World Wars in Post-Conflict Northern Ireland'. *Sociological Research Online* 14 (2009): 1–9.

Say, Rosemary, and Neil Holland. *Rosie's War: An Englishwoman's Escape from Occupied France*. London: Michael O'Mara, 2012.

Shakespeare, Nicolas. *Priscilla: The Hidden Life of an Englishwoman in Wartime France*. London: Vintage, 2014.

Skipwith, Sofka. *The Autobiography of a Princess*. London: Hart David, 1968.

Soussen, Claire. 'Le camp de Vittel, 1941–1944'. *Revue d'histoire de la Shoah* 153 (1995): 104–19.

Steinberg, Madeleine. 'Les camps de Besançon et Vittel (février 1941 à juillet 1944)' Témoignage d'une Internée Civile. *Le Monde Juif* 137 (1990): 6–23.

Two Thousand Women. [Film]. Dir. Frank Launder. London: Gainsborough Studios (1944).

Vormeier, Barbara. 'Les Femmes Allemandes dans la Résistance Française'. In *Les femmes dans la Résistance en France*, edited by Mechtild Gilzmer, Christine Levisse-Touzé, and Stefan Martens, 225–38. Paris: Tallandier, 2003.

Zinovieff, Sofka. *The Red Princess: A Revolutionary Life*. London: Granta, 2007.

10

The internment of British enemy aliens in Fascist internment camps: The case study of *Anglo-Maltesi*

Pierluigi Bolioli

Introduction

The internment by the Italians of the *Anglo-Maltesi*, who had emigrated from Malta to Libya in the second half of the nineteenth century and maintained British citizenship, represented a peculiar case within the Fascist concentration camp system. Due to their provenance, the Fascist regime recognized the privileged status of *Italiani non regnicoli* (non-citizen Italians). The *Anglo-Maltesi* were, therefore, interned in camps because of their British citizenship and their loyalty to the United Kingdom. Most of the *Anglo-Maltesi* were Roman Catholic, and only a few of them were Jews, who were interned immediately after their expulsion from Libya. The number of Jewish *Anglo-Maltesi* is not clear from the archival documents: their religion was often not recorded. Initially, at least, the regime was more interested in the nationality of those it interned. Despite this, we can calculate that at least 5 per cent of the *Anglo-Maltesi* were Jewish.

The *Anglo-Maltesi* represented the majority of British citizens interned in camps in the Italian peninsula and represent the largest individual ethnic group. The Fascist concentration camp system never reached the size and brutality of the Gulag or the Nazi concentration camp system. The camps were mostly small except for those managed by the Royal Army and a few others, like those in Pisticci (in Basilicata), Ferramonti di Tarsia (in Calabria) and le Fraschette di Alatri (in Lazio). The officials of the Ministry of the Interior did not manage to intern all those (including Jews) who were eligible for internment, and for this reason, the camps, however small, were not overcrowded.

This chapter reconstructs the story of the expulsion and internment of the *Anglo-Maltese* colony of Libya, connecting it to the general story of Italian internment policy. The *Anglo-Maltesi*, and their treatment, can be used as an example of this policy where the Fascist regime interned foreigners based on their nationality regardless of their actual capacity for harm. Fascist camps were small and mismanaged, but still a cruel system of controlling groups of peaceful people whose only 'crime' was their citizenship. The *Anglo-Maltesi* were to lose all of their possessions and, some of them, their life. The final part of this chapter connects the absence of heritage of internment camps with a lack of memory of the existence of these camps and the lack of an Italian culture of remembrance. This should not surprise the reader: both the new democratic government of Italy and the Allies preferred not to prosecute these crimes after the war. Genocides, internment camps and other atrocities were forgotten by the Italian population, and knowledge of their existence is limited largely to historians.

The Maltese colony in Libya

The presence of Maltese communities in Libya dates to the century before the Italian occupation. Maltese emigrants to Libya, then part of the Ottoman Empire, jealously preserved their identity and British citizenship. For example, during the Fascist era, a civil servant employed by Tripoli City Hall preferred to lose his job rather than lose his British citizenship[1] Another *Anglo-Maltese*, to show his pro-British sympathies, had the British flag tattooed on his arm.[2] A third, after attempting to enlist in the British Navy, decided to name his newly born child after Churchill.[3] In a report on the Maltese community in Libya, the British consul in Tripoli described the Maltese as 'fanatically attached to their British connection'.[4] The Italians, on the other hand, considered the Maltese to be 'non-citizen Italians', a status not defined by any law, but which guaranteed the possibility of residing in the Kingdom of Italy and voting in local elections.[5] This choice must be seen in the context of the irredentist[6] movement's policy to 'liberate' all historically Italian territories. Non-citizen Italians were defined as 'originating from territories that were ethnically Italian, but politically not part of the Kingdom ... This includes the inhabitants of Nice, Savoy, Corsica et similia'.[7]

Italian colonization of Libya preceded the Fascist period by ten years but, given the hiatus of the Great War, the actual colonization and occupation of the whole country was implemented by Mussolini. Starting from the coast, the only part effectively colonized before the First World War, General Graziani, one of the closest Mussolini allies, conquered the entire country within ten years. The so-called pacification of Libya was nothing less than a genocide: the brutality of the conquest methods and the use of concentration camps awarded Graziani the nickname of 'butcher of Fezzan'.[8] The success of this military operations from the Fascist point of view was complete and, in a few years, Libya was considered a 'safe' place; in 1939, Mussolini annexed it to Italy. Libya was now part of the metropolitan territory and not just a colony, therefore the legislation of the mainland now applied fully to Libyan territory.

The Maltese community in Libya was rather small, about 2,000 people. In February 1934, there were 1,899 Maltese and another 300 or so British subjects in the city of Tripoli. The Maltese resided almost entirely in their own quarter of the old city of Tripoli.[9] The UK was careful to maintain strong relations with these *Anglo-Maltesi*: the Tripoli police reported that on 6 May 1937 the British consulate had summoned the young Maltese living in the city and had 'invited them to perform voluntary military service in Malta, advising them that this was a duty for young men in a position to do so'.[10] The Tripolitan police station also pointed out that, on 12 May, for the coronation of George VI, 'the same consulate would then receive the notables of the *Anglo-Maltesi* community and distribute numerous cash subsidies (from 50 to 100 *lire*) to needy Maltese families'.[11]

Displacement from Libya

On 9 September 1941, Ettore Bastico, the governor of Libya, ordered the expulsion of all foreigners from the colony, men, women and children, to suppress espionage and ease the food supply problems of the civilian population. According to the governor's wishes, over 7,000 foreigners were to be expelled from Libyan territory: about 5,000 from the province of Tripoli, of which 1,900 were *Anglo-Maltesi*, 1,600 were French Jews, 870 were English Jews, 715 Muslims under French protection, 225 Greeks and 155 foreigners of various nationalities and religions. It was also deemed necessary to expel 2,000 foreigners from the province of Benghazi, 150 from the province of Misurata and 100 from the province of Derna.[12] On 17 December 1941, the Ministry of Italian Africa decided, pending the construction of a special internment camp,[13] to send 2,200 foreigners to the Italian mainland, of whom 2,000 were to be sent to hotels and 200 (Jews) to internment camps. The first to be expelled would, therefore, be the 1,900 *Anglo-Maltesi*, plus another 100 foreigners to be sent to hotels, while the 200 Jews with British citizenship (some of whom were the *Anglo-Maltesi*) would be sent to internment camps (listed below).[14] The hotels chosen were in three small spa towns in central Italy: Montecatini (where about 1,000 expellees were to be sent), Fiuggi (500 expellees) and Bagni di Lucca (500 expellees) (Table 10.1).[15] The Ministry of Italian Africa, following the displacement, took care to send to the General Directorate of Public Security relevant information and possible criminal records on displaced persons from Libya.[16]

After this first phase, foreigners living in Libya were transported in small groups, by air or by ship (Table 10.2). A few dozen were transported between January and August 1942. These *Anglo-Maltesi* were housed in convents or with acquaintances in Italy, scattered throughout the Kingdom.

Internment under the Ministry of the Interior

Internment in Italy was a measure aimed at all foreigners capable of bearing arms or otherwise harming the state and was regulated by military law. The *Testo unico delle leggi di guerra e di neutralità* (consolidated text of the laws of war and neutrality) was approved in 1938,[17] and this military law laid down the general guidelines governing internment. Internment could be imposed only by a decree of the Minister of the Interior, although enemy subjects could also be forbidden to stay in a certain place by order of the prefect or the Minister of the Interior.

The internment of prisoners started immediately after the beginning of the conflict in June 1940, but the *Anglo-Maltesi* were deported to Italy and subsequently interned in camps only from the beginning of 1942. Their status as 'non-citizen Italians' seems

Table 10.1 Major Deportations of *Anglo-Maltesi* from Libya

Ship	Day of departure	Port of arrival	Number	Nationalities	Final destination
Monginevro[18]	13 January 1942	Naples	406	68 British and 9 Greek nationals already interned in Libya for political reasons	Bagno a Ripoli internment camp
				139 Greeks	Montecatini Terme Hotels
				190 British Jews	Bagno a Ripoli Internment camp (32)
					Civitella della Chiana Internment camp (51)
					Civitella del Tronto internment camp (107)
Nino Bixio[19]	18 January 1942	Brindisi	515/533[20]	Anglo-Maltesi	Montecatini Terme Hotels (133)
					Fiuggi Hotels (200)
					Bagni di Lucca (200)
Lerici[21]	18 January 1942	Taranto	461/459[22]	Anglo-Maltesi	Montecatini Hotels
Allegri[23]	19 January 1942	Naples	439	Anglo-Maltesi (424)	Montecatini Hotels (274)
					Fiuggi Hotels (145)
					One child, who travelled to Naples with her aunt for medical treatment
				Greeks (5) British Jews (10)	Montecatini Hotels Civitella del Tronto internment camp

likely to have spared them two years of internment because the regime had previously tried to assimilate them, and they were not considered a threat.

The internees had to move within an established perimeter which was different for each camp; they were not allowed to leave without permission. They were also forbidden to leave their location before dawn and had to return home half an hour after sunset. Although there were three roll calls a day, internees were free to take meals either in public establishments or with private families and were expected to exhibit good behaviour. Those without means were paid a daily allowance of 6.5 *lire*. Medicines and health care were paid for by the Ministry of the Interior. Urgent treatment had to be carried out at the nearest hospital and subsequently ratified by the Ministry. For fixed expenses (rent, allowance, maintenance, common medicines), the prefectures had to use the sums made available from the special fund set up for this purpose. All other expenses had to be authorized by the Ministry. The prefectures where the internees resided were responsible for the costs of transferring and accompanying the internees, and they then had to pass them on to the prefectures where the internment

Table 10.2 Secondary Deportations of *Anglo-Maltesi* from Libya

Ship	Day of departure	Port of arrival	Number	Nationalities	Final destination
Monviso[24]	9 March 1942	Palermo	81	*Anglo-Maltesi* (27) and Turk (1)	Fiuggi Hotels
				9 Greeks	Ferramonti di Tarsia internment Camp
				44 British Jews	Bologna Province
Lerici[25]	10 March 1942	Naples	124	*Anglo-Maltesi* (98) and Greeks (26)	
Giuliani[26]	17 March 1942		43	*Anglo-Maltesi* (10), British Jews (29) and Greek (4)	
	17 March 1942[27]		40	*Anglo-Maltesi*	Fiuggi Hotels
Lerici[28]	17 March 1942	Taranto	54	*Anglo-Maltesi* (2) and British Jews (52)	
Bertagna[29]	30 April 1942	Naples	12	*Anglo-Maltesi* (9) and British Jews (3)	
Vettor Pisani[30]	3 July 1942	Taranto	18	*Anglo-Maltesi* (2) and British Jews (16)	

camps were located.[31] The internment camps were inspected monthly by provincial doctors for health checks.[32] The internees were not allowed to have passports, military documents, weapons or radios;[33] they were not allowed to have money over 100 *lire*, and all money had to be deposited in banks or post offices. Authorization was required to make withdrawals and, of course, the amount withdrawn could not exceed the maximum allowed, unless otherwise authorized by the Ministry. Inmates were not allowed to own jewellery or securities, which had to be deposited in safety deposit boxes at the nearest bank. The key was kept by the person concerned and the passbook by the camp director.

The internees were not allowed to get involved in politics and could read only Italian newspapers. The reading of books or newspapers in a foreign language needed the permission of the Ministry. For example, in 1943 the Swiss Legation in Italy, which represented British interests, was authorized to send fifty books to British internees.[34] The *Questure* (provincial office of the Department of Public Security of the Ministry of Interior) then had to check whether the internees had sufficient means of their own to maintain themselves, and if so, any subsidies would be suspended. The *Questure* also had to undertake background checks of dangerous internees or those suspected of espionage to the direction of the camp. The camp director had to examine incoming and outgoing correspondence and parcels. No family members were allowed to live in the camps. Diplomats and journalists were not allowed to enter internment camps or approach internees without permission from the Ministry.[35]

Freedom of worship was granted to all internees, but religious assistance from a priest was only allowed for Catholic internees. In the case of non-Catholics, explicit authorization from the Ministry of the Interior was required. However, it was specified that access to the camps was strictly forbidden to rabbis and that it was pointless to ask for authorization.[36] This provision prohibiting religious assistance to Jewish internees was later revised and rabbis were allowed to assist Jews interned in the camps.[37] The same decree established the conditions under which the internees could be employed in paid work. However, these activities could not be excessive, could not involve participation in warfare and had to be in accordance with the class of the interned person.

The law provided for humane treatment of the internees and protection from violence. It was not possible for internment locations to be in unhealthy places or exposed to enemy fire. The Fascist regime permitted internees to receive support from their government or their families. Interned Jews, for example, enjoyed the support of DELASEM, a Jewish organization authorized by the regime, aimed at helping Jews and assisting their migration.[38] British internees, instead, received financial support from the British government through the American Embassy at first and then the Swiss Legation after the attack on Pearl Harbour and the entry of the United States into the Second World War.[39]

The internment of *Anglo-Maltesi* in camps

At first, the living conditions of the interned *Anglo-Maltesi* were better than those of most of the other internees in Italy. Initial accommodation in hotels was quite acceptable,[40] especially as the accommodation was often beyond the means of the poorest evacuees. In the case of Fiuggi, the Grand Hotel, recently closed due to the conflict but still in good condition, was used for housing the displaced. The situation dramatically worsened with internment in camps. However, the Maltese demanded, and were granted, transfers between the internment camps in order to reunite them with family members in other camps in Italy. Transfers were granted for good conduct if the destination camp was not reserved for the opposite sex.[41] It was also quite common to be able to leave internment for reasons of medical care or 'personal affairs'.[42] *Anglo-Maltesi* internees were sometimes not escorted when moving between camps but only issued with a compulsory travel warrant.[43] An *Anglo-Maltese*, displaced in Fiuggi, who asked to be allowed to resume his work in Tripoli, received a positive reply from the Ministry of Italian Africa if he acquired Italian citizenship.[44] This entailed renouncing his British citizenship and applying for Italian citizenship; given the privileged status of 'non-citizen Italian', he wouldn't have had to meet any other requirement.

However, the living conditions of the *Anglo-Maltesi* were made more difficult by the fact that most of their luggage was lost during the displacement.[45] As for those who were found to have 'Anglophile feelings', the directive was that they should be interned in a camp, while those 'who by conduct, background and feelings of attachment to Italy give the desired confidence' would instead be given the privileged treatment accorded to non-citizen Italians.[46] The pro-Italian *Anglo-Maltesi* were also granted a subsidy of a few hundred *lire* a month, financed by the *fascio* (the local section of the National Fascist Party).⁴⁷

Although the internment of the *Anglo-Maltesi* was a consequence of their loyalty to the UK, it was also provoked by the protests of the local population, outraged by the subsidies they were receiving from the Italian and British governments. The Prefect of Pistoia expressed 'ill-concealed regret for the presence of these guests, whose deplorable personal hygienic conditions and poor health in general, cause reasonable concern for the spread of contagion'. The prefect went on to point out that the spa season began on 1 April and asked the Ministry to have all the expelled Libyans transferred by that date.⁴⁸ In Fiuggi the presence of the *Anglo-Maltesi* sparked protests; on 10 May 1942, the prefect of Frosinone reported that

> the anti-Italian sentiments openly manifested by almost all the *Anglo-Maltesi* evacuees living in Fiuggi; the possession of conspicuous sums of money which they use to buy, even by smuggling, any foodstuff existing in the place; their haughty behaviour, have created in the population of Fiuggi, at first, irritation and antipathy against the unwanted guests; at the present time hatred and contempt: Hatred, because they are considered enemies of our country; contempt, because they are considered starvers of the population.⁴⁹

On 2 June 1942, the *Fascio di combattimento di Malta* (Malta's 'Fasces of Combat' i.e. the Maltese local branch of Fascist National Party) provided the Ministry of the Interior with a list of *Anglo-Maltesi* displaced to Fiuggi, who had 'declared that they wished to share the fate of England of which they were subjects': they would therefore be sent to an internment camp, which would also appease those in the population who made complaints.⁵⁰ In August 1942, those considered by the *Fascio di combattimento di Malta* to have anti-Italian sentiments were sent to an internment camp.⁵¹ The internment camp chosen was the Fraschette di Alatri, in the province of Frosinone, built specifically to house displaced persons from Libya.⁵² On 30 November 1942, the Prefect of Pistoia asked the Ministry of the Interior for all *Anglo-Maltesi* and foreigners displaced to Montecatini to be removed from the city, as Italian evacuees from bombed areas were about to arrive. It would, therefore, have been impossible to control the *Anglo-Maltesi* adequately and there was a risk that the Italians would have suffered greater hardship than the foreigners.⁵³ This request was reiterated again by the new prefect of Pistoia, Francesco Aria, on 12 May 1943. Aria reported that

> with the 20 *lire* they receive from the municipality and the sums they receive from England, the families of these displaced persons live a very good life and do not fail to show off this privileged status in public. This has therefore caused a certain amount of discontent, especially among the compatriots repatriated from Libya and Italian Oriental Africa who enjoy a much lower subsidy ... This situation generates frequent cases in which compatriots publicly point out the unequal treatment with unsympathetic comments. For the above reasons I would propose, therefore, either the removal of the *Anglo-Maltesi* from Montecatini ... or, especially to those who receive subsidies from England, the granting of the

same treatment as our compatriots or, finally, extending to the latter the same treatment as to the former.[54]

On 27 May, the prefect reported to the Ministry his scepticism about the *Anglo-Maltesi* who had declared themselves pro-Italian:

> The reasons that induced the *Anglo-Maltesi* to accept the proposals made to them can be summarised as follows: 1) fear of being expelled from Montecatini Terme and interned in concentration camps, as they had been promised; 2) the desire, for some, to have the immediate release of property and money seized; 3) the poorest ones subordinated their adhesion to the condition that the Italian Government undertook to pass on the full quota of the subsidy they received from the Swiss Legation, while they would have responded negatively if the subsidy in question had been reduced.[55]

For the prefect, the *Anglo-Maltesi* were acting out of self-interest, even though they had not publicly shown any Anglophile sympathies, although nor was there evidence of any 'definite orientation towards Italy'.

On 13 February 1943, the Ministry of the Interior asked prefectures, who represented the Ministry in each province, to list the foreigners expelled from Libya living in their province of competence (Table 10.3).[56] Figure 10.1 shows the locations

Table 10.3 Foreigners Expelled from Libya as Provided by Prefectures in February 1943 on the Request of the Ministry of Interior

Province	Number and nationality	Camps (municipality)	Internment outside camp (municipality)
Arezzo[57]	53 (British Jews and *Anglo-Maltesi*)	Civitella della Chiana	
Ascoli Piceno[58]	237 *Anglo-Maltesi*	Acquasanta; Arquata del Tronto	
Bologna[59]	*Anglo-Maltesi*		Camugnano; Bazzano
Chieti[60]	15		
Florence[61]	22	Bagno a Ripoli	
Frosinone[62]	946 *Anglo-Maltesi*	Fraschette di Alatri	
Lucca[63]	80 *Anglo-Maltesi*	Bagni di Lucca	
Macerata[64]	39	Camerino	
Modena[65]	200 *Anglo-Maltesi* (of which 139 were Aryans' and 61 Jews)		Nonantola; Bastiglia; San Felice sul Panaro; Cavezzo; Medolla[8.5.1942][66]
Parma[67]	17 *Anglo-Maltesi*	Montechiarugolo	
Teramo[68]	At least 117 *Anglo-Maltesi*	Corropoli	

of the main camps used to intern *Anglo-Maltesi*. Note that for military reasons, camps were mostly placed in the centre of the Italian peninsula, far from coasts and borders. Life in the camps was relatively hard, marked by the constant lack of food and precarious and crumbling structures.[69] The population of the poorest areas of Italy, where the camps were usually placed, often suffered from the same problems, but without enjoying the subsidies of *Anglo-Maltesi* from both the Italian and British governments. The condition of those who were subjected to internment outside camps was better, since they were able to obtain food thanks to the help of the inhabitants of the place where they were interned. Jane Cassar, an *Anglo-Maltese*, was interned first in Villa Basilica then in Monte San Savino, in apartments with her parents and relatives. She recalled going to Italian elementary schools and also the music school in Monte San Savino, but she did not mingle with her school mates, probably the parents of her schoolmates advised them to not mingle with her. In her narration she has positive memories, especially of some Italian families who hosted some of her relatives and helped them. After the internment, she came back to Libya, but the possessions of her once-affluent family were looted or stolen. As with many other *Anglo-Maltesi*, her family chose to move to Melbourne, Australia.[70]

The use of the term 'internment camp' can be misleading in describing the 'camps' of the Ministry of the Interior. These were often buildings located in the centre of small towns adapted to the occasion, sometimes with bars on the windows and, when possible, with barbed wire. For example, the Camp in Corropoli[71] in eastern Italy was a former monastery which, at most, could host 180 internees; the camp in Civitella della Chiana[72] in Tuscany was a villa that its owner rented to the government to accommodate between sixty and seventy internees. In most cases, these 'camps' were small structures that housed a hundred internees at most. If very small, the camps were under the administration of the local *podestà* (an unelected mayor during the Fascist period), while the medium-sized camps were administered by a commissioner of public security. In the case of women's camps, the *podestà* and commissioner were assisted by a female director. In the camps of the Ministry of the Interior, there was no lack of hunger and violence, but in general the mortality rate was quite low. Many camps did not have their own kitchen, and this 'forced' internees to go to public inns and trattorias, a real weak point within the theoretical framework of an internment camp that was supposed to provide for the total separation from society and a state of exception for its inmates. The internment camp of Fraschette di Alatri in Lazio, built to host the *Anglo-Maltesi*, was one of the biggest camps of the Fascist regime and, at its maximum, hosted around 4,500 internees. The living conditions in the camp were always harsh since it was never completed, and the camp was often overcrowded. The hygiene was very bad since the sewers were open-air.[73] The *Anglo-Maltesi*, who had gone from 'non-citizen Italians' to 'enemy subjects', were in the best position because they benefited from food help and subsidies paid by the UK through the Swiss Legation. Romeo Cini, in his memoirs, recalled quite favourably his period spent in the Grand Hotel of Fiuggi, while the subject of the narration of his internment in Fraschette was dire: '*Anglo-Maltesi* suffered hunger and cold for months.'[74] The situation improved slightly from 1943 when they started receiving food from the British Red Cross, and after they built a school and a church inside the camp.

Figure 10.1 Map of main camps for *Anglo-Maltesi*
Source: Created by the author with ArcGIS.

This period of relative calm would only last a few months, because of the collapse of the regime and the Nazi invasion of Italy. The *Anglo-Maltesi* could escape because the Fascist guards left, but they preferred not to leave since it was impossible for them to reach their homes in North Africa. At the beginning of 1944, Nazis arrived at the Fraschette camp to capture men for forced labour, so many of the internees fled to the mountains, where they received the help of shepherds. Unfortunately, the camp was close to the Winter Line, where the Nazis and Fascists organized fortifications to slow the Allies' conquest of Italy, and the camp was bombed by the Allies during February 1944.[75] From December 1943, many *Anglo-Maltesi* who were in Italian Social Republic (RSI) territory,[76] including those in Fraschette di Alatri, were deported to Fossoli concentration and transit camp near Carpi. On 1 February 1944, eighty-three *Anglo-Maltesi* of 'Jewish race' were transferred from Fossoli to an unknown concentration camp in Germany.[77]

Repatriation to Libya

The repatriation of the *Anglo-Maltesi* from Italy to Libya cannot be reconstructed precisely. However, the problem was certainly known to the new Italian government[78]. The High Commission for War Refugees had been trying to repatriate refugees from Tripolitania since October 1944, putting pressure on the Ministry of the Interior and the Headquarters of Displaced Persons and Repatriation. However, a subsequent decree restricted the competences of the High Commission and entrusted the administration of Libyan refugees to the Ministry of Italian Africa, which was responsible for all colonial affairs.[79] In any case, in the second half of 1944, most of the *Anglo-Maltesi* began to flow towards the Cinecittà refugee camp in Rome, including the *Anglo-Maltesi* interned in Fossoli camp from July 1944, as the latter was being dismantled.[80]

After a few months, in 1945, they were transferred to the Aversa refugee centre near Naples and from there returned to Libya from 1946.[81] A minority of the *Anglo-Maltesi* were gathered in UNRRA (United Nations Relief and Rehabilitation Administration) refugee camps in the province of Lecce, set up in villas and private houses, where the refugees lived freely, unsupervised.[82] From here, via the port of Bari, some *Anglo-Maltesi* returned to Tripoli.[83] Romeo Cini, in his memoirs, recalled the transfer to the UNRRA camp at Santa Maria di Leuca (in Lecce) and then to Aversa (in Caserta) and finally to Tripoli. However, the hardships were not over; Libya was now inhospitable to these British citizens of Maltese origin because of hostility from the Arab majority, who probably perceived them to be too close to the Fascist colonizers. As a consequence, many *Anglo-Maltese* emigrated to Australia.[84]

The memory of Italian internment camps

The Italian population today is generally unaware of the Fascist regime's internment policy. Italian academics have preferred to focus on other aspects of the Second

World War or of confinement, with the exception of scholars such as Carlo Spartaco Capogreco and Costantino Di Sante.[85]

The website *Campifascisti.it* maps all the internment and concentration camps within the territory under the control of the Kingdom of Italy during the Second World War. It consists of a collection of primary sources from mainly Italian public and private archives. It is a useful research tool for every scholar of internment camps and functions as a way to perpetuate the memory of internment camps and, indeed, Fascist crimes. The site is not yet complete, but it is being continuously updated.

There are signs that the memory of this period is entering a new phase. On 4 March 2021, the Italian Senate approved a bill transforming the internment camp in Servigliano, in the Marche region of Central Italy, into a national monument.[86] Some *Anglo-Maltesi* were interned in Servigliano, but the exact number is unclear.[87] The choice of this camp as a national monument can be attributed to the proposing senator,[88] who resides in the small municipality, and is perhaps not completely justified in terms of historical importance. Despite this, it is a very important step forward for the recognition of the historical importance of internment in Italy.

The Servigliano camp was built during the First World War and was used until after the Second World War to accommodate war refugees. During the 1970s, the camp was destroyed, and the site of the camp is now occupied by a sports ground.[89] In 2001, an association was established to preserve the memory of the camp in a memorial museum in the former train station of Servigliano. This association also provides guided tours of the few remaining ruins.[90] English soldier Keith Killby was also interned in the Servigliano camp. In 1989, he decided to create a trust 'born out of his vision to nurture peace between former warring enemies and the desire to "give something back" to the brave Italian subsistence farmers, the *contadini*, who had protected escaping prisoners of war in Italy after the Armistice in September 1943'.[91] The trust provides bursaries to Italian students willing to spend a period of study in England to learn the language.[92]

The most important camp from a historical point of view, and in terms of the number of internees held, is that of Ferramonti di Tarsia in Calabria (see Figure 10.2), which was destroyed in the 1970s to build the highway from Salerno to Reggio Calabria. The camp was the largest of the internment camps and, given its position in the extreme south of Italy, was likely to have been one of the first camps to be freed by the Allies in 1943. This saved the lives of the Jews interned there as they were too far from Germany to be deported to extermination camps.[93] The camp was used to hold foreigners displaced from Libya, but only Greeks rather than *Anglo-Maltesi*. Since 2004, the site has hosted a memorial museum with various rooms and exhibitions, a library and an archive.[94] Every year, the museum celebrates a Memorial Day on 11 March, the day of the arrival of the first internees.

The camp that hosted the greatest number of *Anglo-Maltesi* is that in Fraschette, in the municipality of Alatri (see Figure 10.3). The camp was specifically built to host *Anglo-Maltesi*. The site is now completely abandoned, and no museum or memorial has been created. In 2016, with the support of a local bank, the municipality placed an artistic installation at the site to remember internees; it was named 'Monumento agli internati' (monument to internees).[95] The camp was never destroyed and many

The Case Study of Anglo-Maltesi 179

Figure 10.2 One of the few remains of the Ferramonti di Tarsia Camp
Source: CC BY 3.0 credits: Salvatore Magliari, 2005.

Figure 10.3 The Fraschette di Alatri Camp
Source: Photo courtesy of Maria Novella De Luca, 2021.

buildings are still standing, so this site would be a better place to create a heritage site than the camps of Servigliano or Ferramonti, which no longer exist. There is still some hope that the camp will be memorialized as, in 2008, the Ministry of Culture designated the 'historical and artistic interest' of the site, which became property of the Italian State. In 2020, the main Italian heritage association, FAI or *Fondo per l'ambiente Italiano* (Italian Fund for Environment), listed the site on its 'census of Italian places not to be forgotten'.[96]

Conclusion

The internment of *Anglo-Maltesi* during the Second World War, with all its peculiarities, did not differ greatly from the internment of other ethnic groups until the collapse of the regime. Of course, the treatment of Jews was harsher, particularly after the Nazi invasion of Italy and the foundation of the RSI. Although the Maltese were at first given privileges by the Fascist regime to buy their loyalty, in the end they suffered discrimination by local populations. To the current lack of acknowledgement of this history, we might also note the lack of a culture of remembrance of the Italian camps as a whole, and the lack of collective consciousness about Italian colonialism and imperialism. This sits alongside the creation of the myth of the '*Italiani brava gente*' (Italian good people).[97] The lack of an Italian 'Nuremberg process' is still considered by historians to be a significant factor in this.[98] All Fascist crimes were pardoned by the Italian government after the war, and Italian courts still tried only Nazi perpetrators, avoiding the connection of these crimes with the necessary cooperation/collaboration of Italian Fascists. The majority of the Italian population is therefore unaware of Italian colonial crimes and of most of the crimes committed during the Second World War.

Italian people and politics have chosen to forget the difficult times suffered during the war and concentrated their efforts instead in reconstruction, industrialization and economic growth: the so-called 'boom' (using the English word, embracing the new pro-American course of Italian politics). This has been reflected dramatically in the preservation of historical sites. The past was painful and embarrassing, and maybe it was better to cover concentration camps with new highways, as happened in Ferramonti di Tarsia, or new sports grounds, as with the camp in Servigliano. Many other camps, far from cities and towns, were just abandoned, as we have seen with the Camp in Fraschette di Alatri.

In the past few decades, things are starting to change. The Vatican archives holding records on the Second World War and the Holocaust are now open to researchers, and public debate around the Holocaust has become common. In 2018, to celebrate International Holocaust Memorial Day, Italian president, Sergio Mattarella, nominated Holocaust survivor Liliana Segre to the position of senator for life. Segre is one of the sponsors of the bill which intends to transform the Servigliano camp into a national monument; a clear sign of change in the memorialization policy of Italian institutions. Despite this, it is still difficult for the Italian population to cope with Italian crimes committed during the Colonial and Fascist period.

Notes

Archival abbreviations used in this chapter:
ACS Archivio Centrale dello Stato, Roma [Central Archive of State, Rome]
ASMAE Archivio Storico del Ministero degli Affari Esteri, Roma [Historical Archive of the Ministry of Foreign Affairs, Rome] also known as Archivio Storico Diplomatico [Diplomatic Historical Archive]
DAGR Divisione generale Affari riservati [General Division for Confidential Affairs]
DGAP Divisione generale Affari politici [General Division for Political Affairs]
DGPS Divisione generale di Pubblica Sicurezza [General Division of Public Security]
MAI Ministero dell'Africa italiana [Ministry of Italian Africa]
MI Ministero dell'Interno [Ministry of Interior]

1. MAI, DGAP (1904–1944), Archivio segreto 1906–1944, b.18, n. 821488-S/1776 del 13/05/1942, ACS, Rome.
2. *Ivi*, n. 821484-S/1768 del 13 maggio 1942, ACS, Rome.
3. MI, DGPS, DAGR, Ufficio internati (1939–1945), A4 bis, Internati stranieri e spionaggio, b. 26, MAI n. 823031 del 25/05/1942, ACS, Rome.
4. (English in the text), Affari politici (1931–1945), b.8, British Consulate Tripoli, 27/09/1933, ASMAE, Rome.
5. Luca Bussotti, 'A History of Italian Citizenship Laws during the Era of the Monarchy (1861–1946)', *Advances in Historical Studies* 5 (2016), 143–67.
6. A form of nationalism aimed at conquering territories that supposedly belong to the country for ethnical, ideological, or historical reasons.
7. Saverio Gentile, *Le leggi razziali: scienza giuridica, norme, circolari* (Milano: EduCatt, 2010), 188.
8. Ali Abdullatif Ahmida, *Genocide in Libya: Shar, a Hidden Colonial History* (London: Routledge, 2020). See also Nicola Labanca, *La guerra italiana per la Libia. 1911–1931* (Bologna: Il Mulino, 2012).
9. Affari politici (1931–1945), b.8, Governo della Tripolitania n. 1506 del 6/02/1934, ASMAE, Rome.
10. MAI, Volume II (1859–1945), posizione 181/76, fascicolo: Cittadinanza italiana ai maltesi in Libia e confinamento maltesi residenti in Tripolitania (segreto) 1922–1952, n. 504166 del 11/06/1937, ASMAE, Rome.
11. Ibid.
12. MAI, DGAP (1904–1944), Archivio segreto 1906–1944, b.18, ministero dell'Africa italiana n. 317032 del 11/09/1941. ACS, Rome.
13. The unnamed camp here is probably that in Fraschette, Alatri
14. *Ivi*, b.18, MAI n. 317941 del 17/12/1941, ACS, Rome.
15. MI, DGPS, DAGR, Archivio generale (1870–1958), Massime, b. 105, Fascicolo 16, Sottofascicolo 1, Ins. 23/1, n. 9271 del 23/12/1941, ACS, Rome.
16. MI, DGPS, DAGR, Ufficio internati (1939–1945), A4 bis, Internati stranieri e spionaggio, b. 75, MAI, n. 8676 del 25 aprile 1942, ACS, Rome.
17. 'RD Legge 8/07/1938 n 1415', *supplemento alla Gazzetta Ufficiale n 211*, 15 Settembre 1938.
18. MAI, DGAP (1904–1944), Archivio segreto 1906–1944, b.18, Governo della Libia, n. 204595 del 13/01/1942 ACS, Rome; also n. 315302 del 22/01/1942, ACS, Rome.
19. MI, DGPS, DAGR, Archivio generale (1870–1958), Massime, b.105, Fascicolo 16, Sottofascicolo 1, Ins. 23/1, n. 2433 del 27/01/1942, ACS, Rome.

20. The documents registering departure from Libya and arrival in hotels state different numbers.
21. *Ivi*, b. 105, n. 012892 del 24/01/1942, ACS, Rome.
22. The documents registering departure from Libya and arrival in hotels state different numbers.
23. *Ivi*, b. 105 n.1892 del 21/01/1942, ACS, Rome.
24. MAI, DGAP (1904-1944), Archivio segreto 1906-1944, b.18, n. 315986 del 10/03/1942 and n. 811749-12/9/8 del 14/03/1942, ACS, Rome.
25. Ibidem. See also MI, DGPS, DAGR, Ufficio internati (1939-1945), A4 bis, Internati stranieri e spionaggio, b. 88, prefettura di Palermo n.05604 del 12/03/1942, ACS, Rome
26. *Ivi*, b. 9, ministero dell'Africa italiana n. 814047 del 6/04/1942, ACS, Rome.
27. MAI, DGAP (1904-1944), Archivio segreto 1906-1944, b.18, n.14341/26315 del 17/04/1942, ACS, Rome.
28. *Ivi*, b.18, n. 316691 del 18/04/1942, ACS, Rome.
29. *Ivi*, b.18, n. 316938 del 1/05/1942, ACS, Rome.
30. *Ivi*, b.18, n. 318134 del 5/07/1942, ACS, Rome.
31. MI, DGPS, DAGR, Massime M4, b. 1, circolare n 442/12267 del 08/06/1940. Vedi Allegato D. ACS, Rome.
32. Simonetta Carolini, ed., *Pericolosi nelle contingenze belliche* (Rome: ANPPIA, 1987), 385.
33. *Ivi*, b. 1, Circolare n 442/14178 del 25/06/1940. Vedi Allegato F and Id, circolare prefettizia n. 02796 del 10 maggio 1943, ACS, Rome.
34. *Ivi*, b. 1, Circolare n. 451/3977 del 16 marzo 1943, ACS, Rome.
35. Carolini, *Pericolosi*, 372.
36. MI, DGPS, DAGR, Massime M4, b. 1, circolare n 442/19427 del 19/08/1940, ACS, Rome.
37. *Ivi*, b. 1 Circolare n. 442/31535 del 8/11/1942; circolare n. 451/31621 del 17/11/1942; circolare n. 451/31621 del 18/01/1943; ACS, Rome.
38. Sandro Antonini, *DELASEM: Storia della più grande organizzazione ebraica di soccorso durante la seconda guerra mondiale* (Genova: De Ferrari, 2000).
39. ASMAE, MAI, Volume II (1859-1945), posizione 180/44, ministero degli Affari Esteri n. 53-3924 del 30 gennaio 1941; see also *ivi*, ministero dell'Africa Italiana n. 315737 del 28 Marzo 1941; See also *ivi*, ministero dell'Africa Italiana n.317462 del 10 Novembre 1941.
40. One of the internees in his memoir describes the period as «bella vita». Romeo Cini, *la nostra storia*, 22, http://campifascisti.it/file/media/romeo%20cini_it.pdf (accessed 5 september 2021).
41. MI, DGPS, DAGR, Ufficio internati (1939-1945), A4 bis, Internati stranieri e spionaggio, b. 75, prefettura di Modena n. 07609 del 8/05/1943, ACS, Rome.
42. MI, DGPS, DAGR, Archivio generale, Categorie permanenti, A16, stranieri (1942-1944), b. 11, ministero dell'Interno, n. 1352 del 14/09/1942, ACS, Rome.
43. MI, DGPS, DAGR, Ufficio internati (1939-1945), A4 bis, Internati stranieri e spionaggio, b. 67, prefettura di Lucca n. 0210 del 11/12/1941, ACS, Rome.
44. *Ivi*, b. 67, MAI n. 319833 del 31/10/1942.
45. *Ivi*, b. 9, Légation de Suisse en Italie, Interessi Britannici n.0045 del 27/07/1942, ACS, Rome.
46. *Ivi*, b. 9, Comando supremo S.I.M. n. B/319482 del 16/08/942, ACS, Rome.
47. *Ivi*, b. 9, Fascio di Combattimento di Malta n.815 del 11/08/1942, ACS, Rome.

48. MI, DGPS, DAGR, Archivio generale (1870–1958), Massime, b. 145, sf.2 Affari per provincia, ins. 51 n. 66 Pistoia, prefettura di Pistoia n. 2444 del 21/02/1942, ACS, Rome.
49. *Ivi*, b. 9, prefettura di Frosinone n. 048896 del 10/05/1942, ACS, Rome.
50. *Ivi*, b. 143, PNF Fascio di combattimento di Malta n. 554 del 2/06/1942, ACS, Rome.
51. *Ivi*, b. 22, Fascio di Combattimento di Malta n. 971 del 12/08/1942, ACS, Rome.
52. MI, DGSG, Affari Generali, b. 87, fascicolo 26331, sottofascicolo internati maltesi a Ascoli Piceno, Fascio di combattimento di Malta n, 1430 del 2 novembre 1942, ACS, Rome.
53. MI, DGPS, DAGR, Ufficio internati (1939–1945), A4 bis, Internati stranieri e spionaggio, b. 5, prefettura di Pistoia, n. 01522 del 30 novembre 1942, ACS, Rome.
54. MI, DGSG, Affari Generali, b. 87, Fascicolo 263/88, Sottofascicolo Internamento di Maltesi residenti a Montecatini Terme, prefettura di Pistoia n 9629 del 12/05/1943, ACS, Rome.
55. MI, DGPS, DAGR, Archivio generale (1870–1958), Categorie permanenti 1894–1958, A16, stranieri ed ebrei stranieri 1930–1956, b. 47, Fascicolo 16/9, prefettura di Pistoia n. 03865 del 27/05/1943, ACS, Rome.
56. ACS, MI, DGPS, DAGR, Ufficio internati (1939–1945), A4 bis, Internati stranieri e spionaggio, b. 9, ministero dell'Interno n. 448/309819 del 13 febbraio 1943.
57. *Ivi*, b. 9, prefettura di Arezzo n. 02735 del 4 marzo 1943. Those interned in the Province of Ascoli Piceno came from the hotels of Montecatini after the population protests: MI, DGPS, DAGR, Archivio generale (1870–1958), Massime b. 105, fascicolo 16, sottofascicolo 1, ins.23/1, n. 01522 del 30/05/1942, ACS, Rome; MI, DGPS, DAGR, Ufficio internati (1939–1945), A4 bis, Internati stranieri e spionaggio, b. 75, prefettura di Pistoia n. 01522 del 1/06/1942, ACS, Rome; *ivi* b. 108, prefettura di Pistoia n. 01522 del 5/06/1942, ACS, Rome.
58. *Ivi*, b. 9, prefettura di Ascoli Piceno.
59. *Ivi*, b. 9, prefettura di Bologna n.03756 del 8 marzo 1943.
60. *Ivi*, b. 9, prefettura di Chieti n.02454 del 15 marzo 1943.
61. *Ivi*, b. 9, pref8 del 8 marzo 1943.
62. *Ivi*, b. 9, prefettura di Frosinone n. 03921 del 14 aprile 1943.
63. *Ivi*, b. 9, prefettura di Lucca n. 04416 del 29 aprile 1943.
64. *Ivi*, b. 9, prefettura di Macerata n.300 del 1 marzo 1943.
65. *Ivi*, b. 9, prefettura di Modena n. 07983 del 12 marzo 1943. The Maltese interned in the province of Modena came from Bagni di Lucca and Fiuggi and were interned for their loyalty to the UK: MI, DGPS, DAGR, Ufficio internati (1939–1945), A4 bis, Internati stranieri e spionaggio, *Ivi*, b. 5, prefettura di Lucca n. 07254 del 30/05/1942, ACS, Rome; *Ivi*, b. 75, PNF fascio di combattimento di Malta n. 272 del 9/04/1942, ACS, Rome; *Ivi*, b. 5, prefettura di Modena n. 012605 del 17/06/1942, ACS, Rome; *Ivi*, b. 22, prefettura di Ascoli Piceno n. 0612 del 16/07/1942, ACS, Rome.
66. ACS, MI, DGPS, DAGR, Ufficio internati (1939–1945), A4 bis, Internati stranieri e spionaggio, b. 17.
67. ACS, MI, DGPS, DAGR, Ufficio internati (1939–1945), A4 bis, Internati stranieri e spionaggio, b. 9, prefettura di Parma n. 02215 del 2 aprile 1943.
68. *Ivi*, b. 143, prefettura di Teramo n. 6886 del 13 luglio 1943.
69. Carlo S. Capogreco, *I campi del Duce. L'internamento civile nell'Italia fascista (1940–1943)* (Torino: Einaudi, 2004), 124–6.
70. The interview to Jane Cassar is available online in the *Campifascisti* website http://campifascisti.it/file/media/Jane%20Cassar_italiano.pdf (accessed 15 November 2021).

71. 235 Costantino Di Sante, 'I campi di concentramento in Abruzzo', in *I campi di concentramento in Italia. Dall'internamento alla deportazione (1940-1945)*, ed. C. Sante, 188-90 (Milano: FrancoAngeli, 2001); See also Capogreco, *I campi del Duce*, 212-13; Geoffrey P. Megargee and Joseph White, eds, *United States Holocaust Memorial Museum Encyclopedia of Camps and Ghettos, 1933-1945. Volume III: Camps and Ghettos under European Regimes, Aligned with Nazi Germany* (Indiana University Press: Bloomington and Indianapolis, in association with United States Holocaust Memorial Museum, 2018), 422.
72. Valeria Galimi, *I campi di concentramento in Toscana fra storia e memoria*, in *I campi di concentramento in Italia*, ed. C. Di Sante, 217-19 (Milano: FrancoAngeli, 2001). See also Capogreco, *I campi del Duce*, pp. 184-5; Megargee and White, *Encyclopedia of Camps and Ghettos*, 418-19.
73. Capogreco, *I campi del Duce*, 198-200. See also Megargee and White, *Encyclopedia of Camps and Ghettos*, 438-9.
74. Cini, *la nostra storia*, available online http://campifascisti.it/file/media/romeo%20cini_it.pdf (accessed 15 November 2021).
75. Ibid.
76. The RSI was a Nazi puppet-state founded in 1943 with Mussolini as head of state and government. It mostly controlled the northern part of Italy.
77. *Ivi*, b. 9, prefettura di Modena n. 06082 del 1/02/1944, ACS, Rome.
78. After the collapse of the Fascist regime, the King instructed General Badoglio to form a new government in the part of Italy freed by the Allies since this was the southern part and the government was temporarily based in Salerno. This period is called by historians *Regno del Sud* (Southern Kingdom).
79. Presidenza del Consiglio dei ministri, Gabinetto, Affari Generali, fascicoli per categorie (1876-1987), 1944-1947, b. 3196, Alto Commissariato per i profughi di guerra, 9/10/1944, ACS, Rome.
80. MI, DGPS, DAGR, Archivio generale, Ufficio internati (1939-1945), A4 bis, internati stranieri e spionaggio 1939-1945, b. 5, Fascicolo 26 (Modena), ACS, Rome.
81. *Ivi*, Categorie permanenti, A16, stranieri (1944-1946) ACS, Rome.
82. MI, Divisione Affari Generali, 1944-1946, b.232, n. 04741 del 5/12/1946 ACS, Rome.
83. MI, DGPS, DAGR, Archivio generale, Categorie permanenti, A16, stranieri (1942-1944), b. 11, questura di Roma, n. 04462 del 22 settembre 1945 ACS, Rome.
84. Romeo Cini, *la nostra storia*, http://campifascisti.it/file/media/romeo%20cini_it.pdf (accessed 5 September 2021).
85. See, for example, Capogreco, *I campi del Duce*, and for more information the complete publications of Carlo S. Capogreco https://polaris.unical.it/browse?type=author&authority=rp40755&authority_lang=en (accessed 10 January 2022); Costantino di Sante, *I campi di concentramento in Italia* and his last book Di Sante, *Criminali del campo di concentramento di Bolzano. Deposizioni, disegni, foto e documenti inediti* (Bolzano: Raetia, 2019).
86. Text of the law available online Senato della Repubblica at http://www.senato.it/service/PDF/PDFServer/BGT/01209148.pdf (accessed 5 May 2021).
87. MI, DGPS, DAGR A4bis, b 358, ACS, Rome.
88. Official Senate page available online http://www.senato.it/leg/18/BGT/Schede/Attsen/00028924.htm (accessed 5 May 2021).
89. C. Di Sante, *L'internamento civile nell'Ascolano e il campo di concentramento di Servigliano (1940-1944)* (Ascoli Piceno: Istituto provinciale per la storia del movimento di liberazione nelle Marche, 1998).

90. La Casa della Memoria https://www.lacasadellamemoria.com/ (accessed 5 September 2021).
91. Monte San Martino Trust https://msmtrust.org.uk/ (accessed 5 September 2021).
92. Ibid.
93. C. S. Capogreco, *Ferramonti. La vita e gli uomini del più grande campo d'internamento fascista, 1940–1945* (Firenze: Giuntina, 1987).
94. Ferramonti di Tarsia Campo di concentramento – Museo della memoria, https://www.campodiferramonti.it/ (accessed 5 September 2021).
95. Ciociaria Oggi, 20/03/2016, https://www.ciociariaoggi.it/news/alatri/15350/alatri-stele-monumento-fraschette.html (accessed 10 January 2022).
96. Fondo per l' Ambiente Italiano https://www.fondoambiente.it/luoghi/campo-di-internamento-le-fraschette?ldc (accessed 8 October 2021).
97. Filippo Focardi, *Il cattivo tedesco e il bravo italiano* (Bari: Laterza, 2013); Angelo Del Boca, *Italiani, brava gente?* (Vicenza: Neri Pozza, 2005); David Bidussa, *Il mito del bravo italiano* (Milano: Il Saggiatore, 1994).
98. Michele Battini, *Peccati di memoria. La mancata Norimberga italiana* (Roma-Bari: Laterza, 2003); Filippo Focardi, *Criminali a piede libero: la mancata Norimberga italiana* (Roma: Viella, 2011).

Bibliography

Ahmida, Ali Abdullatif. *Genocide in Libya: Shar, a Hidden Colonial History.* London: Routledge, 2020.

Antonini, Sandro. *DELASEM: Storia della più grande organizzazione ebraica di soccorso durante la Seconda guerra mondiale.* Genova: De Ferrari, 2000.

Battini, Michele. *Peccati di memoria. La mancata Norimberga italiana.* Roma-Bari: Laterza, 2003.

Bidussa, David. *Il mito del bravo italiano.* Milano: Il Saggiatore, 1994.

Bussotti, Luca. 'A History of Italian Citizenship Laws during the Era of the Monarchy (1861–1946)'. *Advances in Historical Studies* 5 (2016): 143–67.

Capogreco, Carlo Spartaco. *Ferramonti. La vita e gli uomini del più grande campo d'internamento fascista, 1940–1945.* Firenze: Giuntina, 1987.

Capogreco, Carlo Spartaco. *I campi del Duce. L'internamento civile nell'Italia fascista (1940–1943).* Milano: Einaudi, 2004.

Carolini, Simonetta. ed. *Pericolosi nelle contingenze belliche.* Rome: ANPPIA, 1987.

Del Boca, Angelo. *Italiani, brava gente?* Vicenza: Neri Pozza, 2005.

Di Sante, Costantino. *Criminali del campo di concentramento di Bolzano. Deposizioni, disegni, foto e documenti inediti.* Bolzano: Raetia, 2019.

Di Sante, Costantino. 'I campi di concentramento in Abruzzo'. In *I campi di concentramento in Italia. Dall'internamento alla deportazione (1940–1945)*, edited by Costanino Di Sante, 217–19. Milano: FrancoAngeli, 2001.

Di Sante, Costantino. *L'internamento civile nell'Ascolano e il campo di concentramento di Servigliano (1940–1944).* Ascoli Piceno: Istituto provinciale per la storia del movimento di liberazione nelle Marche, 1998.

Focardi, Filippo. *Criminali a piede libero: la mancata Norimberga italiana.* Roma: Viella, 2011.

Focardi, Filippo. *Il cattivo tedesco e il bravo italiano.* Bari: Laterza, 2013.

Galimi, Valeria. *I campi di concentramento in Toscana fra storia e memoria*. In *I campi di concentramento in Italia. Dall'internamento alla deportazione* (1940–1945), edited by C. Di Sante, 207–27. Milano: FrancoAngeli, 2001.

Gentile, Saverio. *Le leggi razziali: scienza giuridica, norme, circolari*. Milano: EduCatt, 2010.

Labanca, Nicola. *La guerra italiana per la Libia. 1911–1931*. Bologna: Il Mulino, 2012.

Megargee, Geoffrey P., and Joseph White, eds. *The United States Holocaust Memorial Museum Encyclopedia of Camps and Ghettos, 1933–1945. Volume III: Camps and Ghettos under European Regimes, Aligned with Nazi Germany*. Indiana University Press: Bloomington and Indianapolis, in association with United States Holocaust Memorial Museum, 2018.

Part Three

Camps in the British Dominions: Continentals interned by the British abroad

11

In detention: Memories of Jewish refugees interned in Atlit near Haifa

Verena Buser

The detention camp in the village of Atlit, around 20 km south of Haifa, existed from December 1939 to December 1948, and was the first encounter with *Eretz Israel* (the Land of Israel) for Jewish immigrants who entered British Mandate Palestine. Today, the site of the camp is regarded as a heritage site where *Ha'apala* (the illegal immigration into Palestine) is commemorated. This chapter will show why Atlit is remembered as a Zionist symbol and will juxtapose this historical narrative with memory discourses of Jews who fled Nazi Europe. It will question the extent to which their specific memories as being refugees expelled from their homeland are included in official ceremonies, the memorial's exhibition and the official narrative. Drawing on memoirs and diaries, this chapter also gauges their conflicting feelings about leaving Europe, their experiences of travel and their imprisonment in Atlit. It will also identify how they felt about the British authorities, and how they lived in a limbo between a threatening past and an unknown future.

The chapter presented here aims to widen the historical narrative. It follows the approach of Israeli researchers Ruth Amir and Leah Rosen, who analysed the creation of a national Jewish identity and challenged the hegemonic Zionist memory discourse through the example of *Youth Aliyah* (a Zionist aid campaign in which Jewish children from Nazi Europe were trained for their immigration to *Eretz Israel* from Romania, Germany or Sweden and other European countries). The authors discuss 'other narratives' which 'sometimes contradict and dispute the official collective memory'. They 'concentrate on the discourse about the past and on the memory which it constructs'. Thus, it is their aim to give a voice to those narratives which are neglected or have barely been acknowledged.[1]

This chapter draws upon ego-documents (documents revealing or providing privileged information about the person who produced it), official sources and oral history testimonies to illuminate an under-researched chapter of history that details the escape from the Holocaust by a particular group of refugees. While the author has carried out research at many archives,[2] it is the testimonies from the University of California Shoah Foundation Archives most especially that illuminate the refugees' perspective on their in-between status. These testimonies and contemporary diaries and letters show the heterogeneous memories about Atlit from the Second World War until the end of the British Mandate period. This chapter argues that these documents and testimonies widen the historical narrative and have been used in the past to enhance a glorifying approach which has turned the Atlit camp retrospectively into a symbol of the struggle of the Zionist movement against the British.

For the former Jewish detainees Atlit also represented their fears and destroyed hopes, suffering while awaiting an unknown future and separation from families. Their emotional struggle with questions of belonging needs further attention: they were living in Atlit in transit, in a status 'in-between': no longer Europeans with a national identity, and not yet Jews with a new homeland. With the later Holocaust survivors of deportation, camps and ghettos they had one thing in common: they were stuck between powerful forces, some of them making decisions on their behalf: the British Mandate authorities, executed through the British Police and Army; their Arab and Jewish auxiliary police and Zionists from Europe; and the *Yishuv* (the Jewish population living in Palestine before the State of Israel was proclaimed in 1948) who wanted to establish a new social order in *Eretz Israel*. In many cases, official and political plans stood against the future plans of individuals.

When the British government published the White Paper of May 1939, which took a 'pro-Arab stance', Jewish immigration was strictly limited to a quota of 1,500 people per month.[3] In the years before, the Mandate power had unsuccessfully tried to implement an appeasement policy with the intention of subdividing Palestine into an Arab and Jewish state.[4] European Zionists collaborated with Zionists in the *Yishuv* to fight the colonial power, and in 1934 initiated what was perceived to be the *Aliya Bet* ('illegal immigration') of Jews.[5] The organization which organized the transfers via land, sea and air was the *Mosad Le-Aliyah Bet* (Organization for Immigration), an enterprise of the Jewish Agency for Palestine (JAFP) to support illegal immigration against the background of its long-term objective to colonize Palestine.[6]

The decision to establish in Atlit a detention camp for 'illegal' Jewish immigrants, of whom the majority came by sea to Palestine, was based on the so-called Palestine (Defence) Order in Council 1937, published with enhancements in August 1939 in the *Palestine Gazette*, the organ of the Mandate government.[7] These regulations were modified into the Defence (Amendment) Regulations (No. 12), 1939. Herein it was laid down that

> any person who is found in Palestine in contravention of the provisions of the Immigration Ordinance shall be guilty of an offence under these regulations and shall be triable by a British Magistrate summarily and on conviction ...] such magistrate shall direct him to be detained during the pleasure of the High Commissioner.

Nevertheless, the illegal immigration of the Zionist enterprise to bring Jews to Palestine had already begun in 1934. Between 1934 and the start of the Second World War, fifty vessels with 20,500 Jewish 'illegal' immigrants arrived at the shores of Mandate Palestine.[8] During the Second World War, around 16,000 immigrants followed on twenty-five ships. Finally, by 1947, twenty additional ships brought 25,000

Holocaust survivors to Palestine.[9] One of the first ships was the *Velos*, which arrived in summer 1934 with young Jews who were trained in agriculture, gardening and other handcrafts by the *Hachshara*, a Zionist emigration preparation program.[10]

Probably the first detainees in Atlit were passengers of the ship *Rudnitchar*, which came from Bulgaria.[11] Armin Schleichkorn arrived with this ship on 8 January 1940 in Haifa harbour with more than 500 others: 'We opened Atlit', he testified in a post-war interview.[12] Other ships arriving with *Ma'apilim* (illegal Jewish immigrants) in 1940 were the *Orion*, *Hilda* and *Sakarya*.[13] According to historian Dalia Ofer, by the end of 1952, some 717,923 Jews had immigrated into Israel.[14]

Official sources in the Israel State Archives in Jerusalem document the construction of a 'Detention Camp for Illegal Jewish Immigrants' in Atlit in 1939.[15] The camp was built with British government funds.[16] The construction works began in early August 1939 on an area of 150 *dunam*; approximately 150,000 m^2. 500 Jewish and Arabic employees worked on the erection of the camp.[17] On 3 December 1939, the *Palestine Post* officially announced that the 'new Atlit Camp ... was ... completed in the record time of about 110 working days. It comprises 60 huts with dormitories, kitchens, dining halls, hospital-bay and sanitary facilities, and can accommodate some 2000 detainees'.[18] It was located midway between what the *Palestine Post* referred to as the 'Gaol Labour Camp' and the sea. Installation works were carried out under the supervision of the district medical officer. Building materials came from nearby Haifa, delivered by Arab and Jewish supplier companies, and included timber, cement and broken stone.[19] In early January 1940, it was finally occupied as a 'place of detention for illegal immigrants'.[20] The external appearance of the camp was described in the *Palestine Post* on 15 January 1941 as follows:

> An alley of tall slender palms leads to the outer camp, which is surrounded by a low fence of barbed wire. Here are the bungalows for the guard and a few small fields. A high fence surrounds the small internees camp itself. Two thousand people have found their first refuge here after nightmare experiences that would have been wholly incredible only yesterday, but are almost commonplace today.

Atlit detention camp was surrounded by barbed wire and divided into two parts by a camp street (see Figure 11.1). On its Western side it was bounded by the Mediterranean, and on its Eastern side, by the Haifa-Tel Aviv Road. It had disinfection facilities and washrooms for its inmates. Barracks could house between thirty and sicty persons, depending on the actual allocations of inmates.

Near the detention camp was Atlit Jail Labour Camp No. 2 for Jewish and Arab prisoners;[21] it also held underground fighters of the *Haganah* (Jewish military organization for self-defence of the labour organization in Palestine).[22] However, Atlit camp, also referred to as a 'clearance camp', served as a quarantine and detention site for Jewish refugees – both legal and illegal – from Nazi-occupied Europe, before immigration procedures took place. Among the most severe problems in Mandate Palestine was the challenge of controlling infectious diseases like malaria, jaundice, typhoid fever, cholera or rabies, as can be read in numerous pages of the contemporary *Palestine Gazette*. Infectious diseases were, unfortunately, an ever-present risk in Atlit.

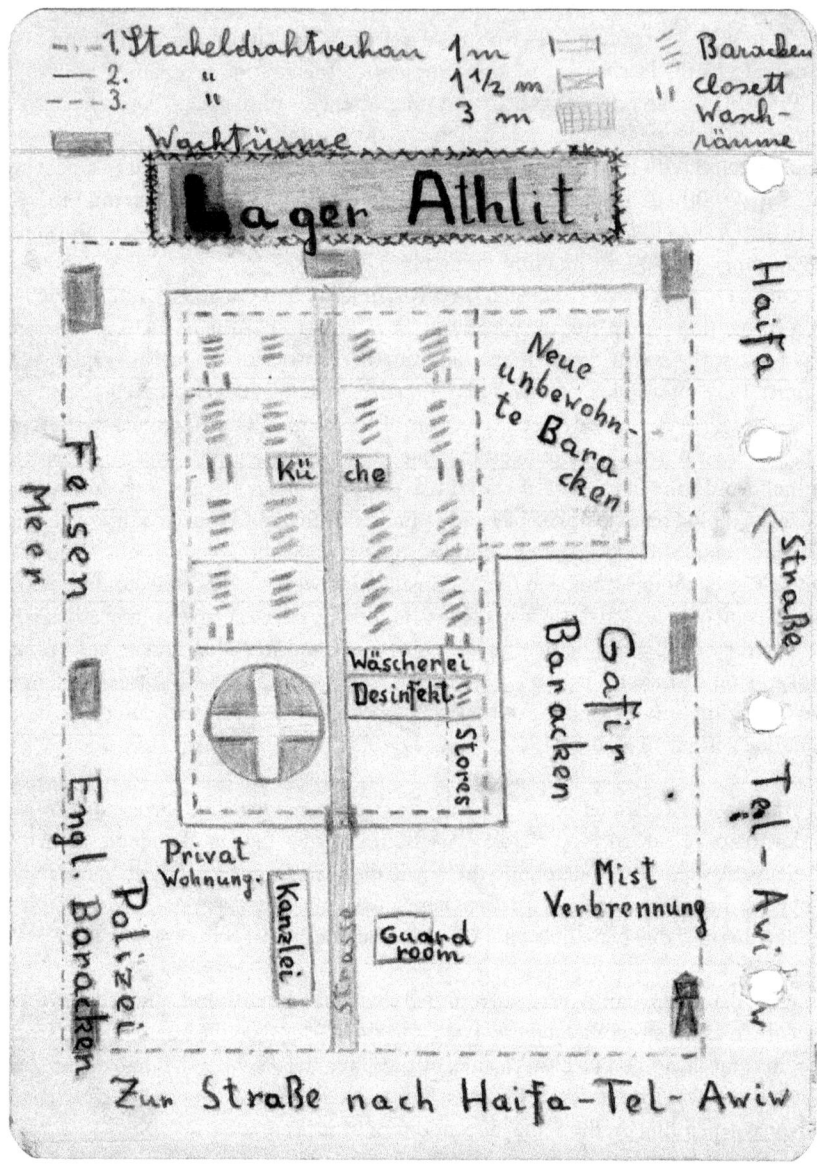

Figure 11.1 Illustrated page from the diary of Egon Weiss showing the layout of Atlit camp, compiled during and immediately after his detention in the camp

Source: © USHMM Photo Collection, image 70188.

At the end of 1940, typhoid broke out. It was said that this was due to new arrivals, and seven people died, including twenty-year-old refugee Alfred Altkorn, who survived the *Patria* disaster referred to later, who died on 17 January 1941.[23]

Illegal refugees – without immigration certificates – were, on the whole, detained in Atlit for a longer time period than those in the possession of permits. Detainees were generally released only on a quota basis. Some of them also came as prospective immigrants from countries like Bulgaria via Syria, or children and teenagers who were transferred by the *Youth Aliya*.[24]

In Atlit, the immigrants were screened not merely for their origins, but were also interrogated to filter out assumed spies. Suspected men were often transferred to the detention camp Sarafand (Al-Sarafand, a former Arab village south of Haifa, in Arabic: الصرفند) or the military prison in Akko, close to Haifa in the North.[25] Suspected women were handed over to the women's prison in Bethlehem. In May 1941, sixteen additional barracks were constructed in Atlit within just one month, most likely because numbers of immigrants were rising.[26]

State of research

Surprisingly, despite the knowledge of the site of Atlit as a heritage site and its original function as a detention camp for immigrants, no study exists of the camp's history and the everyday reality of life inside the camp. Rather, Atlit is mentioned in several studies – elaborated mainly by Israeli researchers – about illegal immigration to Mandate Palestine.[27] Only one publication exists: *The Atlit Camp* by Mordecai Naor, published in 2010, an edited volume written from a Zionist perspective. It discusses the illegal immigration as an enterprise, its protagonists, ships, efforts and sacrifices in pursuit of its final goal: the founding of a Jewish state. Its discussion of Atlit is paradigmatic for a single-sided narrative; the book does not include the very heterogeneous migration experiences of Jews arriving in Mandate Palestine; rather it must be understood within a broader campaign of the Israeli government to promote a Zionist narrative.[28] Generally speaking, the book portrays the 'strong fighters and the weak victims' – the homogeneous mass of Jewish immigrants – quite stereotypically.

There are no publications nor any comprehensive study about the average 'ordinary immigrant', their hopes about or disappointments upon reaching Palestine or their responses to being treated like criminals, often being taken to Palestine under police control. Moreover, there is no examination or study about relations with the Arab population, the auxiliary police or the local Arab population. The only research to date (but without a focus on the detention camp) was published by Ruth Amir about the existence of an Armenian village in Atlit.[29]

Arrival in Atlit

Generally speaking, 'the British' (as survivors referred to them) were the first people met by the refugee immigrants or Holocaust survivors while arriving at the shores of Mandate Palestine. Often, survivor testimonies describe not the actual rank or the correct designation – police, military or army – but more their behaviour towards the immigrants. Negative descriptions are dominant in the testimonies, which must be understood in the context of disappointed and exhausted refugees. Ernest Hoenig remembers that the 'British were chasing people with guns ... police with rifles and guns ... Atlit was some sort of concentration camp with huts, one road in the center, run by police and some *gaffirim*'.[30] Asked during a post-war interview about the attitude of the policemen in charge, he answered that '[they were] very rough'.[31] Ernest Powers, one of the Jewish refugees who worked as a translator for the British, completes this perception: '[The] police were miserable'.[32] Another refugee, Hersch Simon, thought that British police behaved as 'masters of the world'.[33] Yolanda Dicks remembers that after her detention in Atlit, there were 'constantly British police ... Each one was a nothing, but with us they were the bosses'.[34] Ernest Powers thought that Atlit was, in his eyes, 'a very infamous camp ... run by English police with Arab and Jewish policemen, but the ones in charge were always the British ... the rest were natives, bloody natives. We were put in there, all the people that survived the sinking of the Patria'. He described the behaviour of a British police captain while on duty as follows:

> Atlit was not really a summer camp ... Barbed wire, watchtowers ... The food mainly consisted of black coffee, bread and halva. To this day I cannot smell halva and not get sick. ... I was ... an interpreter for the whole camp. ... He had a navy blue uniform, white gloves, and with his white glove finger he would go into the corner of the wooden barrack and he would hold up his white glove finger and would say 'Gentlemen. This is dust. From dust you get lice. From lice you get typhoid fever. And unfortunately from typhoid fever you will die.' I didn't particularly care for the gentlemen too much, but I think it was mutual. [He] didn't care for the Jews too much either.[35]

These negative connotations must surely be read critically and can also be understood by the fact that the immigrants had fled from persecution and harassment, now being deprived of making decisions of their own, being led under police control to a camp, a process with an unknown outcome. M. D., himself a policeman then, remembers that 'when the boats started arriving in full measure, it was greatly resented, because it was we who took them from the boats to the camp, to Atlit. That was bitterly resented'.[36]

Atlit and the *Patria* disaster

The *Patria* disaster received by far the most attention in the press;[37] the *Palestine Post* reported on the catastrophe in Haifa's harbor. The British wanted to deport the refugees who had arrived on board the three 'death ships'[38] – the *Milos, Atlantic*, and the *Pacific* – the majority of passengers coming from Germany, Austria and Czechoslovakia.[39] These ships had sailed from Europe under the most desolate conditions. The Jewish women, men and children had endured weeks and months of starvation, diseases, heavy overcrowding and a lack of firewood on board the ships so that they had to burn the planks of the ship. Passengers of the *Milos* and *Pacific* were brought under British control to the *Patria*, a large steamer, in Haifa harbour. When the *Atlantic* arrived, only some of its passengers were transferred to the *Patria*.

After intensive discussions among *Haganah* leadership and functionaries of the JAFP, it was decided to place a bomb on the *Patria*. The goal of this planned action was to stop the deportation and make the ship unseaworthy, but without harming its passengers. On the morning of 25 November 1941, the ship sank within minutes of the attack. At the time, more than 1,900 women, men and children were on board, and 267 of them drowned in the Mediterranean.[40] Survivors were brought by bus to Atlit. Under the auspices of the High Commissioner, it was decided by the British that those who were not yet transferred to the *Patria* and were still on the *Atlantic* had to be deported to the island of Mauritius. This forced deportation was a shock to the majority of the refugees.

The deportation to Mauritius, some days after the *Patria* catastrophe, was carried out using violence, and was one of the darkest chapters of British Mandate Policy against Holocaust refugees. Survivors bear witness to the events which took place. Liselotte Steckl, who arrived with the *Milos* to Haifa, stated that after some days, the remaining passengers were separated from those who survived the earlier catastrophe. Jewish policemen had informed them in advance that they were being deported. The Jewish men and women, who had just escaped a brutal antisemitic policy in Europe, had, according to Betty Factor who arrived with the *Atlantic*, been told by fighters of the *Haganah* that 'the only thing you have left is passive resistance'.[41] During an interview, Liselotte Steckl remembered that 'some people in the transport decided for passive resistance ... we were all instructed not to dress, to stay naked, not to pack ... it was a primitive way [of resistance]'.[42] According to her testimony, police and military surrounded the camp in the middle of the night. After 8 am they heard screaming and yelling; military and police entered barracks of the single men. They dragged them out of bed, naked or not; the police beat them up very heavily: according to Steckl, 'blood was flooding'. Of those who were still on the *Atlantic*, a group of men were sent to Akko prison, most probably regarded as spies. All the other men, women and children were sent to Atlit.[43]

Everyday life in Atlit

The administrative report of the Palestine Prisons Service for 1940 tells us that Atlit had a 'daily average population' of 1,299 people. The statistics for the detention camp were subsumed under the prison reports. For the year 1940, it stated that 2,039 'illegal immigrants' were detained under the 'Defence Regulations'.[44]

Most of the historic details about everyday camp life can be traced in survivor testimonies and from contemporary articles in the *Palestine Post*. After the *Patria* disaster most especially, in March 1941, official authorization was given for prisoners to receive visitors, including officials of the Haifa rabbinate.[45] Refugees detained in the camp asked visitors to send them toothpaste, soap, shaving cream and razors, as well as cigarettes and reading materials.[46] Private visits were not allowed, however, and appointments had to be arranged via organizations like the Czechoslovak Settlers Association or the German and Australian Settlers Association in Haifa. The number was limited to thirty people a day.[47]

Many former inmates testified to a vivid cultural life despite their uncomfortable and uncertain situation. For example, in March 1941 a commemoration took place at the camp on the occasion of the 91st anniversary of the birth of Tomáš Masaryk, former president of Czechoslovakia.[48] The Czechoslovak and Swedish consuls in Haifa joined this event.

In January 1940, a kosher kitchen operated in the camp, and the Haifa rabbinate was able to visit Atlit.[49] Refugees were keen to receive Shabbat materials, books and papers. Calls in the local Haifa press asked people to support the immigrants with items like books or games of chess. To many of the refugees, the chance to celebrate Passover or other Jewish holidays gave them a sense of security. Oranges were new to many refugees; many of the Jewish refugees mentioned in their testimonies that they saw and ate them for the first time in the camp. Others remembered their first 'encounter' with halva, a sweet made out of sugar, almonds and honey.[50] Some of them fell ill after eating too much; others developed a love for it which lasted all their lives. Others testified later that they could not bear the smell, because they ate too much of it in the camp.

In January 1941, there were seventeen infants in Atlit who had been born in Bratislava or on one of the three refugee ships. One hundred and twenty-eight children were under fourteen years of age, with a further 100 teenagers under eighteen years of age.[51] Jewish organizations sent supplies for the children to Atlit and, for those minors, schooling and kindergarten were organized. The kindergarten was led by Marianne (Miriam) Burstein, a trained kindergarten teacher from Berlin who worked in Atlit in a barrack for mothers and newborns. The children also received footballs and other sports equipment, and were taught Hebrew, mathematics, sport and German. Burstein wrote in her memoirs that 'after a while, I organized a small kindergarten in the camp. I gathered the children, played with them and went for walks throughout the camp'.[52] The camp school was organized by Dr Ella Freund (Figure 11.2).[53] Her school journal is housed in the Atlit Detention Camp database.[54]

In June 1941, the *Palestine Post* reported that training in practical agriculture was included in the school.[55] Later, Lea Grundig, today an artist, and Lena Pfefferkorn, probably a friend of hers, illustrated a children's book in Atlit with the title *Der Scheinwerfer von Atlit* (The spotlight of Atlit), a page of which can be seen in Figure 11.3.[56]

As part of everyday refugee life, young women and men found love and their life partners. These couples started to make future plans. At least two weddings took place in Atlit, during which fellow prisoners held a prayer shawl above the couple, as is Jewish custom. The wedding was celebrated in the office of the police officer in charge of the camp, and representatives of the refugee committee joined the ceremony.[57]

Jewish organizations were also active in the camp.[58] The Zionist Immigration Bureau selected men from among the 530 immigrants who came from Berlin for their specific professional qualifications.[59] Some of them joined later the British Army; among them was Gert (Gideon) Sommerfeld.[60] We do not know how many were due for release at this time, but we know that five months earlier there were 2,100 people in the camp.[61] In August 1941, Mr P. Kohlmann, 'chief of the camp in Athlit' received a letter which

Figure 11.2 Dr Ella Freund
Source: Courtesy and © Yotam Moked.[62]

stated that the Chief Secretary of the Palestine Government agreed to release those who were, by August 1941, still interned in Atlit.[63]

However much we may read accounts of happy kindergartens, love, weddings, we must also remember that the young people in the camp had been forced to part with their parents and relatives, most of them forever, because of hostile circumstances in their homeland. Some felt guilty about planning their future, while their relatives in Berlin were threatened with deportation. Their letters and postcards tell us much today about their personal sufferings and needs, as well as the happy times in the camp.

Atlit and the survivors of the Holocaust[64]

To many Holocaust survivors, who arrived in Palestine in the course of the end of the Second World War and the liberation of the camps, from the summer of 1944 onwards, Atlit served as a first haven after leaving liberated Europe. The *Yishuv* was confronted with those women, men and children who survived the horrors of deportation trains, ghettoization, mass killings, Nazi camps, surviving in hiding or under an assumed identity. Camp names like Auschwitz and Buchenwald, Theresienstadt and Bergen-Belsen, now had a human face, and it was one marked by horrors: children who looked like adults and exhausted passengers who arrived from ships at the shore of Mandate Palestine.

Figure 11.3 A page of the children's book '*The spotlight of Atlit*'
Source: © Atlit Detention Center Database.

The Women's International Zionist Organization (WIZO) installed a 'babies' hut' in Atlit. The *Palestine Post* reported on 24 October 1944 that 144 babies and small children were being cared for, and that numbers were tattooed on the bodies of some of the babies who had been marked for death in Belsen.[65] In the middle of May 1946, there were twenty-three people at the camp hospital, 'mostly suffering from exhaustion'.[66] By the summer of 1946, the British were faced with a 'population explosion'.[67] The detention camps became hugely overcrowded and conditions were unhygienic. By 12 August 1946, they announced that the immigrants would no longer be held in Palestine, but in Cyprus.[68] Between August 1946 and April 1948, they transferred 52,260 immigrants to Cyprus.[69]

Atlit today

The history of Atlit as a detention site for illegal Jewish immigrants ended in 1948, even though the camp was, for many decades, used for Arab prisoners of war.[70] The camp had multiple functions after the State of Israel was born: during the War of Independence in 1948 it housed prisoners of war from Arab states and Palestinian civilians, serving as Camp no. 792. During the 1967 war, it held prisoners from Syria and Egypt, and also held prisoners in the course of the war with Lebanon in 1982. The last prisoners were released in 1985.[71]

The Society for Preservation of Israel Heritage Sites (SPIHS) started to renovate the camp's remaining material traces in the 1980s.[72] In 1987, the *Bintivey Ha'apala* (Clandestine Jewish Immigration Information and Research Center in Memory of Admiral Mordechai [Moka] Limon) was established at the former camp site.[73] On the SPIHS website it states that

> the Atlit Detention Camp, a National Heritage Site, serves as an educational center about clandestine immigration (*ha'apala*) to the Land of Israel. Many Jews who tried to reach the homeland by sea were intercepted by British authorities and incarcerated in the Atlit camp, along with Jews who fought against British rule.[74]

The museum's aim is to educate the public about the illegal immigration efforts between 1934 and 1948.[75] Visitors can examine a model of the original camp, a watchtower, the bus which transferred immigrants to Atlit and the remains of the barbed wire. They can visit the barracks with a fully reconstructed interior, as well as the disinfection facilities. In July 2006, the full-size replica ship *Glina* was transferred from Riga/Latvia to the memorial site. Even though there is no connection between this ship and the historical events recounted here, it is accessible for visitors and serves as a reconstructed model of a *Ma'apilim* ship.[76]

Inside one of the barracks is a multimedia exhibition where visitors can learn about the painful journeys of the former Jewish refugees and Holocaust survivors. The online Atlit Database and Information Center, data from which is mostly only in Hebrew, allows the examination of items like historical artifacts, interviews and video testimonies of immigrants. It also contains a library; more than 700 book entries mention the detention camp, mostly in Hebrew. It provides links to historical sources like artifacts, art and culture, photo albums, diaries and journals, and materials related to topics like the British detention camps in Cyprus.

Conclusion

Today, the former detention camp of Atlit serves as one of the Israeli symbols of the struggle of the Jewish people, represented mostly through a Zionist narrative. Two intertwined, ideologically charged narratives converge here: Palestine as the homeland of the Jewish people (promised in the Balfour Declaration of 1917) and the fight against the British colonial power which conducted a war on immigration against Jews. The historical narrative is that of the Zionist enterprise, where there took place

> a war between the Jewish refugee, standing on a deck of a ship attempting to reach the shores of Palestine after surviving the Holocaust, and the British Royal Navy, which had closed the gates.[It had been] a contest of the weak versus the strong ... David against Goliath.[77]

Several events in the camp which have been used to manifest and create a pure Zionist narrative around Atlit occurred on 10 October 1945. *Palmach* (the military arm of the *Haganah*) fighters broke into the camp and managed to free more than 200 women and men. Later Israeli Prime Minister, Yitzhak Rabin, had planned this raid as a *Palmach* member.[78] The main Jewish organizations and their fight against the British from that period received prominent coverage in Naor's book on Atlit camp. Operation 'Agatha', also known under the term 'Black Sabbath', which was a large military action by the British in 1946 against these organizations, was discussed by Naor. Yet, the actual experiences of the refugees and survivors, their fears and hopes, their further life paths, are still unwritten. In this chapter, I have begun to tell their story, yet further research is needed in order to widen the historical narrative. Further research is needed to illuminate the immigrants' arrival in Mandate Palestine and their acculturation processes in an unknown country, far beyond what German Zionists had promised in Europe. Many friendships from the camp were lifelong, and in many cases, the children and grandchildren of those in the camp are still in contact. Some of the former camp inhabitants had the feeling of 'unstopability' in building *Eretz*; they found their goal in life and fought for their own convictions. Many even lost their lives in the wars that were yet to come, and others left Israel and emigrated into the United States and other countries. The narratives of these people should also be heard.

The museum is closely connected to the Zionist narrative which links the Jewish people to the land. Israeli researcher Ruth Amir stated that one of the narrative's declared aims was to 'redeem the Jews of their long-suffered misery and humiliation in the Diaspora'.[79] Within this narrative, the Jews of Atlit detention camp were the victims of an all-powerful antagonist, namely the British government of Palestine. This narrative reached its peak after the arrival of the Holocaust survivors; they survived absolute evil and were the future settlers who had to establish *Eretz Israel*.

Acknowledgements

I wish to thank Gert Sommerfeld (Haifa) for the many talks which sometimes lasted hours. These encounters deepened my understanding for many Holocaust-related topics and the question of what it meant to be no longer to be 'wanted' in the homeland. He died in September 2020. Gert Sommerfeld was also a detainee in Atlit and was among the last to be released. May his memory be blessed.

Notes

1. Ruth Amir and Leah Rosen, 'Constructing National Identity: The Case of Youth Aliyah', *Israel Studies Review* 21 (2006): 27–51.
2. Materials used for this chapter include sources from the Atlit Information and Research Center; the Ghetto Fighter´s House Museum Archive; Yad Vashem Archives; United States Holocaust Memorial Museum (USHMM) Archives and Photo Collection; The National Archives, Kew; the Joint Distribution Committee Archives; the Leo Baeck Institutes in Jerusalem and New York; the Israel State Archives; the Weizmann Archives; the Central Zionist Archives; the *Palestine Post* and *Palestine Gazette*; the Middle East Centre Archive; and the archives of St Antony's College, Oxford.
3. For British Immigration Policy see Hagit Lavsky, *The Creation of the German-Jewish Diaspora* (München: Oldenbourg Verlag, 2017) or Anita Shapira, *Land and Power: The Zionist Resort to Force, 1881–1948* (Stanford: Stanford University Press, 1999), 233. In 1935, 62,000 Jews immigrated to Palestine, in Shapira, *Land and Power*, 211–12f.
4. In July 1945, the British Labour Party promised to cancel the 1939 immigration policy, but this did not take place.
5. 'Mordecai Naor, ' "Illegal Immigration" to Palestine during the British Mandate', in *The Atlit Camp. A Story of a Time and Place*, ed. Mordecai Naor (Mikveh Israel: Yehuda Dekel Library/Society for Preservation of Israel Heritage Sites, 2010), 17–36. For a more detailed description see Mordecai Naor, ed., *Ha´apala: Clandestine Immigration 1931–1948* (Tel Aviv: Ministry of Defence Publishing House and IDF Museum, 1987) and Bracha Habas, *The Gate Breakers, A Dramatic Chronicle of the Jewish Immigration into Palestine* (New York: Herzl Press, 1963).
6. The JAFP was the representative body of Jews in Mandate Palestine and contact organization for the British Mandate government. See on the question colonization Ilan Pappé, 'Decolonizing Israel-Palestine: A Discourse or a Political Program?', in *Israel: Palestine. Lands and People*, ed. Omer Bartov (New York: Berghahn Books, 2021), 366–81.
7. *The Palestine Gazette*. Official gazette for the government of Palestine, 17 August 1939, Supplement 2, part c, image 149, https://findit.library.yale.edu/catalog/digcoll:2845 212 (accessed on 2 September 2021).
8. Naor, ' "Illegal Immigration" to Palestine during the British Mandate', 18.
9. Starting in summer 1946, the immigrants were interned in camps on Cyprus. Eliana Hadjisavvas works on Cyprus with sources from the Central Zionist Archives (which, due to COVID-19, have not been accessible to the author of this chapter) and the Joint Distribution Committee (available online), also testimonies from the Visual History Archive at the University of California Shoah Foundation (USCSF) and the Fortunoff Video Archives at Yale University.
10. Perez Leshem, *Strasse zur Rettung 1933–1939. Aus Deutschland vertrieben – bereitet sich jüdische Jugend auf Palästina vor* (Tel Aviv: Histadrut, 1973). See also Verena Buser, *The History of Niederschönhausen and its Jewish Trainees* (Melbourne: Jewish Holocaust Centre, 2021), Verena Buser, 'Hachsharot after 1933: Welfare, Child Care and Educational Aspects', in *Jewish horticultural schools and training centers in Germany and their impact on horticulture and landscape architecture in Palestine/Israel*, ed. Tal Alon-Mozes, Irene Aue-Ben-David, and Joachim Wolschke-Bulmahn (München: AVM Edition, 2020), 17–36.

11. The ship brought more than 16,000 immigrants to Mandate Palestine with the *Aliya Bet*.
12. Armin Schleichkorn was born on 5 June 1914 in Hniezdne (then Slovakia), USCSF, Int. Code 54851.
13. See for the whole list of illegal refugee ships 'Bintivey Ha'apala Information Center', http://maapilim.org.il/ (accessed 15 August 2021). The database contains also thousands of names of immigrants from then. See also Naor, *Ha´apala*, Annexe.
14. Dalia Ofer, 'Holocaust Survivors as Immigrants: The Case of Israel and the Cyprus Detainees', *Modern Judaism* 16 (1996): 1–23.
15. 'Israel State Archives', https://www.archives.gov.il/en/ (accessed 15 August 2021).
16. 'British Government Funds for Athlith Camp', *Palestine Post*, 21 August 1939. All quotes from the *Palestine Post*: 'The National Library of Israel', https://www.nli.org.il/en/newspapers/pls. Dunam was a Turkish measure square. One dunam accounts around 1000 m^2.
17. The opening date is not clear: folders in the Israel State Archives date it on 27 September 1939 and talk about its closing on 1 May 1941 as a detention camp. It reopened – the reason for this is also not clear – on 2 May 1941 and closed on 28 December 1946. Moreover, the term 'detention' is used both for illegal Jewish immigrants and for convicted criminals. 2/6/18: Palestine Government, vol. 3, Public Works Department Headquarters, Israel State Archives, Jerusalem.
18. 'New Athlit Camp Completed', *Palestine Post*, 3 December 1939. The spelling of 'Atlit' is not always consistent in the historical sources. In the historical sources and the contemporary press the spelling 'Athlit' or 'Athlith' is also used.
19. 'Athlit Camp', *Palestine Post*, 17 August 1939. Records from the ISA mention, for example, for the supply of stone material by Mr. Samuel Kopelovitz or Mr. Abdel Kader Nijim.
20. CO 814/16-0007: Palestine Sessional Papers. Administration Reports., The National Archives, Kew, 1, https://www.nationallizenzen.de/ (accessed 23 July 2021).
21. 'Palestine Government, Vol. 2, Public Works Department Headquarters, Jaffa-Haifa Road North of Hedera Prison Labour Jail Labour Camp No. 2, opened on 26.11.38 closed on 23.7.47', ISA. The *Palestine Post* published, for example, on 10 August 1938 a small article ('No News of Missing Policeman') about the disappearance of Palestine Constable Ali Saleh, who worked as warden in the Jail Labour Camp.
22. According to a letter of 22 December 1939, the camp was 'again put into use for the accommodation of prisoners' from 24 November 1939. Prisoners worked on the Atlit Antiquity site road. 'Government of Palestine, Director of Public Works, Jerusalem', 4102-5, Israel State Archives. The Jail Labour Camp was opened on 26 November 1938 and closed on 23 July 1947. On 6 December 1938 an unidentified Inspector General of the Palestine Police wrote to the Director of Public Works in Jerusalem, that 'it has been decided by the Central Security Committee that the camp at Athlit shall be converted into a detention camp almost immediately and that steps are being taken to transfer the convicted prisoners from there to other prison establishments'. 'Headquarters, The Palestine Police Force, Jerusalem, to Director of Public Works, Jerusalem, 6 December 1938', inISA.
23. 'Typhoid Death at Athlit', *Palestine Post*, 17 January 1941.
24. '70 Youth Immigrants Released from Camp', *Palestine Post*, 4 April 1941, also '202 Youth Immigrants from Rumania', *Palestine Post*, 26 march 1941, and 'Clearance Camp', *Palestine Post*, 8 May 1941. Ella Hammerschmidt brought a group of *Youth Aliya* children via Vienna, Beirut and Syria to Mandate Palestine. She and the

children, among them three seventeen-year-old boys, were already released after three days in quarantine. Recha Freier Collection: 'Memoirs of Ella Hammerschmidt. Our Exodus, 15.12.1940-15.12.1941', Yad Vashem Digital Collections, 7, 1 https://documents.yadvashem.org/ (accessed 23 July 2021).
25. Several survivors reported about them or their relatives being not sent with their friends and families to Atlit, but to the Old Castle Akko prison: Susi Friedmann who arrived in 1941 (USCSF, Int. Code 17527). She was born on 10 March 1926 in Vienna.
26. 'News in Brief', *Palestine Post*, 22 May 1941.
27. For example, Dalia Ofer, *Escaping the Holocaust: Illegal Immigration to the Land of Israel, 1939–1944* (New York: Oxford University Press, 1990).
28. Judy Jaffe-Schagen, 'Establishing Collections, Building a Nation', in *Having and Belonging: Homes and Museums in Israel*, ed. Judy Jaffe-Schagen (Oxford: Berghahn Books, 2016), 31–55, 134.
29. Ruth Amir, 'Suppression and Dispossession of the Arminian Village of Athlit: A Differend?', *Journal of the Society for Armenian Studies* 25 (2017), 100–22. She also made me aware of the fact that it served as a transit camp for Yemenis.
30. Gaffir was the Jewish police unit that was under British law and legal in order to protect the Jewish settlements; salaries were paid by the British.
31. Ernest Hoenig, Interview USCSF, Int. Code 24504.
32. Ernest Powers, Interview USCSF, Int. Code 16020.
33. Hersch Simon, Interview USCSF, Int. Code 7369.
34. Yolanda Dicks, USCSF Interview, Int. Code 15379.
35. Ernest Powers, Interview USCSF, Int. Code 16020.
36. M. D., 23 March 2006, Interview British Mandate Palestine Police Oral History Project, GB165-0390, At. Antony's College, University of Oxford.
37. For the historical background see Gershon Erich Steiner, *Die Geschichte der 'Patria'* (Tel Aviv: Olamenu, 1973); Meir Chazan, 'The Patria Affair: Moderates vs. Activists in Mapai in the 1940s', *Journal of Israeli History* 22 (2003): 61–95. According to Naor, the bomb was placed by Munia Mardor on the ship (Naor, *Ha'apala*, 35).
38. Theodor F. Meysels, 'Refugees Life at Athlit', *Palestine Post*, 15 January 1941. In the USHMM Archives, the Leo Baeck Institute/Center for Jewish History Archives, and the Yad Vashem and Ghetto Fighter's House Archives, there are hundreds of testimonies in written form in which detention in Atlit and journey on these ships is reported.
39. Generally speaking, the ships were owned by a variety of European shipping companies and usually sailed under false flags.
40. Chazan, 'Patria Affair', 1.
41. Betty Factor, Interview USCSF, Int. Code. 46275.
42. Liselotte Steckl, Interview ibid., Int. Code 24364.
43. Max Kopka, Interview USCSF, Int. Code 6295 reported: 'I and several other men went to the prison camp in Akko'.
44. CO 814/16-0007: Palestine Sessional Papers. Administration Reports., The National Archives, Kew, 1, https://www.nationallizenzen.de/ (accessed 23 July 2021).
45. 'Visits to Refugees Now Permitted', *Palestine Post*, 5 March 1941.
46. 'Soap for Detained Refugees', *Palestine Post*, 15 May 1940.
47. Ibid.
48. 'Matotzh for Detained', *Palestine Post*, 17 March 1942.
49. 'Refugees Visited at Athlit Camp', *Palestine Post*, 18 January 1940.
50. See survivor testimonies in the USCSF.

51. Theodor F. Meysels, 'Refugees Life at Athlit', *Palestine Post*, 15 January 1941.
52. Miriam Marianne Burstein (née Bach) met her future husband Shimon (Hermann) Burstein in Atlit. At the age of eighty-five in Israel, Burstein wrote her memories for her three children and seven grandchildren. I sincerely thank her children Adina Sutlin and Gad Barnea for making these memories available to me. The title is *My Life Story: Memories from My Parents' Home, My Childhood Years, and the Events that Took Place in my Life Thereafter*, 1996. I also thank Avital Barnea, the granddaughter in Washington, DC.
53. For the school also: Margalith (Mali) Lichtenstein, 'Gedanken einer Erzieherin zum 25. Patria Gedenktag', JER 123, Leo Baeck Institute, Jerusalem.
54. This database can be accessed online and provides background information on the history of the illegal immigration. Museum staff are keen to preserve the testimonies of the former refugees and Holocaust survivors, have interviewed a great number of them, and, where biographical information and sources are available, have created an entry on every individual. Ella Freund's journal can be accessed here: maapilim.org.il/notebook_ext.asp?item=55590&site=maapilim&lang=ENG&menu=1 (accessed 17 August 2021).
55. '30-Dunams Farmed by Athlit Refugees', *Palestine Post*, 16 June 1941.
56. '"Der Scheinwerfer von Athlit" –an illustrated book from the Atlit Detention Camp', http://maapilim.org.il/notebook_ext.asp?item=47330&site=maapilim&lang=ENG&menu=1 (accessed 17 August 2021).
57. 'Two Weddings at Athlit: Prayer Shawl as Canopy', *Palestine Post*, 11 March 1941.
58. According to the Mandate draft confirmed and signed in 1923, the British had to cooperate with the Jewish Agency (the Zionist Executive) that represented Jewish interests regarding the National Home. See Lavsky, *The Creation of the German-Jewish Diaspora*.
59. Theodor F. Meysels, 'Refugees Life at Athlit', 15 January 1941.
60. Gert Sommerfeld was born in 1920 in Bromberg (today: Bydgoszcz, Poland) and raised in Berlin. He escaped after the pogroms of November 1938 to Palestine and survived the *Patria* disaster.
61. '50 Visitors Allowed Daily at Athlit', *Palestine Post*, 19 March 1941.
62. 12-2317 (1941): 'Mr. P. Kohlmann, Chief of the Camp, Athlit', Weizmann Archives, Rehovot.
63. Yotam Moked's parents were in Atlit with Ella Freund and were friends of hers; they owned this photograph.
64. A British Pathe newsreel filmed in the camp in 1946 with the title 'Jews Freed by British', https://www.youtube.com/watch?v=kRBziDZm1_s (accessed 19 August 2021).
65. Prisoners were not tattooed in Bergen-Belsen so this is false, but possibly the babies were born in Auschwitz-Birkenau, where they were tattooed.
66. Those were passengers from the M.S. Smyrni (Max Nordau): 'Frontier Control at Athlit', *Palestine Post*, 16 May 1946. Most often, the Holocaust survivors were there only for some days, like the passengers from the *Ville d'Oran*: 'Ville d'Oran Arrivals Released Today', *Palestine Post*, 4 September 1945.
67. Naor, *Ha'apala*, 61.
68. Ibid.
69. Ibid., 68.
70. Salman Abu Sitta and Terry Rempel, 'The ICRC and the Detention of Palestinian Civilians in Israel's 1948 POW/Labor Camps', *Journal of Palestine Studies* 43 (2014): 11–38; see also reports of the International Committee of the Red Cross available

through Wikipedia: https://en.wikipedia.org/wiki/Atlit_detainee_camp. I wish to thank Nadia Fada (Berlin) for help with translations from Arabic.
71. 'The Lebanese prisoners held by Israel', *The Christian Science Monitor*, 1 July 1985.
72. Naor, *Atlit Camp*, 4. The society's homepage shows which other heritage sites in Israel it operates: https://shimur.org/%D7%94%D7%9E%D7%95%D7%A2%D7%A6%D7%94/?lang=en. Here it states that 'the organization was founded for the purpose of preserving and commemorating historical sites related to Israel's pathway to independence'.
73. Limon (born 1924 in Poland) joined the *Palmach* during the Second World War and became a member of *Palyam*, its marine troop. He was the fourth commander of the Israeli Navy, http://webcache.googleusercontent.com/search?q=cache:wZ7Z9bK6fmsJ:www.palyam.org/English/IS/Limon_Mordechai_Moka.pdf+&cd=2&hl=de&ct=clnk&gl=de (18 November 2021).
74. https://shimur.org/sites/atlit-detention-camp/?lang=en (18 November 2021).
75. For a virtual view see https://www.maapilim.org/en-visit-us/ (18 November 2021).
76. Yossi Feldman, 'The Galina: A Reconstructed Model of a Ma'apilim Ship', in *Atlit Camp*, 7–11.
77. Arie Lova Eliav, ' "Illegal Immigration": A Song of Praise, 1945–1948', in *Atlit Camp*, 17–36.
78. There were many important events in the history of the camp which cannot all be discussed and described here.
79. Amir, 'Suppression and Dispossession', 103.

Bibliography

Abu Sitta, Salman, and Terry Rempel. 'The ICRC and the Detention of Palestinian Civilians in Israel's 1948 POW/Labor Camps'. *Journal of Palestine Studies* 43 (2014): 11–38.
Amir, Ruth. 'Suppression and Dispossession of the Arminian Village of Athlit: A Différend?'. *Journal of the Society for Armenian Studies* 25 (2017): 100–22.
Amir, Ruth, and Leah Rosen. 'Constructing National Identity: The Case of Youth Aliyah'. *Israel Studies Review* 21 (2006): 27–51.
Bartov, Omer. *Israel: Palestine. Lands and People*. New York: Berghahn Books, 2021.
Burstein, Miriam Marianne. *My Life Story: Memories from My Parents' Home, My Childhood Years, and the Events that Took Place in My Life Thereafter*. (Unpublished memories, 1996).
Buser, Verena. 'Hachsharot after 1933: Welfare, Child Care and Educational Aspects'. In *Jewish Horticultural Schools and Training Centers in Germany and Their Impact on Horticulture and Landscape Architecture in Palestine/Israel*, edited by Tal Alon-Mozes, Irene Aue-Ben-David, and Joachim Wolschke-Bulmahn, 17–36. München: AVM Edition, 2020.
Buser, Verena. *The History of Niederschönhausen and its Jewish Trainees*. Melbourne: Jewish Holocaust Centre, 2021.
Chazan, Meir. 'The Patria Affair: Moderates vs. Activists in Mapai in the 1940s'. *Journal of Israeli History* 22 (2003): 61–95.
Eliav, Arie Lova. ' "Illegal Immigration": A Song of Praise, 1945–1948'. In *The Atlit Camp: A Story of a Time and Place*, edited by Mordecai Naor, 17–36. Mikveh Israel: Yehuda Dekel Library/Society for Preservation of Israel Heritage Sites, 2010.

Feldman, Yossi. 'The Galina: A Reconstructed Model of a Ma'apilim Ship'. In *The Atlit Camp: A Story of a Time and Place*, edited by Mordecai Naor, 7–11. Mikveh Israel: Yehuda Dekel Library/Society for Preservation of Israel Heritage Sites, 2010.

Habas, Bracha. *The Gate Breakers, A Dramatic Chronicle of the Jewish Immigration into Palestine*. New York: Herzl Press, 1963.

Jaffe-Schagen, Judy. 'Establishing Collections, Building a Nation'. In *Having and Belonging. Homes and Museums in Israel*, edited by Judy Jaffe-Schagen, 31–55. Oxford: Berghahn Books, 2016.

Lavsky, Hagit. *The Creation of the German-Jewish Diaspora*. München: Oldenbourg Verlag, 2017.

Naor, Mordecai. *The Atlit Camp: A Story of a Time and Place*. Mikveh Israel: Yehuda Dekel Library/Society for Preservation of Israel Heritage Sites, 2010.

Naor, Mordecai. *Ha'apala: Clandestine Immigration 1931–1948*. Tel Aviv: Ministry of Defence Publishing House and IDF Museum, 1987.

Naor, Mordecai. '"Illegal Immigration" to Palestine during the British Mandate'. In *The Atlit Camp. A Story of a Time and Place*, edited by Mordecai Naor, 17–36. Mikveh Israel: Yehuda Dekel Library/Society for Preservation of Israel Heritage Sites, 2010.

Ofer, Dalia. *Escaping the Holocaust: Illegal Immigration to the Land of Israel, 1939–1944*. New York: Oxford University Press, 1990.

Ofer, Dalia. 'Holocaust Survivors as Immigrants: The Case of Israel and the Cyprus Detainees'. *Modern Judaism* 16 (1996): 1–23.

Pappé, Ilan. 'Decolonizing Israel-Palestine: A Discourse or a Political Program?'. In *Israel: Palestine. Lands and People*, edited by Omer Bartov, 366–81. Oxford: Berghahn Books, 2021.

Shapira, Anita. *Land and Power: The Zionist Resort to Force, 1881–1948*. Stanford: Stanford University Press, 1999.

Steiner, Gershon Erich. *Die Geschichte der 'Patria'*. Tel Aviv: Olamenu, 1973.

12

The operation, experiences and legacy of the Prem Nagar Central Internment Camp at Dehra Dun in British India, 1939–present

Joseph Cronin

The city of Dehradun lies in the foothills of the Himalayas. In the modern republic of India, Dehradun is the largest city in the northern state of Uttarakhand. It has been a military city since the time of the Mughal Empire, due to its location close to the Chinese and Nepalese borders, although this function expanded considerably under the British Empire. In 1932, the British set up the Indian Military Academy on the outskirts of the city, which still exists today. During the Second World War, some of its barracks were repurposed into internment camps for 'enemy aliens' – citizens of the nations Britain was fighting in the war, principally Germans (including former Austrians) and Italians. Around 1,500 people residing in India became enemy aliens when the war broke out in September 1939.[1] Two camps were set up at Dehradun (spelled Dehra Dun during the British Raj): one, Clement Town, was used for the housing of Italians, the other, Prem Nagar, was used primarily for Germans and Austrians.[2] It is the latter camp, Prem Nagar, that is the subject of this chapter.

The history of internment camps in British India during the Second World War remains a neglected subject. None of the twenty or so camps set up by the British can be considered to hold a place in the public or even scholarly imagination. However, Dehra Dun probably comes closest to this, as it was one of the largest and longest running of the camps. It also hosted some of the war's most famous internees: the mountaineers Heinrich Harrer and Peter Aufschnaiter, and the Buddhist monk Nyanatiloka.[3] The inmates also tended to be educated professionals, some of whom later wrote about their experiences, and this has helped to cement the camp's legacy, at least for historians and interested members of the public.[4] On the other hand, the fact that the camp held Nazi sympathizers alongside Jewish refugees for several years has made its commemoration problematic.

This chapter will first outline the history of internment in British India before taking a more detailed look at the experiences of individual internees and the camp's operation. It will conclude by considering the camp's post-war legacy and why no recent efforts have been made to commemorate the site.

Part one: History of internment in British India

When Britain declared war on Germany on 3 September 1939, Lord Linlithgow, the Viceroy of India, declared war on behalf of India too, without consulting any of India's nationalist politicians. British India was governed as a colony, with a separate government – the Government of India, based in New Delhi – which made decisions separately to the British government in Westminster. Therefore, India did not automatically adopt Britain's policy on internment, and had the power to formulate its own.

The internment policy towards enemy aliens turned out to be much stricter for British India than it was for Britain itself. There were two main reasons for this. The first was that the Government of India was acutely aware of India's vulnerable geostrategic position, with its large land and sea border, that could easily be infiltrated by enemy powers. The Government of India also feared what they called the 'actual or potential disloyalty' of the Indian population.[5] The Indian independence movement had grown considerably since the end of the First World War and enjoyed widespread support by the end of the 1930s. The Government of India therefore believed that, unlike mainland Britain, the Indian population could not *automatically* be relied upon to support the British war effort against Nazi Germany. Added to that, there had been concerns about the spread of Nazi propaganda in India in the years preceding the war, particularly the distribution of Hitler's autobiography *Mein Kampf*.[6]

Considering these factors, the Government of India decided to intern enemy aliens en masse; that is, all men over the age of sixteen. It announced this policy in the 'Enemy Foreigners Order', issued on 3 September 1939 and distributed to local authorities across British India.[7] Several copies of the order are held in the India Office Records of the British Library (Figure 12.1).

As a consequence, 888 German, Austrian and Italian men, of whom around 500 were Jewish refugees, were rounded up from their places of residence and sent first to local camps or prisons before being transferred to a designated 'Central Internment Camp' at Ahmednagar, in Maharashtra, 250 kilometres east of Bombay. On 16 September 1939, the Jewish Relief Association, a Jewish aid organization based in Bombay, wrote to the Government of India asking why Jewish refugees were being interned en masse in India, in contrast to the policy in Britain. Refugees in India were finding it 'difficult to understand the reason for the difference in treatment', the letter stated. It also drew attention to the 'humiliation caused to the Jewish refugees by being interned together with German Nazis, who are responsible for their persecution, the break-up of their homes and careers and the loss of their property'.[8] In early October 1939, the League of Nations High Commissioner for Refugees forwarded these concerns to London's India Office – the Whitehall branch responsible for liaising between Westminster and the Government of India – suggesting that pressure be placed on the Government of India to adopt a tribunal procedure to 'distinguish genuine refugees from others'.[9]

The British government had, in fact, never supported the Government of India's heavy-handed internment policy, not least because it made the release of British subjects from Germany more difficult.[10] The India Office informed the British Foreign

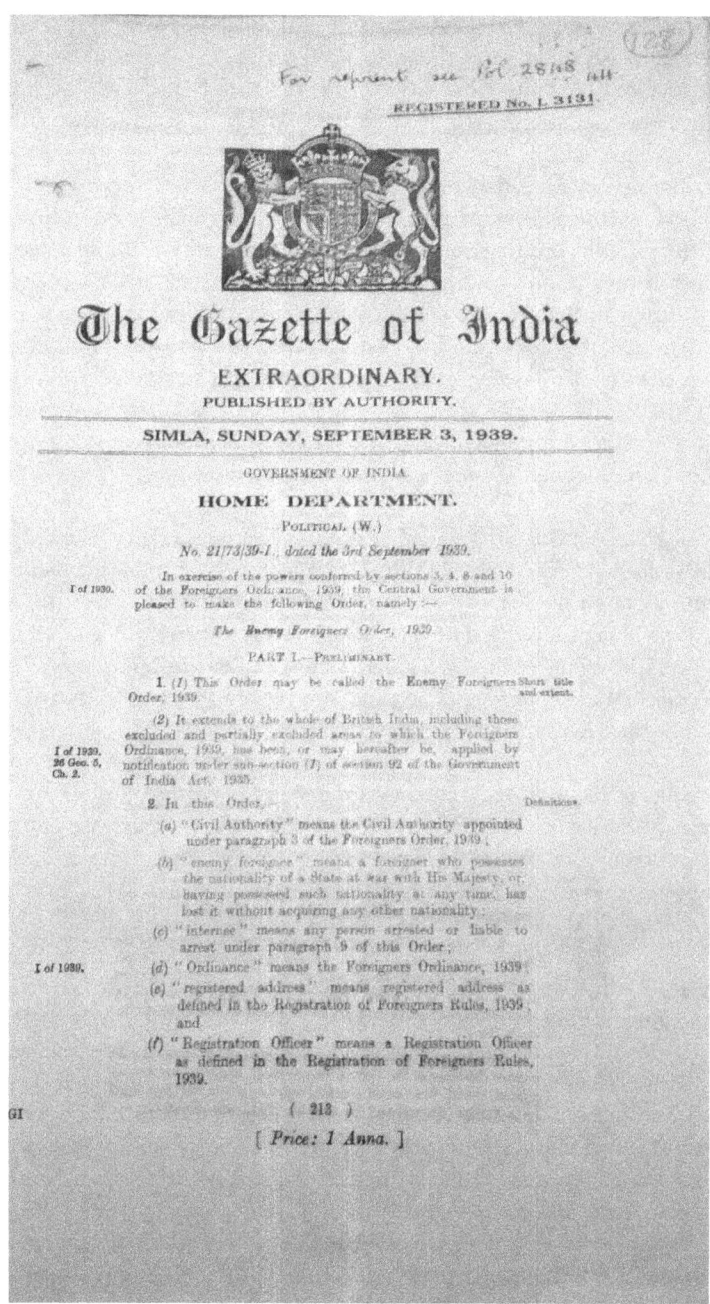

Figure 12.1 The 'Enemy Foreigners Order', copy published in *The Gazette of India*, 3 September 1939. British Library, India Office Records: L/PJ/8/41: 'Coll 101/10B; Aliens in India: Indian Foreigners Orders, Ordinances and Acts; British measures under Aliens Order, 1920'

Source: © The British Library Board.

Office in late September 1939 that there were 'individuals or possibly classes amongst those interned who could, without danger, be permitted to remain at liberty in India'. The Foreign Office then urged the Government of India to 'consider modification' of its internment policy to 'discriminate between' those who could safely remain at liberty in India, those who could be repatriated and those who had to be kept interned.[11]

In response, however, the Government of India doubled down on its policy, justifying its strictness in comparison to Britain's on the grounds that 'enemy powers' had 'set up centres for creating trouble in India' and argued that a 'considerable section' of the Indian population was 'actually or potentially disloyal' to British rule.[12] But, as a concession to the growing demands for clemency towards interned refugees, the Government of India set up the Darling Committee for Interrogation of Alien Internees. Named after its leader Sir Malcolm Darling, the committee was based at the Ahmednagar Central Internment Camp, and its remit was to assess every internee's eligibility for release on an individual basis. The assessment had four stages: first came a questionnaire of some 100 questions, followed by three interviews, the final one presided over by Darling himself.[13]

The Austrian Marxist and geographer Fritz Kolb, who was later interned at Prem Nagar, described his experience with the Darling Committee in his memoir *Leben in der Retorte* ('Life in the Retort'). Having sailed through the first three stages of the process, Kolb became unstuck during the final interview when Darling asked him why he had voted in favour of the Nazi annexation of Austria in March 1938. With his limited English, Kolb realized that he could not explain the complex array of factors that had informed his decision. 'Firstly', he wrote,

> the results of the vote would have been falsified to give the intended outcome anyway. Secondly, our electoral ward was so small that only my wife and I and maybe two or three others would have been suspected of voting no, so it would have been easy to identify us. And thirdly, as members of the [anti-Nazi] resistance, we did not want to take a risk for the sake of a useless protest vote.[14]

Nonetheless, Darling was satisfied that Kolb did not pose a threat to India's security and so released him from internment. By April 1940, when the Darling Committee wound up its operations, 578 of the 888 men interned at Ahmednagar had been released, most of them Jewish refugees.[15]

The Government of India, however, was unhappy with this outcome, believing that the committee had released too many internees. It complained that 'humanitarian considerations' had influenced the committee's decisions 'to a greater extent than was justified'.[16] Subsequently, many of the released internees were re-interned, some with their wives and families in seven dedicated 'parole centres', which offered more space, freedom and better facilities than the internment camps.[17] Following a petition from the Jewish Relief Association in July 1940, the League of Nations High Commissioner for Refugees informed the India Office that refugees should not be confused with enemy aliens, since the former were 'victims of Nazi oppression and therefore opposed to the Nazi regime'.[18] By and large, fewer Jewish refugees were re-interned in 1940 – most of those who were were considered in some way 'suspicious' by the British authorities.

This included, for example, the Austrian graphic artist Kurt Larisch, whose story of escape from Nazi-occupied Europe 'did not ring true' to the advisory committee who interviewed him.[19]

Part two: Operation of the camp and experiences of internees at Prem Nagar

The Prem Nagar camp was divided into seven 'wings'. In 1943, the internee and artist Ernst Messerschmidt drew an impression of Wing 1, the 'German wing', in the style of a sixteenth-century wood engraving. Complete with Latin captions, the illustration shows the 'Campus Teutonicus', which contains fifteen barracks, smaller buildings of different sizes and what appears to be a sports field. To the left and right, separated by strips of land with high barbed wire fencing on each side, one sees the 'Campus Italicus' (not all Italians were held at Clement Town) and the Campus Judaicus – attesting to the fact that Jewish refugees were separated from the main German camp in October 1941 following 'violent clashes' with Nazi sympathizers.[20]

The historian Margit Franz has provided the most complete description of the 'German wing' at Prem Nagar, based on interviews she conducted with former inmates and their descendants, and two visits to the camp's former site in 2003 and 2005.[21] As Franz describes it,

> The camp's appearance resembled that of a typical prisoner-of-war camp. It consisted of living, kitchen and administration barracks, an exercise and sports field, barbed wire fences and watchtowers with spotlights. It also featured ironing and laundry facilities and a tailor's and shoemaker's workshop. There was a camp orchestra, plays were performed and films shown in a makeshift cinema, along with sports – football and hockey – which were played on the camp's sports field.[22]

To complete the picture of relative comfort, Franz notes that there was also a home brewery of sorts, and that camp inmates were allowed to grow vegetables on designated allotment plots, and to pick the fruit of the papaya trees in the camp.[23] Although rudimentary, these facilities were an improvement on other camps, particularly Deolali – a camp in western India – which was deemed by its inmates to be wholly inadequate. Prem Nagar was also intended for longer term accommodation: its barracks were sturdier, the camp had permanent staff who treated the inmates 'humanely' and the camp was run in accordance with the 1929 Geneva Convention's protocols on prisoner-of-war camps.[24]

Inmates who were qualified as doctors and dentists provided their services to other inmates, and academic researchers, such as the medical student Lutz Chicken and the geographers Fritz Kolb and Ludwig Krenek were allowed to conduct their research in and around the camp's grounds. This was based on the camp's 'parole' ethos, which meant that inmates could leave the camp regularly on excursions if they signed an agreement not to speak to anyone, not to use any public transport and, of course, not to try to escape.[25] As one of the inmates, Hans Kopp, described it in his memoirs,

> We were allowed to go for walks outside the camp twice a week, and we had entertainment and sports. Twice a week films were played at a cinema that was built and furnished for us. There was a large library which contained books in almost every language in the world. A school, lectures of all kinds, a theatre, work rooms for every conceivable craft occupation – in short, we had everything a civilized European [sic] needs to be satisfied.[26]

Fritz Kolb also described the lodgings at Prem Nagar in favourable terms:

> From the outset we were housed in barracks, and they were well built. Their main advantage was thick thatched roofs, which provided better protection from the sun than anything else we had known before. They also prevented the interior from cooling down too much during the cold winter nights. Each barrack had a wide veranda on the north and south sides. The northern one was particularly popular in the summer and the southern one in winter. Each barrack housed about 50 men. Then there were a few smaller buildings: for the kitchen, for the showers and one that we set up as a reading room and lounge.[27]

Prem Nagar's population also swelled over the course of the war. A large contingent of new internees arrived at the end of December 1941, following Japan's entry into the war after their attack on Pearl Harbour. The Government of India quickly accepted 2,400 German nationals from the Dutch East Indies, fearing (correctly) that the colony was about to be invaded by Japan.[28] Some of these new arrivals were placed in a separate wing at Prem Nagar.[29]

The records of the India Office, now held at the British Library in London, contain a fragment of the 'nominal rolls' (lists of names) of the inmates at Prem Nagar in August 1943 (Figure 12.2).[30] In this month, there were 1,724 German speakers – all male – interned at the camp in total.[31] The nominal rolls provide a glimpse into the lives of the individuals who were being held at Prem Nagar, where they came from and what they did. The lists themselves are arranged in tables with seven columns, ordered as follows (left to right): security number, registered number, name, date and place of birth, occupation, date and place of arrest, relationship and address of next of kin.

The nominal rolls were divided into two categories: those who were *willing* to have their names 'communicated to their government' and those who were *unwilling* to have their names communicated to their government. Only the list of unwilling names appears in the folder for Dehra Dun, though it seems unlikely that there would have been no inmates willing to have their names communicated, given the aforementioned pro-Nazi sentiments of some of the inmates.

The professions of those who were unwilling to have their names communicated included a Doctor of Chemistry (described as a 'stateless Jew'), a journalist and teacher of languages, a clerk, a ploughing contractor, a missionary, a publisher, a civil engineer and a chemist. Finally, there were four Buddhist monks, all of whom were born in Germany, three of whom were Jewish. The eldest, Nyanatiloka, born Anton Walther Florus Gueth in Wiesbaden in 1878, was one of the first Westerners to have been ordained as a Buddhist monk.

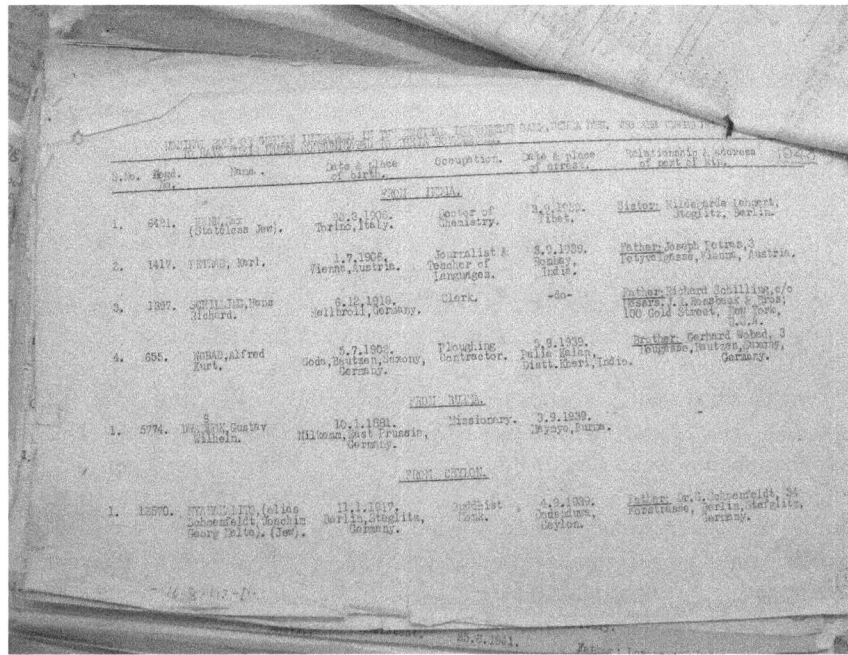

Figure 12.2 British Library, India Office Records: L/PJ/8/31: 'Coll 101/10AA; Nominal rolls of internees and parolees in India'

Source: © The British Library Board.

The nominal rolls also show the places where the internees had been transferred from, which included Burma, Ceylon, Iran and Malaya. This indicates how itinerant the camp's population had become by this point. A good example of this is Hans Grossmann, a Jewish refugee from Berlin who had spent several years travelling east through Europe to the Middle East to escape the Nazis. He had worked for a time in Tehran as a legal advisor. When he arrived in India in 1941, he was immediately interned as a 'suspect enemy alien' due to his previous affiliation with the Zionist movement. He remained interned at Prem Nagar until the end of the war.[32]

The 'security note', the first column on the nominal rolls, provides a clue as to the political affiliations of each internee. The British authorities used it as a means of identifying Nazi sympathizers. The scale ranged from 1 = strongly anti-Nazi to 5 = convinced Nazi.[33] The most prominent of the Nazi sympathizers at Prem Nagar was Oswald Urchs, the self-styled 'NSDAP-Landesgruppenleiter' (Nazi district leader) for India. He had been on the British authorities' watchlist since the mid-1930s, due to his efforts to propagandize the Indian population and also to enlist Germans residing in India to the Nazi cause. One can therefore assume that Urchs was in some way responsible for the 'violent clashes' between German and Jewish inmates that ultimately led to the two groups being separated in October 1941.[34] While the exact size of Prem Nagar's Nazi contingent is difficult to determine, we can be sure that, along with

Urchs, Heinrich Harrer and Peter Aufschnaiter were both party members, while their fellow mountaineers Ludwig Schmaderer, Rolf Magener and Heins von Have were affiliated with the German Alpine Association, a strongly nazified organization that had prohibited Jews from joining since the mid-1920s.[35] Attempts to escape the camp were also, it appears, confined to this group of Nazi sympathizers.

On the night of 29 April 1944, five internees – Peter Aufschnaiter, Heinrich Harrer, Hans Kopp, Friedel Sattler and Bruno Treipl – managed to escape from the camp by 'dodg[ing] the sentries' and 'creeping under the barbed wire fencing', as Treipl later described it.[36] Sattler gave himself up within a few days because he had 'fallen mountain sick' and so 'could not keep pace with the other four', according to the statement he made after his arrest on 12 May.[37] The other four headed east into Tibet, their intention being to travel along the Brahmaputra River 'to reach Burma and join the Japanese there'.[38] As a group of white men, they were quickly spotted by the Tibetan authorities although, for some reason, not arrested. This led to a correspondence between the Tibetan and Indian authorities about how the men should be apprehended and returned to India.[39] A second member of the group, Bruno Treipl, broke away and handed himself in to the police at Chini, a small village in India some 200 kilometres north of Dehra Dun, on 22 July 1944. In a statement to the authorities upon his return to Dehra Dun, Treipl described his experiences over the previous three months. Maintaining that he had escaped alone, Treipl used the first-person pronoun throughout:

> I went up to Gartok in Tibet, after roaming about the hills for about 1 ½ months. I had Rs. 400/- with me at the time of my escape from Dehra Dun. When I was on the road to Gartok I was stopped by a Tibetan Chief, who told me that I could not proceed any further without a permit. As I had no permit and further all the money I had with me was spent I was sent back by the Tibetan Chief accompanied by a Tibetan Military Officer up to Chipki. From Chipki I came to Chini unaccompanied by any officer and there I surrendered myself to the State Police. From Chini I was sent to Rampur Bushehr under police escort. A Military escort was sent for from Dehra Dun by the Rampur State authorities and I have been brought here under that escort. … My idea in escaping from the Dehra Dun Camp was to find my way to Burma via Tibet and from there to my own country (Germany) through Japanese assistance.[40]

Three were left. Kopp broke away from Harrer and Aufschnaiter in November 1944 and was arrested the following month, allegedly after being tricked into going to the British Embassy in Kathmandu to claim asylum. He was returned to Dehra Dun on Christmas Day 1944.[41] The punishment for all the returned escapees was a spell of twenty-eight days in solitary confinement.[42]

The two who were left, Harrer and Aufschnaiter, were the most experienced mountaineers and were ultimately never caught. Although the war ended before they could make contact with the Japanese, they pressed on into Tibet, reaching its capital Lhasa in January 1946.[43] The story of their escape and subsequent journey was described by Harrer in his bestselling book *Seven Years in Tibet*, published in 1952. In 1997 it was turned into a film starring Brad Pitt as Harrer. The fact that Harrer and Aufschnaiter were both Nazi party members and were originally intending to travel back to Nazi Germany with Japanese assistance has gone largely unremarked in treatments of their escape, which tends to be depicted as an example of wartime derring-do.

Part three: Dehra Dun's post-war operation and legacy

The internment camps at Dehra Dun were gradually dissolved at the end of the war and their inhabitants either returned to the lives they had left behind in India, returned to their countries of origin or, more often in the case of Jewish refugees, to new lives in new countries, such as the United States, Great Britain and, after 1948, the newly formed state of Israel. The process of clearing the camp was complete by November 1946; however, those who wished to leave India were not able to do so immediately, since ships leaving India's major ports – Bombay and Calcutta – were booked up for months with British service personnel and colonial administrators leaving the country in anticipation of its independence, which was declared in August 1947. This meant that some of the refugees witnessed the violence that followed India's partition into two separate states, India and Pakistan. As those caught in the 'wrong' state fled across the border, India received a new cohort of Hindu refugees from Pakistan. From autumn 1947, the Dehra Dun camp was used for the sheltering of these refugees.[44] While there was no temporal overlap between European and Pakistani refugees at Dehra Dun, the European refugees had helped to define the concept of a refugee in India, a concept that would subsequently be applied almost exclusively to refugees from neighbouring states.

The British Library's India Office Records reveal another story from the camp's post-war history. It concerns a demobilized British serviceman known as 'Rifleman Reilly' who, in February 1947, wrote the following letter to the India Office:

> I am a returned serviceman from Malaya and whilst on the boat [home] contacted some P.O.Ws from India, who allege that a German Jewish Refugee was interned as a civilian in India around 1940 and because of his outspoken 'Communist' views he was victimised by not receiving the rights of a civilian camp and that to this day he still remains in prison in Dehra Dun, India, yet the camps have all been emptied of their inmates.
>
> They allege also, that Nazi minded German officers have been given the privilege of staying in India as free men so escape their just punishment at the hands of the German workers for ill treating anti-Nazis whilst in prison. As a Socialist and internationalist I am interested in the truth of these allegations and would be grateful if you would enquire into the position. If they are true a grave injustice has been committed and the matter should be immediately rectified.[45]

Five days later, the Labour party politician Arthur Henderson, then junior minister at the India Office, wrote to the Under-Secretary of State for Dominion Affairs, John Parker, in connection with the matter:

> I have looked into the allegations of Rifleman Reilly about the internment in India of a German-Jewish refugee and the release of Nazi-minded officers.
>
> You will appreciate that it would not be possible for me to ask the Government of India to take any action on the vague statements in Rifleman Reilly's letter, which are contrary to the information we possess about both German internees and Jewish refugees in India.
>
> Practically all German internees in India have now been repatriated. The only exceptions are a number of hospital cases and persons who, for one reason or another, e.g. sickness, could not be embarked by the time the repatriation vessels left Bombay; and I have at no time seen or heard a report that Nazi-minded Germans have been given the privilege of staying in India. I do not think, therefore, that the information given to your correspondent can be correct.
>
> On the other hand, a considerable number of Jewish refugees have been allowed to stay on in India. The Government of India, indeed, have treated these Jews with great consideration and kindness; and you may be assured that, if there had been any substance in the allegation that a German Jewish refugee had been interned since 1940 in the Dehra Dun camp for the reason given to Rifleman Reilly, then I should certainly have heard of it. If, however, your correspondent can give me further particulars, I will, of course, have full investigation made into them.[46]

Because the refugee in question was not named in the correspondence, it is impossible to verify the validity of Rifleman Reilly's claims. However, as there are no other documents in this folder, we can assume that no further action was taken.

Over the longer term, the memory of the camp in the post-war period has largely been forgotten. It is of interest only to a small number of scholars and the descendants of those interned. Such neglect is true in both India and Germany, where the memory of the camp raises difficult issues: India's colonial past, on the one hand, and Germany's Nazi past, on the other. The inmates of these camps, indeed the camps themselves, were only there due to a combination of Nazism and British colonialism. After the war and the tumult of partition, the camp eventually reverted to its function as part of the Indian Military Academy. In the 1950s, the West German government erected a memorial to the inmates at Prem Nagar at the Christian cemetery in Dehra Dun, but this has since fallen into disrepair. Margit Franz, who visited the memorial in 2003, described it as follows:

> The memorial garden is an area around ten metres by ten metres. It is enclosed by a low wall around 30 centimetres high. A small opening in this wall marks the entrance from Dehra Dun cemetery. Four park benches made of brick, two on each side of the border to the rest of the cemetery, invite you to linger and enclose the area spatially. A rounded white concrete wall, around 1.5 metres high and seven metres long, dominates the memorial garden. A modern metal construction

is attached to it, which creates nine cross formations from different sized metal elements. In the middle of the concrete curve, a particularly wide metal beam is reminiscent of the Christian crucifix. In front of it, about 2.5 metres away, there is a stone slab on a concrete base, the central stone of the memorial, with the inscription:

Far from their Germans / our dead rest here / from the internment camp Prem Nagar near Dehra Dun / 1941–1946 / the Indian soil lies easy on them

Around four metres away from the central stone, on either side, the names of the dead are listed on two separate stone slabs.[47]

In the past two decades, there have been at least two proposals to renovate the memorial and the camp to make them suitable for tourists and local visitors. In 2003, the German embassy in India stated that it was planning to fund a renovation to the memorial, and that it would also be listed in the database of the German War Graves Commission. Neither of these happened.[48] In January 2015, a *Times of India* article reported that the Uttarakhand state tourism board was 'mulling over the idea of opening up [the camp] for tourists'.[49] A spokesperson for the board commented that the Prem Nagar and Clement Town sites 'would be of immense interest not just for tourists but also students and historians' and that they were 'working out ways on how they can be made more accessible'.[50] The historian Ganesh Saili added that these were 'places of great significance in history' and that the 'tourism department must make intensive efforts to preserve these spots. Not just tourists', he continued, 'but also the descendants of many of the internees would be keen to visit these spots where their ancestors spent time.'[51] As of 2021, however, there is no indication that any of these plans have been put into effect.

As Franz has noted, the fact that the memorial at Prem Nagar is presented entirely in the German language makes it less accessible to local and English-speaking visitors.[52] This may have contributed to its neglect. Additionally, the memorial, with its Christian imagery, appears only to commemorate the Christian German internees and not the Jewish refugees, most of whom were also German. There is a Jewish cemetery at Dehra Dun too, but that has fallen even further into disrepair.[53] The former internment camp at Dehra Dun is also more difficult for tourists to visit than its counterparts in Britain and Europe. It is, furthermore, challenging to present a clear narrative about the camp, as its population was so heterogenous – it contained Nazis alongside Jewish refugees, Buddhist monks, Catholic priests and evangelical missionaries. Nazi inmates perceived the camp as an oppressive prison, something to be escaped. For the refugees, it was a sanctuary. Perhaps the site's significance therefore lies in its multivalence. This quality, however, is unlikely to capture the public imagination, in India, Germany or elsewhere.

Notes

1. Joachim Oesterheld, 'British Policy towards German-Speaking Emigrants in India, 1939–1945', in *Jewish Exile in India: 1933–1945*, ed. Anil Bhatti and Johannes H. Voigt (New Delhi: Max Mueller Bhavan, 1999), 29.

2. Roshen Dalal, 'Dehradun in World War II', https://www.dailypioneer.com/2019/state-editions/dehradun-in-world-war-ii.html (accessed 13 January 2023).
3. See Jared Hohlt, 'Seven Years in Tibet', *Slate*, 10 October 1997, https://slate.com/news-and-politics/1997/10/seven-years-in-tibet.html (accessed 13 January 2023); Sebastian Musch, 'German Migrants and the Circulation of Buddhist Knowledge between Germany and British Ceylon', *Migrant Knowledge*, 18 April 2020, https://migrantknowledge.org/2020/04/18/circulation-of-buddhist-knowledge-between-germany-and-british-ceylon/ (accessed 13 January 2023).
4. The most famous example is Heinrich Harrer's *Seven Years in Tibet: My Life Before, During and After*, trans. Richard Graves (London: Rupert Hart-Davis, 1953). Others include Fritz Kolb, *Leben in der Retorte: Als österreichischer Alpinist in indischen Internierungslagern* (Graz: CLIO, 2014) and Hans Kopp, *Sechsmal über den Himalaya. Fluchterlebnisse eines Deutschen in Indien und Tibet* (Freiburg/Breisgau: Hermann Klemm, 1955).
5. Oesterheld, 'British Policy', 32.
6. British Library (BL), India Office Records (IOR): L/PJ/7/2412: '515; Question in parliament as to why Mein Kampf is permitted unrestricted circulation in India while publications by Ramsay MacDonald are banned' (1939).
7. British India was the part of the Indian subcontinent administered directly by the Government of India. In addition, there were 565 'Princely States' which operated semi-autonomously and had different policies on internment. See Margit Franz, *Gateway India: Deutschsprachiges Exil in Indien zwischen britischer Kolonialherrschaft, Maharadschas und Gandhi* (Graz: CLIO, 2015), 182.
8. BL, IOR: L/PJ/8/65: 'Coll 101/12A; German civilians and other enemy aliens in India; reciprocal release of British and German internees' (1939).
9. Oesterheld, 'British Policy', 31.
10. Ibid., 30.
11. Ibid., 32.
12. Ibid.
13. Franz, *Gateway India*, 184.
14. Ibid., 186.
15. Ibid.
16. Oesterheld, 'British Policy', 35.
17. Ibid., 36; Margit Franz, ' "Passage to India": Österreichisches Exil in Britisch-Indien 1938–1945', in *Jahrbuch 2007*, ed. Dokumentationsarchiv des österreichischen Widerstandes (Vienna: Lit Verlag, 2007), 217.
18. Oesterheld, 'British Policy', 37.
19. National Archives of India (NAI), Home Political (HP): PR_000003011133: 'Recommendation of the A.A.C. Bengal: Case No. 51 Larisch Mr. K. and Wife' (1940).
20. Franz, *Gateway India*, 198–9.
21. Franz, 'Passage to India', 216.
22. Ibid., 216–17.
23. Ibid.
24. Ibid.
25. Ibid., 217.
26. Hans Kopp, *Sechsmal über den Himalaya*, quoted in Franz, 'Passage to India', 217.
27. Franz, *Gateway India*, 199.
28. Oesterheld, 'British Policy', 38.

29. Paul von Tucher, 'Campus Teutonicus at Dehra Dun', http://www.gaebler.info/politik/tucher-11.htm (accessed 13 January 2023).
30. BL, IOR: L/PJ/8/31: 'Coll 101/10AA; Nominal rolls of internees and parolees in India' (1943).
31. Oesterheld, 'British Policy', 39.
32. Franz, *Gateway India*, 192.
33. Oesterheld, 'British Policy', 39.
34. Franz, 'Passage to India', 216; Franz, *Gateway India*, 199.
35. Richard Fuchs, 'Alpine Club Examines Historical Ties to Nazis', *Deutsche Welle*, 2 September 2012, https://www.dw.com/en/alpine-club-examines-historical-ties-to-nazis/a-16214770 (accessed 13 January 2023).
36. NAI, HP: PR_000004009980: 'Escape of German internees from the Premnagar Internee Camp at Dehradun' (1944).
37. Ibid.
38. Ibid.
39. Ibid.
40. Ibid.
41. Roger Croston, 'Prisoners of the Raj', http://www.gaebler.info/india/escape.htm#croston (accessed 13 January 2023).
42. Franz, *Gateway India*, 202.
43. Croston, 'Prisoners of the Raj'.
44. Franz, *Gateway India*, 203.
45. BL, IOR: L/PJ/7/12104: '6530; Allegations of internment of German-Jewish refugees in India and release of Nazi officers in India' (1947).
46. Ibid.
47. Franz, *Gateway India*, 360–3.
48. Ibid., 363.
49. Seema Sharma, 'WWII Prison Camps May Become Tourist Sites Soon', *Times of India*, 25 January 2015, https://timesofindia.indiatimes.com/city/dehradun/wwii-prison-camps-may-become-tourist-sites-soon/articleshow/46014315.cms (accessed 13 January 2023).
50. Ibid.
51. Ibid.
52. Franz, *Gateway India*, 364.
53. Ibid.

Bibliography

Franz, Margit. *Gateway India: Deutschsprachiges Exil in Indien zwischen britischer Kolonialherrschaft, Maharadschas und Gandhi*. Graz: CLIO. 2015.

Franz, Margit. '"Passage to India": Österreichisches Exil in Britisch-Indien 1938–1945'. In *Jahrbuch 2007*, edited by Dokumentationsarchiv des österreichischen Widerstandes, 196–223. Vienna: Lit Verlag. 2007.

Harrer, Heinrich. *Seven Years in Tibet: My Life Before, During and After*. Trans. Richard Graves. London: Rupert Hart-Davis. 1953.

Kolb, Fritz. *Leben in der Retorte: Als österreichischer Alpinist in indischen Internierungslagern*. Graz: CLIO. 2014.

Kopp, Hans. *Sechsmal über den Himalaya. Fluchterlebnisse eines Deutschen in Indien und Tibet*. Freiburg/Breisgau: Hermann Klemm, 1955.

Oesterheld, Joachim. 'British Policy towards German-Speaking Emigrants in India, 1939–1945'. In *Jewish Exile in India: 1933–1945*, edited by Anil Bhatti and Johannes H. Voigt, 25–44. New Delhi: Max Mueller Bhavan, 1999.

13

Civilian internment in the Raj: Central and family internment camps c.1939–43

Alan Malpass

September 1939 marked the beginning of a new chapter in the history of civilian internment in the British Raj. During the Second World War, India reprised the role of 'gaol of Empire'. In addition to interning European enemy aliens present in 1939, thousands more were shipped from the Middle and Far East to camps across India. This chapter provides a survey of the development of the main internment camps where German, Italian and other European nationalities were detained before the opening of the Dehra Dun Central Internment Camp (CIC). It outlines pre-war preparations, the initial arrest of enemy aliens and transfer from local reception camps to the Ahmednagar CIC before their interim stay at Deolali cantonment in the Nashik district of the Bombay Province. The establishment of family camps at Purandhar and Satara, also in Bombay, after the re-internment of enemy aliens in 1940 is discussed, as well as the Deoli camp in Ajmer which briefly held European internees from the Far East.[1] Finally, the current status and legacy of these camps is considered.

'Like Clockwork' – arrest and detention on the outbreak of war

When the issue of dealing with enemy aliens was raised by the looming conflict with Germany in the late 1930s, the Government of India already possessed considerable experience of accommodating detainees during the Anglo-Boer and First World Wars. At the turn of the twentieth century, colonial governments and the War Office looked to India for 'practical precedent and protocol' on the issue of internment.[2] Yet, as Matthew Stibbe contends, 'a kind of selective amnesia descended on the world in respect of civilian internment' after 1918.[3] Following the German occupation of Czechoslovakia in 1938, a review of action to be taken toward enemy aliens highlighted that 'a great deal of confusion would have ensued' due to a lack of information on the number of foreigners in India and an absence of clear instructions regarding the arrest of enemy aliens and disposal of their property.[4] The first step taken to avoid the predicted bedlam was the Registration of Foreigners Act 1939, which required aliens to report their arrival, movements and departure, as well as produce identity documentation.[5]

Furthermore, managers of hotels, boarding-houses, sarai (inns) or similar premises, and those in charge of vessels and aircraft, were obliged to produce lists of foreigners residing in their establishment or using their services. Failure to comply could result in a one-year prison sentence or a fine of 1,000 rupees for foreigners and up to 500 for non-foreigners. Given the severity of the punishment, non-compliance was not to be taken lightly. The second step was taken in August 1939, when new instructions were issued to local police setting out the arrest and dispatch of all enemy aliens aged sixteen years or over to local internment camps upon the outbreak of war. These initial reception sites run by military authorities would temporarily hold internees while the CIC at Ahmednagar was constructed (for the location of the main camps, see Figure 13.1). Twenty-eight local internment camps were earmarked for establishment in 1939, five in Northern Command, eleven in Southern Command, ten in Eastern Command and two in the Western District. The instructions included a general design for a camp or single wing accommodating up to 500 internees. Acknowledging that local conditions varied, the instructions were intended to be flexible and the layout of camps depended upon whether pre-existing buildings were utilized or tents. All camps, however, had to provide living accommodation, ablution and washhouses, latrines and urinals, a cookhouse, guard room and a reception room or tent. At the CIC, internees were classified either as 'A' or 'B' – which corresponded to 'British Officers' and 'British other ranks'. Class A internees, described in the instructions as 'ordinary civilians of good social status', were to provide their own clothing, washing and toilet kit.[6] It was expected that non-interned enemy subjects would be repatriated.

When war was declared, the Defence of India Act 1939 bestowed Central Government with comprehensive legislative controls to maintain internal security. 'As a wartime state', Yasmin Khan notes, 'policemen and civil servants acquired unprecedented power and the state began to use its security apparatus for internal defence'.[7] The Act permitted the arrest and incarceration of individuals 'reasonably suspected of being of hostile origin or of having acted, acting or being about to act, in a manner prejudicial to the public safety or interest or to the defence of British India'.[8] The movement of foreigners was restricted and tribunals to prosecute those who broke the law were arranged. Punishments ranged from imprisonment for several years, a fine or the seizure of property. In more serious cases, individuals could be penalized with transportation for life or execution. By the time the Act had passed, enemy aliens had already been arrested and conveyed to local internment camps. Heinrich Harrer, one of the German mountaineers who would later escape from Dehra Dun internment camp, wrote that 'everything went like clockwork'.[9] Soon after the declaration of war, Harrer and his friends were arrested at a local restaurant and driven to a local reception camp.

Around 850 of the 1,500 Germans who were in India were interned on the outbreak of war, including missionaries and Jewish refugees. In contrast to the United Kingdom, India interned all male enemy aliens aged sixteen years and over. This more stringent and indiscriminate approach was taken due to concerns over subversive Nazi organizations in India and enemy subjects returning to stir unrest after escaping to neighbouring countries.[10] For some, this was a second experience of internment within twenty-five years. In 1914, around 2,000 German subjects were interned or expelled

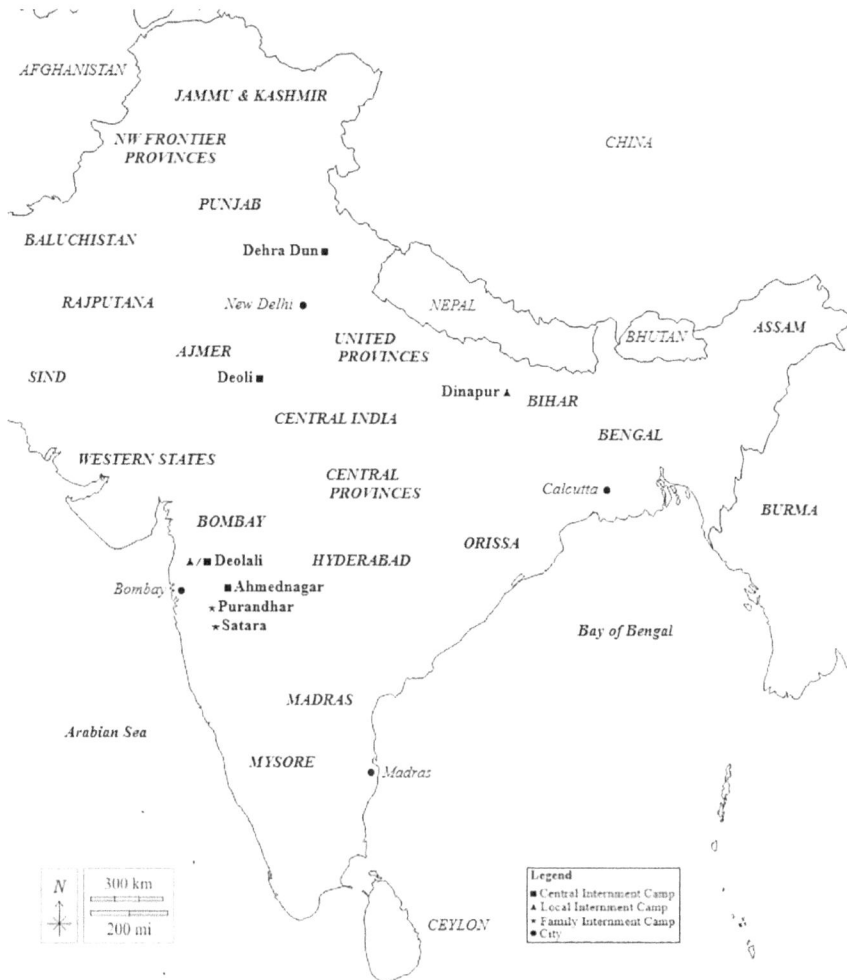

Figure 13.1 Civilian Internment Camps in India c.1939–45

Source: Map adapted by the author from https://d-maps.com/carte.php?num_car=285&lang=en.

from India.[11] *The Times of India* reported that 321 out of 387 German residents in Bombay were arrested in the morning of 3 September and were being transported to Deolali on a 'heavily guarded' train.[12] Elsewhere, fifteen Germans had been arrested in Delhi, six in Darjeeling, four at Ludhiana and Nagpur and two at Agra. Meanwhile forty who had been detained in Bihar, including fourteen residents of Jamshedpur, were being sent to Dinapur military camp.[13]

Cantonments such as Deolali and Dinapur acted as initial reception sites for arrested enemy aliens. Derived from the French 'canton', cantonments were established across India following the Battle of Plassey in 1757. These permanent military bases were unique institutions in India – cantonments were usually temporary encampments – where formations of soldiers were quartered and kept separate from civil settlements. Cantonments were located near to towns and cities but were their own distinct townships. Under military control, they were not subject to municipal regulations and were governed by separate laws. Cantonments soaked up little of the character of the local area and remained considerably different to nearby towns. Neatly organized, with orderly streets and precisely spaced bungalows, British cantonments were similar in design and layout to each other. Larger cantonments held exclusively European military formations tasked with field operations and maintaining order during times of unrest. While boundaries between cantonments and nearby towns were clearly demarcated, these institutions were less isolated from Indian society than remote hill-stations where English officials retreated in order to escape the fierce heat of Indian summertime.

Terence Molloy, an officer in the Northamptonshire Regiment, recalls the arrival of internees to Dinapur. They were held in the isolation hospital within the historic cantonment, around which a barbed-wired fence had been 'hastily erected'. The internees, Molloy tells us, were 'completely inoffensive people' who 'rather objected to having been uprooted from their jobs and put into internment'.[14] Henry Smith, an NCO in the South Lancashire Regiment, assisted in the arrest of enemy aliens in Bombay and their removal to Deolali. Lists of foreign nationals had been made, including information on their dependents and families. 'Somebody pressed a button', Smith describes, 'and out went the troops and the police, fanned out and just simply gathered these people in'.[15] Arrests in Bombay continued through the night of 3 September into the following morning. Taken to Deolali, the internees were accommodated in the barracks the escort troops previously occupied. Now surrounded by wire, they acted as an internment camp. Internees were thoroughly searched, made to bathe, given 'in no uncertain terms' a short back and sides and provided makeshift uniforms.[16] For those arrested, the experience could be disorientating, frustrating and painful as they were separated from their families, not least for the Jewish refugees who had travelled to India to escape persecution. Internees did not stay long at local internment camps and were quickly transferred to the CIC.

Ahmednagar to Deolali

In 1939, a major internment camp was once again established at Ahmednagar, a city long associated with imprisonment. The fort was captured by Arthur Wellesley in 1803 during the Second Anglo-Maratha War and served as a prison throughout the era of the British Raj. Furthermore, 1,000 of the 9,000 Boer prisoners of war (POWs) sent to India between 1899 and 1902 were detained here.[17] During the First World War, German internees, including missionaries, merchant seamen and businessmen, were held at Ahmednagar, their number fluctuating between 1,100 and 1,700. The camp took on a 'symbolic importance for those interned in India as that which Knockaloe held of the Germans interned in Great Britain'.[18] The 1939 camp was located around a mile from the one erected in 1914 and four miles outside Ahmednagar itself. Spanning an eight-acre area, the camp was surrounded by a nine-foot double fence of barbed wire, with another line of wire dividing the camp into two wings, one for Nazis and the other for anti-Nazis.[19] In February 1940, 888 internees were held at Ahmednagar.[20] News coverage emphasized the comforts and privileges granted to internees:

> There is plenty of room for sports and the facilities and amenities provided for the troops stationed there are also available to the internees. Situated on a plateau 2,000 feet above sea level, Ahmednagar has a mild climate throughout the year and includes some of the most beautiful natural scenery in the Deccan.[21]

It was described as a 'healthy camp' boasting a library, well stocked by the German Clubs of Bombay and Calcutta, a hospital and recreational facilities, including a swimming pool. Internees could receive thirty-minute visits from their wives. To prevent the communication of secret messages, 'personal contact' was forbidden. In the pages of the press, Ahmednagar was portrayed akin to a holiday resort or spa rather than an internment camp.[22] Only the barbed wire and sentries indicated the purpose of the site. The contrast between the experience of internment in India and the reports emanating about camps in Germany was underscored:

> Here German nationals who were in India at the outbreak of war are taking a compulsory rest cure for the duration – and a rest cure their sojourn in camp very obviously is when compared with recently published pen pictures of life in concentration and internment camps in their own country.[23]

As the summer approached, in February 1940 it was reported that fans would be installed to combat the heat 'for the comfort of internees'.[24] According to the *Civil & Military Gazette*, there had been no formal complaints as yet received by the internees at Ahmednagar. The speed at which internees were collected and transferred to Ahmednagar, however, meant that conditions were bad and the camps were soon overcrowded and claustrophobic, with tents used initially. 'It was a bad time in the beginning', a former internee remarked:

> because we were all put into tents, four each into one tent at Ahmednagar. There were terrible rains (monsoons), and it went through the tents. And we felt very uncomfortable. But the reason for that was that the barracks were not yet free. First the soldiers had to be removed and then we moved into the barracks; then it became quite a bearable life.[25]

While at Ahmednagar, Jewish internees and missionaries were examined by the Darling Committee. Formed in September 1939 and headed by Sir Malcom Darling, a long-serving member of the Indian Civil Service, the committee screened internees for release.[26] From November, in line with UK policy, India expanded the remit of the Darling Committee to include all internees, not just Jewish refugees. Furthermore, reluctantly, the compulsory repatriation of women and enemy aliens at liberty was abandoned. It was concluded that subversive activity organized by Germans in India was minimal and restrictions imposed on enemy aliens at liberty were relaxed.[27] When policy towards enemy aliens in the event of war with Italy and other countries was reviewed, wholesale internment was abandoned and only suspect individuals were to be interned. The relaxation of regulations was short-lived, however. With the calamitous defeats suffered in Europe, the Government of India followed the UK lead in revising internment policy. On 19 May 1940, the Home Department informed the Provincial Governments of the 'recent manifestations of the subversive activities of German subjects and sympathisers in neutral countries and in the rear of the armies of the allies'.[28] Since the outbreak of war, 920 out of the 950 adult male German subjects in India had been arrested. Twenty-two had been released before internment at Ahmednagar, and 561 had been released following examination by the Darling Committee. Of those released, 330 were Jewish refugees, 123 missionaries or priests and 109 were Aryan Germans. Of the 600 male German subjects at liberty, some 370 were refugees and 230 Aryan Germans, including missionaries. Out of 770 women, 90 had left following the outbreak of war, 450 were nuns, 280 were dependent on refugees and others at liberty and 40 were the wives of internees. At this point, the Home Department decided to re-examine the cases of released internees and explained that the decision to allow them to continue at liberty was to be based not on a lack of evidence to intern them but on the local authorities' satisfaction that they posed no serious security threat.

While the CIC at Dehra Dun was constructed, internees at Ahmednagar, now including Italians, were transferred to an interim camp at Deolali. The setting of the 1970s BBC sitcom *It Ain't Half Hot Mum*, Deolali cantonment was located in the Western Ghats of India near Nashik.[29] Established by the British in 1861, the cantonment served as a transit camp for soldiers leaving or arriving in India during trooping season. Here, British soldiers would acclimatize themselves to the heat, an experience which became notorious. During her stay at the rest centre, former VAD (Voluntary Aid Detachments) nurse Barbara Chambers remembers that it 'could be an inhospitable place and a combination of extreme climates and hard soldiering took its toll'.[30] The term 'doolally' or 'doolali' – slang for an individual who is 'out of one's mind' – is partly derived from the name of the cantonment.[31] It had initially operated as a local camp for arrested enemy aliens from Bombay, and a number had passed through on their way to Ahmednagar already. Driven in a convoy of lorries, the internees arrived at Deolali in February 1941. There were permanent buildings, including barracks, hospitals for British and Indian troops, a chapel, cemetery, police station and stores as well as recreational facilities. Importantly, the Great Indian Peninsula Railway passed through Deolali. Internees were transported here from Ahmednagar so that they could be conveyed by train to the permanent CIC at Dehra Dun once it was completed. While they made no complaints regarding their treatment by the authorities, the internees brought to Deolali were offended by what they considered inhumane conditions:

> They were completely new barracks, but they were, well, for a camp, let's say, when some soldiers have to pass through a space and have to stay for three or four days; then it was all right. But to imagine that one should stay in this camp for the whole duration of the war, absolutely it made us shudder. Aside from that fact, we were terribly limited for space. When you lay in bed, you could touch your neighbour

with the left hand and the other with the right had. You can imagine how close you were.³²

The internees were critical of the unsanitary conditions and limited space. Difficulties were exacerbated by the hot and dry climate. The internees undertook a spontaneous hunger strike in protest over the inadequate conditions. After four and a half days, the camp authorities agreed to move the internees into improved accommodation within the cantonment, 'a proper camp with barracks – a military barracks camp'.³³ The barracks of the new camp were stone built and more spacious with facilities for various sports. Conditions at Deolali cantonment were infamous, but the difficulties were not only faced by internees. In 1946, objections were made in the House of Commons regarding the conditions faced by British troops and there were calls to conduct an official investigation.³⁴ The move of internees into better accommodation certainly made the experience slightly more bearable during their temporary stay. By October 1941, the internees were again transferred, this time to Dehra Dun CIC at the foot of the Himalayas, a three-day train journey via Delhi. Not all internees would travel to the new camp, however. The revised internment instructions issued in May 1940 introduced parole centres where non-interned enemy aliens and the wives of internees were concentrated.

Finding a 'middle course' – re-internment and parole

Along with the re-internment of enemy aliens, wives of internees were forbidden from residing in ports or areas of strategic importance and were required to relocate to suitable townships. Furthermore, it was acknowledged that re-internment might not necessitate male enemy aliens being confined at Ahmednagar. Instead, a 'middle course' of restricting enemy subjects to 'parole settlements' in the provinces was introduced.³⁵ Initially, these centres were 'not envisaged as more than small towns to which non-interned enemy subjects in the more important ports and towns should be required to remove themselves'.³⁶ Parole centres were established at Sabathu, Naini Tal, Hazaribagh, Katapahar, Satara, Yercaud, Kodiakanal and Shillong. The necessity of imposing some restrictions on parolees, including censoring correspondence, 'very soon converted them into camps, where except that they were not fenced, the conditions were similar to those of a quasi-internment camp'.³⁷ All sites were cantonments or hill-stations and accommodation was provided by pre-existing bungalows and housing or military barracks. Where possible, married couples, single males and females were separated. 'Conditions of restriction and living in these settlements', the Home Department reported, 'are generally much easier than those in internment camps and approximate living conditions in hill stations'.³⁸ Initially, only non-interned enemy aliens and suspect foreigners were restricted to parole centres. Following the Allied defeats in Europe and resultant 'spy mania' in spring 1940, however, instructions were issued to restrict all Jewish refugees, now suspected of including spies and saboteurs, to parole centres along with non-interned enemy subjects. In order to supplement accommodation in provincial parole centres, a central parole centre was established at Purandhar. With only limited space within the centres, a new committee was appointed to re-examine Jewish refugees and decide whether they should be released, restricted to parole centres or remain at liberty. Having completed the review, however, 'results were so anomalous' that the Home Department reviewed cases itself in March 1941. Focusing on security concerns alone, the majority of refugees were released or restricted to parole centres after re-examination.[39]

The re-internment of most non-Jewish enemy aliens, new restrictions on internee wives, combined with the internment of Italians following the entry of Italy into the war led to renewed calls for a family camp. Having visited Ahmednagar, the Consulate General of Switzerland in Bombay reported to the Home Department in May 1940 that uncertainty over the formation of a family camp was 'having a very detrimental effect on the morale of the internees'.[40] In November 1939, when the compulsory repatriation of enemy aliens was dropped, the disused military centre at Purandhar fort was earmarked for a family camp. The proposal was abandoned after the Darling Committee found only twenty of the thirty-nine married internees were suitable for release. Maintenance allowances were provided to their dependents instead. In March 1941, the Home Department again put forward proposals to establish a family camp at Purandhar, then operating as a central parole centre. Local police, however, dismissed the suitability of the site for an enclosed camp. Concerns were raised over the water supply, provision of a suitable police guard and lighting. There was no electrical supply on the hill and 'petromax' lamps would be useless during monsoon. It was suggested that an annex be built for families at Dehra Dun or an existing POW camp. The Superintendent of Purandhar emphasized to the Home Department that, with some modification, it was an ideal site for a family camp. He reported that the concerns raised were far from insurmountable and suspected the objections of the Poona District Superintendent of Police were based on his desire to avoid the 'nuisance' of an internment camp.[41] As a result of unfavourable reports, the Home Department surveyed several other sites, including Satara, Tilonia and Deoli. Before a family camp could be established, the influx of evacuees from the Balkans, Middle and Far East had to be dealt with. Following the fall of Singapore in December 1941, 600 Maltese, 1,000 Balkan evacuees and 11,000 Poles were accepted by the Government of India.[42] Several camps accommodated these groups and eventually they were transferred to Coimbatore and Kolhapur. With the transfer of evacuees, the Government of India was able to redistribute the population of parole centres and find sufficient accommodation at Purandhar and Satara to establish combined parole centres and family internment camps.

Family camps

The British occupied Purandhar in 1818 and established a cantonment within the fort which dated back to the formation of the Bahmani Kingdom, the first independent Islamic Kingdom in South India. The fort still stands today on the summit of hills over 4,000 feet above sea level and 2,500 feet above Poona Plain. Described as an 'exceptionally healthy' site, the cantonment included a convalescence centre for soldiers from Ahmednagar and Pune, located on the lower level of the fort called *machi*.[43] Having spent over two years discussing the opening of a family camp, the pressure of accommodating the influx of evacuees and additional internees forced the issue and plans reverted to locate it at Purandhar. Due to a shortage of wire, Purandhar Fort could not be enclosed. The Home Department concluded, however, that Purandhar was an 'isolated hill top from which escape would not be easy' (see Figure 13.2).[44] The threat of being transferred back to the CIC at Dehra Dun was considered a sufficient deterrent. Despite being unfenced, conditions at Purandhar were similar to Dehra Dun.[45] The Superintendent of the Purandhar Parole Centre agreed that, by adapting existing buildings and construction of a new barrack, accommodation could be found for a maximum of 260 adults and seventy children.[46] The existing accommodation needed altering and expanding. It was, the Superintendent noted, 'of a very mixed character' with 'a number of single cubicles with 7' to 8' high wooden partitions', although not 'good enough as a permanency'. Having consulted with the wives of internees, he reported that they were happy to improvise so long as they were reunited with their husbands. Accommodation was allocated based on family size, with the largest families allocated the superior housing.[47] Before the family camp was officially opened, released internees from Ahmednagar and Deolali were transferred here to be with their wives. Conditions at Purandhar became increasingly cramped as internees and parolees were transferred from other sites, including a consignment of German wives from Iran whose interned husbands

Figure 13.2 ICRC Archives (ARR), 1942. Purandhar. Civilian Internees Camp. General view of the camp

Source: V-P-HIST-03480-19A.

had been brought to India. Initially, new arrivals to Purandhar would select whatever rooms were available. Yet, with more arrivals, 'people became more possessive of their space in camp'.[48] In March 1942, there were twenty-eight married couples, eighteen single men, forty-eight single women, eighteen children and 11 infants at the parole centre and the Superintendent was optimistic that the conversion of Purandhar into a family camp would be favourable.[49] The construction of additional accommodation was hampered by the isolated location and short building season, but over the summer of 1942 new barracks were constructed. A former Purandhar resident commented that, 'with a garden, the wonderful climate and the altitude, it was a joy living up there' (Figure 13.3).[50] Within the hillside fort, it proved near impossible to separate married internees and parolees. The Home Department was satisfied that escapes would be unlikely and, therefore, apart from their status, there was little difference between the conditions to which the internees and parolees were subject.

A family internment camp was also opened at Satara, where the additional facilities constructed to accommodate British and European evacuees had doubled capacity of the site. Evacuees were accommodated at Satara as it was at a reasonable distance to Bombay and, therefore, contact with the various consuls responsible for their welfare. Around fifty miles south of Poona, Satara District was annexed by the British in 1848 and remained an important agricultural and business hub in Bombay State. In the beginning, the parole centre here was small and relatively quiet, with German women brought here from the

Figure 13.3 ICRC Archives (ARR), 1942. Purandhar. Civilian Internees Camp. Barrack
Source: V-P-HIST-03480-23A.

Figure 13.4 ICRC Archives (ARR). 1944. Satara, Parole Center. Civilian internees camp. Barracks of the German wing

Source: V-P-HIST-03478-01A.

centres at Yercaud and Kodikanal. When internees were being transferred to Dehra Dun, some were moved from Ahmednagar and Deolali to Satara to join their wives. There were four original military barracks, each divided into eight rooms. Within each there were two bathrooms, two bathtubs and four toilets. As a parole camp for women, each room accommodated a single woman and child or two women. In contrast to Purandhar, three separate camps were established at Satara, with the two family internment camps, one for Germans (see Figure 13.4) and one for Italians, enclosed by barbed wire, as well as a parole centre for non-interned enemy aliens. The new barracks that had been constructed were thought to be inadequate for families and caused tension and irritation between individuals. Those brought from Yercaud and Kodiakanal compared the barracks at Satara unfavourably to the bungalows of the parole centres.[51] By August, the conversion of Satara and Purandhar into combined parole centres and internment camps was complete, with internee families and additional parolees from provincial centres absorbed by them. Over the course of 1942, all married internees from Dehra Dun and other sites in India were transferred to either site.

Deoli

Locating the family camps at Satara and Purandhar was necessary to allow facilities at Deoli (Ajmer) to be expanded. Deoli had been suggested as a site for the family camp but it instead had to be used to accommodate the 2,400 German male internees and 1,250 Japanese internees the Government of India accepted from Sumatra in December 1941.[52] Deoli cantonment was established in 1852, with several battalions raised here in the nineteenth and early twentieth centuries. In 1932, Deoli was used as a detention camp to house Bengali leaders of the Chittagong Armoury raid before closure in 1938. In 1940, the jail was reopened to confine security prisoners, including communists and revolutionaries. While facilities at Deoli were expanded, Japanese internees were held in a tented camp in Purana Qila. European internees from the Dutch East Indies were, meanwhile, held temporarily at Ramgarh POW camp while an appropriate site for a new camp was found. The Home Department had hoped that they could be sent to Dehra Dun, but the Commandant rejected proposals to expand the camp as insurmountable, particularly with regards to the water supply. Ramgarh camp was built in 1940 alongside the military cantonment and was similar in design and style to other civilian internee camps. The internee population at Ramgarh reached around 600 by April 1941; the camp also housed 2,000 Italian POWs in a separate compound. As a comfortable camp, high-ranking Italian officers had been sent to Ramgarh as part of an effort to form anti-fascist battalions. After further consideration, the Commandant at Dehra Dun believed that expansion of the camp was possible and European internees could be transferred to the CIC. Before the move could be completed, however, Ramgarh was required for use as a training site for 10,000 soldiers of the Chinese Expeditionary Force.[53] At this time, Deoli was the only viable camp and European internees from Ramgarh were moved here in July 1942, before being finally transferred to Dehra Dun the following April. The Japanese internees then took their place at Deoli.[54] With the move of the German internees from Deoli to Dehra Dun, there were now four primary internment camps as well as the parole centres dotted across India. In April 1943, the total internee population in India stood at 5,716. Dehra Dun, now the CIC after the closure of Ahmednagar, accommodated 2,477 European adult internees along with 83 merchant seamen. The combined internment and parole camp at Purandhar held 248 European adult and 50 child internees, while 372 European adult and 95 child internees were housed at Satara. Finally, Deoli, now 'a purely Asiatic internees' camp', held 2,216 Japanese adult and 175 child internees as well as 287 Javanese seamen.[55]

Faced with not only interning, and subsequently re-interning or restricting, enemy aliens already present in India, but also finding space for those brought from abroad as well as evacuees, the Home Department, working with the provincial governments, attempted to rationalise the distribution of the internee population of India. In general, individual male internees were detained at the CIC at Ahmednagar, Deolali and, finally, Dehra Dun. Married internees and families were concentrated at Purandhar and Satara. Screening, categorizing and separating Nazi and Fascist internees from Jewish and anti-Nazi internees proved difficult, especially at the latter camps, and tensions and complaints between these groups were not uncommon. While certain sites, such as Purandhar, Satara and Deoli, were utilized to detain enemy aliens throughout the war, the category of inhabitants and number of internees were mutable as the Government of India attempted to accommodate various European evacuees and refugees from the Middle and Far East. Conditions and facilities varied between camps, from the dust-ridden and hot conditions at Deolali to the isolated slopes of Purandhar. All of the main internment camps operated until after the end of the war. The release and repatriation of European internees, some having spent six or seven years in captivity, or who had been originally detained in Iran, Ceylon, Burma, Sumatra or Malaya, would raise further issues for the Government of India, not least the question of who was liable for the substantial costs incurred in building additional camps.

Memorialization and legacy

Regarding the current condition and status of these sites, their memorialization and legacy as places where European internees were held during the Second World War is nominal. Memorials were erected to the Boer POWs who died in India at Ahmednagar and other camps.[56] In the Christian cemetery at Ahmednagar, where the cenotaph to the Boers can be found, is a memorial to the German internees who died here during the 1914–18 conflict. With regards to the Second World War, however, there is no equivalent monument. In post-independence India, Ahmednagar and Deoli are naturally better remembered as places where members of the Indian National Congress were detained rather than the European internees. Furthermore, as many of the sites used for camps were military cantonments, their names are better associated with the different military schools of the Indian forces that currently reside in them. Since 1947, the Armoured Corp of the Indian Army has been located in Ahmednagar. The history of the fort, which is administered by the Corps, is readily associated with the confinement of members of the Congress Working Committee between 1942 and 1945. During his detention at Ahmednagar, Jawaharlal Nehru, the first Prime Minister of India, began writing his *Discovery of India*.[57] Tourists can visit his preserved jail cell, now a museum, the entrance to which has a sign indicating his time interned here. The role Ahmednagar played as the location of the initial CIC in 1939 is marginalized by the fort, which not only dominates the landscape but also memories of civilian internment. Purandhar fort, meanwhile, remains a popular tourist attraction. The church where services were held by interned German missionaries still stands and is a highlight along with a Statute of Murarbaji Deshpande, the Maratha general who defended the fort against the Mughals. In 2017, the *Hindustan Times* reported that the military units of the National Cadet Corp Academy stationed at Purandhar were imposing restrictions on the tourists who hike to the fort to take in the spectacular views. Cameras and mobile phones were prohibited and a strict curfew enforced. The article briefly mentioned that it had once acted as an internment camp for Germans, including the art historian Dr H Goetz.[58]

The Deoli camp would once again receive detainees around twenty years after it had been converted from the Detention Centre into a camp for internees. With the outbreak of the 1962 Sino-Indian War, the result of a long-standing border dispute, Prime Minister Nehru ordered the internment of Chinese-Indians. Prior to Indian independence, The Foreigners Act of 1946 granted the Interim Government of India power to detain aliens and punish those who assisted internees or parolees in escape.[59] On 13 November 1962, India amended the Foreigners Act 1946 so that the government was allowed to detain individuals of 'non-Indian' origin. It was under this Act that some 3,000 Chinese-Indians were interned. Although the Sino-Indian War was short (a ceasefire was declared on 20 November), it marked the beginning of a long internment of Chinese nationals, some remaining detained for five years.[60] Yin Marsh, who was interned with her family in 1962, notes the irony of being taken to Deoli where Nehru, who authorized the internment of Chinese-Indians, had once been held himself.[61]

Historians have emphasized the role India played in the global internment practices of the British Empire in the late nineteenth and early twentieth centuries. Much less has been written on how certain sites were repurposed during the Second World War when European enemy aliens were again interned. The British sought to control foreign and enemy populations in India as they had done in the Anglo-Boer War and First World War. The experience gained and practices honed during these conflicts were applied during the violent processes of decolonization after 1945. Historians of First World War civilian internment have sought to map the routes between the British concentration camps in South Africa and those of the Second World War. As the re-establishment of a camp at Deoli in 1962 suggests, we also need to look beyond 1945 when sites that detained European enemy aliens during the conflict were utilized in the post-colonial world. Memorials and memories of the internment of Europeans in India during the Second World War are certainly marginal, the history of sites at internee camps being subsumed by the longer military histories of the cantonments or the detention of figures associated with the fight for independence, but it is clear that post-war India not only inherited the frameworks and architecture of internment introduced during the British Raj but reclaimed and developed them.

Notes

All references starting with India Office Records (IOR) are held by the British Library, all starting with Home Department are held by the National Archive of India, Delhi.

1. Following the Independence and Partition of India in 1947, the provinces of the British Raj were replaced by states and unions with new boundaries. Certain cities and districts have been renamed since. This chapter uses the place and region names as they appear in contemporary documents during the imperial period.
2. Matthew W. Kennedy, 'The Imperialism of Internment: Boer Prisoners of War in India and Civil Reconstruction in Southern Africa, 1899–1905', *Journal of Imperial and Commonwealth History* 44 (2016): 425.
3. Matthew Stibbe, *Civilian Internment during the First World War: A European and Global History, 1914–1920* (London: Palgrave Macmillan, 2019), 294.
4. IOR L/PJ/8/30B, Home Department, *Civil Internment Manual 1943* (Simla: Government of India, 1943), 1.
5. The Registration of Foreigners Act, 1939. *A Collection of The Acts of The Indian Legislature And of the Governor General for the Year 1939* (Delhi: Manager of Publication, 1939).
6. IOR L/PJ/8/30A, Defence Department, *Military Instructions for the Internment of Enemy Aliens in the event of War, 1939* (Simla: Government of India, 1939).

7. Yasmin Khan, *The Raj At War* (London: Vintage, 2016), 11–12.
8. The Defence of India Act, 1939. *A Collection of the Acts of the Indian Legislature and of the Governor General for the Year 1939* (Delhi: Manager of Publication, 1939).
9. Heinrich Harrer, *Seven Years in Tibet* (London: Rupert Hart-Davis, 1972), 1.
10. CAB 68/1/32, 'Memorandum: India', 2 October 1939, The National Archives, Kew.
11. On the presence of Germans in India before the Second World War see Panikos Panayi, *The Germans in India: Elite European Migrants in the British Empire* (Manchester: Manchester University Press, 2017).
12. 'Germans In India Rounded Up', *The Times of India*, 5 September 1939, 8.
13. Ibid.
14. IWM 19817, Molley, Terence Rupert (Oral History) REEL 1 (1990), Imperial War Museum Sound Archive, https://www.iwm.org.uk/collections/item/object/80018704 (accessed 18 January 2023).
15. IWM 836, Smith, John Henry (Oral History) REEL 5 (1976), Imperial War Museum Sound Archive, https://www.iwm.org.uk/collections/item/object/80000830 (accessed 18 January 18, 2023).
16. Ibid.
17. Kennedy, 'Imperialism of Internment', 429.
18. Stefan Manz and Panikos Panayi, *Enemies in the Empire: Civilian Internment in the British Empire during the First World War* (Oxford: Oxford University Press 2020), 276.
19. 'The Ahmednagar Camp', *The Times of India*, 8 April 1940, 6.
20. 'Camp Under Military Supervision', *Civil and Military Gazette*, 9 February 1940, 8.
21. 'Life in the CIC', *Civil and Military Gazette*, 19 March 1940, 12.
22. 'Interned for the Duration Germans' Life At Ahmednagar Camp', *Illustrated Weekly of India*, 7 April 1940, 20.
23. Ibid.
24. 'Facilities Granted to Enemy Internees', *Civil and Military Gazette*, 8 February 1940, 6.
25. Paul Von Tucher, *Nationalism: Case and Crisis in Missions. German Missions in British India, 1937–1946* (self-published, 1980), 74.
26. 'Release of Enemy Internees', *Civil and Military Gazette*, 24 September 1939, 10.
27. IOR L/PJ/8/30B, Home Department, *Civil Internment Manual 1943* (Simla: Government of India, 1943), 4.
28. Home Department (Political), F/66/3, 'Enemy foreigners at liberty', 19 May 1940.
29. *It Ain't Half Hot Mum* (1974–1981), [TV Programme] BBC1.
30. A2730791, 'Going Deolali 1939–41' (2004), BBC WW2 People's War Archive, https://www.bbc.co.uk/history/ww2peopleswar/stories/91/a2730791.shtml (accessed 18 January 2023).
31. NA Martin, 'The Madness at Deolali', *Journal of the Royal Army Medical Corp*, 152 (2006): 94.
32. Tucher, *Nationalism*, 317.
33. Ibid., 324.
34. Hansard, 25 Feb. 1945, vol. 419, cols. 1568.
35. IOR L/PJ/8/30B, Home Department, *Civil Internment Manual 1943* (Simla: Government of India, 1943), 4.
36. Ibid., 5.
37. Ibid., 7.
38. IOR L/PJ/8/30A, 'Government of India (Home Department) to Secretary of State for India', 14 September 1940.

39. IOR/L/PJ/8/30B, Home Department, *Civil Internment Manual 1943* (Simla: Government of India, 1943), 5–6.
40. Home Department (Political) F/34/61, 'Consulate General of Switzerland (Bombay) to Frampton (Home Department)', 5 May 1940.
41. Home Department (Political) F/154/40, 'Note on the suitability of Purandhar as a site for a family internment camp', 8 November 1941.
42. Dominions Office (DO) 133/107, 'Memorandum of important and useful information concerning European evacuees in India' (1947), The National Archives, Kew.
43. Sidney Toy, *The Fortified Cities of India* (London: Heinemann, 1965), 40.
44. Home Department F/154/40. 'Memorandum: Family Internment Camp', 9 January 1942.
45. Home Department F/154/40. Home Department to Superintendent, Parole Centre (Purandhar), 17 January 1942.
46. Home Department F/154/40. 'Purandhar: Conversion into a Family Internment Camp', 3 February 1942.
47. Home Department F/154/40. Superintendent, Parole Centre (Purandhar) to Home Department, 2 March 1942.
48. Tucher, *Nationalism*, 380.
49. Home Department F/154/40. Superintendent, Parole Centre (Purandhar)to Home Department, 3 March 1942.
50. Tucher, *Nationalism*, 385.
51. Ibid., 415–16.
52. Home Department F/154/40, 'Memorandum: Family Internment Camp', 9 January 1942.
53. Yin Cao (2020), 'Establishing the Ramgarh Training Center: The Burman Campaign, the Colonial Internment Camp, and the Wartime Sino-British Relations', *Trans-Regional and -National Studies of Southeast Asi*a, 9/1, 5.
54. Christine de Matos and Rowena Ward, 'Forgotten Forced Migrants of War: Civilian Internment of Japanese in British India, 1941–6', *Journal of Contemporary History* 56/4 (2021): 1102–125, https://doi.org/10.1177/0022009421997913 (accessed 18 January 2023).
55. IOR L/PJ/8/30B, 'Administration of Internment Camps in India: General', 3 August 1943.
56. Isabel Hofmeyr, 'South Africa's Indian Ocean: Boer Prisoners of War in India', *Social Dynamics*, 38/3 (2012): 363–80.
57. Khan, *The Raj at War*, 281.
58. Ashish Phadnis, 'No Cameras, no Mobiles on Purandar Fort in Pune', *Hindustan Times*, 26 October 2017, https://www.hindustantimes.com/pune-news/no-cameras-no-mobiles-on-purandar-fort-in-pune/story-VC5HpnSYObemxjTsiLT7qI.html (accessed 18 January 2023).
59. The Foreigners Act 1946. *A Collection of the Acts of the Central Legislature and Ordinances of the Governor Generals for the Year 1946* (Simla: Government of India, 1947).
60. Joy Ma and Dilip D'Souza, *The Deoliwallahs: The True Story of the 1962 Chinese-Indian Internment* (London: Macmillian, 2020).
61. Yin Marsh, *Doing Time with Nehru: The Story of an Indian-Chinese Family* (Chicago: UCP, 2016).

Bibliography

Cao, Yin. 'Establishing the Ramgarh Training Center: The Burman Campaign, the Colonial Internment Camp, and the Wartime Sino-British Relations'. *TRaNS: Trans-Regional and -National Studies of Southeast Asia* 9, no. 1 (2020): 1–10.

Harrer, Heinrich. *Seven Years in Tibet*. London: Rupert Hart-Davis, 1972.

Hofmeyr, Isabel. 'South Africa's Indian Ocean: Boer Prisoners of War in India'. *Social Dynamics* 38, no. 3 (2012): 363–80.

Kennedy, Matthew W. 'The Imperialism of Internment: Boer Prisoners of War in India and Civil Reconstruction in Southern Africa, 1899–1905'. *Journal of Imperial and Commonwealth History* 44, no. 3 (2016): 423–47.

Khan, Yasmin. *The Raj At War*. London: Vintage, 2016.

Ma, Joy, and Dilip D'Souza. *The Deoliwallahs: The True Story of the 1962 Chinese-Indian Internment*. London: Macmillian, 2020.

Manz, Stefan, and Panikos Panayi. *Enemies in the Empire: Civilian Internment in the British Empire during the First World War*. Oxford: Oxford University Press, 2020.

Marsh, Yin. *Doing Time with Nehru: The Story of an Indian-Chinese Family*. Chicago: University of Chicago Press, 2016.

Martin, NA 'The Madness at Deolali'. *Journal of the Royal Army Medical Corp* 152 (2006): 94–5.

de Matos, Christine, and Rowena Ward. 'Forgotten Forced Migrants of War: Civilian Internment of Japanese in British India, 1941–6'. *Journal of Contemporary History* 56, no. 4 (2021): 1102–125.

Panayi, Panikos. *The Germans in India: Elite European Migrants in the British Empire*. Manchester: Manchester University Press, 2017.

Sidney, Toy. *The Fortified Cities of India*. London: Heinemann, 1965.

Stibbe, Matthew. *Civilian Internment during the First World War: A European and Global History, 1914–1920*. London: Palgrave Macmillan, 2019.

Tucher, Paul Von. *Nationalism: Case and Crisis in Missions. German Missions in British India, 1937–1946*. self-published, 1980.

14

The British sent them to Australia from around the World: The internment of enemy aliens in the Second World War at Tatura Camps 1 to 4

Alan Morgenroth

At the request and expense of the British government, the Australian government agreed to take an unspecified number of Germans, Austrians and Italians who had been interned by the British in the United Kingdom and elsewhere, who the British were unable or unwilling to accommodate in their current locations. In 1940–1, 4,234 internees were sent to Australia by the British: 2,546 from the United Kingdom aboard HMT *Dunera*; 301 from Singapore aboard RMS *Queen Mary*; 512 from occupied Persia aboard SS *Rangitikei* and 875 from Mandated Palestine aboard RMS *Queen Elizabeth*. The internees were all considered by Britain to be civilian 'enemy aliens'; they comprised men, women, children and families with pro-fascist German nationalists alongside anti-Nazi refugees. With so many different groupings and conflicting loyalties there were frequent disputes within the internment camps, giving the Australian authorities the logistical nightmare of keeping opposing groups apart. In consequence, the internees were regularly moved from one camp or compound to another to split feuding groups, accommodate new arrivals or to the make best use of the extra capacity as new camps were finished.

This chapter focuses on internees deported to Australia by the British and their time in Tatura Internment Camps 1 to 4. The military prisoner-of-war (POW) camps in the region are not covered in this chapter. This chapter consists of four parts: the first is an analysis and explanation of the circumstances behind each of the deportations; the second describes the structure and history of Tatura Camps 1 to 4; the third section is dedicated to legacy and heritage; with the fourth section discussing selected memory and the interpretation of history (Figure 14.1).

Deportations to Australia: UK internment and deportations to Australia – HMT *Dunera* July 1940

Until May 1940, internment of male enemy aliens in Britain had been restricted to those who were Category A and considered a threat to national security. While the

240 British Internment and the Internment of Britons

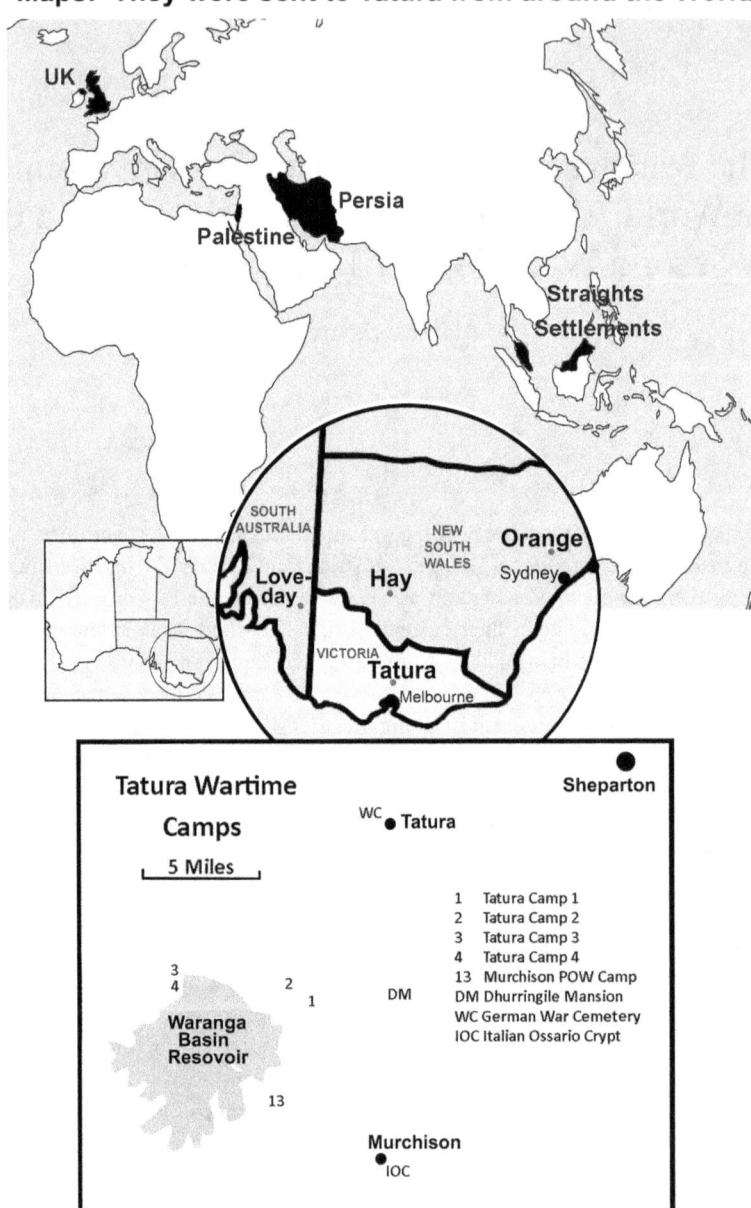

Figure 14.1 Points of departure of internee deportations to Australia and locations of wartime camps and memorials in the Tatura district

Source: © Alan Morgenroth.

Category A aliens were interned immediately, the aliens placed in Categories B and C, who were predominately refugees from Nazi oppression, remained at liberty. In his report to the War Cabinet on 29 April 1940, Sir John Anderson, the Secretary of State at the Home Office, argued against any further or general internment.[1] However, from April to June 1940, circumstances changed dramatically as the situation in the theatres of war deteriorated and public opinion turned against the Germans and Austrians still at liberty. On 9 April, Nazi Germany occupied Denmark and invaded Norway, which was overrun within a month, and this success was attributed, in part, to a fifth column of Nazi sympathisers. When France was invaded on 10 May, coinciding with Winston Churchill becoming Prime Minister, the threat of invasion was very real, as was the perception of a British fifth column. Consequently, the pendulum swung in favour of further internment. On 12 May, the arrest commenced of four to five thousand Category B and C male enemy aliens aged sixteen to sixty years living in coastal areas believed at greatest risk of invasion.[2] Four days later, the remaining Category B men were interned, followed on 28 May by the c.3,500 Category B women plus their dependent children.[3] Housing and feeding all these internees became an immediate issue; so to alleviate the problem, the British government had already approached Canada and Australia, requesting that they should take the most dangerous. Canada agreed to take up to 7,000 and Australia an undefined number.[4]

By 4 June 1940, British forces had been evacuated from Dunkirk and, on 10 June, Italy entered the war, precipitating the internment of 3,700 Italian men. Within five weeks, the enemy alien internee population had increased from around 2,850 to over 17,000.[5] Then, just as the transports to Canada were about to start, the decision was made, on 21 June, to intern a further 25,000 Category C enemy aliens aged between sixteen and seventy years, but since accommodation was not immediately available, this was planned in three phases starting on 25 June. At the end of June, deportations to the colonies was the easiest and fastest method to alleviate the problem of chaotic and overcrowded domestic internment camps. By 4 July, four transports had left the United Kingdom with internees and POWs bound for Canada, including the ill-fated SS *Arandora Star* which was torpedoed on 2 July, with the loss of 175 German and 446 Italian internees.[6] However, this tragedy did not immediately precipitate an end to the overseas transports. With the quota for deportations to Canada filled, urgent instructions were sent to the camps to select around 2,500 internees to fill a ship to Australia. Those selected included 251 Category A German and 200 Italian survivors of the *Arandora Star*. The commandant of Huyton camp, near Liverpool, selected nearly 1,000 internees; a further 800 came from Onchan, Central Promenade Douglas and Mooragh camps on the Isle of Man, with another 300 coming from Lingfield racecourse camp in Surrey.[7] In total, 2,546 internees set sail on the HMT *Dunera* on 10 July in miserably overcrowded conditions for a nightmare nine-week journey to Australia. During the journey, the internees were robbed and mistreated by the British guards, for which the internees were later compensated and three of the guards were court martialled.[8]

Of the 2,542 who arrived in Australia, the 250 German and 200 Italian survivors of the *Arandora Star* plus 95 Category 'B' and 'C' internees were disembarked in

Table 14.1 Internees Deported from the United Kingdom on HMT *Dunera*

HMT *Dunera* deportations[9]	Cat. A	Cat. B & C	Returned to United Kingdom/Died	Total arrived in Australia	Disembarked in Melbourne for Tatura Camp 2	Disembarked in Sydney for Hay NSW Camps 7 and 8
Germans ex-*Arandora Star*	251		-1	250	250	
Italians ex-*Arandora Star*	200			200	200	
German internees		2,095	-3	2,092	95	1,997
Embarked 2,546 Landed 2,542	451	2,095	-4*	2,542	545	1,997

*3 Died en-route and 1 German diplomat was disembarked at Cape Town and returned to the United Kingdom.

Melbourne and transferred to Tatura Camp 2 with the remaining 1,997 disembarked in Sydney and transferred by train to Hay Camps 7 and 8 in New South Wales, as shown in Table 14.1.

Deportations to Australia: Enemy aliens from the Straits Settlements Singapore – RMS *Queen Mary* September 1940

The Straits Settlements, of which Singapore was the capital, had been a Crown Colony of the British Empire since 1867, directly overseen by the Colonial Office in Whitehall. In July 1940, the authorities in Singapore informed all resident Germans, Austrians and Italians that they would be expelled, giving them a choice of moving to a neutral country or being deported to another country under British control.[10] Correspondence held in The National Archives, Kew, shows that the Colonial Office had a different attitude to the 'problem' of these enemy aliens compared to that of Stanley Jones, Colonial Secretary of the Colony.[11] By September, the British government was looking to release enemy alien refugees from internment rather than to intern more. However, Jones wanted to wash his hands of the problem by deporting them to Australia; Lord Lloyd, Secretary of State for the Colonies, reluctantly acquiesced.[12]

On 18 September 1940, 220 Germans and Austrians (predominately Jewish), with 45 Italians, were embarked on RMS *Queen Mary* for the voyage to Australia.[13] Unlike the conditions on the *Dunera*, the Singapore internees arrived in Australia in relative luxury and on 25 September they were transported by truck and train to the recently constructed Tatura Camp 3. There were two further small deportations from Singapore to Australia in 1941.[14] Table 14.2 provides the breakdown of the ships and their internee passengers.

Table 14.2 Internees Deported from Singapore[15]

Internees from Singapore	Germans				Italians				Total
	Men	Women	<16	Total	Men	Women	<16	Total	
RMS *Queen Mary*	133	68	29	230	24	11	10	45	275
MS *Boissevain*	1	1		2	1	1	2	4	6
SS *Rangitikei*	12			12					12
Born in internment			10	10			8	8	18
Singapore totals	146	69	39	254	25	12	20	57	311

Table 14.3 Internees Deported from Palestine to Australia[16]

Internees from Palestine	Germans				Italians				Total
	Men	Women	<16	Total	Men	Women	<16	Total	
RMS *Queen Elizabeth*	239	189	235	663	106	25	19	150	823
Born in internment			43	43			9	9	52
Palestine totals	239	189	278	706	106	25	28	159	875

Deportations to Australia: Internees from Palestine – RMS *Queen Elizabeth* July 1941

Germans living in British Mandated Palestine in September 1939 included members of the Temple Society, a German religious sect who had broken away from the Lutheran Church in the mid-nineteenth century, and who, in 1869, had established their first settlement at Haifa in the Holy Land. Over the next eighty years they were instrumental in reclaiming and improving the land and were pioneers in establishing settlements in the region, a decade before the first large-scale Jewish Zionist migrants from Russia arrived.[17] This German-speaking community retained their German citizenship, along with strong affiliations and allegiances to their homeland with the youngsters returning to Germany for study, and after 1933, these youngsters enthusiastically embraced Nazism.[18] In August 1939, 249 men from the community answered the call to return to Germany to join the Wehrmacht.[19] When Britain declared war on Germany the following month, the authorities in Palestine moved to intern the German enemy aliens. On 31 July 1941, the authorities deported 663 Germans, mostly Templers, and 150 Italians from Palestine for internment in Australia.[20] Table 14.3 details provides the breakdown of gender and nationality of the internees from Palestine.

Deportations to Australia: German civilians interned in Persia – SS *Rangitikei* September 1941

By the outbreak of war, the Third Reich, through its civilian German expatriate community, had created significant influence and control in Iran having developed substantial trade, with Berlin's share in Iran's foreign trade growing from 8 per cent in 1932–3 to 45 per cent in 1940.[21] There was a thriving and wealthy German community which had the backing of Reza Shah, who wished to counter the imperial ambitions of both the British and the Russian Empires. The community was overtly pro-Nazi and there were a considerable number of 'agents' of the Third Reich living and working in Iran. The situation became increasingly difficult when Germany invaded Russia on 22 June 1941 and on 19 July 1941 the British and Soviet governments sent diplomatic notes to the government of Iran demanding the expulsion of the Germans in Iran.[22]

There were many other strategic reasons why the British and Soviets wanted to occupy Iran, including protecting India from German invasion, protecting the strategic oil fields and controlling the supply routes to Russia.[23] However, the presence of the Germans in Iran was seen as the pretext most acceptable to the international community to justify an invasion.[24] The demands to expel Germans were ignored, and on 25 August, 'Operation Countenance', the joint Anglo-Soviet invasion of Iran commenced, encountering relatively little resistance. German and Italian civilians were rounded up across the country, including merchant seamen who were captured after the night-raid of 24 August 1941 on the Port of Bandar Shahpur, on the Persian Gulf.[25] The British authorities were in contact with Australia as early as 26 August, requesting that the Australians take up to 1,000 internees, including men, women, and children; their request was accepted by telegram on 9 September.[26] Meanwhile, in London, the War Cabinet minuted the following under the heading 'Persia … Internment of Germans':

> The Foreign Secretary added that he had received a message, through the Swiss Government, that the Germans proposed as a reprisal, to seize and intern British subjects from the Channel Islands equivalent in number interned by us in Persia… The War Cabinet took note of this statement.[27]

The German Ambassador in Tehran, Erwin Ettel, negotiated with the British, Soviet and Iranian authorities to resolve the fate of the German civilians in Iran. It was finally decided that the German women, children, embassy officials and men unfit for service could leave for Germany via Turkey, if the single men accepted being interned and sent to the British camps in Basra in neighbouring Iraq.[28] The British took 595 German and Italian internees from Iran to Basra, including six German women who had opted for internment with their husbands, accompanied by four children. On 17 September, those to be repatriated to Germany left Iran via Turkey.[29]

This compromise did not appease Hitler, who immediately ordered the internment of all British subjects in the Channel Islands; however, this was not undertaken until September 1942, when 2,011 British men, women and children were deported to the continent for internment.[30] Once in Basra, the German internees were interrogated by the British before being transferred to the steamer *Rohna*, which then set sail for Bombay, where the Italians and one sick German were disembarked.[31] The remaining Germans were transferred to the SS *Rangitikei*, and sailed for Australia via Singapore, arriving in Adelaide on 19 November 1940. Table 14.4 summarizes the movements of enemy aliens captured in Persia and sent for internment in India and Australia.

Table 14.4 Internees Detained by the British in Iran September 1941[32]

Internees detained by the British in Persia November 1941	German/ other* men	German women & *children	Italian men	Total
Sent to Basra from Iran	506	10	79	595
Died in Basra	-1			-1
Transferred to Palestine	-21			-21
Boarded SS *Rohna* to Bombay	484	10	79	573
Disembarked Bombay	-1		-79	-80
Boarded SS *Rangitikei* to Australia	483	10	0	493
RMS *Queen Elizabeth* to Australia	17			17
Arrived in Australia	500	10	0	510
Transferred to Tatura Camp 3	6	10		16
Transferred to Loveday Camp 10	494			494
Born in internment		2		2
Total in Australia	500	12	0	512

*Includes 18 Hungarians, 2 Czechs, 1 Pole and 1 Belgian

Tatura internment: The third Military District – Prisoner-of-War and internment camps

The area around Tatura was chosen as a major centre for internment and POW camps, to be administered by the Australian third Military District covering Victoria, principally because it was far from the coast and therefore considered secure, with plenty of water provided by the Waranga Reservoir to facilitate ample food production.[33] The area already contained the first temporary camp set up in September 1939 at Dhurringile Mansion. Tatura 1, located on the eastern side of Waranga Reservoir, was Australia's first purpose-built internment camp, opening in January 1941, with Camps 2 and 3 opening in early September 1940 and Camp 4 in May 1941. Camps 2, 3 and 4 used a similar hexagonal blueprint and were paid for by the British. Across the four camps there were twelve separate compounds, each designed to be self-contained; consequently, the dynamic and style of the camps and compounds altered every time there was a change in occupancy.

The memory and descriptions of the four camps understandably follows the occupants who were resident for the longest. Camp 1 became known as the 'Nazi Camp' for single men, Camp 2 housed single Italian men for the majority of the war, but it is also known for the *Dunera* internees who resided there from July 1941 until their release in 1942 and 1943. Camp 3 was the family camp, and Camp 4 was used for a variety of German and Italian groups for fifteen months from May 1941 but became known as the 'Japanese Family Camp', as they occupied the camp for the next four to five years. When the German *Dunera* refugee internees left Hay in NSW (Camps 7 and 8) in 1941, they were mostly sent to Tatura Camps 2, 3 and 4 with 400 internees, for whom there was no room at Tatura, sent to Camp Orange, northwest of Sydney, for eight weeks before moving to Tatura. There has been very little effort (until now) to distinguish between Camps 2, 3, and 4 at Tatura. However, since the majority of the internees were in Camp 2, and for the longest period, it very often assumed that when a *Dunera* internee talks about being interned at Tatura, he is talking about Camp 2. A consequence of this is that the memory of the camps has become confused.

The 2018 book *Dunera Lives: A Visual History* prefaces the chapters dedicated to the Tatura Camps with the comment that 'tracing the movements of internees at Tatura can be difficult. In many cases we do not know who was held in which camp at what time'. The subsequent pages of the book have just a handful of references to specific camps.[34] Whilst it is impossible to track every individual internee's trajectory through the Australian internment camps, Table 14.5 below presents, for the first time, the most significant movements of different groups, providing a greater understanding of the changing nature of the camps as their occupancy changed over time.[35]

Tatura: Internment Camp 1

Tatura housed male civilian internees, initially those of German origin resident in Australia at the outbreak of war, and Italians when Italy joined the Axis Alliance in June 1940. The camp opened on 25 January 1940, and internees were initially housed in Compound A in fourteen unlined army huts, with sixteen men to each hut. Over time, the camp expanded with more huts and a second compound. By 1943, conditions improved when the latrines and washrooms were connected to a sewerage plant and proper sanitation was provided.[36]

The internees were left to run their own affairs and held democratic elections for the camp leader. However, a chronicle written by an unidentified internee recounts how members of the Nazi party controlled the hustings using strong-arm tactics to stifle dissent to ensure that their candidate, Dr Haslinger, won.[37] It is not surprising, then, to learn that the camp became known by the authorities as the 'Nazi Camp'.

Compound B was established on the eastern side of the camp when 640 local German internees were brought to Camp 1 from the rest of Australia, along with Category A internees and survivors of the *Arandora Star* who had been brought to Australia on the *Dunera*, and who were transferred from Camp 2 in January 1941.[38] The population of the camp remained relatively unchanged for the next four years until February 1945, when many of the Persian internees were transferred from Loveday Camp.

The camp established their own well-stocked canteen, educational classes and workshops, with gardening being a popular pastime. Café *Wellblech* (corrugated iron) was created early in 1942 with a three-foot-high stone promenade to the entrance, a feature which, although decayed, can still be identified on the original site. On summer nights, an area was reserved for the orchestra, and smartly dressed waiters served black coffee and German cakes to the clientele. Inside the café, the panelled walls were painted with scenes of the Rhine Valley and Berlin, with tables and chairs to accommodate some thirty diners. Behind the counter, the shelves were heavily stocked with preserved foods and delicacies.[39] Photographs of daily life in the camp are reproduced in Figure 14.2.

Table 14.5 Tatura Internment Camps: A Guide to the Use and Occupancy of Each Camp and Compound 1940 to 1947

Tatura Camp 1	Compound A	Compound B
1.40 to release	Pro-Nazi internees arrested from NSW and Victoria at the outbreak of war	
1.41 to release	Pro-Nazi survivors of the *Arandora Star* ex-*Dunera* from Tatura 2 (224)	
1.41 to release	Pro-Nazi internees arrested in other areas of Australia	
2.45 to 1.47	Germans from Persia ex-*Rangitikei* transferred from Loveday camp 2.45	

Tatura Camp 2	Compound A	Compound B
3.9.40 to 1.41	German Nazi ex-*Dunera* and *Arandora Star* (224)	Italians ex-*Dunera* (200)
9.40 to 25.9.40	German Anti-Nazi ex-*Dunera* (125)	
10.40 to 17.5.41	German internees, origin unknown	
19.5.41 to 12.43	*Dunera* internees ex-Hay Camp 7	*Dunera* Internees ex-Hay Camp 8
24.7.41 to 12.43	*Dunera* internees ex-Orange camp	
1944 and 1946	Re-designated as 'Rushworth' POW Camp No. 19	

Tatura Camp 3	Compound A	Compound B	Compound C	Compound D
9.40 to 1.41	Compound empty	Compound empty	Anti-Nazi ex-*Dunera*, some ex-*Arandora Star* (125) and single men ex-*Queen Mary*	German/Italian Families mostly from Singapore ex-*Queen Mary*. Some domestic Australian enemy aliens.
1.41 to 5.41	Compound empty	*Dunera* infirm (ca.100) Ex-Hay Camps 17.1.41		
5.41 to 8.41	*Dunera* (200) ex-Hay Camp 7/8, 5.5.41	*Dunera* Orthodox Group 21.5.41		
9.41 to 1946	Germans and Italians families ex Palestine and Iran predominately Templers from Palestine.			

Tatura Camp 4	Compound A	Compound B	Compound C	Compound D
5.41 to 7.41	German Nazi seamen from Tatura Camp 1	Italians from Tatura Camp 2	*Dunera* (219) Pioneer Corp Volunteers Ex-Hay Camp 8	*Dunera* (196) Pioneer Corp Volunteers Ex-Hay Camp 7
7.41 to 8.42	Various groups transferred from Tatura 3. However, the makeup of the groups occupying each compound is still being researched.			
9.42 to 1946	Japanese family internees			

Key (123) = approximate numbers of internees

| Empty | Anti-Nazi | Anti-Nazi families | Italians |
| Japanese families | Nazi/fascist families | German Nazis | Prisoners of war |

Figure 14.2 'Tatura Camp 1'

Source: Annotated compilation of official photographs c.1943 now in the public domain courtesy Australian War Memorial.

Tatura: Internment Camp 2

Tatura 2 was the first of the camps paid for by the British to open, and in September 1940 the two compounds were occupied with Germans and Italians who had disembarked from the *Dunera* at Melbourne. Within a short time, the Italians demanded to be separated from the Germans and the gates between the two compounds were locked, leaving a mix of pro- and anti-Nazis in the German compound for two weeks until the anti-Nazis were moved to Camp 3.[40] However, Victor Tolaini, one of the Italians who remained in the camp for eighteen months, recalls free movement between the compounds during the day.[41]

The Italians created a Catholic Chapel, *La Nostra Chiesetta a Tatura* (our little church in Tatura) in one of the communal huts. However, this is an excellent example how the character of the camps altered immediately once their occupancy changed, since as soon as the *Dunera* internees arrived from Hay in May 1941 this hut was reutilized as a workshop.[42]

Gunther Sondheim arrived in July 1941 from Camp Orange, and in his diary he writes, 'The camp did not look too nice, crowded, and noisy … corrugated iron huts each with twenty-eight bunks, with little space in-between … the lavatories were horrible'. The two compounds were open to each other during the day, but the gates were locked at 10 pm.[43] In general, the relationship between the guards of the Tatura garrison and the internees was very good. There was a considerable diversity of German and Italian internees held across the Tatura camps, with both pro- and anti-Nazi sympathies; however the camp regulations were the same for each camp or compound. The *Dunera* internees who arrived in the Tatura camps from Hay in January, May and July 1941 were frustrated at being subjected to up to four roll calls a day, having been used to just one.[44]

Tatura: Internment Camp 3

Tatura Camp 3 was the first camp designed to take family groups and differed from Camp 2 in that the residential huts were divided into twelve rooms, each created to take two adults with their own door to the outside. The camp was intended to take up to 1,000 internees and was subdivided into four compounds, isolated from each other by a track with barbed-wire fences on either side. Although physically separated, the compounds were close enough for communication between them and it was possible to open gates between the compounds so the residents could associate if the authorities saw fit. When the camp first opened in September 1940, the residents in Compound D included the family groups of German and Italians who had been interned domestically within Australia, and these were joined by the *Queen Mary* Singapore families who arrived at the end of the month. At the same time, the anti-Nazi *Dunera* internees transferred from Camp 2 were put in Compound C. Rainer Radok, as part of this group, recalls arriving in Camp 3 on 25 September 1940. He also noted that, two days later, the internees from Singapore arrived in the camp and fifty-six single men joined them in Compound C, with the family groups put in the adjacent Compound

D. Radok celebrated the 'new' blood, which he recalled included a jazz band and other musicians, a dentist and two doctors.[45]

The *Dunera* group included survivors of the *Arandora Star*, and on 2 July 1941, the first anniversary of the tragedy, the internees dedicated a memorial to those who had died, carved out of local stone by internee artist Robert Braun. Fellow internee Leonhard Adam produced a watercolour of the memorial, which depicted a giant wave.[46] In 1947, once the camp closed, the land reverted to its original owner and the memorial was destroyed. However, funds were raised to create a replica memorial sculpted by Jason Huntley, which was placed at the entrance to the Tatura Wartime Camps Museum and was unveiled 7 May 2017 by 94-year-old Bern Brent (a former *Dunera* internee) who had witnessed the dedication of the original, seventy-six years earlier. The new memorial was dedicated to the internees who lost their lives not only on the SS *Arandora Star* but also those internees who perished returning to the United Kingdom when their ships, the MV *Abosso* and SS *Waroonga*, were torpedoed in 1942 and 1943.[47] The new memorial and plaque are illustrated in Figure 14.3 along with a watercolour by Leonard Adam of the original.[48]

One anecdote recounted by Ludwig Baruch in his memoirs was that he and a few other communist tailors set up a business in the camp which the Australian guards would utilize to alter their ill-fitting army uniforms. However, when they only offered to pay for the work in camp currency, their uniforms were held to ransom until they agreed to pay for them in Australian currency, which was illegal within the camp. It is interesting to note that this group then donated £32 (equivalent to over £1,500 today) to support the war effort, not for the British or Australians, but for the Russians![49]

Compounds A and B were not utilized until 1941, when transfers were made of groups of *Dunera* internees from Hay in January and May 1941.[50] In August 1941, the single men were moved to other camps to make way for the families of Germans and Italians from Iran and Palestine, including over 500 Templers. They were placed in Compounds A, B and C and, and being predominately pro-Nazi/fascist, they requested and were granted permission to amalgamate the three compounds with free access between them. The original family groups in Compound D were unaffected and still contained a troubled mix of mainly Jewish refugees, Italian families from Singapore plus the Germans and Italian families arrested in Australia early in the war, some of whom were pro-Nazi. In Compounds A to C there were a few anti-Nazi families, including some Jews in mixed marriages who, unsurprisingly, were ostracized by the pro-Nazi majority and were not allowed to join the camp entertainments, which included performances of Shakespeare and Wagner, and puppet shows by the Italians.[51]

The Nazi Youth in the Compounds A to C held celebrations, especially around the equinox and solstices, and would march up and down the camp singing nationalist and Nazi songs. On one such occasion on 29 September 1941, they paraded in front of the boundary of Compound D, and Waldemar Weber, a pro-Nazi occupant in the Compound D, raised a Nazi salute and shouted, 'Bravo, Bravo'. A riot ensued with the Jewish occupants attacking Weber while an occupant of Compound C tried to scale the fence to come to his aid. Warning shots were fired by the guards to regain control. From the official report, it is apparent that the commandant of the camp, Lieutenant-Colonel Tackaberry, and his deputy, Major Sproat, turned a blind eye to these Nazi provocations and no action was taken against Weber, while another internee, Tilly Heimann, who had been abusive to Weber's wife, was gaoled in the punishment cell. Ultimately, Heimann was released and twenty-seven pro-Nazis, including the Webers, were removed from Compound D.[52]

In 1942, most of the male Jewish Internees from Singapore were, if fit, recruited to labour schemes in Australia, whilst the unfit men, women and children were released in Australia. The vast majority of the Templer internees remained interned in Camp 3 until they were released in Australia after the war. Since the single-male *Dunera* internees occupied only part of the camp for a few months in 1941, Camp 3 is best remembered and is generally described as the 'family camp'.

Tatura: Internment Camp 4

This camp was built just a mile from Camp 3, utilizing internee labour from Camp 3, and was on higher ground with views of the Warranga Basin reservoir. In almost all respects it was similar to the design of Camp 3, with four compounds and huts containing rooms designed for married couples/families. It opened in May 1941, with Compounds A and B accepting the Germans and Italians from Camp 2. Compounds C and D were occupied between 19 May and 21 August 1941 by *Dunera* internees from Hay Camps 7 and 8, respectively, who had elected to return to the United Kingdom to join the Pioneer Corps and were awaiting suitable transport.[53] When this did not materialize, they were shunted to Loveday Camp 10 to make room for transfers from Camp 3 of *Dunera* internees who were, in their turn, making room for the family groups from Persia and Palestine. In January 1943, the entire camp was prepared for Japanese families interned in Australia or its territories who took up residence for the remainder of the war. By this time, most of the *Dunera* internees had been either returned to the United Kingdom, emigrated, or joined the Australian Labour Battalion, or been released in Australia with those who remained in internment being transferred to Camp 2. The camp is best remembered as the Japanese Family Camp.

The legacy and heritage of the Tatura internment camps

The greatest legacy of the deportation of civilian internees to Australia by the British has been the unintended migration to Australia of a significant number of Germans, Austrians and Italians. From the four transports bringing some 4,200 internees to Australia, nearly 50 per cent remained, and of these about half were refugees from Nazi oppression, with the remainder made up of Italians, Templers from Palestine and German nationalists from Iran.[54] The Templers' community in Australia was further bolstered by the emigration of the remaining Templers from Palestine in the period up to 1948; today there are about 1,300 Templers in Australia and just 700 in Germany.[55]

After the camps closed, the land was either sold or reverted to the original owners; consequently there is no public access today. In the camps themselves, only the concrete footings of the more permanent buildings such as guard houses and shower blocks remain. Tatura Camp 1 has the most visible remains, where some of the structures that the internees created to landscape their environment, such as garden walls and ornamental ponds, still exist.[56] Tatura Camps 2 to 4 were all built as temporary structures and the buildings were sold and transported to new locations around the Shepparton area so there is little or nothing on the original sites to record their wartime usage. Only on the site of Camp 1, which was built as a more permanent army-style camp, are there visible signs of the original camp. These archaeological remains are emotive symbols of internment; however, more can be learned from the surviving art, ephemera and testimony left by the internees than the scant remains of the buildings.

Husband and wife team, Lurline and Arthur Knee, were founding members of the Tatura and District Historical Society in 1984 and helped establish the Tatura Irrigation and Wartime Camps Museum which now houses a collection of over 1,800 artefacts from the diverse groups held in the camps. The museum was recognized by Victoria Heritage Council in 2017 as being of 'cultural heritage significance'; the couple themselves received the Heritage Council of Victoria award for outstanding volunteer service to heritage.[57] They have published two books incorporating their accumulated knowledge: *Marched In* and *The Nazi Camp*.[58] In 2020, the Museum was significantly enlarged and extended and a large mural was added to the new exterior wall. The artwork transitions from a monochrome watchtower and bank of accommodation huts behind barbed wire to a colourful depiction of a family internment hut surrounded by well-tended gardens, with the tower of Dhurringile Mansion appearing on the horizon above the gum trees. There is also a family of internees and a nurse from the camp hospital, and on close inspection, you can see a POW appearing from an escape tunnel. Completing the work is one of the specially minted internment camp tokens which were used as currency within internment and POW camps in both Australia and New Zealand from February 1943 (Figure 14.3). In May 2021, the mural won an award for 'Interpretive Signage' from the Greater Shepparton Cultural Heritage organization.

Additionally, the Australian War Memorial in Canberra, a museum and records collection, holds over 500 contemporary official photographs of the camps including daily life in Camp 1 taken in 1943 (Figure 14.2).[59] In 1956, the Australian War Graves Commission constructed the official German War Cemetery at Tatura and the interred remains of forty-eight internees and eleven POWs from the Second World War who were relocated to the site from other parts of Australia.[60] In 1966, 128 Italians who died while imprisoned around Australia were re-interred in the Italian Ossario Crypt at Murchison.[61] For locations in relation to the camps, see Figure 14.1.

The artistic record is an obvious and particularly impactful legacy left to us by those who recorded their experiences in drawings, paintings, sculptures, poems and music, although due to their high visual and emotional impact, the artistic internees are often disproportionately represented in the historical record. The arts played an important role in the daily life of the camps, keeping the spirits of the internees high in the face of their indefinite confinement. Most of the art that survives from the internment camps has a positive and amusing reflection on internment. Cartoon artists Fritz Lowenstein (Fred Lowen) and Fritz (Fred) Schonbach created many humorous cartoons which they recreated and sold as souvenirs to their fellow inmates. These often made light of the conditions and treatment they had received on the *Dunera*.[62] The musical and theatrical reviews performed by the internees were also recorded with the creation of painted or printed souvenir tickets, invitations and programmes. Of note are those produced by Emil Whittenberg, Paul Glass, Hein Heckroth and Alfred Landauer.[63] The original 1929 artistic director of the Bauhaus, Ludwig Hirschfeld-Mack, along with Alfred Landauer, was almost certainly responsible for introducing woodcut printing to other internees. This favourite Bauhaus technique was good for reproducing large numbers of prints and was used to create souvenir prints of the camps and camp life as well as theatrical programmes, Christmas cards and the like.[64]

The selected memory and interpretation of the history of the Tatura internment camps

The memory of the camps is very much segmented by the various groups involved and the circumstances leading to their internment; in consequence, each narrative is often biased to each groups' perspective. As the number of survivors diminish, any commentaries inevitably move to individuals from the second and third generations, who tend to view their forebears' experiences in isolation without reference to the wider picture of internment in the global conflict. This results in their predisposition to view the actions of the British and Australian authorities far more harshly than their forebears. Fortunately, there are many contemporary diaries and oral histories, created by the internees themselves, in archives around the world which can be studied to produce a balanced view.[65]

The *Dunera* Association has represented the *Dunera* and *Queen Mary* refugees and their descendants since the early 1980s and publishes regular newsletters, organizes reunions and events and maintains a website and Facebook group.[66] Most of the Jewish refugees settled in and around Melbourne, where they were affectionately described as 'the *Dunera* Boys'. Such has been their impact on Australian life, particularly in academic and artistic circles, that the *Dunera* has often been described as the largest boatload of talent ever to have arrived on Australia's shores. Their story and lives have been chronicled with a somewhat sensationalized TV mini-series and film.[67] Bern Brent is one of the very few surviving *Dunera* Boys (he celebrated his 100th birthday on 17 December 2022) and has a truly remarkable memory of the events from over eighty years ago and orates his knowledge in a considered and impartial way. In a recorded interview in 2019, he was scathing of the *Dunera* Boys mini-series and film, which he described as 'frightful' and 'ridiculous', complaining about the exaggerated portrayal of mistreatment aboard the *Dunera*. He blames this view on a 'vocal minority' and the fact that the media is only interested in 'bad news' because it sells.[68] Countless books have been written on the *Dunera* of which *Dunera Lives, Part 1: 'A Visual History'* and *Dunera Lives, Part 2: 'Profiles'* are the latest significant contributions.[69] In 2021, a heritage exhibition was established at Jones Warf in Sydney, which commemorated the arrival of the boat in Sydney on 6 September 1940, and included a model of the *Dunera* made by Tom Wolf, the son-in-law of a *Dunera* Boy which is shown as part of Figure 14.3.

The Italians, survivors of the *Arandora Star*, find their voice through Italian family history groups and the *Arandora Star* Facebook Group.[70] The deportation of internees from Palestine will always be a part of the Templer community's heritage and they maintain their own website.[71] Until recently the internees from Persia had virtually no representation. However, since August 2019, Pedram Khosrenejad, an Iranian academic, who is currently adjunct professor at Western Sydney University, has created a website called 'German Civilians of Persia', which contains the history of German influence in Persia and the personal memoirs and ephemera from internees and their families.[72]

The Australian *Dunera* internees' experiences are far better remembered and documented compared with those who remained in the United Kingdom or those deported to Canada. Although many of the official records regarding internment and internees were previously supressed, these are now either becoming available either through the expiration of embargos or through freedom of information requests. When reviewing the security service files at the National Archives in the United Kingdom or in Australia, it is now possible to see why the authorities believed mass internment was justified in the short term to remove the threat posed by a small minority of suspect individuals.[73] The deportation and shipment of internees around the globe was expensive in manpower and resources, and repatriation back to the United Kingdom was expensive and dangerous. Since the Australian government refused to countenance release in Australia, many of the refugee internees who could not or did not wish to return to the United Kingdom were left in internment until there was a change of Australian government at the end of 1941. In February 1942, some of the internees were permitted to leave the internment camps to pick fruit on farms and later to enlist in the Australian Labour Battalion; the older internees not fit enough to do this work were permitted to be released in Australia. In 1943, the Italians were permitted to join the Civilian Alien Corps. Many of these internees who served in the armed forces chose to remain in Australia.

Whilst the memory and heritage of these internees are well represented in Australia, this is not the case in the United Kingdom. In Australia the internees became big fish in smaller ponds. They were a significant part of the Australian Jewish communities, had disproportionate influence on Australian academic and cultural life and were, in general, concentrated in Melbourne and Sydney. Those in the United Kingdom, on the other hand, were geographically more dispersed and constituted a much smaller proportion of the Jewish immigrant population. Many of those in the United Kingdom joined the Pioneer Corps and were later able to join combat units including the special forces, facilitated by their fluency in German which also gave rise to important roles as translators at the Nuremberg Trials. Consequently, many chose to celebrate their important military careers rather than mark the trials and tribulations of internment.[74]

The true legacy of this episode of internment belongs to the individuals and groups who were interned; their lives were disrupted and transformed, not only by actions of the Third Reich and the ensuing global conflict, but also by the policies of both the British, who sent them to Australia from around the world, and the Australian authorities who, after initial reluctance, accepted many of them as valued citizens.

Above: The new mural outside the Tatura Wartime Camps Museum, Middle: The new Arandora Star Memorial with the plaque unveiled by Bern Brent and detail from the Leonhard Adam watercolour of the original in camp three in 1940. Below; New model of HMT *Dunera* by Tom Wolf on display at the Jones Wharf Tribute Museum, Sydney.

Figure 14.3 Tatura Irrigation and Wartime Camps Museum; Mural and *Arandora Star* Memorial and HMT *Dunera* Model

Source: Compilation of images by Alan Morgenroth. Leonard Adams Arandora Star memorial watercolour reproduced courtesy of Mary-Clare Adams.

Notes

Archival abbreviations used in this chapter
The UK National Archives, Kew = TNA
The Australian National Archives = NAA
Imperial War Museum (United Kingdom) = IWM
Manx National Archives = MNA
Victoria Heritage Determination = VHD
United States Holocaust Memorial Museum = USHMM

1. War Cabinet Minutes April 29, 1940. Control of aliens, memorandum by the Home Secretary John Anderson. TNA, CAB 67\6\15.
2. War Cabinet Minutes May 11, 1940. Item 4. Invasion of Britain, Internment of enemy aliens in the Eastern Counties. TNA, CAB67\6\15.
3. War Cabinet Minutes May 24, 1940, Item 11. Invasion of Britain, Security measures: control of aliens. TNA CAB 65\7\32.
4. Rachel Pistol, 'Remembering the Internment of "Enemy Aliens" During the Second World War and the Isle of Man, and in Australia and Canada', in *The Jews, the Holocaust, and the Public: The Legacies of David Cesarani*, ed. Larissa Allwork and Rachel Pistol (London: Palgrave Macmillan, 2019), 96.
5. 2,673 Category A men were deported overseas (TNA, PREM 3/49) plus 175 Category A women. 17,000 = 2,850 Category A, 4,000–5,000 East Coast, 3000 'B' Men 3,500 Women and Children, 3,700 Italians. Mooragh Camp opened w/e 28 May, Onchan and Central Promenade Camps w/e 15 June 1940. (MNA MS 06472). Rushen Camp 29 May 1940. Doreen Moule et al., *Friend or Foe: The Fascinating Story of Women's Internment during WWII in Port Erin & Port St Mary, Isle of Man* (Rushen, Isle of man: Rushen Heritage Trust. 2018) 23.
6. Maria Serena Balestracci, *Arandora Star: From Oblivion to Memory*, 3rd ed. (Parma, Italy: Fondazione Monteparma, 2020). 230.
7. Alan Morgenroth, database analysis of *Dunera* embarkation lists based on TNA HO 215/1 and Home Office File on Discrepancies HO 215/260 cross referenced with TNA of Australia series MP1103/1 and MP1103/2 Internee Records.
8. 'Steamship "*Dunera*" (Internees' Claims) – Tuesday 5 August 1941 – Hansard – UK Parliament', https://hansard.parliament.uk/Commons/1941-08-05/debates/32569 a92-1f6d-4f61-ab74-892aa45659e1/SteamshipDunera(InterneesClaims)highlight=dun era+court+martial (accessed 5 August 2021).
9. Alan Morgenroth, database analysis of *Dunera* embarkation lists: 2,543 is the total number of internee records prefixed with 'E' (for England), 1 died before landing.
10. Seumas Spark cited TNA CO 323/1799/1 during his presentation as part of a webinar *The Queen Mary 80th Anniversary of Arrival in Australia – Webinar Recording*, 2020, https://www.youtube.com/watch?v=LCBY4ghP6co (accessed 5 August 2021).
11. Ibid.
12. Ibid.
13. Alan Morgenroth, database created from Internee Records NAA series MP1103.
14. Ibid.
15. Ibid., 301 is the total number of internee records prefixed with 'Z' (for Singapore).
16. Ibid., 875 is the total number of internee records prefixed with 'P' (for Palestine).

17. Raffi Berg, 'The Templers: German Settlers Who Left Their Mark on Palestine', *BBC News*, 12 July 2013, https://www.bbc.com/news/magazine-22276494 (accessed 5 August 2021).
18. Ibid.
19. Ibid.
20. Alan Morgenroth, database created from Internee Records NAA series MP1103.
21. George Lenczowski, ed., Iran Under the Pahlavis (Stanford: Hoover Institution Press, 1978) cited by Nikolay A. Kozhanov, 'The Pretexts and Reasons for the Allied Invasion of Iran in 1941', *Iranian Studies* 45/4 (2012), 489.
22. F. Eshraghi, 'Anglo-Soviet Occupation of Iran in August 1941', *Middle Eastern Studies* 20/1 (1984): 39.
23. Ibid., 49.
24. Ibid.
25. Five German and three Italian merchantmen were captured in 'Operation Bishop' spearheaded by the Australian Navy 'Naval-History.Net', http://www.naval-history.net/xDKWW2-4108-35AUG02.htm (accessed 22 June 2021).
26. 'Internees from Iran' NAA MP508/1, 255/702/1547 (1941): 136.
27. 'War Cabinet Minutes 11 September 1941 TNA, CAB 65/19/28. Item 6 Internment of Germans.
28. Pedram Khosrenejad, 'German Civilians of Iran WWII', https://www.german-civilians-of-persia-wwii.com (accessed 14 May 2021).
29. Ibid.
30. Deportation lists in TNA, WO 311/13.
31. 'Internees from Iran' NAA MP508/1, 255/702/1547 (1941), 49–66.
32. 'Internees from Iran – Correspondence from British Military in Iran to Australia, NAA A433 1945/2/6034 and MP1103 Records, 1941, and Alan Morgenroth, database created from internee records NAA series MP1103: 512 is the total number of internee records prefixed with 'R' (for Iran).
33. Lurline Knee and Arthur Knee, *The Nazi Camp: The Story of a WW2 Internment Camp at Tatura, Victoria*, 2019, 15–16.
34. Ken Inglis, Seumas Spark, and Jay Winter, *Dunera Lives: A Visual History* (Clayton, Victoria: Monash University Publishing, 2018), 195–306.
35. There are no official records of the occupancy of individual camps or compounds at Tatura. Table 14.5 has been pieced together using a wide variety of sources including Internees' record cards NAA MP1103/1, 'Internees from Iran' Memo from Secretary Military Board to Southern Command, and instructions to reorganize camps at Loveday and Tatura to accept new arrivals from Iran. NAA MP 508/1 255/702/1547 16 September 1940, 130–1. Diaries, memoirs and personal papers have been invaluable including those of Kurt Lewinski, Leonhard Adam, Gunther Sondheim, Peter Lowensberg, Victor Tolaini, Hans Rosenbluth and Kurt Morgenroth.
36. Knee and Knee, *The Nazi Camp*.
37. Chronicle found after the war in a Sydney Hotel cited in Knee and Knee, *The Nazi Camp*, 27.
38. Ludwig Baruch, 'Lou Baruch – Reminiscences' family papers.
39. 'Recommendation of the Executive Director and assessment of cultural heritage significance under Part 3 of the Heritage', http://heritagecouncil.vic.gov.au/wp-content/uploads/2018/07/ED-RECOMMENDATION-MURCHISON-POW-CAMP-INCLUDE.pdf (accessed 5 August 2021).

40. Rainer Radok, 'Before and after the Reichskristallnacht: The History of a Königsberg Family' (Radok, Rainer, 1999), http://mpec.sc.mahidol.ac.th/radok/life/ECONTE NTS.HTM?fbclid=IwAR2Bahap53RYHsbI2Dq80ffQlsKKikh-vf-R__iF1Y4NOEbn ZGXfeTXER_A (accessed 5 August 2021).
41. Victor Tolaini, 'Private Papers of V Tolaini' (1940 to 1945), Manuscripts, 11298 Imperial War Museum.
42. Christopher Wolkenstein, 'Private Papers of Christopher Wolkenstein' (1940 to 1941), Family Archive.
43. Gunther Sondheim, 'The Diaries of Gunther (Mike) Sondheim Part 3 Tatura. 24 July 1941 to 7 March 1942. P187-231', Tatura, Victoria: Tatura War Camps Museum, n.d..
44. Ibid
45. Radok, Königsberg Family.
46. *Leonhard Adam: From the Spree to the Yarra Aquarelles 1911–1955* (Tatura, Victoria: Tatura Historical Society, 1996), 23.
47. '(5) Tatura Museum – Posts | Facebook', 7 May 2017, https://www.facebook.com/permalink.php?story_fbid=1647729051921166&id=398091246884959 (accessed 5 August 2021).
48. '(5) Tatura Museum – Posts | Facebook'.
49. Ludwig (Lou) Baruch 'Reminiscences' Private papers
50. Kurt Lewinski, '19 Wasted Months: Diary and notes of my internment', n.d., USHMM. He arrived at Tatura 5 May 1941.
51. Samuel Koehne, 'A Cultural Battlefront in the Total War: Theatre in Australian Internment Camps', *Terror, War, Tradition: Studies in European History*, https://www.academia.edu/1646227/A_Cultural_Battlefront_in_the_Total_War_Theatre_in_Australian_Internment_Camps (accessed 7 April 2021).
52. Samuel Koehne, '"Disturbance in D Compound": The Question of Control in Australian Internment Camps During World War II', *Melbourne Historical Journal* 34 (2006), 71–86.
53. Private family papers of Hans Rosenbluth (Caryl Ross) and Kurt Morgenroth.
54. Author estimates, from United Kingdom 800, from Singapore 300, from Palestine, 600, and from Iran 300.
55. 'Temple Society Australia Heritage', https://www.templesociety.org.au/heritage.html (accessed 15 May 2021).
56. 'VHD Tatura Camp No.1', https://vhd.heritagecouncil.vic.gov.au/places/12699 https://heritagecouncil.vic.gov.au/2017/04/heritage-volunteer-award-2/ (accessed 5 August 2021).
57. 'VHD 'Tatura World War II Internment and POW Camps Collection' (Victoria Heritage Council, 3 August 2017).
58. Lurline, Knee and Arthur Knee, *Marched In: Seven Internment and Prisoner of War Camps in the Tatura Area during World War 2* (2008); Knee and Knee, *The Nazi Camp*.
59. 'Australian War Memorial', https://www.awm.gov.au/search (accessed 5 August 2021).
60. 'Tatura World War II Internment and POW Camps Collection'. Tatura German War Cemetery, heritagecouncil.vic.gov.au (accessed 8 September 2021).
61. Knee and Knee, *Marched In*, 152.
62. Alan Morgenroth, 'The souvenir artworks of Hay Internment Camps 7 and 8'. Paper presented to the Insiders Outsiders/Monash University Antipodean Connections Conference. 1 October 2021, https://www.youtube.com/watch?v=3rMyABfYiXI (accessed 23 January 2023). Total duration 3hr 38min Extract starts at 1hr 57min duration 26min.

63. Ibid.
64. Alan Morgenroth, unpublished research on the woodcut prints of Hay and Tatura internment camps including Ludwig Hirschfeld-Mack collection National Gallery of Australia and the Alfred Landauer artworks in the Landauer family archive.
65. Including National Library of Australia, IWM London, Jewish Museum of Australia, Jewish Museum Melbourne, Wiener Holocaust Library London and the United States Holocaust Memorial Museum.
66. 'Friends of the Dunera Boys', https://www.facebook.com/groups/281170982833; 'Dunera News' – First edition May 1984. Volume 110 June 2021; 'Dunera Association' available online https://www.duneraassociation.com (accessed 5 August 2021).
67. 'The Dunera Boys' TV Mini-series and Film. Written and directed by Ben Lewin, 1985.
68. 'Interviewing Bern Brent', https://www.dunerastories.monash.edu/dunera-stories/112-interviewing-bern-brent.html (accessed 19 May 2021).
69. Inglis, Spark and Winter, *Dunera Lives. A Visual History* and Ken Inglis et al., *Dunera Lives. Profiles* (Melbourne: Monash University Publishing, 2020).
70. 'Anglo Italian Family History Society', https://www.facebook.com/groups/AncestralChimes/?multi_permalinks=4742309782450852; 'Arandora Star Facebook Group', https://www.facebook.com/groups/67868197405/?multi_permalinks=10158196515432406 (accessed 5 August 2021).
71. 'Temple Society Australia, https://www.templesociety.org.au/about-temple-society.html (accessed 5 August 2021).
72. 'German Civilians of Iran WWII', Germansinpersia, https://www.german-civilians-of-persia-wwii.com (accessed 5 August 2021).
73. TNA Security Service Files Series FV and NAA Series A367, correspondence files of Commonwealth Investigation Service. 1939 to 1945.
74. Publications on the Pioneer Corps: *The King's Own Enemy Aliens Leighton Langer*, 2006 and *The King's Most Loyal Enemy Aliens Helen Fry*, 2008.

Bibliography

Adam, Mary-Clare. *Leonhard Adam: From the Spree to the Yarra Aquarelles 1911–1955*. Tatura, Victoria: Tatura Historical Society, 1996.

Balestracci, Maria Serena. *Arandora Star: From Oblivion to Memory* (3rd edn). Parma, Italy: Fondazione Monteparma, 2020.

Eshraghi, F. 'Anglo-Soviet Occupation of Iran in August 1941'. *Middle Eastern Studies* 20, no. 1 (1984): 27–52.

Inglis, Ken, Bill Gammage, Seumas Spark, Jay Winter and Carol Bunyan. *Dunera Lives. Profiles*. Melbourne: Monash University Publishing, 2020.

Inglis, Ken, Seumas Spark, and Jay Winter. *Dunera Lives: A Visual History*. Clayton, Victoria: Monash University Publishing, 2018.

Knee, Lurine, and Arthur Knee. *Marched In: Seven Internment and Prisoner of War Camps in the Tatura Area during World War 2*. Tatura, Victoria: Lurine and Arthur Knee, 2008.

Knee, Lurine, and Arthur Knee. *The Nazi Camp: The Story of a WW2 Internment Camp at Tatura, Victoria*. Tatura, Victoria: Lurine and Arthur Knee, 2019.

Koehne, Samuel. 'A Cultural Battlefront in the Total War: Theatre in Australian Internment Camps'. *Terror, War, Tradition: Studies in European History*. https://www.academia.edu/1646227/A_Cultural_Battlefront_in_the_Total_War_Theatre_in_Australian_Internment_Camps (accessed 7 April 2021).

Koehne, Samuel. ' "Disturbance in D Compound": The Question of Control in Australian Internment Camps During World War II'. *Melbourne Historical Journal* 34 (1 November 2006): 71–86.

Kozhanov, Nikolay A. 'The Pretexts and Reasons for the Allied Invasion of Iran in 1941'. *Iranian Studies* 45, no. 4 (2012): 479–97.

Moule, Doreen, Pamela Crowe, Alison Graham, David Wertheim, Sandra Davidson, Jane Saywell and Hugh Davidson. *Friend or Foe: The Fascinating Story of Women's Internment during WWII in Port Erin & Port St Mary, Isle of Man*. Rushen, Isle of man: Rushen Heritage Trust, 2018.

Pistol, Rachel. 'Remembering the Internment of "Enemy Aliens" During the Second World War and the Isle of Man, and in Australia and Canada'. In *The Jews, the Holocaust, and the Public: The Legacies of David Cesarani*, edited by Larissa Allwork and Pistol, Rachel, 93–114. London: Palgrave Macmillan, 2019.

Sondheim, Gunther. 'The Diaries of Gunther (Mike) Sondheim Part 3 Tatura. 24 July 1941 to 7 March 1942. P187-231'. Tatura, Victoria: Tatura War Camps Museum, n.d.

Wolkenstein, Christopher. 'Private Papers of Christopher Wolkenstein', Family Archive, n.d.

15

Grass growing is like forgetting: A case study of the heritage of the Second World War–internment camp B-70 New Brunswick, Canada

Todd E. Caissie

Site of Former Internment Camp B-70 (Ripples Internment Camp) 1940–1945. Sponsored by the New Brunswick Internment Camp Committee.[1]

These are the words printed on a large sign in Ripples, New Brunswick (NB), at the edge of the forest alongside Canadian Highway 10 between the small village of Minto and the provincial capital city of Fredericton.[2] Adjacent to the sign stands the remains of the superstructure base of a water tower (Figure 15.1). These two objects are the only physical markers left to indicate this is the original site of Second World War–internment camp B-70. That sign, however, was not erected until 1995, roughly fifty years after the end of the war and closure of the internment camp. Prior to that marker, there were no on-site visual indicators that this location once served as a former internment camp. For generations, the story behind this isolate solitary concrete cube frame along the side of the road was mostly forgotten.[3]

This chapter focuses on the memory, memorialization and heritage of camp B-70 from its closure to the present time, a span of roughly seventy-five years. My analysis of camp B-70's history frames an examination of how Canada has negotiated its difficult heritage as well as how visitors to the original site, and the New Brunswick Internment Camp Museum (NBICM), experience that heritage today. Additionally, I analyse how aspects of the past have been addressed and sometimes ignored both nationally and locally. The chapter title, 'Grass Growing is Like Forgetting', derives from a quote by a foreign visitor to the Zeppelin building in front of the Hitler podium in Nuremberg Germany who, while pointing to weeds 'flourishing' in the cracks of the building, said he felt the site was being neglected 'because the Germans do not want to remember it'.[4] At the abandoned site of camp B-70 in Ripples, NB, the grass also grew, and grew, until the entire fifty-two acres of internment camp was swallowed by forest. Although the history associated with Nuremberg and Hitler is more egregious, in both instances

Figure 15.1 Photograph of the superstructure base of the water tower next to the sign indicating location of the original camp.

Source: Image © Todd Caissie.

nations wished to forget, marginalize or ignore shameful or negative aspects of their past.

The history of the NB internment camp can be aptly described as being associated with difficult heritage as well as negative heritage. Sharon MacDonald defines difficult heritage as 'a past recognised as meaningful in the present but that is also contested and awkward for public reconciliation with a positive self-affirming contemporary identity'.[5] Lynn Meskell coined the term 'negative heritage' to refer to places that become repositories of traumatic memory in the collective imaginary.[6] Negative cultural heritage sites are described as places that may be interpreted by a group as commemorating conflict, trauma and disaster.[7] The terms 'difficult heritage' and 'negative heritage' may sometimes overlap and are not mutually exclusive and both can both apply to the NB internment camp. For the purposes of this chapter, however, to avoid confusion, I use 'difficult heritage', in part because my research springs from Macdonald's view that by looking at difficult heritage, rather than at 'that which can be celebrated or at least comfortably acknowledged' as part of a nation's valued history, unsettled assumptions and constructed narrative selection can be considered within the discourse of public representation and reception.[8]

The case study begins with a brief historical overview of internment camp B-70, the only such camp located in the Maritime Provinces (New Brunswick, Nova Scotia, Prince Edward Island), and its interned population, followed by an examination of the physical state of the site over the past seventy-five years and related heritage commemoration or preservation actions, including the formation of a dedicated museum in the nearby village of Minto. The challenge for the NBCIM in some ways mirror those of Nuremberg, as well as other former prisoner-of-war (POW) camps, in that both memorialize a place imbued with difficult heritage. In Canada's example, 'grass growing' was certainly deliberate and intentional.[9] Outside of people directly impacted by internment, Canadian Second World War internment was largely excluded from school curricula, and largely forgotten by the public for almost five decades. Moreover, the physical structures of the camp itself were purposefully removed.

By analysing the museum's efforts and examining the life of the site since its abandonment at the end of the war, I frame a discourse on material remains, both *in situ* and removed, with the commemoration and physical marking of difficult heritage spaces. Post-war interventions by various actors include the destruction, relocation and repurposing of material remains, followed by late-twentieth-century preservation efforts, including a museum and a heritage trail adorned with commemorative markers. For the purposes of this chapter, particular emphasis is given to the memory and memorialization of the camp's 711 Phase I internees (1940–1941), mostly German and Austrian Jews, who had previously fled Nazi-occupied territories to Great Britain.[10]

The war and internment

There are various terms used to describe facilities used for incarceration in times of war: prison camp, internment camp, concentration camp, death camp, labour camp, relocation camp and refugee camp, to name a few of the most widely used labels. During the earliest years of the Second World War–internment program, the Canadian government labelled camp B-70 and other camps POW camps, but eventually switched to the less harsh categorization 'internment'. Hegemonic authorities in the United States and Canada have often used 'internment camp' as a euphemistic term to make incarceration of a particular group more acceptable or palatable to the public, that, while technically correct, may evoke a softer reaction towards this difficult heritage.[11]

Being a member of the British Empire, Canada officially entered the Second World War with Britain in September 1939.[12] During the early stages of hostilities, the Canadian government built and operated twenty-six internment camps throughout Canada. Camp populations included an estimated 40,000 dissenters, consisting of Canadian citizens, captured enemy soldiers and roughly 7,000 British transfers, many of whom were Jewish refugees from Nazism to Britain.[13] An estimated 2,284 of the British transfers were refugees from Nazism referred to as 'camp boys' (meaning men under the age of twenty-five), and close to 5,000 were British subjects of Italian descent, among others.[14] Additionally, Canada incarcerated more than 22,000 Japanese Canadians in separate dedicated internment camps.[15]

Camp B-70 in Ripples, NB, was surrounded by five rows of barbed wire and six machine gun towers encircling fifty-two buildings. The entire site covered 23 hectares, including a 6.07 hectare fenced in compound, supporting two phases of activity.[16] The first phase ran from 1940 to 1941 and the second from 1941 to 1945, the year it was closed. Phase I involved the incarceration of 711 prisoners, mostly German and Austrian Jews who had fled Nazi Germany to Britain before British authorities arranged for them to be transported to Canada for incarceration. The Jewish internees, many highly educated, ranged from sixteen to sixty years of age, including lawyers (Dr Adolf Brumberg), dental surgeons (Dr Ernst Bustin) and psychotherapists (Dr Ernst Bien).[17] Of the 711 Phase I prisoners, 175 had British school or university education and 373 held labour permits in Britain, like Viennese Egon Stark, who had come to England as a teenager to work the farms in Hampshire and Essex before he was arrested on May 15 1940 and forced into a detention centre.[18] During Phase II, the government imprisoned 1,200 captured Italian and German merchant marines, along with many Canadians who had spoken out against the war and some deemed to be fascist or Nazi sympathizers.[19] Most of the Canadian citizen–Phase II population were of Italian or German ancestry and categorized as POW Class 2 (non-combatant). Some of these Canadians were members of the Canadian branch of the German Labour Front or members of known fascist organizations, but others were rounded up unjustifiably.[20]

Camp life

Life in camp B-70 had all the trappings of prison. Former prisoner Heribert Poelmann even said their nickname for the camp was 'The Zoo', 'because we were caged, while the animals came out of the forest and looked at us through the surrounding fence'.[21] The fundamental difference between modern prisons and internment or POW camps is, unlike prisons, internment camps regularly detain individuals without a scheduled release date, although both employ forced labour. During incarceration, prisoners participated in various types of labour, both forced and voluntary. The camp plan identifies several buildings associated with penal labour including a trades hut, a recreation hut as well as a detention hut used to punish prisoners who refused to work.[22] Canada's history of state-enforced confinement is deeply intertwined with issues of work and labour and all Canadian Second World War–internment camps had some variety of labour programs which operated according to the terms of the Geneva Convention.[23] This information, however, does not indicate how different types of labour co-existed within the microcosm of these camps. The work landscape within the camp was, in fact, nuanced and complex.

For internees, work was at times forced and at times voluntary, internal and external, paid and non-paid, physical and cerebral, hobby and commercial. For example, they were required to work without pay to provide for basic camp functions such as administration, cleaning and cooking, but any labour beyond camp maintenance was, in a certain sense, 'voluntary' in that they had some choice of assignment, and were paid, usually, at a daily rate of twenty cents.[24] The prisoners worked five and a half days a week with only Saturday afternoons and Sundays off.

The choice for internees to select working assignments was limited, but it appears there was some choice. Trade work for tailors, cobblers and barbers was organized, but anyone without a trade would most likely end up chopping wood out in the forest for eight hours a day, often during brutal Canadian winters.[25] In all of Canada's Second World War–internment camps, craft workshops were important to the functioning of the camps, the maintenance of discipline and the mental health of the internees. Some jobs were relatively easy, such as sweeping, cooking and managing the canteen, while other jobs were physically difficult, such as wood cutting and road repair, which often exposed prisoners to harsh NB winters.[26] Prisoners also sold or bartered various arts and crafts they created in their free time to stave off boredom and to obtain money.

Prisoners on a work crew were given an axe to cut firewood on the 22,500 acres woodland belonging to the Acadia Research Forest that surrounded the camp. From this effort, they transported over 2,000 cords of wood a year to feed the camp's 100 large wood-burning stoves.[27] Even though most of the Jewish refugees had never wielded an axe before, each internee was still expected to cut one cord of wood per day.[28] According to Forestry Officer Byron C. Wile, the majority of prisoners at camp B-70 did not take to forestry work. Wile noted that they worked with 'great inefficiency, being untrained, unwilling, and poorly equipped'.[29] One example of an internee's negative memories of incarceration in Ripples is a vivid oral history by former internee Gerry Fry. Fry recalls dreading woodcutting duty and that, during one particularly brutal winter's day, he concocted a plan to attempt to evade the freezing outdoor work duty. His plan was to intentionally cut his foot, only slightly, with his axe in order to be sent to the warm confines of the infirmary. Although he intended to simply nick his foot, Fry miscalculated and accidentally cut his foot so deeply he required two full days in the infirmary (although he still referred to those two days as 'heaven' in the 1995 video interview). Upon recovery, Fry pleaded for indoor work duty, but the only available option, which he accepted, was cleaning the latrines.[30]

Prisoners also planted and tended the gardens, at least in part, to provide fresh ingredients for meals, which the internees prepared themselves. Interestingly, internees commented that initially camp food was intolerable, until the Italian Canadian internees, during Phase II, took over the camp kitchen and started to use fresh ingredients from their own vegetable gardens. According to former prisoner Heribert Poelmann, music was permitted, and he noted at least one hut had a gramophone with 'wonderful records, [and] most symphonies'.[31] Prisoners performed concerts and plays as well. The performances were varied and happened often, from vaudeville-style concerts, piano recitals to cabarets. At least one concert at camp B-70 included a piano, two violins, a viola, a cello and two flutes.[32] For internees, music not only inspired hope and resistance, but it created a sense of collective identity. According to Helmut Kallmann, the concerts were also therapeutic and 'provided eagerly craved spiritual nourishment'.[33] In camp B-70, perhaps the most important labour, aside from cutting wood for heat, involved wood workshops.[34] The museum's collection includes many prisoner woodworks, but arguably the most impressive is the large prisoner-made pine chest. The dark-stained pine chest is carved with intricate decorative patterns and the initials A.M.S. on the center front panel. Robert Saunders, a woods foreman at the Acadia Research Forest, who was, for a time, responsible for supervising work crews of POWs from camp B-70 commissioned the chest from a prisoner for his wife Alicia M. Saunders (A.M.S) as a Christmas present in 1941 or 1942.[35]

A large corpus of these carceral labour accounts can be found in three books devoted exclusively to the history of camp B-70: Ted Jones' two volume, *Both Sides of the Wire* (1988, 1989), and Andrew Theobald's *Dangerous Enemy Sympathizers* (2019).

These personal accounts, combined with official records, diaries and newsletters reveal the place's multivalent levels of states of being, including an environment of peaceful resistance, obedience or, conversely, reluctant acceptance to blatant refusal. As previously mentioned, outside work was often demanding and conducted in harsh weather. According to Theobald, 'Internee leadership initially refused to support outside work. This position, far from unanimous, invariably shifted to reluctant acceptance.'[36] A military entry in late November even noted an 'escort [was] called into compound to deal with a party of Orthodox Jews who had refused [work] duty'.[37] An 8 October 1940 entry in Phase I Jewish-internee Helmut Kallman's diary expresses his sense of helplessness, 'I am with a work party, digging and grading. Forced!'[38] In a later entry, Kallman compared the working conditions to 'like being a slave'.[39] Conversely, Henry Kreisel wrote in his diary that 'I go out to work in the woods. It is beautiful. We are three and work by ourselves without a guard. One almost feels free. Free! Freedom!'[40]

Even though the prisoners were paid for certain labour, Mario Duliani notes that legal tender (paper and coins) was not permitted in camp.[41] Instead the camp operated a system which involved each internee opening an account through the 'Official Accountant', who acted as a sort of bank. In addition to any wages being recorded, prisoners could also receive money from family members which would also be credited to their accounts. Each prisoner, therefore, had a ledger and could request money against this account. In addition, internees could earn money informally by doing camp chores, like laundry, for others.[42] When not on work duty, some prisoners continued their education and read prodigiously.[43] Kallmann, wrote in the *Ex-Internees Newsletter* 2 in 1997 that he inherited the position of Camp B librarian in early 1941, so some form of library or book borrowing program was in place.[44] The Phase I prisoner population included a impressive number of intellectuals who even formed a camp 'school'. The school, headed by Dr Alfons Rosenberg, offered plethora of courses ranging from thermodynamics to art history that were taught by accomplished experts like physicist Dr K.M. Guggenheimer, a former assistant to Albert Einstein.[45] Canada's McGill University in Quebec even sponsored matriculation exams at the camp.[46]

Difficult heritage, negative heritage and marginalized voices

In examining the difficult heritage of camp B-70, sensitivity to alternate conceptions of the past is of paramount importance. I follow Robert Layton's heritage studies article, 'Who Needs the Past? Indigenous Values and Archaeology', which argues that marginalized voices and sensitivity to alternative conceptions of the past – especially those of disenfranchised groups – is both necessary and desirable.[47] Layton's message reinforces the importance of NBICM's mission and collection to Canadian history and carceral history more broadly. Even between prisoners interned at camp B-70 at the same time, the selective nature of historic memory differs, not to mention those between guards and prisoners, and certainly between families affected by incarceration and those who were not. Phase I internee, Egon Stark astutely noted, 'If there were some 700 internees at Camp B and you ask each one for his story, you would get *Rashomon* [conflicting or differing versions, perspectives, or interpretations] multiplied by 700.'[48]

Jonathan Webber explains the challenges of multiple constructed narratives in his analysis of dealing with difficult memories of genocide at the Auschwitz–Birkenau Memorial and Museum. He says, 'There is no single narrative, nor a holistic outlook on what happened. Building up a multifaceted picture of Auschwitz out of those fragments and partial views parallels the site's status as simultaneously being a symbol, a cemetery, a pilgrimage site, a museum, a theater, and a place of "dark" tourism.'[49] Camp B-70 heritage, although in no means as horrible as that of Auschwitz, faces similar challenges being a museum as well as a place of trauma and pain, and a symbol of oppression.

The internment camp post-war

After camp B-70 was formerly closed on 31 August 1945, the government sold most of the fifty-two original camp buildings, considered Crown assets, in 1947, to individuals and institutions.[50] As Macdonald notes in her study of negotiating the Nazi past in Nuremberg, 'One approach to difficult heritage is to obliterate it-to remove it from view.'[51] The Canadian government took a similar approach, post-war, to dealing with the NB internment camp, by removing as much of it from view as possible. Trinidad Rico's writes,

> The survival of some heritage places over others should not be seen as accidental or natural. The heritage record at any point in time is a product of a selective appreciation and safeguarding of meanings and values, associated with a certain perception of the past and informed by identity politics, nation-building agendas, and other factors.[52]

This attempted erasure of the physical remains, and, in turn, the memory, was not accidental and took two forms: divestiture and destruction.

Divestiture took the form of an auction of internment camp buildings to be relocated across the province and away from the original site. One purchaser, the University of New Brunswick (Figure 15.2), acquired a section of the camp's H-shaped mess hall, which they converted to a biology hall on their Fredericton campus. Unfortunately, the biology building was torn down in 1994 to make way for a new childhood education centre, but the original windows, along with the architectural plans, were donated to the NBICM. As of 2021, both the windows and camp plans are currently on display in the museum.

Many of the original buildings were purchased by individuals and repurposed into a variety of new uses, including a church and a law office, shedding their original carceral meanings.[53] One camp building became a meeting lodge for the Canadian Legion in Nackawic, NB, while another structure was transported to Chipman, NB (thirty-two kilometres away) to become the Star Inn Dance Hall.[54] There is also one recorded instance of a camp building being moved twice. After the Second World War, it was first purchased by local businessman Ashley Colter and remained relatively intact until

Figure 15.2 Four photographs of University of New Brunswick Biology Hall
Source: Image © Todd Caissie.

the building came under ownership of the City of Fredericton. Until then 'nothing had been done to it. It looked like it had just come out of the camp after the camp had closed', said Ed Caissie, the founder of the NBICM.[55] In 2015, during construction of a parking lot in Fredericton, the building was relocated again. According to Caissie, the structure, which may have originally been the camp hospital or possibly a bunkhouse, was then purchased by a second individual and relocated to Maugerville, NB, to be used for equipment storage.[56]

When buildings were too large for a truck bed or too large to fit under the nearby covered bridge that straddled the Little River, they were sectioned into smaller pieces. George Merrill recalls the large camp B-70-H-shaped hut being purchased and relocated by another nearby Legion, this time in Marysville. He said, 'The building was sawed apart in sections, trucked in, and set up in sections.'[57] A Minto resident purchased two of the smaller camp buildings which he relocated to his property. Interestingly, he did not want to damage his buildings by cutting them into pieces to fit through the Little River covered bridge, so he waited until the river froze and hauled both structures, intact, across the ice.[58] Although there are no extant buildings at the original site, perhaps as many as fifteen of the original structures, now scattered across the province, still exist, albeit in repurposed forms which have lost their original meaning within their new contexts.

In contrast to the auctioning of the internment camp's physical structures, most of the camp's movable objects were intentionally destroyed. According to Theobald, 'the military systematically destroyed its contents: dishes were smashed or buried, books burnt, and other objects simply disappeared, scavenged by locals eager to make use of the military waste at the abruptly forsaken site'.[59] Veteran Guard Clarence Wade recalls, 'When the Camp was closed, a military delegation from #7 District was appointed to destroy the contents, and that they did, stacking the dishes, pots, pans, etc., seeing who could break the most with one blow'.[60] Several examples of deliberately damaged camp pots and pans are on display in the NB internment camp museum.[61]

The birth of a museum

The story behind the foundation of the NBICM is an extraordinary example of local actors positively impacting the preservation and memorialization of difficult heritage. In 1993, almost thirty years after the last building was removed from the site, local Minto teacher, Ed Caissie, who was developing alternate programs for at-risk students at Minto Elementary Junior High School, decided to bring some students to the site for a 'hands-on' educational experience as part of a class project.[62] By then, the original site was completely overgrown with only the water tower superstructure visible. Caissie began by mentoring a class of twelve at-risk students, but the project team eventually expanded to sixty students. This project required the students, among other assignments, to dig for artifacts at the site and to construct a scale model of the twenty-three-hectare internment camp complete with all fifty-two buildings (Figure 15.3).[63] The project was a resounding success in raising awareness of the camp's history and, by 1995, via a traveling exhibit across the province, had been seen by over 15,000 people.[64]

Excavated artifacts and the to-scale camp model were placed in display cases at the school, which it was thought at the time constituted the end of the project. However, numerous parents and various other visitors to the school who saw the display indicated that they also had artifacts from the camp, including rosary beads, a prisoner-carved wooden shark sculpture, a ship in a bottle and various other paraphernalia, which they were willing to lend or donate to the collection. Before long, Caissie and his team accumulated so many objects that they far exceeded the display case capacity, and the idea of a dedicated museum emerged. Having reached this tipping point, Caissie sought out a group of local individuals to form a non-profit organization (The NB Internment Camp Heritage Committee) to manage and preserve the story and physical remains of the camp, which eventually led to the creation of the NBICM in June 1997. All these developments were privately driven rather than provincially or federally funded initiatives. The lack of federal financial support is notable since Canada considers itself at the forefront of acknowledging historical wrongs and addressing issues of social justice.

Moreover, Canada currently has only two museums dedicated exclusively to preserving the history of Second World War internment, the NBICM and the Nikkei Internment Memorial Centre in British Columbia. The Nikkei Internment Memorial Centre is devoted exclusively to the Japanese Canadian internment experience,

Figure 15.3 Photograph of students building scale model of the internment camp
Source: Image © Todd Caissie.

whereas the NBICM focuses on the history of camp B-70, as well as managing the original internment camp B-70 site in nearby Ripples. NBICM is the only Canadian museum dedicated exclusively to the history and memory of non-Japanese Second World War–internment camps, and the collection includes over 650 artifacts and objects associated with the original camp.[65] Special emphasis is given to the experience of incarceration, constitutional issues, violations of civil liberties and civil rights as well as the broader issues of race and social justice.[66] The museum is home to a mosaic of memories much like the camp itself, which held a mosaic of prisoners including Jews, Protestants, Catholics, Canadians and German and Italian merchant marines. In historical terms, this kaleidoscope of prisoners results in a complexity of events and narratives with multivalent meanings, with the practices and policies towards incarcerating Jewish refugees vis-a-vis German and Italian soldiers perhaps being the most obvious example and challenge for the museum.

I contend this more complex approach is preferable, a viewpoint supported by Susan Ashley in her article, 'State Authority and the Public Sphere: Ideas on the Changing Role of the Museum as a Canadian Social Institution'. She wrote that a museum must be cognizant of tempering homogeneity and single points of view, while encouraging complexity and pluralism.[67] The NBICM curatorial decisions admirably push against such homogeneity. For example, although the museum has multiple narratives and material examples of internees who were treated well and feeling 'fortunate' even to be interned in Canada, they also educate visitors on crueler aspects of incarceration, including the grueling working conditions, especially in winter. Interestingly, the museum itself is not located on the site of the original camp; rather, it is housed in a 2,000 square-foot space in the basement of the Minto Village Hall building. The committee therefore must grapple with various problematic issues associated with managing two geographically separate sites. This multi-site dynamic is worthy of further research and analysis, but beyond the scope of this chapter.

The place where it happened

The conservation and presentation of the cultural heritage of the original camp site created additional challenges as well as opportunities for stakeholders. For example, the NBICM created a short historical trail in 2006 that would be open year-round (although snowshoes are often required during winter) and snake through the foundations, overgrown roads and other scattered markers of the original site.[68] The purpose of the trail was also to offer visitors of the museum (roughly sixteen km away) a cohesively curated multi-site experience. A brief perambulation reveals several extant remains including two cement manholes with pipes, large rocks that formed the base of the grandstand and the previously mentioned water tower base. A few years later, they added signage along the trail to mark the locations of several original camp buildings, which adds greatly to the educational value and visitor experience.[69]

As David Lowenthal acknowledges, the problematics of how to remember (or to forget) historical events can make heritage a minefield for curators and conservators.[70] The museum, in many ways, acts as a conduit between academia and the general public in that the matters of civil injustices 'remain socially barren and culturally useless unless shared with the wider community'.[71] As is often the case with the history of internment, camp B-70's heritage is complicated and nuanced and museum professionals are charged with the responsibility of deciding which works are displayed or left in storage, and how each object interacts with the accompanying collection in a gallery. The challenges are amplified when curating the difficult heritage of internment and the marginalized voices of Second World War internees. By highlighting prisoner narratives of Canadian oppression, the museum, in a way, shatters some of the idealized perceptions Canadians have about their collective past.

The NBICM, a project driven exclusively by local actors, presents a rich, layered history that benefits from ongoing creative reimagining to reveal multivalent issues of social and civil justice. I argue that the various interventions shaped the perception and collective memory of the local populations who formed its sense of identity and distinctiveness from the historicity that came from the knowledge of the camp existence and purpose or lack thereof. The construction and eventual destruction of the camp altered the material reception of place while shaping the landscape and collective memory of the local population for decades. The destruction of the camp led to the creation of a new heritage structure and a constructed narrative of absence, a narrative which eventually engulfed the history of the camp until the memory and original purpose were diligently revisited in 1993. That original purpose faded from collective memory to be replaced by new values in the relocated structures, which became the public identity of these buildings, thus constructing an additional layer of heritage on these structures. I hope this brief analysis of the difficult heritage of the Canada's only non-Japanese Second World War–internment camp museum encourages a deeper and broader consideration of the issue of reception and historical impermanence and that even though time may move relentlessly forward, history sometimes, does not.

Notes

1. The camp had many names, both official and unofficial, including B, 70, B-70, Little River, Ripples, and Fredericton. I chose to use B-70 because that is the term most used at the NBICM.
2. According to Canada statistics, in 2016 Fredericton and Minto had populations of 58,220 and 2,305, respectively. 'Statistics Canada', https://www.statcan.gc.ca/eng/start (accessed 10 June 2019).
3. Tim Porter, 'Internment Camp Project Gets Boost', *The Daily Gleaner*, November 1995. For more on the absence of the topic in schools see Alexandra Wood, 'Japanese-Canadian see: Challenging History: Public Education and Reluctance to Remember the Japanese Canadian Experience in British Columbia', Historical Studies in Education. CHEA Conference, 2012.
4. Sharon Macdonald, *Difficult Heritage: Negotiating the Nazi Past in Nuremberg and Beyond* (New York: Routledge, 2009), 8.
5. Ibid., 1.
6. Lynn Meskell, 'Negative Heritage and Past Mastering in Archeology', *Anthropology Quarterly* 75/3 (2002): 557–74. Robert Preucel and Regis Picos, 'Place: Cochiti Pueblo, Core Values, and Authorized Heritage Discourse', in *Heritage Keywords* (Boulder: University Press of Colorado, 2015), 224.
7. Trinidad Rico, 'Negative Heritage: The Place of Conflict in Negative Heritage', *Conservation and Management of Archaeological Sites* 10/4 (November 2008): 344.
8. Macdonald, *Difficult Heritage*, 1.
9. Ibid., 8–9.
10. David Carter, *POW-Behind Canadian Barbed Wire* (Elkwater: Eagle Butte Press, 2004), 5. For the events surrounding the transfer of those interned in Britain in general, see Paula Draper, 'The Paradox of Survival Jewish Refugees Interned in Canada 1940–43', in *Civilian Internment in Canada: Histories and Legacies*, ed. Rhonda Hinther and Jim Mochoruk (Winnipeg: University of Manitoba Press, 2020), 309–32.
11. For more about contested terminology discourse see *Power of Words Handbook: A Guide to Language about Japanese Americans in World War II*. National JACL (Japanese American Citizens League) Power of Worde II Committee 27 April 2013, https://static1.squarespace.com/static/5e8e0d3e848b7a506128dddf/t/5ffc86174 1448928cd131066/1610384921163/POW-Handbook-Rev2020-V4.pdf (accessed 21 October 2021) and Andrea Pitzer, *One Long Night: A Global History of Concentration Camps* (Little Brown, 2017), 5–6.
12. Carter, *Behind Canadian Barbed Wire*, 42–3. Canada's first internment occurred 4 September 1939, only three days after Germany entered Poland.
13. Ted Jones, *Both Sides of the Wire: The Fredericton Internment Camp*, vol. 1 (Fredericton: New Ireland Press, 1988), 1. Rachel Pistol, 'Remembering the

Internment of Enemy Aliens', in *The Jews, the Holocaust, and the Public: The Legacies of David Cesarani*, ed. Larissa Allwork and Rachel Pistol (Switzerland: Palgrave Macmillan, 2019), 96.
14. Maryse Bedard, 'From One Island to Another: The Internment of the Italian-British in Montreal, 1940–1943' (Paper presented at the Civilian Internment in Canada Workshop, Winnipeg, Manitoba, 17–19 June 2015). Christine Whitehouse, 'Camp Boys': Privacy and the Sexual Self, in *Civilian Internment in Canada: Histories and Legacies*, ed. Rhonda Hinther and Jim Mochoruk (Winnipeg: University of Manitoba Press, 2020), 131–49. Jewish refugees in Britain under the age of twenty-five, many of whom ended up in Canadian camps, are often referred to as 'camp boys'.
15. Rob Mickleburgh, 'Trio of Cabins Marks Japanese Internment Camp', http://www.theglobeandmail.com/news/british-columbia/trio-of-cabins-marks-japanese-internment-camp/article13337889/ (accessed 1 August 2019).
16. Todd Caissie and Ed Caissie, 'The New Brunswick Internment Camp Museum: Preserving the History of Internment Camp B-70', in *Civilian Internment in Canada: Histories and Legacies*, ed. Rhonda Hinther and Jim Mochoruk (Winnipeg: University of Manitoba Press, 2020), 268–9.
17. Jones, *Both Sides of the Wire*, vol. 1, 25, 47.
18. Ibid., 11, 58. Leo Inslicht, the man who compiled these statistics, formerly worked with British Hotel and Tourism.
19. For information on the Italian internees transferred to Canada see Bedard, 'From One Island to Another'.
20. Theobald, *Dangerous Enemy Sympathizers* (Fredericton: Goose Lane, 2019), 83–5.
21. Jones, *Both Sides of the Wire*, vol. 2, 712.
22. Andrew Theobald, *Dangerous Enemy Sympathizers*, 40. Library and Archives Canada (LAC) 8328–652.
23. Ibid., 59. Jones, *Both Sides of the Wire*, vol. 1, 158, 169. Jones notes the daily rate later was raised from 20 to 30 cents. Remuneration reports are contested and sometimes contradictory. Kallman, for example, notes cleaning was only 10 cents while trench digging 20 cents.
24. Jones, *Both Sides of the Wire*, vol. 1, 158, 169.
25. Ibid., 173.
26. Ibid., 170. Prisoners were also tasked with fighting the great fire of 1944.
27. Theobald, *Dangerous Enemy Sympathizers*, 60.
28. Ibid., 61. The cord of wood was to be a 4 foot by 4 foot by 8 foot pile.
29. Ibid., 69.
30. Video Interview, Internee Gerry Fry. NBICM archives.
31. Jones, *Both Sides of the Wire*, vol. 2, 673.
32. Three internees, Newmark, Homburger, and Kraemer, were all made Officers of the Order of Canada in 1974, 1984 and 1987, respectively, for their musical impact on Canada.
33. John Beckwith and Robin Elliott, eds, *Mapping Canada's Music: Selected writings of Helmut Kallmann* (Waterloo: Wilfrid Laurier University Press, 2013) 129.
34. Anne Marie Lane Jonah, 'Port Royal Reproductions', internal Parks Canada research notes, 2015. Internees in camp B-70 during Phase II became renowned for their fine crafts and, for example, produced the stunning furnishing reproductions for Port Royal, NS. According to Lane Jonah, the curatorial records of forty-five reproduction items in the Port Royal furnishings collection include the statement, 'Made at the Acadian Forest Internment Camp'.

35. Saunders paid the internee for the commission, but the exact fee is unknown.
36. Theobald, *Dangerous Enemy Sympathizers*, 59.
37. Jones, *Both Sides of the Wire*, vol. 1, 173.
38. Ibid., 169.
39. Ibid., 170.
40. Theobald, *Dangerous Enemy Sympathizers*, 68.
41. 'Prisoner's Receipt for Cash Fredericton Internment Camp, 1 Jan 1943', http://www.italiancanadianww2.ca/collection/details/licea2012_0002_0013 (accessed 7 January 2020).
42. 'Prisoner's Receipt for Cash, http://www.italiancanadianww2.ca/collection/details/licea2012_0002_0013 (accessed 7 January 2020).
43. NBICM has several course completions certificates of courses, such as thermodynamics and trigonometry, from the camp's first phase.
44. Helmut Kallmann Ex-Internees Newsletter, Number 2, February 1997. Kallmann notes he also became librarian for Camp A and went on to work at the National Library of Canada and co-edit the Encyclopaedia of Music in Canada.
45. Theobald, *Dangerous Enemy Sympathizers*, 63–4.
46. Ibid., 65.
47. Robert Layton, *Who Needs the Past? Indigenous Values and Archaeology* (London: Routledge, 1994), 17–18.
48. Jones, *Both Sides of the Wire*, vol. 1, prologue.
49. Jonathan Webber, 'The Kingdom of Death as Heritage Site: Making sense of Auschwitz', in *A Companion to Heritage Studies*, ed. William Logan, Máiréad, Nic Craith, and Ullrich Kockel (Chichester, West Sussex: John Wiley, 2016), 130.
50. Theobald, *Dangerous Enemy Sympathizers*, 146. UNB purchased some of the buildings, which were literally relocated via trucks to the University's Fredericton campus. According to Ed Caissie some of the buildings sold for as little as $200 CAD.
51. Macdonald, *Difficult Heritage*, 52.
52. Rico, Negative *Heritage*, 148.
53. The Bethel Baptist church is still a functioning place of worship as of this writing.
54. Jones, *Both Sides of the Wire*, vol. 2, 719.
55. 'Ripples internment camp building moved to new home', https://www.cbc.ca/news/canada/new-brunswick/ripples-internment-camp-shed-1.3264105 (accessed 20 September 2017).
56. Ibid. The modern green paneling was added to the exterior of the shed in the late 1990s or early 2000s.
57. Jones, *Both Sides of the Wire*, vol. 2, 718.
58. Discussion with MBICM museum guide Griffin Mountan, January 10 2020.
59. Theobald, *Dangerous Enemy Sympathizers*, 145–6. See also Jones, vol. 2, 716–17.
60. Jones, *Both Sides of the Wire*, vol. 2, 717.
61. NBICM website, http://www.nbinternmentcampmuseum.ca (accessed 7 May 2021).
62. Ed Caissie is the author's father. The building has since burned down.
63. For his efforts, Caissie received a Hilroy Fellowship national teacher's award for innovations in teaching.
64. Porter, 'Internment Camp Project Gets Boost'.
65. The second museum is the Nikkei Internment Memorial Center in New Denver, BC.
66. Caissie and Caissie, 'The New Brunswick Internment Camp Museum', 273.

67. Ashley, Susan, 'State Authority and the Public Sphere: Ideas on the Changing Role of the Museum as a Canadian Social Institution', *Museum and Society* 3, no. 1 (March 2005): 5–17.
68. Kirkpatrick was on the board of the NBICM and the Park Ranger overseeing the Crown land upon which the original camp now rests.
69. Parts of a road are noticeable by an absence of vegetation as well. During the war, ashes from the camp stoves were dumped on the road, which formed a hard floor where little can grow.
70. David Lowenthal, *Stewarding the Past in a Perplexing Present*, in *Values and Heritage Conservation* (Los Angeles: The Getty Conservation Institute, 2000), 19.
71. Ibid., 23.

Bibliography

Ashley, Susan. 'State Authority and the Public Sphere: Ideas on the Changing Role of the Museum as a Canadian Social Institution', *Museum and Society* 3, no. 1 (March 2005): 5–17.

Beckwith, John, and Robin Elliot eds. *Mapping Canada's Music: Selected Writings of Helmut Kallmann*. Waterloo: Wilfrid Laurier University Press, 2013.

Caissie, Ed, and Todd Caissie. 'The New Brunswick Internment Camp Museum: Preserving the History of Internment Camp B-70'. In *Civilian Internment in Canada: Histories and Legacies*, edited by Rhonda Hinther and James Mochoruk, 267–82. Winnipeg: University of Manitoba Press, 2020.

Carter, David. *POW-Behind Canadian Barbed Wire*. Elkwater: Eagle Butte Press, 2004.

Draper, Paula. 'The Paradox of Survival Jewish Refugees Interned in Canada 1940–43'. In *Civilian Internment in Canada: Histories and Legacies*, edited by Rhonda Hinther and James Mochoruk, 309–32. Winnipeg: University of Manitoba Press, 2020.

Duliani, Mario. *The City Without Women: A Chronicle of Internment Life in Canada During World War II*. Oakville: Mosaic Press, 1994.

Graham, Brian, Greg Ashworth and John Tunbridge. *A Geography of Heritage: Power, Culture and Economy*. London: Hodder Arnold, 2004.

Jones, Ted. *Both Sides of the Wire: The Fredericton Internment Camp*, vol. 1. Fredericton: New Ireland Press, 1988.

Jones, Ted. *Both Sides of the Wire: The Fredericton Internment Camp*, vol. 2. Fredericton: New Ireland Press, 1989.

Kallmann, Helmut. Ex-Internees Newsletter, Number 2, February 1997. New Brunswick Internment Camp Museum Archives.

Layton, Robert. *Who Needs the Past? Indigenous Values and Archaeology*. London: Routledge, 1994.

Lowenthal, David. 'Stewarding the Past in a Perplexing Present'. In *Values and Heritage Conservation*, edited by Erica C. Avrami, Randall Mason and Marta De la Torre, 18–25. Los Angeles: The Getty Conservation Institute, 2000.

Macdonald, Sharon. *Difficult Heritage: Negotiating the Nazi Past in Nuremberg and Beyond*. New York: Routledge, 2009.

Pistol, Rachel. 'Remembering the Internment of Enemy Aliens During the Second World War on the Isle of Man, and in Australia and Canada'. In *The Jews, the Holocaust, and* the Public: *The Legacies of David Cesarani*, edited by Larissa Allwork and Rachel Pistol, 93–114. Switzerland: Palgrave Macmillian.

Pitzer, Andrea. *One Long Night: A Global History of Concentration Camps*. New York: Little Brown, 2017.

Rico, Trinidad. 'Negative Heritage: The Place of Conflict in Negative Heritage'. *Conservation and Management of Archaeological Sites* 10, no. 4 (November 2008): 344–52.

Robert, Preucel, and Regis Picos, 'Place: Cochiti Pueblo, Core Values, and Authorized Heritage Discourse'. In *Heritage Keywords*, edited by Kathryn Lafrenz Samuels and Trinidad Rico, 221–42. Boulder: University Press of Colorado, 2015.

Theobald, Andrew. *Dangerous Enemy Sympathizers*. Fredericton: Goose Lane, 2019.

Thompson, Erin. 'Destruction of Art'. In *Encyclopaedia of Aesthetics*, Online: Oxford University Press, 2014, 3.

Webber, Jonathan. 'The Kingdom of Death as Heritage Site: Making Sense of Auschwitz'. In *A Companion to Heritage Studies*, edited by William Logan Máiréad, Nic Craith, and Ullrich Kockel, 115–32. Chichester, West Sussex: John Wiley, 2016.

Whitehouse, Christine. 'Camp Boys': Privacy and the Sexual Self. In *Civilian Internment in Canada: Histories and Legacies*, edited by Rhonda Hinther and Jim Mochoruk, 131–9. Winnipeg: University of Manitoba Press, 2020.

Index

18B, Defence Regulation 3, 20, 106

Abosso MV 250
Abyssinia 48
Acquasanta 174
Adler, Fritz 87
Ahmednagar 208, 210, 221–2, 224–9, 231–3
Akko 193, 195
Albany Street Barracks 18–19
Aliens Act, 1919 38
Aliyah 189–90
Anderson, Sir John 101–2, 104, 241
anti-Italian Sentiment 49, 58, 173
antisemitism 6–7, 35, 37, 130, 195
Arandora Star SS 4, 8, 25, 47, 49–50, 53, 55, 57–9, 72, 241–2, 246–7, 250, 254–5
Arquata del Tronto 174
art 25, 34, 74–6, 92–4, 105, 110, 152, 199, 233, 252–3, 265–6
Ascot 18, 20, 25
Ashton, Gwen 123–4, 126, 131
Association of Jewish Refugees (AJR) 7, 41–2
Atlantic SS 194–5
Aufschnaiter, Peter 207, 214–15
Auschwitz-Birkenau 6, 118, 122, 125, 143, 151, 154, 157–8, 161, 197, 267
Australia 2–5, 7, 13, 23–4, 32, 42, 71–2, 118, 175, 177, 239–55
Auxiliary Military Pioneer Corps (AMPC) 38–40, 89, 247, 251, 254

Bagni di Lucca 169–70, 174
Bagno a Ripoli 170, 174
Balfour Declaration 199
barbed wire 2, 7, 14, 18, 20–1, 23, 25, 40, 68, 74–6, 84–91, 106, 121–5, 151, 175, 191, 194, 199, 211, 214, 225, 231, 249, 252
Barthel, Kurt 73

Bastico, Ettore 169
Bell, Bishop George 72–3
Bell, Sir Stuart 56
Bentwich, Helen 41
Bentwich, Norman 32, 39, 41
Besançon 5, 150–1, 157–60
Bethlehem 193
Beverley Barracks 18
Biberach 118, 120, 126, 131
Bland, Sir John 102
Bloch, Martin 90, 92–4
Board of Deputies of British Jews 36–7
Boer War 221, 224, 233–4
Bombay (Mumbai) 208, 215–16, 221, 223–8, 230, 244–5
Bondy, Paul 72–4
Borchard, Ruth 108, 111
Bouget, Beryl 126
Bougourd, Doris 123–4, 126, 131
Brehm, Eugen 71–3
Brighton racecourse 20
British Expeditionary Force (BEF) 57, 102
British Union of Fascists (BUF) 20, 35–6
Buchelt, Oberleutnant 140
Burma (Myanmar) 213–14, 233
Burstein, Marianne (Miriam) 196
Buxton College 84

Caissie, Ed 268–9
Calcutta (Kolkata) 215
Canada 2, 4, 7, 13, 23–4, 72, 151, 241, 254, 261, 263–4, 269–70
Caserne Vauban 150, 157–8
Catholic 56, 73, 110, 167, 172, 217, 249, 270
Cazalet, Victor 3
Central British Fund for German Jewry (CBF) 31
Central Promenade 92, 241
Ceresa, Edoardo 50, 55, 58
Chamberlain, Neville 102

Channel Islands 6, 117–20, 123, 125, 127, 129, 131, 244
  Guernsey 118–24, 127, 129
  Jersey 118, 118–24, 126
  Sark 117–18, 120–1, 125, 127
Chelsea Barracks 18
Chicken, Lutz 211
Churchill, Winston 39, 51, 67, 102, 104, 151, 168, 241
citizenship 1, 7, 90, 167–9, 172, 175, 177, 207, 243, 254, 263–4
Civitella della Chiana 170, 174–5
Clacton (Butlin's) 14, 16, 24
Clague, Alec 103
Clement Town 207, 211, 217
Cobham, Viscount 102
communist 13, 50, 73–4, 121, 143, 215, 232, 250
concentration camps 6, 31–4, 39–40, 68, 76, 117, 122, 125, 127, 129–30, 137, 142, 151, 161, 167–8, 174, 177–8, 180, 194, 225, 234, 263
Corropoli 174–5
Cowley Barracks 18
Craigmillar's Hostel 14
Cresswell, Yvonne 92
Cruickshank, Dame Joanna 104–9
Cuthbert, Chief Inspector Cyril 105–6
Cyprus 198–9

Dachinger, Hugo 34, 74
Dalheim, Martin 68, 73
Dalston Hospital 108
Daniel, Capt H. O. 92
Darling, Malcolm 210, 225–8
David, Werner 83–5, 94
Defence of India Act (1939) 222
Dehra Dun 207, 209, 212, 214–17, 221–2, 226–9, 231–2
DELASEM 172
Deolali 211, 221, 223–7, 229, 231–3
Deoli 221, 228, 231–4
demolition 5, 7, 40, 109, 111, 127, 178, 190, 250, 269
deportation 2–4, 6–8, 23, 48, 50, 59, 68, 71–3, 117–25, 127–31, 154, 157–61, 169–71, 177–8, 190, 194–7, 239–44, 251, 254
Dhurringile Mansion 245, 252

Dinapur 223–4
discrimination 48–9, 51, 55, 59, 106, 154, 180
Donington Hall 14
Donaldson's School, Edinburgh 14
Douglas (Isle of Man) 6–7, 73, 83, 86, 90–2, 104–7, 110
Duchess of York SS 72
Dunera Association 253
Dunera HMT 4, 7–8, 71–2, 239, 241–2, 245–7, 249–51, 253–5
Duquemin, Elisabet 118, 125

education and training 17, 20, 32, 34–6, 38–9, 41, 74, 83–4, 87–92, 105, 108–9, 127, 130, 196, 232, 264, 266–7
emigration 8, 32, 47, 49–51, 54, 57, 59, 73, 168, 191, 251
Enemy Aliens: Category A 13, 84, 101, 103, 239, 241, 246
  anti-Nazi 14, 17, 74, 109, 210, 213, 215, 225, 232, 239, 247, 249–50
  Category B 13, 18, 84, 101–3, 241
  Category C 13, 18, 20, 84, 102, 241
  Merchant Seamen 13–14, 17–18, 24, 224, 232, 244, 264, 270
  pro-Nazi 21, 212, 239, 244, 247, 250–1
Enemy Foreigners Order (September 1939) 208–9
Enoch, H. 19
expatriates 57, 73, 151, 243

family camps 142, 221, 228–31, 245, 251
Farnham, K. H. 20
fascism 8, 36–7, 48–50, 54, 167–8, 172, 175, 177–8, 180, 232, 247, 250, 264
fascio/fasci 48, 173
Fechenbach, Hermann 23
Fenham Barracks 18
Ferramonti di Tarsia 5, 167, 171, 178–80
Fifth Column 3, 38–9, 102, 241
First World War 21, 31, 34, 38, 102, 104, 111, 121, 136, 168, 178, 208, 221, 224, 234
Fiuggi 169–75
food 6, 14, 18–21, 23, 25, 34, 69, 71–2, 87, 104, 107–9, 121–5, 137–8, 141–2, 152–4, 169, 175, 191, 194, 245–6, 265
Foreigners Act (India 1946) 233

Fossoli di Carpi 177
Frankenschwerth, Kurt 19
Franklin, Alan 92
Franz, Margit 211, 216–17
Fraschette di Alatri 167, 173–5, 177–80
Fredericton 261, 267–8
Freund, Ella 196–7
Frontstalag 122, 121–2, 124
Frontstalag 14, 25, 149–50
Fürnberg, Louis 74

Gaffirim 194
Gaiety Theatre, Douglas 88
Gainsborough 14, 18
Gál, Hans 69, 71, 73–4, 85
Gask, Jeanne 136, 143
Giromagny 143
Gliwice (Polish) / Gleiwitz (German) 135–6
Godfrey, Margaret 123, 131
Goetz, Dr Hermann 233
Golden Cage 149, 152
Goldsmith, John 69, 76
Gombrich, Ernst 75
Gordon-Canning, Captain Robert 35
Gornitzky, Manfred 87–90
Gottfurcht, Hans 75
Government of India 208, 210, 212, 216, 221, 226, 228, 232–3
Grand Hôtel 155–6, 172, 175
Gregson, George 138–42
Grossmann, Hans 213
Grundig, Lea 196
Guillemette, Louis 119–20, 131

Hadda, Gerhard 74
Haganah 191, 195, 200
Haifa 4, 189, 191, 193–6, 200, 243
Halifax, Lord 102
Hallgarten, Katherine 111
Harrer, Heinrich 207, 214–15, 222
Have, Heins von 214
Hay (New South Wales) 4, 242, 245, 247, 249–51
Heaume, Una 124
Hemsby 14
Henig, Baroness 111
Hitler, Adolph 3, 67, 73–4, 76, 151, 208, 244, 261

Hollitscher, Wilhelm 69, 72–4, 88
Holloway Prison 17, 20, 103, 107
Home Department (Government of India) 226–32
Home Office 32–3, 38–9, 50, 71, 101, 103, 105–8, 159, 241
Hôtel de la Providence 156, 160
Hughes, Terry 76
Hutchinson 7, 34, 83, 88, 90–2, 94
Huy 137–41, 143
Huyton 4–5, 23–5, 67–77, 83–8, 91, 94, 241

Ilag VIII 135–7, 140, 142–4
immigration 51, 56, 58, 130, 189–200, 254
imperialism 180, 244
Indian National Congress 6, 233
India Office (Whitehall, London) 208–213, 215–16
International Committee of the Red Cross (ICRC) 3, 74, 108, 120, 122–3, 137, 141–3, 149–50, 152–4, 175
Iran 3, 213, 229, 233, 239, 243–7, 250–1, 254
Irredentism 168
Isle of Man 4, 6–7, 13, 17, 20, 23–5, 34, 40, 68–9, 72–4, 83–7, 91–2, 94, 101–11, 241
Italian Social Republic (RSI) 177
Italy 5–8, 47–59, 67, 168–78, 180, 226, 228, 241, 246

Jacobsthal, Paul 18
Japanese 24, 214–15, 232, 245, 247, 251
Japanese Canadian 263, 269
Jewish Museum, London 41
Jewish Relief Association 208, 210
Jondorf, Wilhelm 22

Kallmann, Helmut 265–6
Kathmandu 214
Katowice 135
Keller, Hans 89
Kempton Park 19–21, 24, 72
Kindertransport 2, 31, 41, 101
Kitchener camp 4, 7, 31–42
Kitchener Descendants' Group 8, 41–2
Knockaloe 102, 111, 224
Kolb, Fritz 210–12
Kopp, Hans 211, 214

Kosher 108–9, 111, 196
Krägel, Sybille 143–4
Krakow 135
Krenek, Ludwig 211
Kreuzburg (German) / Kluczbork (Polish) 120, 146
Kristallnacht 31–2

Larisch, Kurt 211
Laufen 117, 120, 126
Lawrence, Marjorie 126, 131
Layton, Julian 39–40
League of Nations 208, 210
Leale, John 118–19
Le Feuvre, Nellie née Gallienne 120–6, 131
Lehmann-Russbueldt, Otto 71–3
Leiser, George 19
Libya 5, 167–78
Liège 135, 137, 141
Lille 135, 137
Lingfield Racecourse 14, 17–21, 24, 241
Little River 268
Liverpool 4–5, 23, 48, 55–6, 67–77, 84, 94, 103–4, 143, 241
Lloyd, Esther Pauline née Silver 125
Lloyd, Lord 242
Lomnitz, Alfred 71–2, 74
Loos 137
Lorand, Arnold 88
Lutheran 108, 243
Lütkens, Gerhard 75

Magener, Rolf 214
Malta 167–8, 173
Maltese 167–9, 172–5, 177, 180, 228
Manchester 50, 58, 73, 83–4, 87, 89, 109
Manx Museum 91, 111
Manx National Heritage 91–2, 94
Marsh, Yin 234
Mauritius 195
May, Jonas 34
May, Phineas 34
Maynard, Michael 83, 87, 89, 94
McArd, Keith 111
McCrum, Robert 137
McGahy, Arthur 123–5
memory 1–2, 4–5, 7–8, 41, 47, 49–59, 67, 77, 84, 86, 90–1, 131, 136, 143–4, 149–50, 157–61, 168, 178, 189, 199, 216, 239, 245–6, 253–4, 261–3, 266–7, 270–1
Merchant Seamen 13–14, 17–18, 24, 224, 232, 244
Messerschmidt, Ernst 211
Methodist 110
MI5 13–14, 48, 102
Milos SS 194–5
Ministry of the Interior 167, 169–70, 172–7
Ministry of Italian Africa 169, 172, 177
Minto 261, 263, 268–9, 271
Monte San Savino 175
Montecatini Terme 169–70, 173–4
Montechiarugolo 174
Mooragh 74, 92, 241
morale 20, 23, 25, 39, 67, 70–3, 89, 228
Moser, Claus 75
Munzer, Elfrieda and Kurt 111
Mussolini, Benito 48, 168

Nazi 2–3, 6–7, 13–14, 17, 20–1, 32, 38, 41, 68, 73, 84, 101–2, 109, 127, 135–7, 140, 143–4, 146, 149–51, 157, 159, 167, 177, 180, 189, 191, 197, 207–17, 222, 225, 232, 239, 241, 243–52, 263–4, 267
Nehru, Jawaharlal 6, 233–4
Nessler, Walter 74, 76
Neumann, Robert 69, 72, 85
New Brunswick Internment Camp Museum (NBICM) 4, 261
newspapers 2, 17, 20, 35, 37–8, 41, 50–1, 69–71, 73, 88, 92, 106–7, 110, 140, 171
Nissel, Siegfried 71
NKVD 6, 143–5
non-citizen Italians 167–9, 172, 175
nuns 151–2, 155, 226
Nyanatiloka (Anton Gueth) 207, 212

Olympia 14
Onchan 86, 88, 91–2, 94, 241
Operation Countenance 244
Orange Camp 247
Ord, Reverend Douglas 119–20
Orthodox 73, 108, 247, 266
Ossario Crypt (Murchison) 252
overcrowding 4, 18, 23, 69, 71, 139, 143, 167, 175, 194, 198, 225, 241

Pächt, Otto 75
Pacific SS 194–5
Paignton (Dixon's) 14, 16–17, 24
Pakistan 215
Palestine 4, 32, 38, 189–91, 193–200, 239, 243, 245, 247, 250–1, 254
Palmach 200
Parole 210–11, 213, 227–33
Patria SS 193–5
Pearson, Lady Grace 35–6
permission to leave camp 33
Persia (*see* Iran)
Pevsner, Nikolaus 75
Pfefferkorn, Lea 196
philanthropy 33
Pioneer Corps (*see* Auxiliary Military Pioneer Corps)
Poelmann, Heribert 264–5
Port Erin 94, 103–11
Port St Mary 94, 103–11, 113
Prees Heath 21–2, 84
prejudice 48, 51, 55, 106
Prem Nagar 207, 210–17
Prinses Josephine Charlotte HMS 103
Prisoners of War 1–3, 24, 47, 137, 142, 178, 199, 224, 232–3, 241, 247, 252, 265
propaganda 74, 151, 169, 208
Purana Qila 232
Purandhar 221, 228–33

Quakers 41, 70, 74, 108
Queen Elizabeth RMS 239, 243, 245
Queen Mary RMS 239, 242–3, 247, 249, 253
Quin, Wilhelmina 122

Rabin, Yitzhak 200
Radok, Rainer 14, 18, 249–50
Ramgarh 232
Randall, Robert 121–3, 126
Rangitikei SS 239, 243–5, 247
Rathbone, Eleanor 3, 21
Rawicz, Maryan 73
Reading, Lord 38, 40
Registration of Foreigners Act (India) 1939 221
repatriation 143, 154, 173, 177, 210, 216, 222, 225, 228, 233, 244, 254
resistance 54, 119, 130, 149–50, 157–8, 160, 195, 210, 244, 265–6

Retzlaff-Kresse, Bruno 73
Richborough 31, 41–2
Rieger, Dr Hans Christoph 110–11
Ripples (Canada) 261, 263, 265, 270
Rosenbaum, Sebastian 144
Rosenstrauch, Arnold 20, 23
Royallieu-Compiègne 117, 121, 127
Rushen 4, 7, 17, 20, 83, 92, 94, 101, 103–7, 111
Rushen Heritage Action Team 4, 7, 101, 111

Sandwich, Kent 4, 7, 31–2, 35–7, 40–2
Sarafand 193
Sarginson, Tom 136–43
Satara 221, 227–8, 230–2
Sattler, Friedel 214
Schmaderer, Ludwig 214
Schonfeld, Rabbi Solomon 72, 88
Seaton (Warner's) 14, 16–19, 24
Sefton Hotel 6, 83, 86, 91–2
Service Exchange 108
Servigliano 5, 178, 180
Shah, Reza 244
Shakespeare, Nicolas 149, 158, 250
Sherwill, Ambrose 119, 121
Singapore 228, 239, 242–4, 247, 249–51
Sino-Indian War (1962) 233–4
Skipwith, Sofka 159–60
Slatter, Lt. Col. S. W. 72–3
Snaefell SS 104
Society of Friends (*see* Quakers)
Sondhelm, Walter 87
Special Operations Executive (SOE) 150, 159
Spier, Eugen 14
Spiro, Ludwig 19
Sproat, Iain 136
Stadlen, Peter 74
Still, Ruby 121, 124, 126
Sutton Coldfield 21
Swanwick 17

Tatura, Camp 1 239, 247–8, 252
  Camp 2 239, 242, 245, 247, 249, 252
  Camp 3 239, 242, 245, 247, 249
  Camp 4 239, 245, 247
Tatura Irrigation and Wartime Camps Museum 252, 255

Templers 243, 247, 250–1, 254
Tibet 214–15
Times Mill 14
Tost (German) / Toszek (Polish) 5–6, 135–46
Townend, Bill 140
Traczl, Boguslaw 144
transit camps 4, 6, 21, 23, 25, 32, 35, 41, 68, 71–2, 76, 117, 121–2, 130, 151, 158, 177, 190, 226
training 32, 34–9, 196, 232
Treipl, Bruno 214
tribunals 13, 38, 84, 101–2, 105, 110, 208, 222
Tripoli 168–9, 172, 177
Turner, Frédérik 136
Twemlow, Fanny 158

Uhlman, Fred 20, 34, 85, 88
Upper Silesia 135–8
United Nations Relief and Rehabilitation Administration (UNRRA) 177
United States of America (USA) 32, 38–9, 42, 151, 172, 200, 215, 263
UOKG 143

Urchs, Oswald 213–14
Uttarakhand 207, 217

Vajda, Steven 20
Veteran Guard 269
Vichy 150, 154
Vittel 5–7, 149–60

Waroonga SS 250
Warsaw 136, 151
Warth Mills 21, 23, 25–7
Weeting Hall 14
Wegrzyn, Dariusz 144
Wellington Barracks 18
White, Madeleine 159
White Papers 7, 190
Wiener Holocaust Library 2, 41–2
Wodehouse, Ethel 142
Wodehouse, P. G. 5, 135–45
Woolfall Heath 67, 75, 77
Wroclaw 135–6
Wurmser, Leo 88

York Racecourse 18
Youth Aliyah (*see* Aliyah)

www.ingramcontent.com/pod-product-compliance
Lightning Source LLC
Chambersburg PA
CBHW071807300426
44116CB00009B/1224